MW01062901

CEDAR MOUNTAIN
TO ANTIETAM

A Civil War Campaign History
of the Union XII Corps,
July–September, 1862

M. Chris Bryan

Savas Beatie
California

Library of Congress Cataloging-in-Publication Data

Names: Bryan, M. Chris, 1978- author.
Title: Cedar Mountain to Antietam : a Civil War campaign history of the
    Union XII Corps, July-September 1862 / by M. Chris Bryan.
Description: El Dorado Hills, CA: Savas Beatie LLC, [2021] | Includes
    bibliographical references and index. | Summary: "Cedar Mountain to
    Antietam: A Civil War Campaign History of the Union XII Corps,
    July-September 1862 is the first detailed analysis of the Union Twelfth
    Corps, examining the corps' initial campaigns, including the battle of
    Cedar Mountain, the Second Manassas Campaign, and the battle of
    Antietam, with thorough accounts of the corps' opponents as well as army
    and theater-wide strategic context. This study fills a historiographical
    gap of a little-studied yet consequential corps"– Provided by publisher.
Identifiers: LCCN 2021037167 | ISBN 9781611215779 (hardcover) | ISBN
    9781611215786 (ebook)
Subjects: LCSH: United States. Army of the Potomac. Corps, 12th--History. |
    United States—History—Civil War, 1861-1865—Regimental histories. |
    United States--History—Civil War, 1861-1865—Campaigns. | Antietam,
    Battle of, Md., 1862. | Cedar Mountain, Battle of, Va., 1862.
Classification: LCC E493.1 12th .B79 2021 | DDC 973.7/41—dc23
LC record available at https://lccn.loc.gov/2021037167

First Edition, First Printing

Savas Beatie
989 Governor Drive, Suite 102
El Dorado Hills, CA 95762
Phone: 916-941-6896 / (E-mail) sales@savasbeatie.com

Savas Beatie titles are available at special discounts for bulk purchases in the United States. Contact us for more details.

Proudly published, printed, and warehoused in the United States of America.

For Jen, Sophie, and William.

Thank you for your support and patience.

Table of Contents

Table of Contents (continued)

List of Maps

Archival Sources

AMP—Antietam National Military Park Archives, Keedysville, MD
APD—Antietam Papers, Rauner Library, Dartmouth College, Hanover, NH
BA—Boston Athenaeum, Boston, MA
BHM—Buffalo History Museum, Buffalo, NY
CHA—Cincinnati History Library and Archives, Cincinnati, OH
CLSC—Confederate Memorial Literary Society Collection, Virginia Historical Society, American Civil War Museum, Richmond, VA
DU—Rubenstein Library, Duke University Library, Durham, NC
ECHS—Erie County Historical Society, Erie PA
FNMP—Fredericksburg and Spotsylvania National Military Park Archives, Fredericksburg, VA
GC—Gettysburg College, Gettysburg, PA
GNMP—Gettysburg National Military Park, Gettysburg PA
GA—Georgia Archives, Morrow, GA
HL—The Huntington Library, San Marino, CA
HSP—Historical Society of Pennsylvania, Philadelphia, PA
HLHU—Houghton Library, Harvard University, Boston MA
IHS—Indiana Historical Society, Indianapolis, IN
ISL—Rare Books and Manuscripts, Indiana State Library, Indianapolis, IN
LC—Library of Congress, Washington, DC
LV—Library of Virginia, Richmond, VA
MHS—Massachusetts Historical Society, Boston, MA
NA—National Archives, Washington, DC
NA-AS—Antietam Studies, RG 92:707, National Archives, Washington, DC
NL—Newberry Library, Chicago, IL
NYPL—Ezra Ayers Carman Papers, New York Public Library, New York, NY
OHC—Ohio History Connection, Columbus, OH
OCHS—Orange County Historical Society, Orange, VA
PSA—Pennsylvania State Archives, Harrisburg, PA
RIHS—Rhode Island Historical Society, Providence, RI
RU—Special Collections and University Archives, Rutgers University, New Brunswick, NJ
SCL-USC—South Caroliniana Library, University of South Carolina, Columbia, SC
SHC—Southern Historical Collection, University of North Carolina, Chapel Hill, NC
SLCHA—St. Lawrence County Historical Association Archives, Canton, NY
TSLA—Tennessee State Library and Archives, Nashville, TN
UM—William L. Clements Library, University of Michigan, Ann Arbor, MI
USA—U.S. Army War College, Carlisle, PA
UVA—Small Special Collections Library, University of Virginia, Charlottesville, VA
WCHS—Warren County Historical Society, Warren, PA
WHS—Wisconsin Historical Society, Madison, WI

Introduction

... [N]o official reports or histories give us credit at Antietam any more than they do any where else. I used to get mad but now I smile somewhat, thinking that it won't make much difference some hundred years from now. Some few historical names will live; the rest of us will come under the general head, "and the army moved" and "Gen. Banks with 1,000,000 men a la Xerxes, arrant of Persia, marched up the hill, etc.[1]

— Lewis Stegman, 102nd New York

In April 1863, Brig. Gen. Alpheus S. Williams wrote to the erstwhile Army of the Potomac commander, Maj. Gen. George Brinton McClellan, to solicit credit for the performance of the XII Corps at Antietam. Williams had commanded the corps during most of the battle. In the letter, he explained the roles of his various brigades. He reserved the greatest plaudits for Brig. Gen. George Henry Gordon's brigade of Williams's own division and for two brigades of Brig. Gen. George Sears Greene's division, commanded by Lt. Col. Hector Tyndale and Col. Henry J. Stainrook.

Two of Williams's arguments are worth noting. First, as the corps entered the battle, it was badly depleted. It went into battle, according to Williams:

Without coffee or food, and after an almost sleepless night. It was a small corps strangers for the most part in your army. The 1st Division had but little over a month previously at Cedar Mountain, lost all the Field Officers and all the adjutants of one of its two brigades, and its ranks so reduced that several of the old regiments numbered but little over one hundred men, and were commanded by captains. There were in this division five new regiments but two weeks from home officers and men without drill or military instruction. The second division (Greene) less than two thousand strong, had lost three General officers wounded and prisoners at Cedar Mountain, and one or more of its brigades were commanded by majors. The whole corps had been for six weeks in continuous daily marches except four days. When General Banks left the command, his whole staff followed him, and my own was so reduced that I had but one aide (acting as adjutant

---

1 Lewis Stegman to John M. Gould, February 29, 1892, John Mead Gould Papers, APD.

general) and one quartermaster during our march through Maryland and afterwards while in command of the corps.[2]

These men were not only strangers to the Army of the Potomac, but also largely to each other and their commanders. Formed in late June 1862, the corps was designated the II Corps, Army of Virginia. It experienced an exsanguinating near-victory-turned-crushing defeat at Cedar Mountain in early August, and a wearying, demoralizing, yet mostly bloodless ordeal during Maj. Gen. John Pope's Second Manassas campaign at the end of that month. As the corps passed Washington during the first week of September, Gordon's and Brig. Gen. Samuel Wylie Crawford's brigades received five embryonic regiments, unknown to both warfare and the corps. The following week, the corps was renamed the XII Corps, Army of the Potomac.

Rough handling by Maj. Gen. Thomas J. "Stonewall" Jackson at Cedar Mountain left the corps woefully understaffed. Many trusted leaders were killed, captured, or severely wounded; junior officers stepped into unaccustomed roles. The soldiers greeted some of the new brigade and division commanders with suspicion and, occasionally, contempt. While Jackson had decimated the corps's numbers, Pope's mishandling and disdain for logistics left it physically devastated.

The corps endured a physically and mentally depleting experience during Pope's August campaigns, and its men plumbed the depths of low morale as they approached the forts outside of Washington on September 2. Their physical state, however, was by no means worse than that of the Confederate soldiers they would soon meet at Antietam In fact, they were in better shape by some measures. Nevertheless, they had not received a real chance to recover from the hardships of Cedar Mountain and Second Manassas, and unlike the Confederates, they did not have a string of past successes from which they could draw confidence.

The other noteworthy point in Williams's letter to McClellan was the dearth of credit for the XII Corps in McClellan's preliminary report on Antietam. Moreover, Williams felt that the meager references that McClellan made of the corps contained an overinflated and misplaced emphasis on Crawford's brigade. This did not sit well with Williams, who thought little of Crawford's contribution on September 17 or at Cedar Mountain six weeks earlier. To Williams, the brigades and leaders that did the hard fighting at Antietam went unnoticed.

---

2 Alpheus S. Williams to George B. McClellan, April 18, 1863, Antietam Battlefield Board Papers, NYPL.

Over the years, McClellan's report seems to have perpetuated itself. To this day, the efforts of the XII Corps do not figure prominently in the literature on the battle. This lack of attention is curious since the two men with arguably the greatest influence on developing the picture of what happened at the battle, Ezra Ayers Carman and John Mead Gould, were both XII Corps soldiers. Both men corresponded exhaustively with veterans to understand what, when, and where events occurred. Carman led the government's effort to develop an atlas of the battle and to place tablets on the battlefield, and he did an outstanding job with both tasks. Both men left behind a goldmine of primary sources.

In his manuscript on the battle, Carman hinted that he was disappointed with the scant attention given to the XII Corps's efforts in the official reports. One plausible reason for this is its limited numbers. The whole corps fielded scarcely 7,200 men on September 17, 1862, and Greene's two brigades, which had the greatest success on that day, contained just over 1,700 men.[3] These low numbers, combined with a string of defeats and recent privations in Virginia, made the corps an unlikely candidate for remarkable feats at Antietam.

This book tells the story of the soldiers of XII Corps, beginning with the corps's formation just before it marched toward Cedar Run and a fight that gave the locally known Slaughter's Mountain the new moniker of "Cedar Mountain." It ends with the battle of Antietam.

3 Ezra Carman, The Maryland Campaign of September 1862, Vol. II: Antietam, Thomas G. Clemens, ed. (El Dorado Hills, CA, 2012), 141, 583-584.

"We are going to whip them to-day."

The sound of gunfire shook the men of the XII Corps awake before dawn on September 17, 1862. When the distant skirmishing gave way to volleys and cannon fire, they struggled to their feet after just three hours of sleep under a light rain and began a fitful march toward the fighting.

Officers called a halt that lasted nearly an hour, and they rested in formation. It was not yet 6:30 a.m. The head of the column was west of Samuel Poffenberger's woods. The soldiers distracted themselves as best they could, some trying to brew coffee. Hecklers mocked the knots of men retreating past them. Memories of past disappointments, particularly those suffered during the past six weeks, were hard to shake off. A little after 7:00 a.m. the rumbling sounds of battle grew more menacing as they rose toward a crescendo. Word spread that the Confederates were counterattacking the army's I Corps under Joe Hooker.

An older mounted officer rode to the edge of the woods on high ground to observe the fighting. He soon returned at a gallop, his white hair and beard flowing behind him. His men knew this meant action, jumped to their feet, and grabbed their stacked arms. The Hoosier veterans of the 27th Indiana cheered as the general thundered past. "That's right, boys; you may well cheer," he shouted while waving his hat. "We are going to whip them to-day!" The Indiana boys cheered louder. As one onlooker would later recall, the words "Enthused every man with the old General's spirit. We felt for the first time that we had a corps commander capable of leading us to victory."[4]

---

4 Edmund R. Brown, *The Twenty-Seventh Indiana Volunteer Infantry in the War of the Rebellion, 1861-1865*, (1899), 241; John Bresnahan, "Battle of Antietam," *National Tribune*, February 21, 1889.

Part I

II Corps, Army of Virginia
From Little Washington to Washington, DC
July 28 to September 3, 1862

"When sorrows come, they come not single spies
But in battalions."
— Hamlet, Act 4, Scene 5

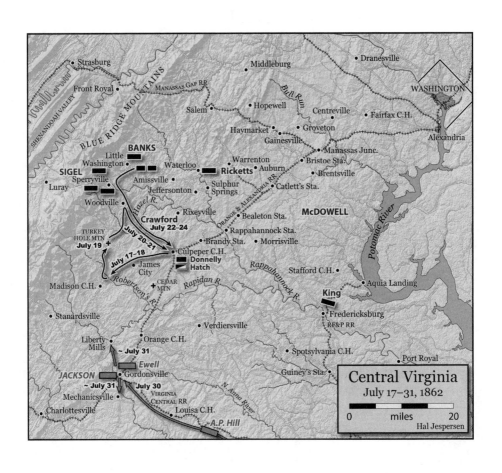

Strasburg

Front Royal

SHENANDOAH VALLEY

BLUE RIDGE MOUNTAINS

MANASSAS GAP RR

Middleburg

Dranesville

WASHINGTON

Salem

Bull Run

Hopewell

Centreville

Fairfax C.H.

Haymarket

Groveton

Alexandria

Gainesville

Manassas Junc.

BANKS

Little
Washington

Waterloo

Warrenton

Bristoe Sta.

SIGEL

Sperryville

Amissville

Ricketts

Auburn

Brentsville

Luray

Jeffersonton

Sulphur
Springs

Catlett's Sta.

ORANGE & ALEXANDRIA RR

Woodville

Hazel R.

Rixeyville

Bealeton Sta.

McDOWELL

Crawford
July 22–24

Rappahannock Sta.

TURKEY
HOLE MTN
July 19

July 20–21

Brandy Sta.

Morrisville

Potomac River

July 17–18

Culpeper C.H.
Donnelly
Hatch

Stafford C.H.

Aquia Landing

James
City

Rappahannock R.

Madison C.H.

Robertson's R.

CEDAR
MTN

Rapidan R.

King

Stanardsville

Verdiersville

Fredericksburg

RF&P RR

Liberty
Mills

Orange C.H.

Spotsylvania C.H.

Port Royal

~ July 31

Ewell

JACKSON

Gordonsville

Guiney's Sta.

~ July 31

July 30

VIRGINIA
CENTRAL RR

N. Anna River

Mechanicsville

Charlottesville

Louisa C.H.

A.P. Hill

Central Virginia
July 17–31, 1862

0   miles   20

Hal Jespersen

Chapter 1

"The stupidity of past follies must be atoned for by energetic blows."[1]

— James Gillette, 3rd Maryland

Banks's Corps from Little Washington to Culpeper Court House

July 28–August 7, 1862

On the clear morning of July 28, 1862, near their camp outside the rolling hills near Little Washington, Virginia, Maj. Gen. Nathanial P. Banks's forces underwent extensive drills. Banks arrayed 5,000 infantrymen on a 60-acre field, and the troops stood in defensive squares, confronting both charging cavalry and the sweltering Virginia heat. The Yankee cavalry failed to disperse the infantrymen, twice charging furiously and not breaking off until nearly on their comrades' bayonets.

Alonzo Quint, chaplain of the 2nd Massachusetts, described these Napoleonic-era anachronisms as "sham fights" that occurred after Banks reviewed and drilled all the units in his camp: 12 infantry regiments and 50 artillery pieces. A Pennsylvanian described the men as being "in good trim and all alacrity to obey the commands," which Banks issued in his "clear, deep tone of voice."[2]

---

1 James Gillette to Mother, August 7, 1862, James Gillette Papers, LC.

2 Alonzo H. Quint, *The Record of the Second Massachusetts Infantry, 1861-1865* (Boston, 1867), 101-102; *The Warren* [PA] *Ledger*, August 13, 1862; Julian Wisner Hinkley, Diary, July 28, 1862, Julian Wisner Hinkley Papers, WHS; John O. Foering, Diary, July 28, 1862, HSP; William A. Armor to brother, July 29, 1862, William A. Armor Papers, PSA. Different accounts place the

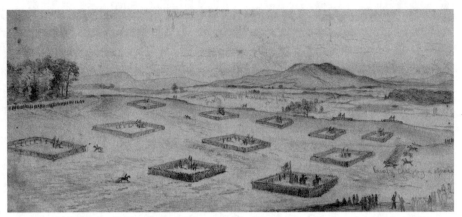

"Grand Review of N. P. Banks' Corps at Little Washington, Va," on July 28th, 1862, Edwin Forbes. *Library of Congress*

Banks was proud that he had personally directed the entire command and told his wife he felt as if he had been doing it all his life. This was not so. Despite his lofty rank, Banks lacked military experience. He was a "political general," a former Speaker of the U.S. House of Representatives and Governor of Massachusetts who gained his major general's commission via his political connections. Before properly learning the mechanics of his new trade, he had seniority over most other major generals. Banks's military service began in Baltimore, where he successfully quelled secessionist rumblings. He was then given command of the Department of the Shenandoah, furtively dispatching the 3rd Wisconsin to Frederick, Maryland, to arrest a cabal of secessionist state delegates.[3]

The following spring, Banks followed Stonewall Jackson south, up the Shenandoah Valley, and established a garrison down the valley at Strasburg, Virginia. In late May, Jackson threatened Banks's lines of communication, precipitating the latter's unnecessarily tardy withdrawal to Winchester. Banks and Brig. Gen. Alpheus S. Williams, commanding the sole division present, entered

---

number of regiments present at 11 and 14-15, the number of men at 5,000-8,000, and 48-75 artillery pieces. Subtracting Crawford's brigade and the Ohio portion of Geary's brigade, which had not yet arrived, leaves no more than 12 regiments. Though Banks wrote to his wife (July 29, 1862, Banks Papers, LC) of 10,000 men present, he had less than 7,000 at Cedar Mountain after those eight regiments had rejoined the command.

3 Banks to wife, July 29, 1862, LC; Ezra J. Warner, *Generals in Blue: Lives of the Union Commanders* (Baton Rouge, 1992), 18; Fred Harvey Harrington, *Fighting Politician: Major General N. P. Banks* (Philadelphia, 1948), 57-60.

Winchester that evening. Units that had fought rearguard actions on the retreat showed up later. The 27th Indiana and 28th New York finally arrived at 11:00 p.m., and the 2nd Massachusetts dragged in at 2:00 a.m. Williams's brigade commanders, Cols. George H. Gordon and Dudley Donnelly, stayed on the field all night, preparing for possible Rebel attacks.[4]

When Jackson, who outnumbered Banks three to one, arrived at dawn, he turned Banks's flank and pursued the Northerners through the streets of Winchester while citizens fired at the Yankees from windows. After a grueling, day-long march from Strasburg and a demoralizing drubbing at Winchester, Banks's troops now trudged another 35 miles to safety on the Potomac's north shore at Williamsport, Maryland. Though many of his soldiers still firmly trusted Banks, this latest experience soured others. Captain Richard Cary, a company commander in the 2nd Massachusetts, wrote disgustedly in late June that, "Being under Banks is very much like being in company with a drunken man who flourishes a revolver. You may be shot at any moment & then not have the satisfaction of knowing it was intentional but owing merely to your excited friend not knowing what he was about."[5]

Banks soon returned to Virginia, and when Maj. Gen. John Pope's Army of Virginia was created on June 26, Banks's reorganized, two-division command became its II Corps. Banks made widespread changes in corps leadership during this time. After the Winchester defeat, Brig. Gen. Samuel Wylie Crawford supplanted Col. Donnelly in command of Williams's 1st Brigade. Donnelly reassumed command of the 28th New York. The brigade's soldiers, who invariably thought well of Donnelly, resented this change. Two brigades, which constituted two-thirds of Brig. Gen. Christopher C. Augur's 2nd Division, joined the command near Amissville on July 10. Brigadier Generals Henry Prince and George S. Greene assumed command of these brigades, neither of which had seen serious action. Augur also had recently joined his command, which reached Little Washington on July 19, two days after the rest of Banks's corps. On August 1, a final brigade, under Brig. Gen. Erastus Tyler, was placed in Augur's division. Brigadier General John W. Geary assumed command of the brigade, and Tyler left

4 Harrington, *Fighting Politician*, 67-70; George H. Gordon, *Brook Farm to Cedar Mountain: In the War of the Great Rebellion, 1861-1862* (Boston, 1883), 207; Edwin E. Bryant, *History of the Third Regiment of Wisconsin Volunteer Infantry, 1861-1865* (Madison, 1891), 62.

5 James G. Hollandsworth, Jr., *Pretense of Glory: The Life of General Nathaniel P. Banks* (Baton Rouge, 1998), 67; Richard Cary to wife, June 25, 1862, Richard Cary Letters, MHS.

the corps. Geary's former command, the 28th Pennsylvania, joined four veteran Ohio regiments that had fought Jackson at Kernstown and Port Republic.[6]

In late June and early July, Banks's troops devastated the ubiquitous cherries and blackberries growing in the region. On the march to Amissville on July 7, each man in the company marching ahead of the 10th Maine slung a cherry tree bough over his shoulder, reminding Lt. John Gould of the moving forest fulfilling the witches' prophecy to Macbeth. Tragic allusions aside, it was a relaxing time for Banks's corps. Gould and his comrades enjoyed a "picnic life" in the forest near Amissville. All were cheerful and rations plentiful. "The woods ring continually with a thousand laughing voices, or echo the tunes of the bands." Colonel George Cobham, who could hear the dozen regimental bands playing within earshot, thought the evenings "very pleasant." A staff clerk's mistake, however, briefly halted this relaxing time, resulting in the corps marching toward Warrenton rather than its correct destination of Little Washington, north of the Rappahannock. The corps found a "cheerless and devastated country." In but six weeks hence, they would be here again.[7]

After reaching Little Washington, Williams's division began complaining about its placement. Captain Richard Cary griped, "We have got a beastly camp ground on the side of a steep hill & just where the line of battle is intended to be in case of a fight. . . . Neither Crawford nor Gordon wanted to camp here." One of Banks's aides quashed these protests, and the division remained there until July 25, when it moved to a spot closer to the 60-acre drill field. Except for the oppressive heat, Cary was mostly satisfied with the new camp. He wished he had a, "Scientific interest in bugs of which I have always on hand—or rather all over me—in my tent a very large & choice assortment including every variety."[8]

At its new camp, the soldiers affected more than the population of cherries. General Gordon sympathized: "Our camps generally were established in the neighborhood of quiet farms, which we occupied and overran, until we became a great unnatural plague to the people. We filled their woods with our tents, we killed

6 Hinkley Diary, July 17, 1862, WHS; Gordon, *Brook Farm*, 272; Gould, *10th Maine*, 156; Chandler Gillam to wife, June 27, 1862, Chandler B. Gillam Papers, LC; Warner, *Generals in Blue*, 515.

7 Gould, *10th Maine*, 155-157. George A. Cobham, Jr., to sister, July 14, 1862, WCHS, transcript copy at GNMP; Richard Eddy, *History of the Sixtieth Regiment New York State Volunteers, From the Commencement of its Organization in July, 1862, to its Public Reception at Ogdensburgh as a Veteran Command, January 7th, 1864* (Philadelphia, 1864), 135.

8 Quint, *2nd Massachusetts*, 102; Cary to wife, July 16/18, 26, 1862, MHS.

Maj. Gen. John Pope, Army of Virginia
Library of Congress

their sheep and calves, and substituted, for the 'drowsy tinkling of their lowing herds,' the beating drum, the ear-piercing fife, and all the loud alarum of war." According to its regimental history, darkness brought, "in some way," a variety of livestock and vegetables into the 60th New York's camp. Lieutenant James J. Gillette, commissary officer for Prince's brigade, heartily disdained his fellow soldiers' behavior:

> Straggling soldiers have been known to rob the farm houses and even small cottages. The homes of the poor of every ounce of food or forage contained in them. Families have been left without the means of preparing a meal of victuals. . . .The anxieties, privations and discomforts of those removed from the scene of wars conflicts, away from the path of armies know nothing of the suffering or inconveniences compared with the horrors undergone by the people of Virginia. . . .The lawless acts of many of our soldiery are worthy of worse than death. The villains urge as authority: Gen Pope's order.[9]

* * *

Major General John Pope graduated from West Point in 1842 and was twice brevetted in the Mexican War. He achieved success in the Western Theater in the early days of the Civil War, capturing New Madrid, Missouri, and Island Number 10 on the Mississippi River. Lincoln brought him east during the Army of the Potomac's glacially slow march up the York-James peninsula, southeast of Richmond. Pope's mission was to coordinate and focus the scattered and hitherto ineffective forces operating in and around the Shenandoah Valley. Their common opponent, Stonewall Jackson, had temporarily quit the Valley to support Robert E.

---

9   Gordon, *Brook Farm*, 266; Eddy, *Sixtieth New York*, 132; Gillette to Mother, July 31, 1862, LC.

Lee's defense of Richmond. On June 26, the commands of Banks and Maj. Gens. John C. Fremont and Irvin McDowell were consolidated into Pope's Army of Virginia. East of Richmond, Lee's forces were fighting the "Seven Days" battles, which resulted in Maj. Gen. George B. McClellan's "change of base" from the York to the James River.[10]

The Army of Virginia was charged with covering Washington and relieving the pressure on McClellan's Army of the Potomac at Harrison's Landing on the James by threatening Lee's supply line on the Virginia Central Railroad near Gordonsville. Pope concentrated his army on a line from Sperryville to Fredericksburg. Major General Franz Sigel, Fremont's replacement, camped at Sperryville. Banks was southeast of Little Washington, to Sigel's east, and yet further east, McDowell's corps was strung out along the Rappahannock River from Waterloo Bridge to Fredericksburg. Pope remained in Washington and issued a flurry of orders. Pope directed his men to subsist off the land in order to "secure efficient and rapid operations," but his orders gave rise to the unrestrained foraging that Union officers struggled to constrain. General Orders Nos. 7 and 11 decreed draconian measures, such as burning houses of civilians from which Union troops were ambushed, executing oath violators, and forcing the populace to repair guerilla damage.[11]

Pope's orders, sanctioned by the Lincoln administration, stirred up a storm and provided angry Virginians further cause for acrimony. Uncharacteristically eager to punish his adversary, Lee told Jackson on July 27, "I want Pope to be suppressed. The course indicated in his orders, if the newspapers report them correctly, cannot be permitted and will lead to retaliation on our part. You had better inform him the first opportunity." During a foraging expedition to gather horses, one resident uttered prayers that Jackson would come to their rescue and shoot every one of the Yankee riders. Sergeant Washington L. Hicks, the 28th New York's clerk, lamented, "Union feeling here was not in the ascendant," and "the ladies feeling secure in the liberty accorded to their sex were very bitter and sometimes insulting in their language to our troops."[12]

---

10 Warner, *Generals in Blue*, 376; Joseph L. Harsh, *Confederate Tide Rising: Robert E. Lee and the Making of Southern Strategy, 1861-1862* (Kent, OH, 1998), 89-97.

11 *The War of the Rebellion: A Compilation of the Official Records of the Union and Confederate Armies*, 128 vols. (Washington, DC, 1880-1901), Series 1, vol. 12, part 2, pages 21, 23, 50-52, hereafter cited as *OR*. All references are to Series 1 unless otherwise noted.

12 *OR* 11, Pt. 3, 359; *OR* 12, pt. 3, 500-1, 919; Joseph Kerns to Banks, July 14, 1862, Banks Papers, LC; Washington L. Hicks, Diary, 6, Chandler Gillam Papers, LC. The Hicks Diary,

2nd Lieutenant Julian Wisner Hinkley,
3rd Wisconsin
Wisconsin Veterans Museum (Madison, WI)

Hoping to inspire the army, Pope issued an instantly infamous circular:

I have come to you from the West, where we have always seen the backs of our enemies; from an army whose business it has been to seek the adversary and to beat him when he was found; whose policy has been attack and not defense.. . . dismiss from your minds certain phrases, which I am sorry to find so much in vogue amongst you. I hear constantly of "taking strong positions and holding them," of "lines of retreat," and of "bases of supply." Let us discard such ideas. The strongest position a soldier should desire to occupy is one from which he can most easily advance against the enemy. Let us study the probable lines of retreat of our opponents, and leave our own to take care of themselves.[13]

Some of Pope's new soldiers viewed his hortatory declarations favorably at first, while others found them patronizing.[14]

On the day Pope issued this order, he wrote Banks, trying to drive his point home. He began with his strategic intentions. Pope wanted his three corps in position to concentrate within 24 hours for an advance either on the railroad at Gordonsville or against the Confederate flank. He then explained that he did not intend to assume, "Strong positions . . . to defend them. . . . I shall push forward and do the attacking myself . . . the attack will hereafter always be made by us." This letter, Pope's bombastic orders, and Banks's humiliating experience two months

contained in the Gillam Papers, uses page numbers more consistently than dates of entry. Its pagination restarts in June 1862, and that is the page range referenced throughout this narrative.

13 *OR* 12, pt. 3, 473-474.

14 Hicks Diary, 9-10, LC; William Shimp to Anna, July 28, 1862, CWDocColl, USA; Quint, *2nd Massachusetts*, 100-101.

earlier and concern for public sentiment would interact disastrously in the coming weeks.[15]

*   *   *

From his excellent vantage point near the viewing platform, officer of the guard Lt. Julian Hinkley thought Banks's July 28 grand review presented a "splendid appearance." "[T]he immense superiority of Gordon's brigade in drill and soldierly appearance was apparent to every officer," he wrote. That brigade, to which Hinkley belonged, had a reputation for discipline and thorough drilling. This was especially true in the 2nd Massachusetts, which had been molded by its erstwhile commander, Brig. Gen. George H. Gordon.[16]

A West Point classmate of George McClellan, Gordon had seen heavy fighting as a dragoon in the Mounted Rifles during the Mexican War. Twice wounded, Gordon earned a brevet to first lieutenant for gallantry at Cerro Gordo. He later attended Harvard and practiced law in Massachusetts. After securing approval from Governor John Andrew and President Lincoln to handpick its officers, Gordon formed the 2nd Massachusetts Infantry after Lincoln's initial call for volunteers after Fort Sumter. He intended to craft the best volunteer regiment in the army. Well-equipped, modeled on the Regular Army, and meticulously prepared, its officers came from prominent Boston families. One of these, Capt. Richard Cary, deemed Gordon, "The best military man I have seen in the valley, he is quicker & has more decision than the others I have had an opportunity of seeing."[17]

Unfortunately Gordon's decisiveness came with an apparently insolent manner that caused problems up and down the chain of command. The 27th Indiana despised him. Its Midwestern farmers initially perceived an "air of contemptuous superiority" toward them from the 2nd Massachusetts. Though their angst toward the Bay Staters cooled in time, the Hoosiers still loathed Gordon, an educated and experienced officer but one, "So supremely stuck on

15 John Pope to Banks, July 14, 1862, Banks Papers, LC.

16 Hinkley Diary, July 28, 1862, WHS.

17 Warner, *Generals in Blue*, 177; Gordon, *Brook Farm*, 2-3, 9; John H. and David J. Eicher, *Civil War High Commands* (Stanford, CA, 2001), 259, 517; George W. Cullum, *Biographical Register of the Officers and Graduates of the U. S. Military Academy at West Point, N.Y. from its Establishment, in 1802, to 1890 with the Early History of the United States Military Academy, Vol. II* (Boston, 1891), 291-292; Cary to wife, July 16/18, 1862, MHS.

Brig. Gen. George Henry Gordon
Library of Congress

himself that he could not be respectful to superiors, considerate of subordinates, or learn anything from anybody." Indeed, one man thought the regiment would have been better off had a "stalking pestilence" visited it. Their relations worsened when Gordon's Winchester battle report claimed the Indianans broke without orders after being flanked. Conversely, the lumbermen and raftsmen of the 3rd Wisconsin quickly overcame an initial aversion to the 2nd Massachusetts's transfer into the brigade in March 1862, and eventually formed a close friendship with the regiment.[18]

Gordon also had several run-ins with Banks. The previous year, Banks withdrew guards he had promised Gordon after the latter punished an enlisted man from another regiment by stringing him up by his thumbs. According to one officer, this episode proved Banks could not "throw off the politician," since he removed the guards in response to his clamoring soldiers. Banks also observed that, though he was too outspoken with superiors and regularly failed to restrain contempt for his politician commander, Gordon's personal courage and dash inspired his men. Their strained relationship came to a head on the eve of Banks's retreat from Strasburg. When Jackson threatened the Federal line of communication with Winchester, Gordon and Banks disagreed about when to abandon the town. According to Gordon, Banks initially balked at the suggestion of leaving, citing public opinion. Gordon apparently shared details of the conversation with his 2nd Massachusetts officers, who bristled at the incident. "You can imagine how pleasant it is to stand in a rain of bullets & think not that it is to save your country or from stern military necessity," explained a disgusted Capt. Cary, "but because the general who commands you fears that the public will not

---

18 Brown, *Twenty-Seventh Indiana*, 106, 165-168; Julian Wisner Hinkley, *A Narrative of Service with the Third Wisconsin Infantry* (Madison, WI, 1912), 15, 18. After the battle of Winchester, General Green superseded him, but Gordon received his star in June and returned to the brigade.

Capt. Richard Cary, 2nd Massachusetts,
Company G
U.S. Army Heritage and Education Center

understand why he retreats unless the reason is explained to them thro' the medium of a long list of dead, wounded & missing."[19]

With thoughts of Winchester fresh in their minds, Gordon's men drilled intensively on the 60-acre field throughout late July. Two days after Banks's grand review, Gordon led the whole brigade in some novel advanced maneuvers. The regiments conducted firing practice, but Lieutenant Hinkley's midwestern woodsmen scarcely needed to hone their shooting skills.[20]

* * *

After the review, Banks extolled the "fine and soldierly appearance" of Brig. Gen. John White Geary's mixed Ohio/Pennsylvania brigade. Geary told his wife that "all passed off satisfactorily."[21]

Lieutenant Colonel Hector Tyndale, a former Philadelphia ceramics and glass importer, commanded the 28th Pennsylvania, Geary's former regiment. In mid-May, Tyndale led a detachment of three companies and a cavalry detail at Front Royal while Banks garrisoned Strasburg. He wired Banks that the Luray Valley appeared to be filling with Confederates, intelligence that Banks

---

19 Gordon, *Brook Farm*, 50-53, 192-193; Cary to wife, September 6 and 21, 1861, and June 18, 1862, MHS.

20 Hinkley Diary, July 30, August 2 and 4, 1862, WHS; Gordon, *Brook Farm*, 273; William Wallace, Diary, August 4, 1862, WHS.

21 Foering Diary, July 28, 1862, HSP; John Geary to wife, July 29, 1862, Geary Papers, HSP.

disregarded. A few days later, Jackson's men overwhelmed Tyndale's relief regiment, the 1st Maryland, before menacing Banks's supply line.[22]

Tyndale drove his men hard and became acutely unpopular. William Roberts, Jr., of the 28th Pennsylvania wrote that on a sizzling day in early July, "That miserable beast . . . urged the men on until many dropped exhausted [and] if a man left the ranks for a drink of water when a halt was not ordered this wretch would make them pour it out. Every man hates him bitterly . . . on this inhuman march, 400 men only out of 1200 . . . reached camp." Robert M. Erwin thought the men had been "done out" on that march. He declined to say what was "generally thought" of Tyndale, but did not think the regiment would long "stand its present usage." Geary warned Tyndale that he would be cashiered if he ever marched his men like that again. The next day's march was slow with many long rests.[23]

After Banks's review, Tyndale ordered Company K to fall in and, in full view of the rest of the regiment, dressed its men down as, "A set of worthless vagabonds ... Skulks. [A] disgrace to the Regt. Scoundrels and Cowards." He then threatened to chain their wrists and march them before the regiment like slaves with the officers following, swordless. Such behavior naturally alienated men he would soon lead into combat, and fellow officers eventually brought charges against him for "tyrannical and capricious conduct unbecoming an officer and a gentleman."[24]

*   *   *

The 60th New York of Greene's brigade faced troubles of its own. An outbreak of typhoid fever developed in its camp near Amissville, and while on the march toward Little Washington on July 17, a drenching rain caused a freshet on the Rappahannock River as the men reached it. They crossed the river on a log bridge and their accompanying battery forded it, but their supply trains could not cross. Left without food or cooking utensils, they were forced to forage. The Rappahannock continued to rise and eventually submerged the wagons for twelve

22 Warner, *Generals in Blue*, 517; John M. McLaughlin, *A Memoir of Hector Tyndale, Brigadier-General and Brevet Major-General, U. S. Volunteers* (Philadelphia, 1882) 11-12. Another facet of Tyndale's character was revealed on the eve of the radical abolitionist John Brown's execution in 1859. He accompanied Brown's wife to Harper's Ferry for the hanging and then escorted her and the remains to New York.

23 William Roberts, Jr., to father, July 8, 1862, William Roberts, Jr., Papers, HSP; transcript, Robert M. Erwin to father and mother, July 14, 1862, USA.

24 "28th Pennsylvania Volunteer Papers, 1861-1863," HSP.

hours. At midday on July 20, teamsters recovered waterlogged and muddy papers, blankets, and uniforms.[25]

On July 21, the 60th New York hailed the return of four detached companies that had been guarding the B&O Railroad. The regiment had spent the first year of war on railroad duty and was just entering active field service. The returning detachment, under Maj. Edward James, performed well en route. On July 17, discovering that they missed the crossing of the swollen Rappahannock, James continued upstream to Waterloo Bridge, which had been washed away after the river rose 18 feet over its banks. With Banks nearby and 200 wagons filled with stores for his and Sigel's corps engulfed by the river, James's men worked to save many wagons and dray animals. Banks thanked them for averting famine in the corps.[26]

After the detachment's return, disease proliferated in the 60th. On July 22nd, 64 troops were being treated—and deaths occurred almost daily. By August 4, the sick numbered 311. The next morning, Greene ordered the regiment to move to Fauquier White Sulphur Springs, south of Warrenton on the Rappahannock. At sunset, with General Greene, his staff, and representatives of other units present, the 60th buried two of its lieutenants. That evening, two more died. "[T]he drum and fife constantly sounding the death march," wrote General Gordon, "made the evenings feel sad and solemn." If the corps was not meeting Pope's order to live off the land, "We were doing the next best thing—we were dying on it." Lieutenant James Gillette simply observed: "the bands were ever playing the dirge."

Because of its waters' supposed medicinal qualities, the Sulphur Springs resort was a popular and well-known destination. The 60th New York, residing in its brick buildings and cottages and using its pavilions for a hospital, would recuperate there and miss the coming battle. But Colonel Goodrich and his men would soon return to action.[27]

*　*　*

Portions of Banks's command were absent during the concentration at Little Washington. As part of his effort to disrupt Lee's connection with the Shenandoah

---

25 Eddy, *Sixtieth New York*, 132, 135.

26 Ibid., 139, 141-142.

27 Ibid., 143-151, 156; Gordon, *Brook Farm*, 277; Gillette to Mother, August 7, 1862, LC.

Valley via the Virginia Central Railroad, Pope ordered Banks's cavalry, under Brig. Gen. John Porter Hatch, and "sufficient infantry" south to occupy the "trim little village" of Culpeper. On July 14, Pope directed Hatch to proceed south from Culpeper, occupy Gordonsville, and destroy the tracks for 10–15 miles east toward Richmond. That same day, Banks sent Colonel Donnelly and the 28th New York, along with the 46th Pennsylvania of Crawford's brigade, forward with two days' rations. They marched at sunset, passed through Warrenton, and forded the Rappahannock at Sulphur Springs. By the morning of July 16, they were encamped near a Confederate cemetery, one mile south of Culpeper.[28]

Donnelly's detachment broke camp early on July 17 and followed Hatch's cavalry through a heavy downpour. The cavalry and artillery had badly churned the muddy roads and it was a sluggish, tiring march. The expedition continued through James City to Robertson's River, where the cavalry could not ford the swollen stream. The field on which they camped was ankle-deep in water, and Donnelly's men spent the night and the next day there.[29]

On July 19, the column waded the river near Madison. Rumors spread that two brigades under Confederate Maj. Gen. Richard Ewell were nearby. Constantly on the alert for suspected threats, Donnelly's detachment changed direction and withdrew over "mountainous and unfrequented roads" to Turkey Hole Mountain, up a "precipitous mountain path," and through brambles "in the bottom of some deep and dark ravine."[30]

After reaching Turkey Hole Mountain, Donnelly's rations ran out. Soldiers collected chickens and vegetables from nearby residences, and a makeshift charge by some cavalrymen killed eight to ten enemy geese. The quixotic dash amused the infantrymen, many of whom habitually accused the cavalry of having a reputation for "charging rearward." Leaving Turkey Hole Mountain, the column passed through Woodville before reaching Culpeper on July 21.[31]

---

28 Pope to Banks, July 14, 1862, Banks Papers, LC; George Townsend, *Campaigns of a Non-Combatant and His Romaunt Abroad During the War* (New York, 1866), 239; Hicks Diary, 6, LC.

29 Hicks Diary, 7, LC.

30 Charles Boyce, "A History of the 28th Regiment, New York State Volunteers," Charles H. Boyce Papers, LC, 107, 110; Chandler Gillam to Sarah Gillam, July 23, 1862, LC. The Boyce manuscript appears to be a copy, largely verbatim, of the Washington Hicks Diary. Boyce added details in a few instances; otherwise, Hicks is referenced.

31 Boyce, "28th Regiment," 108.

Pope was not pleased. He expected Hatch to be in Charlottesville, and had earlier directed Banks to spur his cavalry chief along. Hatch might push on to the James River, twenty miles south of Charlottesville, the commanding general added, to destroy a canal. Pope was unaware that Hatch had brought an infantry escort for his cavalry raid and that they were still encamped at Culpeper. On July 18, Banks forwarded to Pope a dispatch Hatch had sent the day before, which betrayed the makeup of his expedition. The confounded Pope immediately directed Banks to recall the infantry and its trains. "I fear the whole object of the expedition is frustrated by the terrible delay occasioned by this strange misapprehension," he seethed, which could "possibly lead to serious consequences." Moreover, Hatch's circuitous march failed to occupy Gordonsville, let alone Charlottesville. Worse still, Lee ordered Stonewall Jackson, with his former division and another under Ewell, to Louisa Court House and on to Gordonsville "if practicable." Jackson accomplished the first leg of this assignment on the rails that Hatch had been ordered to destroy. Ewell's division arrived in Gordonsville on July 15. Hatch blamed the delay in carrying out his mission on poor roads.[32]

On July 20, Pope explicitly instructed Hatch to proceed to Charlottesville and destroy the rail lines from there to both Gordonsville and Lynchburg, an effort Hatch abandoned shortly after starting. As a result, Pope replaced Hatch with Brig. Gen. John Buford, an assistant inspector general. Buford, who would gain fame at Gettysburg 11 months hence, found a dilapidated command with no records beyond inaccurate morning reports and troopers who misunderstood their duties as cavalrymen. Pope pressed his mounted arm to harass the enemy energetically, but cavalry detachments were scattered across the map and Buford could not make sense of his units' positions easily or quickly. He recalled detachments and requested infantry support from Sigel's I Corps, in front of which the II Corps cavalry operated. By August 7, Buford's cavalry picketed the Rapidan between Barnett's Ford and the Blue Ridge, still screening Sigel's corps. Brigadier General George Bayard's four cavalry regiments from McDowell's corps, sent by Pope to Culpeper to support Hatch on July 16, remained in front of Culpeper. While

---

32 OR 12, pt. 3, 476, 481, 484, 915; OR 12, pt. 2, 24; John S. Clark, Report to Banks, August 3, 1862, Banks Papers, LC; McHenry Howard, *Recollections of a Maryland Confederate Soldier and Staff Officer Under Johnston, Jackson and Lee* (Baltimore, 1914), 161; Jubal Anderson Early, *Autobiographical Sketch and Narrative of the War Between the States* (Philadelphia, 1912), 92. With an eye to retreat routes, Col. John S. Clark of Banks's staff reported on August 3 that the roads south of the Rapidan in Orange, Louisa, and Spotsylvania counties could be considered generally good, but those north of the Rapidan, in Culpeper County, were "bad very bad" and undependable.

occupying a position along the Rapidan between Raccoon Ford to the east and linked with Buford at Barnett's Ford to the west, Bayard's men screened, and occasionally cooperated with, Banks's infantry.[33]

When Colonel Donnelly's two-regiment demi-brigade returned to Culpeper on July 21, it found abundant provisions. Though supply wagons from Warrenton proved insufficient, local residents begrudgingly met the balance of their needs with plentiful potatoes, honey, ham, butter, and milk. Many soldiers bought supplies with Confederate money, which the residents preferred. For the Yankees, this was the same as appropriating them. The regiments also had the good fortune to camp next to a large cornfield, which the men liberally plundered. The owner's complaints to Donnelly precipitated a heated discussion and a Northern victory. If the plaintiff was a Union man, the colonel said, he, "Ought to be willing to give a few ears of corn to half-starved soldiers, fighting to preserve the Union; and if, as I suspect, you are a rebel, you deserve to lose your entire crop."[34]

This compulsory largesse elicited no warmth, and the locals openly disdained the soldiers. One scowling woman on a veranda jeered "Scum!" through clenched teeth at a passing regiment. Others turned their backs to soldiers and detoured off sidewalks to avoid walking under the United States flag. When Confederate prisoners arrived in town after a few days, the townspeople effusively attended to their needs. A sergeant in Capt. Joseph M. Knap's Battery E, Pennsylvania Light Artillery, observed that women and their slaves brought whatever "delicacies" the Rebels needed at all hours of the day, but would claim that nothing was available when Northerners asked.[35]

The Federal concentration near Culpeper, meanwhile, continued to develop. The two-regiment balance of Crawford's brigade left Little Washington before dawn on July 22, their mountainside camp aflame behind them. They joined Donnelly's detachment two days later. Crawford assumed command, deploying heavy pickets to thwart Confederate cavalry raids and posting Capt. Jacob

33 OR 12, pt. 2, 24 and pt. 3, 490-491; John Pope to Banks, July 14, 1862, Special Order No. 31, August 2, 1862, and John Buford, Report, August 4, 1862, Banks Papers, LC.

34 Gould, *10th Maine*, 161; Chandler Gillam to Parents, July 25, 1862, and C. Gillam to S. Gillam, July 28, 1862, LC; Charles W. Boyce, *A Brief History of the Twenty-eighth Regiment New York State Volunteers* (Buffalo, NY, 1896), 34.

35 Boyce, *Twenty-eighth New York*, 34; Townsend, *Campaigns of a Non-Combatant*, 242; David Nichol to family, August 7, 1862, David Nichol Letters, USA.

Maj. Gen. Nathaniel Prentiss Banks and staff. Col. John S. Clark is on Banks's left.
National Archives Records Administration

Roemer's Battery L, 2nd New York Light Artillery, east of town, covering the roads from Orange.[36]

On August 1, Roemer's artillerymen marked former President Martin Van Buren's death by firing once a minute until they recognized all 26 states that were part of the Union during Van Buren's term. The troops could clearly observe the townspeople flying into hysterics after the first shot, thinking they were being shelled. This amusement alone was worth the onerous guard duty.[37]

* * *

The situation at Culpeper tried Pope's patience. In addition to Hatch's inactivity, Banks communicated little about what was occurring in his front. On July 23, Pope exhorted Banks to pay attention to developments there and report them to headquarters daily. That same day, he confided to Irvin McDowell that he felt Banks knew nothing about military affairs. Not satisfied with Banks's July 24

36 Gould, *10th Maine*, 159; Hicks Diary, 9, LC; Jacob Roemer, *Reminiscences of the War of the Rebellion, 1861-1865* (Flushing, NY, 1897), 35.

37 Roemer, *Reminiscences*, 36.

report, Pope began coaching him on July 25. He cautioned Banks about blindly trusting his commanders and suggested he send a trusted staff officer to Culpeper to manage matters. The next day, Banks dispatched Col. John S. Clark, who collected intelligence for the next few weeks, at times providing important information. Finally, Pope cautioned against "the grave consequences which result from carelessness in our front," apparently a thinly veiled reminder of the Strasburg-Winchester debacle. Banks likely perceived it as such.[38]

Banks was not the only officer being prodded from above. Echoing Pope's dispatches, Banks began putting spurs to Crawford on July 26. As a result, scouting parties started to penetrate the Rapidan fords, though their incursions were usually brief. The urgency and frustration of Banks's communications with Crawford grew until the end of July, when he pushed Crawford to conduct wider reconnaissances beyond the river. On July 29, Clark reported the, "Universal ill feeling here among the officers against Gen. Crawford so much so as seriously to impair the efficiency of the troops." Clark said he would explain this to Banks "when I see you," adding that Crawford felt it "not at all safe" for anything less than a brigade of infantry to cross the Rapidan.[39]

On July 31, Clark passed intelligence, gathered from slaves, that Confederate infantry was no closer than Gordonsville and their cavalry was heavily picketing the river. More importantly, trains from Richmond had deposited a large body of infantry on July 30. The 1st New Jersey Cavalry's commander substantiated this on the same day, reporting a skirmish with Rebel pickets northwest of Orange at Barnett's Ford. He also reported hearing trains constantly moving at Gordonsville, which was Maj. Gen. A. P. Hill's division arriving from Richmond to reinforce Jackson's two divisions. Colonel Clark worried that his scouting parties were too far from the enemy to be effective. In response, Banks reiterated the need for vigilance at the front and requested that Clark communicate his desires to Crawford, who in turn responded by going forward himself.[40]

Samuel W. Crawford, a native of Franklin County, Pennsylvania, graduated from the University of Pennsylvania's medical school in 1850. He served as an army surgeon on the frontier until being assigned to a fortuitous billet at the Charleston forts in 1860. After a short stay at Fort Moultrie, Crawford moved to Fort Sumter, where he commanded a battery during the Confederate

38 OR 12, pt. 3, 499-500, 506-507.

39 OR 12, pt. 3, 510-511, 521-522; John S. Clark to Banks, July 29, 1862, Banks Papers, LC.

40 Clark to Banks, July 31, 1862; Joseph Karge to John Hatch, July 31, 1862, Banks Papers, LC.

Brig. Gen. Samuel Wylie Crawford
Library of Congress

bombardment in April 1861. As was common, Crawford received outsized recognition for being in the right place during the war's opening events. By the spring of 1862, he was a brigadier general serving under Banks in the Shenandoah Valley. He was unassigned until after Winchester, when he displaced Donnelly as commander of Williams's 1st Brigade.[41]

On August 1, Crawford directed Bayard to hold Barnett's Ford upriver. The next day, Crawford accompanied two of Bayard's cavalry regiments upriver from Raccoon Ford, crossed at Somerville Ford, and continued southwest to Orange. At the junction with the Fredericksburg Road, a mile northeast of Orange, Crawford advanced two companies of the 1st Vermont and a squadron from the 5th New York as skirmishers. They discovered and drove in about 50 Confederate pickets. Company F of the 17th Virginia Cavalry Battalion under Capt. Foxhall Daingerfield advanced to high ground half a mile east of town.[42]

The Federals brushed aside Daingerfield's men, killing one and wounding another. Beneath them, the Fredericksburg Road entered Orange, becoming Main Street and continuing west toward Liberty Mills. At the eastern edge of the town, the Orange & Alexandria Railroad, oriented roughly north-south, crossed Main Street. Farther west on Main Street, a road extended north to Barnett's Ford and Madison. The courthouse stood at the northwest corner of this intersection, with the station and depot southeast of the courthouse. West of the courthouse, the Gordonsville Road began, coursing south-southwest from Main Street.[43]

---

41 Warner, *Generals in Blue*, 99.

42 OR 12, pt. 2, 111-113; Samuel Crawford to Banks, August 2 and 3, 1862, Banks Papers, LC; William N. McDonald, *A History of the Laurel Brigade* (Baltimore, 1907), 78.

43 Steaman Ruggles, "From the Vermont Cavalry," *Montpelier* [VT] *Green Mountain Daily Freeman*, August 13, 1862; Frank S. Dickinson, "Fifth New York Cavalry at Culpeper," in *The*

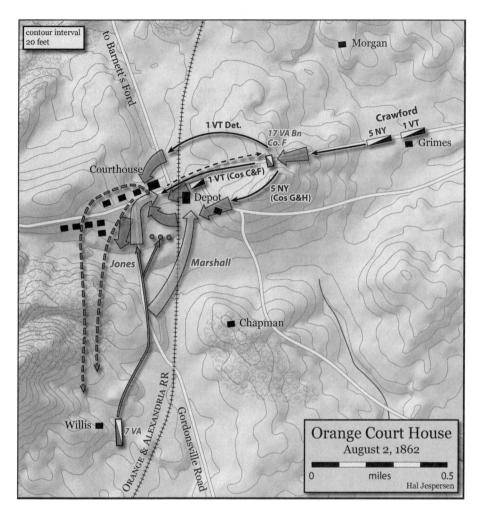

contour interval
20 feet

to Barnett's Ford

Morgan

Crawford

1 VT Det.

17 VA Bn
Co. F

5 NY   1 VT

Grimes

Courthouse

1 VT (Cos C&F)

Depot

5 NY
(Cos G&H)

Jones   Marshall

Chapman

Willis   7 VA

ORANGE & ALEXANDRIA RR

Gordonsville Road

Orange Court House
August 2, 1862

0   miles   0.5
Hal Jespersen

Crawford sent Capt. John Hammond and two companies from the 5th New York left to cross the Gordonsville Road south of town. A Vermont detachment headed right to approach Orange from the north. The main column entered town and headed west on Main Street. A New Yorker remembered "a stillness like that

Maine Bugle Campaign 1, Call 3 (Rockland, ME, July 1894), 247; S. Howell Brown, U.S. Army Engineering Corps, *Map of Orange Court House, 1863*, OCHS.

of death seemed to reign all around." Just ahead of them, the deserted street intersected the Gordonsville Road.[44]

Meanwhile, Col. William E. "Grumble" Jones arrived from Gordonsville with the 7th Virginia Cavalry. Reaching the Willis property three-quarters of a mile southwest of Orange, he learned of the Federal approach. A little farther on, Jones encountered Daingerfield's men streaming from town. Impressed by the situation's urgency, Jones immediately deployed Capt. John H. Magruder's company as sharpshooters and sent a detachment under Maj. Thomas Marshall (a descendant of the first chief justice of the United States Supreme Court) toward the Union left flank by way of the depot. As Crawford's main body neared the Gordonsville Road intersection, Magruder's men opened fire. Turning onto Main Street with sabers drawn, Jones's force collided with the head of Crawford's column. One of the Virginians remembered "yelling like demons" as he and his comrades attacked.[45]

Jones's charge threw Crawford's force into disarray, driving most of it to the eastern edge of town. Fortunately for the Federals, the 1st Vermont detachment approached and fired into Jones' left, stalling the Virginians in the narrow street. A few stalwart clutches of men broke through the jam to rejoin Jones's vanguard. Despite the Confederates' confusion, about a dozen Vermont troops found themselves outnumbered and surrounded.[46]

As the main Federal body fell back, Captain Hall directed the 1st Vermont's 5th squadron, Companies C and F, to do so as well. Captain William Wells, commanding Company C, was behind Hall's Company F and instead pushed those men forward, toward the Confederates, at the point of his saber. Hall, seeing his company return to the front, ordered his troopers to ignore his last order and charge. The two companies surged forward into the teeth of the Rebel force.[47]

Around this time, Captain Hammond and Companies G and H of the 5th New York crashed into the right flank of Marshall's flanking force near the depot. A desperate close-quarters fight between the opposing flanking parties resulted in

44 Louis N. Boudrye, *Historic Records of the Fifth New York Cavalry* (Albany, NY, 1865), 37-38; "O.P.Q.," "From the Vermont Cavalry" *Montpelier Green Mountain Daily Freeman*, August 12, 1862.

45 *OR* 12, pt. 2, 111-113; John Blue, *Reminiscences*, Unidentified publication, Copy at FNMP, 50; Crawford to Banks, August 3, 1862, Banks Papers, LC.

46 *OR* 12, pt. 2, 113; Dickinson, "Fifth New York Cavalry," 247; "O.P.Q.," "From the Vermont Cavalry."

47 Ruggles, "Vermont Cavalry."

Major Marshall's capture after a saber blow—a "terrible cut . . . clove" to his skull—knocked him unconscious. The Union flankers then charged the right and rear of Jones's column but were stalled by a counterattack. The Yankee cavalry opened the fight with their revolvers. Most of the Confederates, who relied on their sabers, consequently enjoyed a brief advantage when the Northerners had to change from emptied pistols to swords. A nasty fight with men slashing each other ensued in the congested streets of Orange. Frightened residents pulled the wounded into their houses. Jones's vanguard, which had initially driven the main Union column, now faced superior numbers and was nearly surrounded. Using alleyways, the men made what escapes they could. Many of them gathered on a hill on the Willis property, while Jones reported rallying one mile from town.[48]

Though no general pursuit occurred, a few bands of Federals chased the fleeing Rebels as far as three-quarters of a mile from Orange. Captain Wells and a handful of his men followed the Confederates across a barnyard, a hill, and another lot, before several Virginians made a stand at a culvert and were captured. Wells pursued a bit too far and was nearly captured himself before retreating.

Crawford satisfied himself with securing the town, cutting telegraph wires, and dismantling some railroad track. A Vermont sergeant allegedly saw Crawford and the 1st Vermont's Colonel Tompkins on a hill at a "safe" distance from the fighting. Crawford reportedly messaged his men after the battle ended, encouraging them to "keep to work." English correspondent George A. Townsend described this post-engagement "work" as raiding "henroosts and private pantries." After a couple of hours, the Federals, hastened by the sound of cheers accompanying the 6th Virginia's arrival at the 7th's rallying point, withdrew. The Confederates pursued Crawford as far as the railroad bridge across the Rapidan. The Federals crossed at Raccoon Ford and headed to Culpeper. Neither Crawford's messages to Banks nor Colonel Tompkins's after-action report list Union losses. Grumble Jones, however, estimated 11 Federals killed, 30 wounded, and 12 missing. Of the approximately 200 Confederate cavalrymen, Jones reported 10 wounded and 40 missing. Union commanders estimated 25 Confederates killed

---

48 OR 12, pt. 2, 112-113; McDonald, *Laurel Brigade*, 78; *John Hammond: In Memoriam* (Chicago, 1890), 54; Blue, *Reminiscences*, 50-51; Crawford to Banks, August 3, 1862, Banks Papers, LC; Townsend, *Campaigns of a Non-Combatant*, 243; David Humphreys, *Heroes and Spies of the Civil War* (New York, 1903), 103.

Culpeper Court House with Confederate prisoners from the skirmish at Orange Court House on balcony, photo by Timothy O'Sullivan.
Library of Congress

and reported bagging 52 prisoners, whom Crawford delivered to Col. Clark in Culpeper for questioning.[49]

On August 4, Clark reported details from interrogations and from Union prisoners who had returned after confinement in Lynchburg. He correctly determined that two new Alabama regiments had joined Brig. Gen. William B. Taliaferro's three-regiment Virginia brigade. With typical Federal proclivity for overestimating the size of Confederate armies, he declared that the enemy numbered about 36,000 men, including 10,000 under A. P. Hill. Actually, Jackson's total force was approximately 20,000 fewer than Clark's estimate. Clark also discovered trains at Gordonsville delivering ordnance from Charlottesville, and

49 OR 12, pt. 2, 113, pt. 3, 525; Ruggles, "Vermont Cavalry"; Crawford to Banks, August 3, 1862, Banks Papers, LC; Townsend, *Campaigns of a Non-Combatant*, 243. Sergeant Steaman Ruggles wrote that Crawford was one mile from town, but the high ground half a mile east of Orange is more likely.

reported finding "occasional straws" pointing to McClellan's evacuation of the York-James peninsula. He was unsure however, of the extent to which fighting east of Richmond were affecting the Confederate movement westward.[50]

Clark's assertion that Jackson's advance was connected to events on the Peninsula was dubious. Jackson's arrival with two divisions and a cavalry brigade was actually in response to Pope's probes toward Gordonsville. Lee's July 13 order to Jackson was merely to "oppose the reported advance of the enemy." Five days later, he alluded to seeking opportunities to strike the Union flank if Pope moved against either Charlottesville or Richmond. When Lee sent A. P. Hill's division and Brig. Gen. William Starke's brigade west at the end of July, it was to strengthen Jackson sufficiently to strike and then return to Richmond. He did not learn of McClellan's departure from the Peninsula until several days after Clark's August 4th dispatch. Indeed, on the 7th Lee tried to determine whether a strong probe by McClellan to Malvern Hill was a fresh movement or a feint to cover an advance from McDowell at Fredericksburg, or by Pope's army farther west. It is thus unclear how any junior or field-grade Confederate officers captured at Orange on August 2 would know any better. Finally, after recounting with middling accuracy the perceived locations of Jackson's forces, Clark stated an opinion firmly rooted in Shenandoah Valley experience. He was "positive they will all be found in one body at the proper time."[51]

While Clark interviewed Crawford's prisoners in Culpeper on August 3, Pope arrived at Little Washington. Banks's corps formed up at 8:00 a.m. for the commanding general's inspection, but the soldiers waited in the heat well beyond the prescribed time. "Napoleon did not fail to keep his appointments to review his troops," one of Gordon's staff officers bantered. "Nor did Wellington," another shot back, apparently skeptical that Pope would live up to either of those men despite his self-proclaimed laurels. On the heels of these remarks, the men observed a dust cloud announcing the arrival of Pope and his abundant staff. In front of each brigade, the regiments formally received their new commander. When he got to Gordon's brigade, the 27th Indiana had recurring problems executing the regulation formalities. Indisposed to reserve, Pope launched into a

50 Clark to Banks, August 3 and 4, 1862, Banks Papers, LC; Robert Krick, *Stonewall Jackson at Cedar Mountain* (Chapel Hill, NC, 1990), 45.

51 *OR* 12, pt. 3, 915, 919, 925, 928-929; Clifford Dowdey and Louis H. Manarin, eds., *The Wartime Papers of Robert E. Lee* (Boston, 1961), 232-233, 238, 247; Clark to Banks, August 4, 1862, and a second letter that Clark started on the 3rd, to which he added on the 4th, Banks Papers, LC.

profane censure rivalling the corps's coarsest leaders, Alpheus Williams and the 46th Pennsylvania's Col. Joseph Knipe.[52]

The deficiencies of other regiments raised concerns as well. In late June, the 3rd Maryland's Lieutenant Gillette griped, "I am disgusted with the men and officers. . . . I am determined, if possible, to separate from the regiment until it shows better sign of efficiency and discipline. . . . From the Colonel down, all is confusion and discontent owing to inefficiency of officers and the newness of the regt." Another Maryland infantry unit, the Purnell Legion, also had difficulties. Banks sent it to the rear after a handful of dispatches between Banks and Pope's chief of staff, Col. George Ruggles, on August 4. Ruggles inquired whether it would "settle matters" in the Purnell Legion if it was sent to guard the Orange & Alexandria Railroad bridge over the Rappahannock. Banks replied that, "The Purnell Legion, officers and men, will accept 'with great pleasure' the position assigned to them." The ensuing move scattered the Legion's companies over a 25-mile stretch of railroad from Culpeper to Catlett's Station. Another regiment in Greene's now sharply abridged brigade, the 3rd Delaware, was on garrison duty at Front Royal and would miss the upcoming battle.[53]

* * *

Following reports of Jackson's gathering forces, Pope began concentrating near Culpeper. On August 4, Colonel Ruggles asked Banks whether the roads would support a direct march to Woodville and if not, directed his men to repair the worst spots. In the spirit of his commanding general, Ruggles then offered the optimistic guidance that Banks's men would have to travel that road once and would only need to make sufficient repairs for that trip. Banks agreed, so long as the route was via Sperryville. On August 5, Pope ordered Banks's corps to move the next morning to where the Sperryville-Culpeper Road crossed the Hazel River.[54]

Before departing Little Washington, Banks issued an order safeguarding a local planter's crops and livestock. The farmer, Thomas Fletcher, had furnished 650

---

52 Gordon, *Brook Farm*, 274-276.

53 *OR* 12, pt. 3, 533; Ruggles to Banks, August 4, 1862, Banks Papers, LC; August 15, 1862 letter from "Howard," in *Danbury* [CT] *Times*, August 21, 1862.

54 *OR* 12, pt. 3, 533, 536-537; George Ruggles to Banks, August 4, 1862, and Charles Nordendorf to Banks, August 5, 1862, Banks Papers, LC.

bushels of wheat, 400 bushels of oats, and 100 cattle for Banks's corps during its three-week stay. As a result, 350 bushels of wheat, 20 barrels of flour, 500 pounds of bacon, and 150 bushels of old wheat would remain inviolate for the use of Mr. Fletcher and his 40 family members.[55]

Reveille sounded at 3:00 a.m. on August 6, and Williams's division marched before sunrise. It passed Sigel's I Corps encampment at Sperryville and reached Woodville at 4:00 p.m. Augur then leap-frogged Williams's division and went into camp, much to General Gordon's chagrin. Gordon wanted to set out at 3:00 a.m. and end before midday in order to avoid having to march in the midst of a punishing swelter. Augur's movement meant Gordon's men would have to wait. Temperature readings at Georgetown on August 7 reached 92°, and it was 98° on the day of the battle of Cedar Mountain.[56]

Before marching on August 7, Banks's men deposited their knapsacks in wagons, per an order from Pope. Gordon's disappointment with his 8:00 a.m. start worsened after his troops marched just about 50 yards. Passing a curve in the road, Gordon discovered Augur's wagon trains halted. After fifteen minutes, he pushed his men past this roadblock. But after another quarter mile, they encountered another stopped wagon train. Unwilling to have his soldiers waste time roasting in the road, Gordon ordered them into the woods, where they remained until noon when the road cleared. During the halt, supply wagons issued 100 rounds of ammunition per man. With the sun at its zenith, Gordon's brigade hit the road again. "[C]louds of dust hung over us, there was not a breath of air, and the road was like a furnace," he recalled.[57]

Meanwhile Ricketts's division of Irvin McDowell's corps moved from Waterloo Bridge on the upper Rappahannock to Culpeper. Rickett's men arrived late on August 6 and camped north of Crawford's detachment. Pope's army now occupied a line along the road from Sperryville to Culpeper. Bayard had informed Crawford on August 4 that his cavalry was insufficient to properly cover the length of river assigned to them. The troopers' ability to screen Pope's force while it concentrated was about to be tested.[58]

55 Banks, order, August 5, 1862, Banks Papers, LC.

56 Krick, *Stonewall Jackson at Cedar Mountain*, 17, 34, 48; Hinkley Diary, August 6, 1862, WHS.

57 Gordon, *Brook Farm*, 277; Hinkley Diary, August 7, 1862, WHS.

58 *OR* 12, pt. 2, 24; Bayard to Crawford, August 4, 1862, Banks Papers, LC; Gordon, *Brook Farm*, 278; Gould, *10th Maine*, 165.

After covering six grueling miles, Banks's corps camped on the Hazel River on August 7. Lieutenant Colonel David Hunter Strother of Pope's staff rode to Banks's bivouac and beheld a "most beautiful" scene. Mountains rose to the east and west, and a large covered bridge crossed the river, which was "alive with bathers, joyous and noisy," recovering from their scorching march. The heat exacerbated the sickness that gripped parts of the corps, and many soldiers dropped exhausted by the side of the road to Culpeper.[59]

Several officers in the 2nd Massachusetts were sick as the march began. Captain Richard Goodwin applied for but failed to receive a furlough for an illness that had persisted for two months. Before leaving Little Washington, he anxiously wrote to his wife, "The medical Director says mine is rather a case for Resignation than for Furlough. Resignation! I think I would rather die out here first. I should have to be much sicker than I am now before I should take such a step. . . . I shall have to do my marching in an ambulance, at present, for I am quite weak."[60]

Captain Goodwin's indefatigable spirit was common in Banks's corps. Commissary officer James Gillette wrote from the Hazel River, "Events are crowding upon us and we must meet them manfully–the stupidity of past follies must be atoned for by energetic blows & iron will in following them up if successful." They would meet these "crowding events" in two days.[61]

59 Cecil D. Eby, Jr., ed., *A Virginia Yankee in the Civil War: The Diaries of David Hunter Strother* (Chapel Hill, NC, 1961), 74.

60 Richard Goodwin to Lucy Goodwin, August 5, 1862, Goodwin Family Papers, MHS.

61 Gillette to Mother, August 7, 1862, LC.

Chapter 2

"... the shot came along as if they had wings and were flying."

— John Mead Gould, 10th Maine Infantry

Jackson Moves on Culpeper

August 7 to 5:45 p.m. on August 9, 1862

Two parties entered Culpeper by early on August 8. General Pope arrived with his staff to direct operations. He had spent August 7 in Sperryville with Sigel's corps until reports from the front precipitated further progress to Culpeper. Meanwhile, some of George Bayard's cavalry straggled from the front. They brought the Union forces in Culpeper what Sergeant Hicks called the "unlooked for intelligence" that Jackson was across the Rapidan.[1]

After taking position at Gordonsville in mid-July, Jackson maintained a defensive posture while observing Pope. After A. P. Hill arrived in late July, Ewell's division was detached to Liberty Mills on the Rapidan, where it stayed until Jackson advanced into Culpeper County. Jackson's division remained a few days near Gordonsville and then retired to Mechanicsville in Louisa County. After spending a week in the lush pastures of the Green Springs district, Jackson's division advanced to Oliver H. P. Terrell's farm and James Magruder's plantation, on the road between Gordonsville and Liberty Mills.[2]

---

1 OR 12, pt. 2, 25, and pt. 3, 544; Hicks Diary, 10, LC; Townsend, *Campaigns of a Non-Combatant*, 247.

2 G. Campbell Brown, "Military Reminiscences, 1861-1863," Brown-Ewell Papers, Box 2, Folder 4, TSLA, 81; Early, *Autobiographical Sketch*, 92; Archie McDonald, ed., *Make Me a Map of*

Late on August 7 Jackson's three divisions moved toward Culpeper Court House in response to intelligence that part of Pope's army was heading there. Ewell's division crossed the Rapidan at Liberty Mills as if heading for Madison but then turned right over primitive farm roads and fields toward Barnett's Ford, where it bivouacked. After fording the Rapidan at several points, Brig. Gen. Beverly H. Robertson's cavalry screened Ewell's left flank. Hill's and Jackson's divisions headed for Orange Court House. Robertson pushed back Federal pickets, who reported these movements to Pope in Sperryville.[3]

Jackson's force did not live up to its reputation for exceptional marching on August 8, and heat was not the sole culprit. Jackson ordered Ewell to follow Robertson on the road from Barnett's Ford to Culpeper; Hill would follow Ewell, with Jackson's division in the rear. Due to a misunderstanding, Hill waited in Orange before dawn, looking for Ewell's column. Ewell, moving north of the river, never showed up. Jackson's division and its wagon trains passed before Hill moved. Slowly struggling behind Jackson's trains instead of marching ahead of Jackson's division, Hill's troops did not cover the miles Jackson prescribed. As a result, the majority of Jackson's infantry had marched only to the Rapidan by the time Banks's corps reached the Hazel River, about eight miles northwest of Culpeper. Robertson's cavalry was more successful, pushing back Northern troopers at Locust Dale, south of Robertson's River, and at Crooked Run Church, where it captured a Federal camp. By midnight on August 8, Jackson's lead elements, Ewell and Robertson, were bivouacked north of the Rapidan near Crooked Run Church.[4]

That night Brig. Gen. John Buford's cavalry created mischief. Pope had directed Buford to "feel down cautiously" with his cavalry near Jackson's left at Barnett's Ford and look for an opportunity to "dash in vigorously" on the rear and flank of the Rebel wagon train. Buford's probe brought much of Jackson's division under arms and into line that night. A spattering of bullets cut through tree branches, under which ailing Brig. Gen. Charles Winder of the Stonewall Brigade

---

the Valley: The Civil War Journal of Stonewall Jackson's Topographer (Dallas, 1973), 62-65; Howard, *Maryland Confederate*, 161; Krick, *Stonewall Jackson at Cedar Mountain*, 16.

3 OR 12, pt. 2, 182, 210-211; OR 12, pt. 3, 926; Early, *Autobiographical Sketch*, 93; Samuel Buck, *With the Old Confeds: Actual Experiences of a Captain in the Line* (Baltimore, 1925), 44; Brown, "Military Reminiscences," 82; McDonald, *Make Me a Map*, 65; Thompson A. Snyder, "Recollections of Four Years with the Union Cavalry, 1861-1865," 10, FNMP.

4 OR 12, pt. 2, 180-181, 214-217; McDonald, *Make Me a Map*, 65-66.

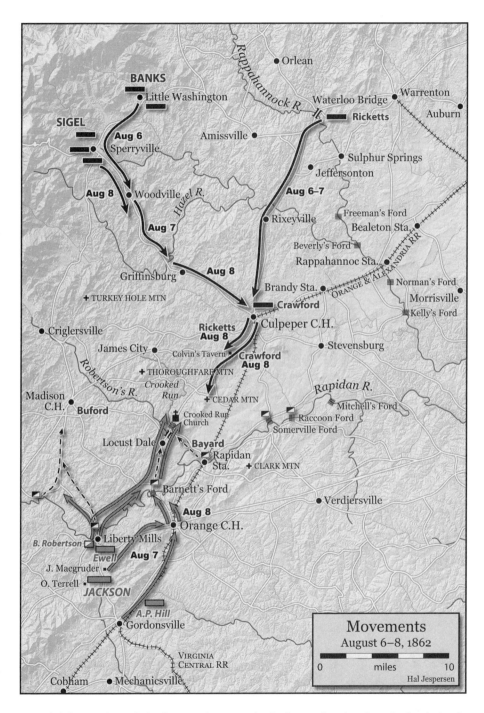

rested. This action elicited enough pause in Jackson that he detached a brigade under Brig. Gen. Alexander Lawton at dawn on August 9 to guard the trains. The order that precluded Lawton's participation in the coming battle also directed Winder to command Jackson's division.[5]

*   *   *

When Pope arrived in Culpeper early on August 8, he put his army into motion in response to picket reports. Pope ordered Crawford's brigade to march south in an hour in order to support Bayard's cavalry. Stragglers from Bayard's command poured into the south end of Culpeper in small groups and then in whole companies. Pope's staff struck the headquarters tents it had recently erected a mile south of Culpeper and moved north. At this time, Lieutenant Colonel Strother of Pope's staff witnessed a demoralizing sight. Two hundred cavalrymen streamed north toward town, looking "miserably thin and jaded." Strother's spirit improved abruptly when the sound of beating drums drew his attention to town.[6]

Crawford's men headed south "in gallant array" and with flags fluttering in the hot breeze. Strother had served with the brigade in the Valley, and Crawford gave him an enthusiastic salute as his regiments poured through side roads into the main street. The 10th Maine received new uniforms that morning, and the soldiers accoutered themselves with whatever fresh items they could manage in the time available. Regimental bands joined singing troops, creating a cacophony in the streets. As the column reached the courthouse, officers allowed the men to draw cold water from a pump on the shade-covered square. An unfamiliar colonel, probably from Pope's staff, diligently worked the pump to help the men.[7]

The residents of Culpeper were indignant. Some peered from behind windows, while others, in high spirits over word of Jackson's advance, openly taunted the Federals. A Connecticut soldier heard such things as, "Old Jack will give you all you want," "You will come back tomorrow on the double quick if you come at all," and "You'll be whippeed out o'yere right smart." It was a little after 1:00 p.m.[8]

---

5 OR 12, pt. 2, 182; 12, pt. 3, 548; Howard, *Maryland Confederate*, 164-165.

6 OR 12, pt. 2, 25; Hicks Diary, 10, LC; Eby, *Virginia Yankee*, 75.

7 Eby, *Virginia Yankee*, 75; Gould, *10th Maine*, 166; Edwin E. Marvin, *The Fifth Regiment Connecticut Volunteers: A History Compiled from Diaries and Official Reports* (Hartford, 1889), 151-152; John M. Gould, *History of the 1st, 10th, and 29th Maine Regiment* (Portland, ME, 1871), 166; Townsend, *Campaigns of a Non-Combatant*, 248-249.

8 Marvin, *Fifth Regiment*, 151.

Within the first mile, the heat took a toll on the brigade. All around Lieutenant John Gould, soldiers "blanched and reeled over," creating obstacles for those who pressed on. In spite of the heat, the heckling from townspeople, and the threat of looming battle, the men remained sanguine. English correspondent George Townsend reported, "A continual explosion of small arms, in the shape of epithets, jests, [and] imitations," characterized the march. Officers called halts in the shade. After men collapsed in the dusty roadway, they would have a drink, wipe away the sweat, and joke and bellow.[9]

Despite these buoyant appearances, the men knew what awaited them. Crawford's brigade, which included the 5th Connecticut, 46th Pennsylvania, 28th New York, and 10th Maine, had fought alongside Gordon's brigade at Winchester and endured the miserable retreat from that battle. A battery of three-inch rifles, commanded by Capt. Jacob Roemer, and two sections of Capt. Joseph M. Knap's battery of 10-pounder Parrott rifles, totaling 10 pieces, joined the brigade. One private with a sense of foreboding approached Townsend and asked him to write a note to his wife. It read, "My dear Mary, we are going into action soon, and I send you my love. Kiss baby, and if I am not killed I will write to you after the fight." He never sent another letter.[10]

Heading south on the Orange Road, Crawford found Bayard beyond Colvin's Tavern at approximately 4:00 p.m. At the same time, a messenger delivered orders from Pope, placing Crawford in command of all forces on the field. Some of Bayard's cavalrymen were still beyond Cedar Run near a schoolhouse. Observing advanced elements of Jackson's army in their front, Crawford chose a defensive line in the edge of a belt of woods behind Cedar Run's north branch. This position was about two miles behind Bayard's cavalry at the schoolhouse. Crawford advanced the two cavalry regiments accompanying him, and his infantry continued on the road from Colvin's Tavern, heading south and descending toward the creek. The foot soldiers filed off the road and formed a well-concealed line in the woods along the run. Strong pickets advanced beyond the main line. Crawford placed his 10 guns about 200 yards beyond the run. Four of Roemer's pieces were on the right of the road, while his third section joined Knap's two sections on the left. The 10th Maine and 5th Connecticut supported Knap, and the 28th New York and 46th

---

9 Gould, *10th Maine*, 167; Townsend, *Campaigns of a Non-Combatant*, 251.

10 Townsend, *Campaigns of a Non-Combatant*, 251; George Leonard Andrews, "The Battle of Cedar Mountain, August 9, 1862," *Papers of the Military Historical Society of Massachusetts, Volume II* (Wilmington, NC, 1989), 410.

Pennsylvania were north of the road behind Roemer. A more commanding piece of ground stood less than a mile ahead.[11]

At this point, the Orange Road ran west-southwest. The Mitchell Station Road abutted it a quarter mile in front of Cedar Run, heading south. Approximately 1,100 yards west of this intersection, a small lane, two-thirds of a mile long, leading from the Orange Road to the Crittenden house, paralleled the Mitchell Station Road. Both thoroughfares were atop ridges. The ground between those roads and the Orange Road to the north was largely cleared and under cultivation. From the Mitchell Station Road, cornfields, hereafter known as "the Cornfield," stretched for about 550 yards toward Crittenden Lane. Beyond the Cornfield, another cleared space of similar size rose to the lane. This undulating field sloped to the south, where it drained into the southern branch of Cedar Run, which formed the southern boundary of this space. A small tributary of the north branch of Cedar Run flowed from the northwest corner of this area to the southeast corner, causing a depression between the lane and the Mitchell Station Road. A gate stood at the junction of the Crittenden Lane and the Orange Road, around which much Confederate activity would occur during the upcoming fight. West of the Crittenden Gate, woodlots bordered each side of the Orange Road for a short distance. At the other end of the lane, northeast of the Crittenden house, a prominent copse of cedar trees stood upon a small hillock.[12]

A significant wood, beginning just west of the Mitchell Station Road, stretched north of the Orange Road, interrupted only by a recently harvested wheatfield. This field contained shocks of wheat and a few rock piles, and it stretched for about 600 yards along the Orange Road, which bounded it to the south. Approximately 400 yards separated the Crittenden Gate and the western edge of what would be memorialized as "the Wheatfield." Woods, between 800 and 600 yards and edged with fences, formed the Wheatfield's eastern and western boundaries. The Wheatfield was widest at the road, narrowing toward the north, where it was approximately 200 yards wide. A low ridge at its northern boundary separated it from a smaller field, overgrown with what the history of the 5th Connecticut

11 OR 12, pt. 2, 149-150, OR 51, pt. 1, 121; Gould, *10th Maine*, 168; Hicks Diary, 10, LC; Samuel Wylie Crawford, *U.S. Army Generals' Reports of Civil War Service, 1864-1887*, Record Group 94, NA, 7; Roemer, *Reminiscences*, 39-42. Accounts conflict as to the location of their bivouac; Hicks wrote that they crossed Cedar Run in the morning. Gould wrote that they did so on August 8. Crawford wrote only that they were protected by the bank.

12 OR 12, pt. 2, 203; Krick, *Stonewall Jackson at Cedar Mountain*, 68, 73-75. Battlefield landmarks such as the Cornfield, the Wheatfield, Crittenden Lane, the Scrub Field, and the Crittenden Gate will be capitalized in the descriptions of the battle of Cedar Mountain.

described as "low shrub oaks and brush of a couple of years' growth, rising to the height of men's shoulders." The Wheatfield and this latter clearing, the "Scrub Field," shared the same fenced forest as their eastern boundary. To the west, the Scrub Field continued around the corner of the western woods. The Wheatfield was roughly rectangular running north-south, and so was the Scrub Field, running nearly east-west. Together, they approximated an inverted, backward "L"-shaped cut from the woods. Like the topography between the Mitchell Station Road and the Crittenden Lane, the Wheatfield sloped downward from the woods on its eastern side and then sharply upward again toward the western side, due to a tributary that fed Cedar Run. This tributary began at a spring in the woods on the western side of the Wheatfield near the Orange Road and flowed southeast across the field until it crossed the road. From there, it continued southeast and entered the north branch north of a millrace near the Mitchell Station Road. Though slight, this rivulet created an undulation in the terrain that made that portion of the Wheatfield marshy. This was about three-quarters of the distance from the woods on the eastern side toward the western side. Prior to the terrain sloping downward to the rivulet, a low ridge in the field rose one-third of the distance from the woods on the east. The ground between the Wheatfield and Cedar Run became increasingly wooded and steep moving north from the road. Northeast of the field a pleasant cottage belonging to a "Mrs. Brown" stood atop a high knoll. This hill was about 1,200 yards north of the point where the Orange Road descends to the run, and was more than three-quarters of a mile from the Wheatfield and well right of Crawford's position. Finally, the eminence that gave its name to the coming struggle, Slaughter's Mountain, rose abruptly south of the Crittenden house and to Crawford's left front. The elevation was named for the Reverend Philip Slaughter, whose house sat on its eastern slope.[13]

Camp sounds filled the evening air. Soldiers dismantled fences to allow free movement of the cavalry and artillery, then tried to find food. While some smoked pipes and played cards, others were left with their thoughts. Second Lieutenant Gould of the 10th Maine recalled that the evening's suspense wrought great stress upon body and soul. Captain Roemer, commanding the battery north of the Orange Road, was anxious about leading his artillerymen into battle for the first

---

13 OR 12, pt. 2, 151; Krick, *Stonewall Jackson at Cedar Mountain*, 100, 144-145; Gordon, *Brook Farm*, 284-285; Boyce, *Twenty-eighth New York*, 35; Marvin, *Fifth Regiment*, 155. Locals and Confederate veterans referred to the battle as "Slaughter's Mountain," or "Cedar Run," while Northerners conflated the mountain with Cedar Run, calling it "Cedar Mountain," which is most widely used today.

time. Shortly after midnight, he walked to Cedar Run behind his battery. He watched fish in the moonlit water and prayed.[14]

The balance of Pope's army marched on August 8. Brigadier General James Ricketts's division of McDowell's corps was ordered to move a few miles south of Culpeper. Pope ordered Franz Sigel's corps to march from Sperryville, following Banks's corps to Culpeper. That morning, before orders arrived, the ever-preparing 2nd Massachusetts conducted battalion drill. Corporal Calvin H. Blanchard of the 111th Pennsylvania had returned to duty on August 7 after a bout of measles. He described the August 8 advance as a "forced march" that was "scorching hot and dusty." First Lieutenant Edwin E. Bryant of the 3rd Wisconsin thought it the "most wearisome of marching," with halts every few minutes in the blazing heat. Augur's division reached Culpeper around 10:00 p.m., and Gordon's brigade reached camp at midnight. The sky was clear, the moon radiant. Henry Prince's brigade bivouacked ominously in a graveyard outside town. After ensuring his division was encamped, Brigadier General Williams located a tollhouse room outside town and shared it with a dozen officers.[15]

The morning of August 9 "broke clear and pleasant," according to one New Yorker. At the front, Crawford's command rose early. Jacob Roemer's battery quietly passed reveille by word at 4:00 a.m. Walking toward the front about thirty minutes later, Roemer spotted Union cavalry, and a group of officers hailed him. Crawford approached, greeted Roemer, and offered him a pork chop and a musket cartridge. Crawford said, "Captain Roemer, we have no salt this morning, and as you will have to smell powder today, you may as well eat some this morning." He retold lore that gunpowder was helpful in firing the blood. Roemer finished several seasoned pork chops and told Crawford his battery would be ready at 5:00 a.m.[16]

Early that morning, Bayard informed Crawford that Confederate cavalry was advancing toward the Union left. Crawford pushed his regiments beyond the creek bank, where they stacked arms and rested in line of battle. Skirmishing parties

---

14 Gould, *10th Maine*, 168; *National Tribune*, April 22, 1886; Roemer, *Reminiscences*, 40.

15 OR 12, pt. 2, 25; Gordon, *Brook Farm*, 278-279; C. H. Blanchard, "Memoir," ECHS, copy at GNMP, 3; William Roberts, Jr., to sister, August 10, 1862, Roberts Papers, HSP; Quint, *2nd Massachusetts*, 103; Milo Quaife, ed., *From the Cannon's Mouth: The Civil War Letters of General Alpheus S. Williams* (Detroit, 1959), 99; *2nd Annual Report of the State Historian of the State of New York* (Albany, 1897), 101.

16 Hicks Diary, 10, LC; Roemer, *Reminiscences*, 41. Roemer was given to exaggeration. He described his battery halting a fictional Confederate cavalry charge led by Brig. Gen. Winder that resulted in Winder's death. This breakfast anecdote should perhaps be taken with a grain of salt.

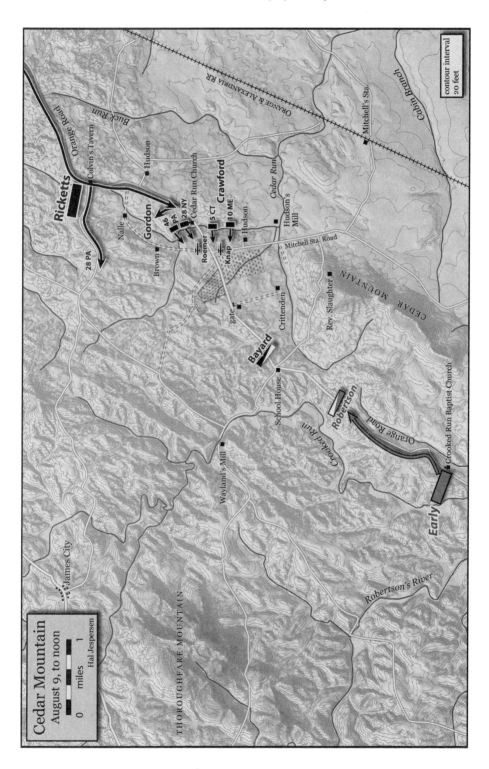

Cedar Mountain
August 9, to noon

0   miles   1

Hal Jespersen

contour interval
20 feet

deployed, and north of the road, Capt. Erwin A. Bowen took Company D of the 28th New York forward. Bowen had been ill for days but stayed with his men. Eager for something to do, some infantrymen scampered to the crest of the ridge in front to have a look at mounted Confederates moving near the base of the mountain. Captain Joseph Knap, commanding the battery ahead of the 10th Maine, assigned a guard to keep the foot soldiers from the ridge. The Maine men then outflanked the battery, at which point their regimental commander, Col. George Beal, ordered them to stop.[17]

Confederate artillery fired briefly between 11:00 a.m. and noon, eliciting a few rounds from Roemer's and Knap's batteries in response. Though Crawford thought these shots came from the mountain, they were actually fired from the south end of the valley between the mountain and the Orange Road. The Rebels were not gunning for Crawford's infantry or artillery at all; rather, their target was the Union cavalry that stood on the Crittenden ridge blocking the Confederates' way.[18]

Bayard's cavalry remained in Beverly Robertson's path. In the early morning, Ewell's lead brigade, under Brig. Gen. Jubal A. Early, caught up with Robertson and was ordered to clear the Federal cavalry as soon as Winder's division was sufficiently close to follow. At 2:00 p.m., Winder notified Early that he could move, and his brigade advanced north of the Orange Road. Taking advantage of a ridgeline and the woodlot west of the Crittenden Lane, it passed obliquely to the right, crossed the Orange Road, and emerged in line over the ridge, catching the Federal horsemen off guard. The troopers dashed rearward while Early's brigade crossed the Crittenden Lane and occupied the ridge.[19]

*   *   *

---

17 *OR* 12, pt. 2, 150; Hicks Diary, 10, LC; Gould, *10th Maine*, 170.

18 *OR* 12, pt. 2, 150, 161, 226, 237; Roemer, Reminiscences, 42. Crawford's after-action report and his postwar statement both suggested that Confederates opened fire from the mountain and that Knap (identified as Roemer in the postwar statement) replied, driving off the Rebel battery. Roemer's reminiscence suggested that his battery fired the first Union shot of the battle. Fire from the mountain would not have occurred until later, because Confederate infantry advanced to disperse Union cavalry in the valley west of the Crittenden Lane and occupied the mountain before artillery arrived there. The Southern infantry did not start moving until 2:00 p.m.

19 Early, *Autobiographical Sketch*, 95.

While these events transpired, Pope, McDowell, and Ricketts sat together under a shade tree in Culpeper. Ricketts then left, and Pope reclined, smoking a cigar. According to Capt. Daniel Jones of Rickett's division, Pope lounged, "with as much sangfroid as if the country was at peace and he at peace with all the world *and the rest of mankind.*" McDowell gazed upon the ground with his hands between his knees, "roling" his thumbs. Suddenly a dust-covered rider galloped up. With Pope's and McDowell's staffers watching, the officer passed news to the two generals. As they huddled over a map, an orderly arrived and thrust a note into McDowell's hands. After digesting its contents, McDowell passed the note to Pope. In an instant, all the staffers scattered in different directions to put in motion a fresh round of corps movements.[20]

After a brief rest in Culpeper on the night of the 8th, Nathaniel Banks received reports and orders that shaped his decision-making throughout August 9. At 8:40 a.m., he got a dispatch from John Buford, whose cavalry operated against the Confederate left. Buford, who thought he was cut off from the main body, stated that he had withdrawn from Madison, that Confederate cavalry were on both flanks and in his rear, and that he was retreating toward Sperryville. The Confederate cavalry, however, was only a screen for Ewell, who was not threatening Madison. Nevertheless, Buford's message likely concerned Banks and Pope. The road from Madison could lead a Confederate force to Colvin's Tavern, in Crawford's rear.[21]

Banks's corps, meanwhile, was ready to march south. At 8:00 a.m., he received orders to move, but they were countermanded 30 minutes later. Gordon's brigade was then told to fall out and set up camp. Likewise, Captain O'Neil W. Robinson's 4th Battery, Maine Light Artillery, was ready to move at 9:00 a.m. but was told to unharness its horses. The drivers led the animals to a pasture to graze.[22]

At 9:45 a.m., Col. Louis Marshall of Pope's staff arrived at Banks's headquarters. Colonel John Clark, Majors Louis Pelouze and Delavan Perkins, and other members of Banks's staff were on hand. Marshall passed along a verbal order to Banks: "General Banks to move to the front immediately. Assume command of all forces in the front. Deploy his skirmishers if the enemy approaches and attack him immediately as soon as he approaches and be reinforced from here." Banks

---

20 D. D. Jones to John Jordan, Jr., August 11, 1862, Daniel D. Jones Papers, HSP.

21 *OR* 12, pt. 2, 55; Andrews, "Cedar Mountain," 410.

22 Quint, *2nd Massachusetts*, 104; *History of the Fourth Maine Battery Light Artillery in the Civil War, 1861-1865* (Augusta, ME, 1905), 17.

directed Marshall to give the order to Pelouze, his assistant adjutant general. Marshall walked to Pelouze, who was seated at a desk, and repeated the order. Pelouze transcribed it, repeated it to the group, and got Marshall's concurrence. Brigadier General Alpheus Williams received word of this movement by 10:00 a.m., and, accompanying Gordon's brigade, was on the road shortly thereafter. The soldiers left their tents standing, as Crawford's men had done the day before. Augur's division followed Gordon's brigade. Robinson's battery hustled to collect its grazing horses and join the column. Passing Pope's headquarters in Culpeper, Hoosiers in Gordon's brigade noticed the general and his staff, whose sangfroid had returned, lounging on the front porch "in apparent unconcern."[23]

Banks's men believed, with varying degrees of accuracy, that other corps displayed a similar lack of concern. After a few miles, Gordon's brigade passed Ricketts's division at Colvin's Tavern, where the road from Madison terminated. Ricketts's men relaxed beneath tents, guarding the approach from Madison. Banks's men would resent the fact that Ricketts remained there, even though his troops were quite close to where the upcoming battle was fought.[24]

Ricketts's division was not the only force to reach the battlefield later than Banks's men thought appropriate. Franz Sigel received orders to march from Sperryville to Culpeper on August 8. Early that evening Sigel asked Pope to clarify his route. Pope was incredulous at what he described as "General Sigel's singular uncertainty" on the question; a stone turnpike directly connected the two points. After a night march, Sigel reached Culpeper without rations in the late afternoon of August 9 and needed to have food from McDowell's trains cooked before he could proceed. This further needled Pope, whose orders had directed that all commands be ready to march at a moment's notice, with each soldier carrying two days'

23 Quint, *2nd Massachusetts*, 104; *Joint Committee on the Conduct of the War, 38th Congress* (Washington, DC, 1894-1927), 3: Miscellaneous, 45; Written statement of Louis H. Pelouze dated January 23, 1865, Banks Papers, LC. The original transcription of Pope's verbal order to Banks is attached to Pelouze's statement; Quaife, *From the Cannon's Mouth*, 99-100; *History of the Fourth Maine Battery*, 17; Brown, *Twenty-Seventh Indiana*, 195.

24 OR 12, pt. 2, 26; Gordon, *Brook Farm*, 281-282. Many correspondents, both contemporaneously and postbellum, remarked with bitterness on the proximity of Ricketts's men. Their enmity was not necessarily aimed at the troops themselves, but at those they thought had left them there. Irvin McDowell became the chief scapegoat, especially following Second Manassas; Pope's official report indicated that he had placed Ricketts there to guard the approach from Madison Court House, which was appropriate given the perceived threat. Perhaps Banks did not consider Ricketts's men to be available to call upon during the battle. But by the time his situation became critical, Pope was also on the field.

rations. Those two delays kept Sigel's corps from arriving at the battlefield until after night fell.[25]

Gordon's march to Cedar Run, like Crawford's the day before, was over a road containing little shade and no water, but with a surfeit of dust and debilitating heat. The pace was brisk, and the men seldom halted. Gordon described the midday air as "hot as a bake oven." As on August 8, scores of men dropped and several suffered heat strokes. An artilleryman from Maine saw infantrymen with sunstroke drop like logs. A soldier from the 27th Indiana described men falling and "frothing at the mouth, rolling their eyeballs and writhing in painful contortions." A new recruit in the 2nd Massachusetts, Pvt. Thomas Carey of Company F, dropped dead from the heat; a party buried him by the roadside. A robust soldier in the 3rd Maryland reportedly died from the heat. First Lieutenant Aaron Bates of the 102nd New York lay unconscious in the woods along the road until awoken by cannon fire. Like many of the heat-related casualties, Bates got up and pressed on, rejoining his regiment in time for the fight. Unfortunately, he discovered that someone had lightened his burden by pilfering his sword.[26]

After Augur's division had marched a few miles south of Culpeper, Banks dashed toward the front, passing the 28th Pennsylvania. Brigadier General Geary rode back to his former regiment and stopped at the colors. He ordered a halt and told the men that two Confederate regiments had driven a signal corps detachment from Thoroughfare Mountain. The signalmen notified Culpeper that one cavalry regiment surrounded them. Banks, tasked by Pope with regaining the mountain and protecting the detachment, assigned the mission to the 28th Pennsylvania, accompanied by a cavalry squadron. It is easy to imagine why that regiment was chosen. Raised from throughout the state and organized in Philadelphia, the 28th Pennsylvania contained 15 companies instead of the normal 10. Moreover, because it had not yet experienced a large engagement, it was near full strength and appeared as a brigade to regiments that had seen hard fighting. Geary told the men that they were to take and hold the mountain "at all hazards." He said he knew they could do it and that the brigade would come to the mountain from another direction to make an attack to relieve them. Thoroughfare Mountain was west of the battlefield, so Lieutenant Colonel Tyndale turned his large regiment west at

25 OR 12, pt. 2, 25-26; Gordon, *Brook Farm*, 281.

26 Gordon, *Brook Farm*, 281-282; Quint, *2nd Massachusetts*, 105; Brown, *Twenty-Seventh Indiana*, 195; *History of the Fourth Maine Battery*, 17; Abraham Marks, Diary, transcribed and edited by Henrietta E. Mosley, August 8, 1862, FNMP; *2nd Annual Report*, 102.

Col. Thomas Ruger, 3rd Wisconsin
Library of Congress

Colvin's Tavern. With weapons loaded, the men marched along the wooded road toward James City. In an instant, Geary's brigade lost over half its strength as his Buckeye regiments continued toward Cedar Run.[27]

*   *   *

About noon, Gordon's brigade descended the final half mile toward Cedar Run; Slaughter's Mountain came into view on the left. The men saw Crawford's skirmishers in the woods ahead. Gordon ordered a halt. His men slaked their thirst in warm, muddy water, dunked overheated heads, and filled canteens. Brigadier General Benjamin Stone Roberts was there, overseeing Banks's deployment in Pope's stead. Gordon had kept a keen eye on the surrounding ground as his brigade approached the field. When he spotted Roberts, he seized what he thought was an opportunity. The fastidious Massachusetts general directed Roberts's attention to a commanding position about three-quarters of a mile to the right of the road, saying, "That should be held by our right. Shall I take it?" Roberts assented. Gordon had indeed found the best spot on the Union side of the field. Unfortunately, the intervening distance was too great for Williams's division to fill. Roberts took the decision about Gordon's deployment away from Banks, who was still on the road and never sufficiently ascertained the position of his right. Gordon's brigade filed northward until it reached Mrs. Brown's cottage, picturesque atop a substantial hill with verdant turf bounded by a fence. Behind the house, to the east, stood a wooded grove. To the southwest, the land descended to Cedar Run, beyond which the steep upward slope became thickly wooded and briar-filled. This belt of woods

27 OR 12, pt. 2, 144; Robert G. Davis to father, August 14, 1862, LV; Ambrose Henry Hayward to sister, August 17, 1862, Ambrose Henry Hayward Papers, GC; Roberts to sister, August 10, 1862, HSP; Foering Diary, August 9, 1862, HSP; McLaughlin, Memoir of *Hector Tyndale*, 63-64.

began at the Orange Road as a point and widened to the north to become 400 to 600 yards wide.[28]

As Gordon's brigade deployed around the Brown cottage, the matron and her relatives, all women and children, repeatedly asked Gordon what they should do. Gordon told them to leave immediately, but, too frightened to accept his answer, they remained. Carrying on his deployment, Gordon placed the 27th Indiana on the right. The 2nd Massachusetts, joined by a company of the colorfully uniformed *Zouaves d'Afrique*, was on the Hoosiers' left, followed by the 3rd Wisconsin. Captain George Cothran's Battery M, 1st New York Light Artillery, was on the far left. It contained six 10-pounder Parrott guns. Colonel Silas Colgrove sent Companies C and F of the 27th Indiana under 1st Sgt. John M. Bloss a half mile right to another hill as flankers. Gordon deployed six 3rd Wisconsin companies forward and left, nearly to the Wheatfield.[29]

Colonel Thomas H. Ruger, commanding the 3rd Wisconsin, accompanied the detachment. Ruger, who graduated third at West Point in 1854, was an engineer in the prewar army, and after resigning, he successfully practiced law. In 1861, after a week on the governor's military staff, he accepted the lieutenant colonelcy of the 3rd while it formed at Fond du Lac. With his West Point background, he taught tactics to the inexperienced junior officers. He was reliable, levelheaded, and suffered hardships without outward appearance. According to the regimental history, "profane or indelicate language never passed his lips." The men thought of him as a strict yet fair and humane disciplinarian.[30]

The rest of the regiment's senior leadership also joined the detachment. Lieutenant Colonel Louis H. D. Crane had been a lawyer in Wisconsin since 1850. He had a pleasant manner and had earned the trust and respect of his men. Prolonged illness had made Crane increasingly morose, and he entered battle on August 9 with a strong feeling that he would not survive. When the second order to march came that morning, he turned to his non-combatant brother and ominously

28 Gordon, *Brook Farm*, 282, 284-285; Brown, *Twenty-Seventh Indiana*, 196; "A. W. Account," August 13, 1862, *Milwaukee Sentinel*, in Quiner Scrapbook, WHS. On August 17, Williams wrote that after seeing the field, he sent a message to Banks stating that the position was poor.

29 OR 51, pt. 1, 123; Gordon, *Brook Farm*, 287; Brown, *Twenty-Seventh Indiana*, 199. It is curious that a first sergeant commanded a two-company detachment at this stage of the war. Bloss, who would be promoted to 1st lieutenant in September, was "ably counseled and assisted" by 2nd Lt. Jacob A. Lee. It is possible that Bloss, to whom Brown refers as "Lieutenant Bloss," was an acting second lieutenant. But in the dramatic discovery of Lee's lost order in September, Bloss was described as a first sergeant. See Brown, *Twenty-Seventh Indiana*, 199, 579, 597.

30 Bryant, *Third Wisconsin*, 367-368.

Capt. Moses O'Brien,
3rd Wisconsin, Company I
Bryant, Third Wisconsin

said "I knew it was coming." Major John W. Scott and Captains Moses O'Brien and William Hawley also moved forward with the detachment.[31]

Of Irish extraction, Moses O'Brien was a large, resilient officer who often relieved the load of a fatigued or ill soldier. Though a trained civil engineer, O'Brien ran a burgeoning legal practice in April 1861. Then, during a meeting to register recruits for the nascent war, this grandson of a soldier who had died leading cavalry in Ireland in 1798 was the first to sign the roll, declaring, "I learned to love liberty in the land of my birth; I came to America to enjoy it; I can fight to defend it. Give me the pen." He led the 3rd Wisconsin's Company I down the hill in front of Mrs. Brown's house and crossed Cedar Run.[32]

Captain William Hawley was, like Colonel Ruger, a New Yorker. Grandson of a major in the War of 1812, Hawley enlisted as an artillerist in the Mexican War and was promoted to sergeant. In April 1861, he raised Company K of the 3rd Wisconsin. He was energetic, erudite, and solicitous about his soldiers' well-being. Hawley's Company K was on the right flank.[33]

The 2nd Massachusetts, commanded by Col. George Leonard Andrews, waited back at the Brown cottage. Andrews graduated first in the West Point class of 1851 and served as an engineer until resigning from the army in 1855. He left a large Boston business house and passed up a colonelcy in another regiment to become lieutenant colonel of the 2nd Massachusetts.[34]

---

31 Bryant, *Third Wisconsin*, 377-378; James Crane to mother and sister, August 14, 1862, published in unidentified newspaper, Quiner Scrapbook, WHS.

32 Bryant, *Third Wisconsin*, 379.

33 Ibid., 372-373.

34 Quint, *2nd Massachusetts*, 476.

Andrews's major, James Savage, had replaced the regiment's first major, Wilder Dwight, who was taken prisoner at Winchester. Savage was a Harvard graduate whose lineage included the commander of Massachusetts forces in King Philip's War. He was sensitive, earnest, and joyous, but he was prone to illness, and his constitution could not support his desire for action. Two of the 2nd Massachusetts's captains, Richard Cary and Richard Goodwin, and 2nd Lt. Stephen Perkins were thoroughly debilitated on August 9 and rode toward the action in ambulances. Unwilling to stay away from the fight, they got out when they neared the battlefield.[35]

*   *   *

Augur's division, with Banks in tow, arrived on the field at about 1:30 p.m. General Roberts suggested that they were currently in the best available position. Banks agreed and placed the rest of his command on Crawford's line. Apparently, their discussion did not include Gordon's precise location. Banks thought Gordon was behind the woods on Crawford's immediate right. But there was a significant gap between the two: Gordon's brigade was behind Cedar Run, far to Crawford's right and rear.[36]

While Banks did not ascertain Gordon's position from this meeting, he did take another message from it. According to Banks, Roberts stated numerous times that "there must be no backing out this day." Whether Pope gave positive instructions or whether Roberts spoke on his own initiative is unclear, but the message hit its mark. Combined with Pope's past instructions to the army and to Banks personally, this must have impacted Banks's attitude that day. Testifying before the Joint Committee on the Conduct of the War, Banks would attest, "I was a little desperate, because we supposed that General Pope thought we did not want to fight."[37]

*   *   *

35 Quint, *2nd Massachusetts*, 482-483; *Harvard Memorial Biographies*, vol. 1 (Cambridge, 1866), 380.

36 *OR* 12, pt. 2, 150; Gordon, *Brook Farm*, 282-283, 286.

37 *Joint Committee on the Conduct of the War, 38th Congress*, 3: Miscellaneous, 46.

While Banks and Roberts conferred, Brig. Gen. Jubal Early prepared for battle. After driving Bayard's cavalry, Early's brigade advanced across the Crittenden Lane to the crest of the ridge. He correctly suspected that Union infantry was concealed behind the opposite ridge. After three Union batteries that he spotted fired at him, Early put his soldiers under cover behind the ridge and sent word to Charles Winder to bring up his division. Early's right was to the left of and a little behind the copse of cedar trees, and his left was a few hundred yards to the right of the road. Meanwhile, the other brigades in Ewell's division, under Col. Henry Forno and Brig. Gen. Isaac Trimble, advanced at 2:00 p.m. They broke south of Early's advance, remaining right of the southern branch of Cedar Run, and moved up the mountain, joined by two batteries, totaling six guns, under Capt. Joseph W. Latimer and Lt. Nathaniel Terry. These batteries were in place by 3:30 p.m.[38]

The rest of Ewell's artillery began arriving at Early's position. A three-inch rifle under Capt. William D. Brown and two of Capt. William F. Dement's 12-pounder Napoleons went to the high ground near the cedars. Dement's two remaining Napoleons and three guns under Capt. Louis E. D'Aquin deployed just southwest of the cedars. Early detached the 12th Georgia slightly to the right to support these batteries and to attempt, in a very meager way, to fill some of the distance between his right and the rest of Ewell's division on the mountain. Dement's rear section at the cedars had a shaky start, with the section commander ordering his two guns forward before the cannoneers mounted. When they caught up, one broke a sponge head off in one of the gun barrels and loaded a shell on top of it before discovering his error. The crews had to extract both under fire.[39]

Brigadier General Charles Winder arrived at the Crittenden Gate around this time. Dismounted and in his shirtsleeves, the ailing general personally directed the guns' deployment. He initially called on his artillery chief, Maj. Richard Snowden Andrews, to position one rifle in front of the gate. Shortly after it arrived, two rifles of Capt. William Poague's Rockbridge Artillery joined it. The three pieces immediately went into action, provoking a substantial Federal response. Soon after, Andrews repositioned these rifles to higher ground 250 to 400 yards to the right and front. He ultimately sent a total of four rifled pieces and one 12-pounder Napoleon from Poague's, Capt. William Caskie's, and Lt. Joseph Carpenter's batteries. Within 15 minutes, Carpenter received a head wound that would prove

---

38 OR 12, pt. 2, 235, 238; Early, *Autobiographical Sketch*, 96.

39 OR 12, pt. 2, 238; Early, *Autobiographical Sketch*, 97; Tom Kelley, ed., *The Personal Memoirs of Jonathan Thomas Scharf of the First Maryland Artillery* (Baltimore, 1992), 32-33.

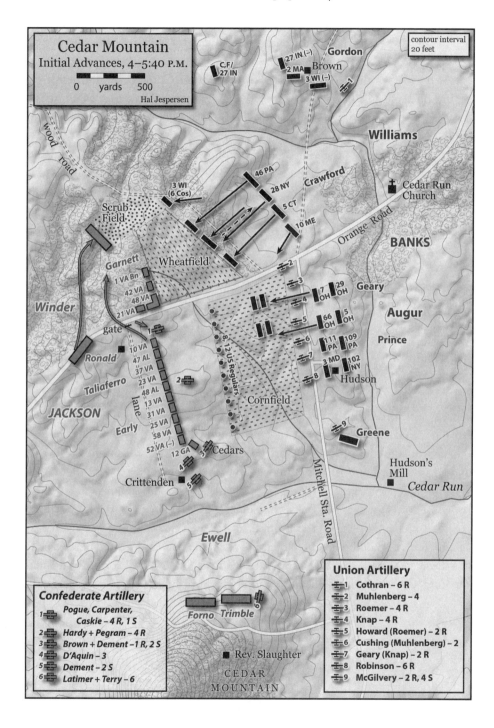

Cedar Mountain
Initial Advances, 4–5:40 P.M.

0   yards   500

Hal Jespersen

contour interval
20 feet

27 IN (–)
C,F/
27 IN
Gordon
2 MA
3 WI (–)
Brown

wood
road

Williams

46 PA
28 NY
Crawford
5 CT
10 ME
Cedar Run
Church

3 WI
(6 Cos)

Scrub
Field

Orange Road
BANKS

Garnett
Wheatfield
1 VA Bn
42 VA
48 VA
21 VA
7
OH
29
OH
Geary
Augur
66
OH
5
OH
Prince

Winder

gate
1
10 VA
47 AL
37 VA
23 VA
48 AL
13 VA
31 VA
25 VA
58 VA
52 VA (–)
Ronald
2
Taliaferro
lane
JACKSON
Early
8, 12 US Regulars

Cornfield

3
4
5
6
111
PA
109
PA
7
3 MD
8
102
NY
Hudson

9
Greene

12 GA
4
3
5
Cedars
Crittenden

Hudson's
Mill
Cedar Run

Mitchell Sta. Road

Ewell

Confederate Artillery

1	Pogue, Carpenter, Caskie – 4 R, 1 S
2	Hardy + Pegram – 4 R
3	Brown + Dement – 1 R, 2 S
4	D'Aquin – 3
5	Dement – 2 S
6	Latimer + Terry – 6

Forno   Trimble
6

Rev. Slaughter

CEDAR
MOUNTAIN

Union Artillery

1	Cothran – 6 R
2	Muhlenberg – 4
3	Roemer – 4 R
4	Knap – 4 R
5	Howard (Roemer) – 2 R
6	Cushing (Muhlenberg) – 2
7	Geary (Knap) – 2 R
8	Robinson – 6 R
9	McGilvery – 2 R, 4 S

fatal in a few weeks. After a half hour of firing, Poague withdrew one rifle, which had been rendered unserviceable.[40]

As the guns at the cedars, followed by those at the Crittenden Gate, increased the fire on Banks's artillery between 3:00 and 4:00 p.m., Winder sent infantry to Early's left. His first brigade, commanded by Lt. Col. Thomas Garnett, entered the woods north of the road and moved east to within 20 yards of the Wheatfield. To support the batteries at the Gate, Garnett's brigade deployed irregularly into the wooded right angle formed by the Wheatfield and the Orange Road. Garnett's left, which included the 1st Virginia Battalion, the 42nd Virginia, and part of the 48th Virginia, fronted the Wheatfield. His right, comprised of the rest of the 48th and the 21st Virginia, faced the road, the open space in front of the Confederate batteries, and the Cornfield beyond. Shortly before the Federal assault, Brig. Gen. William B. Taliaferro's brigade crossed the Crittenden Lane and deployed between Early's left and the batteries in front of the Gate. From right to left, Taliaferro's line consisted of the 48th Alabama, the 23rd and 37th Virginia, the 47th Alabama, and the 10th Virginia. Winder kept the Stonewall Brigade, commanded by Col. Charles A. Ronald, in the rear as a reserve. Behind Winder's deploying division, A. P. Hill's division was still on the road from the Rapidan, creating a long dust cloud that Crawford's soldiers could see rising threateningly in the distance.[41]

The artillery duel continued for roughly two hours, plowing turf, ripping treetops, and producing a few casualties on each side. A falling tree limb struck Captain Caskie, commanding one of the Crittenden Gate batteries, in the back and knocked him to the ground. Before Andrews's batteries repositioned, General Winder stood next to Poague's leftmost gun with his hand to his mouth attempting to shout directions over the din. A Federal shell passed through his left side and arm, ripping his torso as far back as his spine. Winder fell backward, his body fully extended and shuddering on the ground. Several men carried him on a stretcher to the grove of a schoolhouse three-quarters of a mile rearward, where he died. His loss threw into confusion any immediate efforts to execute Jackson's closely held intention for an advance against the Union right. Shortly after this, Major Andrews,

---

40 OR 12, pt. 2, 186, 213-214; Howard, *Maryland Confederate*, 167-168; Edward A. Moore, *The Story of a Cannoneer under Stonewall Jackson* (New York, 1907), 95; Monroe F. Cockrell, ed., *Gunner with Stonewall: Reminiscences of William Thomas Poague* (Jackson, TN, 1957), 33.

41 OR 12, pt. 2, 188-189, 200, 206, 210; Charles W. Turner, ed., "Major Charles A. Davidson: Letters of a Virginia Soldier," *Civil War History*, vol. 22, no. 1 (1976), 28; John H. Worsham, *One of Jackson's Foot Cavalry* (New York, 1912), 111; Howard, *Maryland Confederate*, 169; Marvin, *Fifth Regiment*, 154; Krick, *Stonewall Jackson at Cedar Mountain*, 84-85.

commanding Winder's artillery, also received a wound, which those present thought was mortal. A fragment of a bursting shell tore apart his abdominal wall. Pressing his hand to the wound to keep his entrails from spilling out, Andrews slid from his horse. He lay by the side of the road for hours until A. P. Hill found him and sent for an ambulance. He was captured after the battle when Jackson withdrew to the Rapidan, but miraculously survived the war.[42]

In Dement's Maryland battery, one man lost an arm at the shoulder and another lost both legs. The impact flung one leg into the air, while the other hung from a sinew. Both died. A shell fragment hit a sergeant in Dement's forward section in the face, and an ambulance detail carried him from the field with blood streaming from the wound. Neither these casualties nor the battery's earlier mistakes materially limited its efficiency. Its rate of fire, combined with the excessive heat, caused the water on the sponge head to sizzle when men swabbed the barrels. They prudently ceased firing for a time to let the guns cool.[43]

Though Confederate artillery casualties were grievous, Northern batteries were at an unquestionable disadvantage. All the positions from which the Confederate artillery fired were higher than their Union targets. A common opinion among the Federals was that the batteries on the mountain were a higher caliber. They were not. The men were experiencing the physics of fire plunging from elevated batteries. Second Lieutenant Gould observed that the "shot came along as if they had wings and were flying."[44]

* * *

Meanwhile, Lt. Col. Hector Tyndale and his 28th Pennsylvania continued on the road to Thoroughfare Mountain, over a rolling, sylvan country. They marched into the unknown, unable to see more than a mile in any direction. Tyndale halted frequently, scouting the woods to avert an ambush. The oppressive heat caused extra concern, for he found it difficult to keep his men in close order in the uncertain territory. If he needed to bring them rapidly into line, he would have trouble. As the column continued alone, concussions from the opening artillery fire

---

42 Howard, *Maryland Confederate*, 169; Moore, *The Story of a Cannoneer*, 95; Cockrell, ed., *Gunner with Stonewall*, 33; Tunstall Smith, ed., *Richard Snowden Andrews, Lieutenant Colonel Commanding the First Maryland Artillery Confederate States Army, A Memoir* (1910), 54-55.

43 Kelley, *Scharf Memoirs*, 33; John W. F. Hatton, "Memoir," 309, FNMP.

44 Gould, *10th Maine*, 171.

Brig. Gen. Christopher C. Augur
Library of Congress

suddenly intensified, immediately drawing the men's attention to their left rear. The sound of firing escalated into a nearly constant string of discharges, quashing any lingering presumption that Geary would soon arrive to save the day. Tyndale halted his command and consulted with his senior officers about whether it would be better to continue as ordered or cross overland to reach the battlefield. He decided that his given objective may have been a key position in a larger plan involving Pope's entire army, and the regiment distractedly continued toward the mountain.[45]

*   *   *

While the Confederate deployment and the artillery duel occurred, Banks finalized his own troop dispositions. After Augur arrived around 1:30 p.m., Banks shuffled units so that Augur's division was south of the road and Williams's division was to its north, or right. Geary's brigade deployed with its right 100 yards behind and across the road from Lt. Edward D. Muhlenberg's Battery F, 4th U.S. Artillery. The brigade extended to the south and was in place by 2:00 p.m. In front of its extreme left regiment, Geary's son, Lt. Edward R. Geary, commanded one section of Knap's battery. The artillery went to work shortly after the brigade's arrival. It was still under fire, though concealed from Confederate view, as the men double-quicked by the right flank at 3:30 p.m., redeploying in two lines nearer the road. The first line contained the 66th Ohio on the left and the 7th Ohio on the right. The 5th and 29th Ohio formed the second line.[46]

45 Robert G. Davis to Father, August 14, 1862, Robert G. Davis Letters, LV; McLaughlin, *Memoir of Hector Tyndale*, 64.

46 *OR* 12, pt. 2, 160, 165. Additional guns were in front of Geary and are described later.

Arriving behind Geary, Henry Prince's brigade filed left down the creek bed for three-quarters of a mile and halted. Prince then received word to detach the battalion of 8th and 12th U.S. Regular troops under Capt. Thomas Pitcher to the front as skirmishers. Pitcher's men covered the entire division front. Augur also directed Prince to form the rest of his brigade in two lines on Geary's left. His front line contained the 3rd Maryland on the left and the 111th Pennsylvania on the right. Prince placed the 102nd New York to the left and the 109th Pennsylvania on the right as his reserve. Captain Pitcher addressed his men within earshot of the 111th Pennsylvania before advancing. He announced that they were going into battle in front of volunteer troops and they should set "a regular soldier's example." Major Thomas McCormick Walker commanded the 111th and had been its only field-grade officer since the third week in July. Walker studied at Princeton before the war and according to the regimental history, he possessed "unusual ability and promise." On the heels of Pitcher's comments, the 28-year-old Walker brought his troops to attention and gave his own speech:

> Men of the One Hundred and Eleventh: You have heard Captain Pitcher's soldierly words to his battalion. I want to say to you as you go into this fight, that as they remember they are regulars, so you are to remember that you are volunteers, and while you can load and fire a musket you must not allow regular soldiers, the enemy, or anyone else to outfight you! Do you hear?

The Pennsylvanians had to wait their turn, however. Private James T. Miller of Company D recalled that, "For three long weary hours we lay on our faces on the ground about four rods to the rear of the canon but in all time our regiment only had only four men wounded." While lying there, another member of Company D had fun at the company pariah's expense. Corporal Calvin H. Blanchard had enlisted in January as a 16-year-old runaway. He discovered a "lowse about the size of a wheat kernel" crawling up the soldier's back. Blanchard offered, "We'll soon be in it now, boys, Andy is deploying his skirmishers."[47]

The 8th and 12th Regulars emerged from the edge of the Cornfield and exchanged a lively, sustained fire with Early's and Taliaferro's brigades. The

---

47 OR 12, pt. 2, 167-168; John Richards Boyle, *Soldiers True: The Story of the One Hundred and Eleventh Regiment Pennsylvania Veteran Volunteers, and of its Campaigns in the War for the Union, 1861-1865* (New York & Cincinnati, 1903), 12, 41-44; Roger D. Hunt and Jack R. Brown, *Brevet Brigadier Generals in Blue* (Gaithersburg, MD, 2010), 646; James T. Miller to Brother, August 13, 1862, James T. Miller Letters, UM; Blanchard, "Memoir," 3. Four rods equal 66 feet.

Regulars, according to word sent to General Augur after the battle from a captured officer in Richmond:

> Excited the admiration of the enemy, who inquired if they were not regulars, as they had never seen such skirmishing. They were out during the whole battle . . . and annoyed him so as to turn the attention of his guns away from more distant firing with shot and shell, and caused him to waste canister upon the ground of the skirmishers.

Confederate artillery arrived near the Cornfield just before Pitcher. Two of A. P. Hill's batteries, under Capt. "Willie" Pegram and Lt. William B. Hardy, rolled southeast from the Crittenden Lane to within 150 yards of the Cornfield. They deployed en echelon ahead of Taliaferro's right, with Pegram's guns in front and to the right of Hardy's, unaware that Federal skirmishers were nearby. Early double-quicked his brigade in order to secure the battery, which opened on Pitcher's men with canister. Nevertheless, the skirmishers held at the edge of the Cornfield until relieved by the general advance.[48]

Captain O'Neil W. Robinson's battery had a disorderly start. As soon as it arrived, Prince placed Robinson under arrest. The men were unaware why, but the infraction apparently was less consequential than the impending hazard. Within half an hour, Prince released Robinson, who led his battery half a mile across an open field while shells passed harmlessly overhead. Nevertheless, they were wary of lingering. They parked behind haystacks near the Hudson house, which stood behind the Mitchell Station Road. Robinson's guns and the house were to the left rear of the already engaged batteries. The nearest guns were Lieutenant Geary's section of Knap's battery. A Confederate shell landed in a nearby group of calves, causing a minor stampede and a laugh among the men. More menacingly, soldiers began carrying casualties from the batteries rearward. After 15 minutes, (about 3:15 p.m.), Robinson's guns moved forward and went into battery to the left of Geary's section. While climbing the ridge, they spotted some of Geary's dead horses sprawled on the ground.[49]

Robinson's men immediately came under fire. A shell struck Pvt. Abel Davis in the leg. Private Charles Salley replaced Davis and received a severe scalp wound.

---

48 OR 12, pt. 2, 158, 187, 226; Early, *Autobiographical Sketch*, 98.

49 *History of the Fourth Maine Battery*, 18; United States Army, Corps of Topographical Engineers, and J. Schedler, *Map of Culpeper County with parts of Madison, Rappahannock, and Fauquier counties, Virginia* (Washington, DC, 1863); Krick, *Stonewall Jackson at Cedar Mountain*, 302. There was a second Hudson house, farther to the Federal rear, near which reinforcements from McDowell's corps formed in the evening.

Capt. Joseph Knap, Independent Battery E, Pennsylvania Light Artillery
Library of Congress

No one got an opportunity to carry him to the rear, however, because he ran away so fast that he could not be caught. The section on the right, under 1st Lt. Lucius M. S. Haynes, was on higher ground. Being more visible, it received the heaviest fire. Robinson posted himself with the section on the left.[50]

After Lieutenant Haynes's section fired about 50 rounds per gun, a Confederate projectile struck a gun wheel, ricocheted, and removed part of Pvt. Newell Byron Phillips's chin and shoulder. He died a few hours later at the Hudson house. A shell struck the axle of another piece, disabling it and wounding several cannoneers with splintered wood. A piece of shrapnel from a case round passed through Pvt. Hannibal Powers's boot. Assuming he was injured, he started for the rear, but was told to look at the wound. With his boot off, the iron rolled out, and the unharmed Powers resumed his duties. By 5:00 p.m., Lieutenant Haynes had repositioned left, personally working his section's one serviceable gun. The non-combatants in charge of the battery's wagons and forge brought water to the gunners, who were suffering intensely from their exertions in the heat. Shortly after Robinson's battery was in place, Capt. Freeman McGilvery's 6th Battery, Maine Light Artillery, went into position south of the Hudson house.[51]

George Sears Greene's tiny brigade and Captain McGilvery's battery of two three-inch rifles and four 12-pounder Napoleons formed the left flank. Greene's brigade consisted of the 78th New York and a battalion of the 1st District of

---

50 *History of the Fourth Maine Battery*, 19.

51 Ibid., 19-20.

Columbia. Both Greene and McGilvery guarded Banks's left from Ewell's two brigades on the mountain, which was ahead of and to their left.[52]

Knap's battery, on the right of Robinson's, suffered similarly gruesome casualties. As happened with many batteries that day, Knap's cannoneers were soon exhausted, and many fell out. The captain's servant-cook worked the number one gun. A Confederate shell removed the top of his head.[53]

With Augur in place, Crawford's brigade reunited north of the road; the 10th Maine was on the left, followed by the 5th Connecticut, the 28th New York, and the 46th Pennsylvania. The brigade occupied the woods west of Cedar Run. Gordon was far beyond Crawford's left rear, behind the run. Both divisions were well covered when the main artillery duel began between 3:00 and 4:00 p.m.[54]

After the infantry redeployed, Banks's artillery south of the road was arranged as follows from left to right: McGilvery's six guns; Robinson's six rifles; two of Knap's rifles, commanded by Lieutenant Geary; a section of Lieutenant Muhlenberg's U.S. Battery under Lt. Harry Cushing; two rifles of Captain Roemer's battery, commanded by Lieutenant Howard; Knap's remaining four rifles, which were still in their original position; and Roemer's remaining four rifles. The balance of Lieutenant Muhlenberg's battery sat north of the road. Finally, Capt. George Cothran's Battery M, 1st New York Artillery, supported Gordon's brigade at Brown's cottage.[55]

Behind Pitcher's skirmishers, Geary's brigade moved forward about 200 yards, 100 yards in advance of the batteries, between 4:00 and 4:30 p.m. After crossing the Mitchell Station Road and entering the Cornfield, the troops took to the ground in a depression and awaited orders under heavy artillery fire that killed and wounded several men. Prince's brigade remained behind the batteries and the Mitchell Station Road. Colonel Henry Stainrook of the 109th Pennsylvania was among Prince's wounded. By this time, 1st Lt. Aaron Bates had recovered from the heat and rejoined the 102nd New York, which was northeast of the Hudson place.[56]

52 OR 51, pt. 1, 121; George Sears Greene, "Official Reports, August 14, 1862," Banks Papers, LC.

53 David Nichol to family, August 11, 1862, and James Stewart to mother, August 11, 1862, USA.

54 OR 12, pt. 2, 150; Gordon, *Brook Farm*, 282; Hicks Diary, 10, LC.

55 OR 12, pt. 2, 160-161; Andrews, "Cedar Mountain," 415-416.

56 OR 12, pt. 2, 160, 165, 167-168; *2nd Annual Report*, 102, 112; *Cleveland Morning Leader*, August 18, 1862.

North of the road, Banks directed Crawford to advance a regiment of skirmishers to guard against Confederate skirmishers that were seen approaching stealthily. The 28th New York's six right companies deployed; the balance followed as a reserve. They reached the Wheatfield without contact. Crawford became concerned that a single regiment was insufficient to deal with enemy skirmishers and requested reinforcements. At about 5:00 p.m., Williams forwarded Banks's order to Crawford to advance his brigade into the woods and prepare to move against Jackson's left.[57]

Crawford recalled the 28th New York and advanced the brigade across an open field at the double-quick, his men hurrahing enthusiastically. Before reaching the belt of trees that bordered the Wheatfield, they slowed to a walk and then disappeared from view into the tangled woods. Each line became broken. Officers could not see the next regiment through the undergrowth. The brigade halted about 40 yards from the fence at the edge of the woods. The men waited there nearly an hour for orders, but Crawford's entire brigade had not gone forward. Banks retained the 10th Maine to guard Muhlenberg's battery, and a staff officer led the 10th forward and to the left. With their left resting on the road, the men nervously lay behind the outgunned battery, which reportedly received six shots for each one that it fired.[58]

At some point between Crawford's redeployment and his move forward, Brig. Gen. Alpheus Williams joined the regimental commanders of his old brigade, Crawford's, for a lunch of "coffee, ham, etc." After the meal, they all reclined under a shade tree and, in a carefree manner, shared stories from their prior service together. Colonel Donnelly, a lawyer from Lockport, New York, who was known for his droll personality, was in a lighthearted mood. Donnelly exuberantly cracked jokes with his friends during this peaceful, hot afternoon *fête* above the creek.[59]

---

57 OR 12, pt. 2, 55, 146, 150-151; Hicks Diary, 10-11, LC; *Joint Committee on the Conduct of the War, 38th Congress*, 3: Miscellaneous, 46.

58 OR 12, pt. 2, 151; Hicks Diary, 11, LC; Gould, *10th Maine*, 171.

59 Quaife, *From the Cannon's Mouth*, 100; Roger D. Hunt, *Colonels in Blue: Union Army Colonels of the Civil War, New York* (Atglen, PA, 2003), 107. This was likely a late lunch, sometime between 1:30 and 3:00 p.m. Williams wrote that it occurred after his units were positioned, and Crawford would not have moved until Augur arrived at 1:30. The account in Marvin wherein Crawford's two left regiments crossed the road to reunite the brigade between 4:00 and 4:15 is likely inaccurate. Further, it was reported as a relaxing meal, so it probably occurred prior to the start of the main artillery duel at 3:00. Given reports of another, more hurried, prebattle meeting at Antietam, described in John Gould's letter to Ezra Carman (January 7, 1898, APD), it is possible that the "etc." included something more invigorating than gunpowder.

Chapter 3

"The Sable Raven Bellowed for Revenge."[1]

— Thomas Anderson, 12th U.S. Infantry

Banks Attacks at Slaughter's Mountain

5:45 to 6:15 p.m., August 9, 1862

Loving country more than life,
More than kindred, home or wife;
'Neath the flag they loved so well,
Nobly, foremost fighting fell.[2]

— Sylvester S. Marvin, 28th New York, 1902

The sun plunged swiftly toward the horizon in front of Gordon's brigade. A general engagement seemed less likely. Doing their best to recover from the torrid march, some men slept. Soon, a few rose from their coffee or shaded repose to peer toward the Cornfield. Banks ordered the artillery to pause at 5:00 p.m. Gordon's men heard musketry building as Augur's line relieved Pitcher's skirmishers. Suddenly, between 5:45 and 6:00 p.m., a jarring explosion of musketry

---

1 T. M. Anderson, "Civil War Recollections of the Twelfth Infantry," *Journal of the Military Service Institution of the United States, Vol. XLI* (Governor's Island, 1907), 386. Anderson, referring to Banks, loosely paraphrased *Hamlet* (Act 3, Scene 2), "the croaking Raven doth bellow for revenge."

2 Horatio King, *Dedication of the Monument to the 28th New York Volunteers, Culpeper, Va., Aug. 8, 1902,* 26.

in the Wheatfield reverberated over the undulant terrain to the ears of Gordon's brigade. Writing after the war, several competent observers, who were at several different locations during the battle, described it as the most thunderous volleying they ever heard. When the artillery resumed firing, musketry muted the sound of shells thudding against trees. Lieutenant John Gould remembered that "rising higher and more terrible than all was the hurrah of the boys."[3]

*   *   *

Crawford's officers had conferred during their halt in the woods an hour earlier. Colonel Joseph Knipe, commanding the 46th Pennsylvania, pressed for an advance, suggesting that it would be an easy thing to capture the battery near the Crittenden Gate. Others voiced concerns; they had little knowledge of Confederate strength in their front. The men in the 28th New York could see this congress of brigade leaders; the few discernable words and the animated gesticulating made it clear that a charge was imminent. Meanwhile, a Union scouting party, led by a sergeant, advanced into the Wheatfield as far as the rivulet depression. From this position, they discovered Garnett's Confederates in the woods and returned without drawing fire.[4]

While Crawford and Knipe were keen to assault, the decision rested with Banks. He acted without developing the Confederate presence in his front, without consulting Pope, and without calling for Ricketts's division, which was then guarding the approach from James City. Banks's decision to attack, according to historian Robert Krick, was done "in almost reflexive annoyance with Confederate artillery." There may be truth in that statement, but David Hunter Strother's postwar writings contained at least as much accuracy regarding Banks's judgment at Cedar Mountain. Strother, who was on Banks's staff before and after Cedar Mountain, alleged that Banks was dissatisfied with public opinion regarding his performance that spring in the Shenandoah Valley. Strother wrote that Banks was "burning for an opportunity to wipe away unmerited opprobrium." Whatever the accuracy of this assessment, Pope's and Roberts's goading statements, in person

---

3 OR 51, pt. 1, 120; Gordon, *Brook Farm*, 298; Quint, *2nd Massachusetts*, 109; Andrews, "Cedar Mountain," 423-424; Gould, *10th Maine*, 172; Brown, *Twenty-Seventh Indiana*, 201.

4 Marvin, *Fifth Connecticut*, 154; Boyce, *Twenty-eighth New York*, 36; Boyce, "28th Regiment," 119-120.

and in writing, could not have helped Banks's ability to restrict himself to a defensive posture.[5]

Waiting for Banks's decision near the Wheatfield, Crawford worried about the distance across which his brigade would have to advance in order to reach the opposite woods. He sent an aide to Banks requesting a section of Muhlenberg's Napoleons to clear the opposite tree line. Before the aide returned, Williams's assistant adjutant general, Captain William Wilkins, arrived and pressed Crawford to advance immediately. Besides spurring Crawford, Wilkins did the Pennsylvanian a service.[6]

The 3rd Wisconsin battalion that Gordon had sent forward under Colonel Ruger was in the woods about 100 yards from the Wheatfield astride an old wood road when Crawford's brigade had advanced toward the Wheatfield. The 46th Pennsylvania passed through the 3rd's line, its right reaching Ruger's Company D, fourth from the left. The brigade paused a few minutes and then continued toward its position near the Wheatfield and out of sight. Captain Wilkins of Williams's staff rode up, carrying an order from Crawford to join his advance. Ruger demurred. He was under Gordon's orders, and any change needed to come from a higher authority than Crawford. Soon after that, Wilkins returned, claiming to have similar orders from Banks. Orders to that effect also passed from Williams to Gordon. Colonel Ruger marched his six companies toward the right far enough to achieve what he supposed was sufficient distance beyond the 46th Pennsylvania. He then called a halt for a short speech. He told his men they were to charge a battery and that the honor of the regiment was in their hands. They then pressed forward as close to double-quick as possible over the difficult terrain and briar-filled undergrowth. Emerging from the woods into the Scrub Field, they discovered that they were alone. Their path had diverged from that of the 46th Pennsylvania on their left. A slight ridge separated the two fields.[7]

To the left, when Wilkins delivered orders for Crawford to advance, officers hurriedly mounted and rode to their positions. The men sprang to their feet. Captain William Cogswell, an aide to Crawford on loan from the 5th Connecticut,

5   Krick, *Stonewall Jackson at Cedar Mountain*, 143. Strother's article from the August 1867 edition of *Harper's Monthly* was quoted in Gordon, *Brook Farm*, 346.

6   OR 12, pt. 2, 151.

7   OR 51, pt. 1, 124; Gordon, *Brook Farm*, 202; Hinkley, *Third Wisconsin*, 33; Bryant, *Third Wisconsin*, 82; Julian Wisner Hinkley, "Handwritten Essay on the Civil War," Julian Wisner Hinkley Papers, WHS, 19-20; *National Tribune*, February 28, 1895.

passed the order to the 5th. In an instant, most of the regiment was over the fence and in the field. Colonel Chapman called them back; the brigade would advance together. Chapman, who had manufactured pistol components for Samuel Colt before the war, stood behind the colors. He told his men to remember their good name and do credit to themselves and their state. Color Sergeant James Hewison noticed that Chapman had no revolver and offered him the one he was carrying. Chapman replied that he valued Hewison's life as much as his own and prepared to charge across the field with just his sword. Upon receiving the order to go forward, officers shouted, "Fix bayonets and charge. . . . Charge, charge and yell."[8]

*   *   *

Just before the Federal advance, Brig. Gen. William Taliaferro took command of Jackson's division, replacing the mortally wounded Charles Winder. Unaware of Jackson's and Winder's plans, which called for a flanking movement against the Union right, Taliaferro decided to reconnoiter in front of Garnett's brigade for signs of Yankees. Taliaferro characteristically concerned himself with defense rather than opportunities to attack. Finding no evidence of the enemy, he returned to the right of the division, where he discerned Union infantry in the Cornfield. Garnett's right, the 21st and 48th Virginia, engaged these troops, which were at the roadside Virginians' left oblique. Taliaferro ordered his former brigade, now under Col. Alexander Galt Taliaferro, to advance into the open field beyond the Crittenden Lane. This brigade-and-a-half now focused its attention strictly on the Cornfield, initially against Pitcher's Regulars and then on Augur's main advance.

As the brigade advanced, word reached General Taliaferro regarding Northerners in front of Garnett's left. He directed the 10th Virginia to move to the left of the 1st Virginia Battalion on Garnett's extreme left. He also ordered Col. Charles Ronald, whose Stonewall Brigade was in reserve, to move rapidly left to support Garnett's brigade. Before advancing, Ronald muddled through the dense woods, deploying into line, into column of regiments, and back into line. After vacillating between formations through the gnarled forest under fire from Federal artillery, Ronald's Stonewall Brigade slogged through the morass in line of battle, attempting to find Garnett's left.[9]

8 Boyce, "28th Regiment," 120; Marvin, *Fifth Connecticut*, 7, 157-158.

9 OR 12, pt. 2, 189, 192, 200; Jed Hotchkiss to G. F. R. Henderson, July 30, 1896, Hotchkiss Papers, LC, typescript copy at FNMP; Worsham, *One of Jackson's Foot Cavalry*, 112.

Shortly after Taliaferro reconnoitered the left, Jackson sent his chief engineer, Capt. J. K. Boswell, there to determine the feasibility of a turning movement. Major John Seddon, commanding the 1st Virginia battalion, told him they had seen Northerners near the fence across the Wheatfield. Boswell moved beyond Seddon's dangling left flank, inching to the harvested Wheatfield with his companion, Lt. T. T. L. Sneade. He soon heard heavy musketry to his right, the same gunfire that had surprised Gordon's men at the Brown cottage. A long Federal line appeared, traversing the fence on the east side of the Wheatfield. Boswell and Sneade mounted and raced to Jackson, who was then behind the Crittenden Lane. Lieutenant Charles A. Davidson of the Virginia Battalion observed Yankees in a "beautiful line" across the field. To Major Seddon, the Federal line appeared to extend indefinitely in both directions. This troubled him, since his left was in the air. The 10th Virginia and the Stonewall Brigade were still en route.[10]

*   *   *

Across the Wheatfield, Crawford's men sprung over or toppled the fence on its eastern edge, then paused briefly to reform their line. Crawford's three isolated regiments gave a deep shout and double-quicked with bayonets fixed. Unsupported and with no knowledge of the force in their front, they manfully faced odds that soon became heavily lopsided. For Crawford, the odds were worse than he had expected; he had believed that Gordon's brigade would support his right during this charge.[11]

Gordon, whose troops were three-quarters of a mile to the right and rear, was too far away to support Crawford and had not yet received word to do so. Alpheus Williams's official report stated that Gordon's brigade was to "be in readiness to re-enforce Crawford's brigade in case of necessity." Ten to 15 minutes before Crawford advanced, about 5:30 p.m., an aide from Williams arrived and told Gordon to observe the hill behind the woods through which Crawford had passed. Williams was there and was clearly visible from Gordon's position. He would wave a handkerchief as a signal to advance. Gordon stared through his glass, waiting for a signal that never came. He remembered that Crawford's brigade "swept like a

---

10 OR 12, pt. 2, 205; J. K. Boswell, "Unpublished Report," Hotchkiss Papers, LC, copy at FNMP; Turner, "Major Charles A. Davidson," 29.

11 OR 12, pt. 2, 150-151; Boyce, *Twenty-eighth New York*, 36-37; Hicks, Diary, 11, LC.

Colonel Dudley Donnelly, 28th New York
William L. Clements Library, University of Michigan

torrent across the wheatfield." He grew impatient as the musketry intensified. Straining at his slip, he finally bellowed, "Fall in!" By this time, most of the men were already on their feet, peering toward the Wheatfield. They now stood formed, awaiting the order to follow Crawford's men.[12]

Crawford, for his part, remained in the woods on the Union side of the Wheatfield. Several accounts, while not confirming Crawford's whereabouts, indicate that he was somewhere other than with his brigade and provided no direction beyond the initial order to advance. Colonel Donnelly became the brigade's de facto commander.[13]

Lieutenant Colonel Edwin F. Brown of the 28th New York was, like Donnelly, strict yet kind to his men. Brown rode a fine black horse, one of 20 the regiment had captured at Point of Rocks, Maryland, the previous year. The ailing Captain Bowen led Company D as he had throughout the day. Company B began the day commanded by 1st Lt. John C. Walsh. Their erstwhile commander, Capt. William W. Bush, was under arrest and awaiting a court-martial for charges of cowardice at Winchester in May. Ten minutes before the regiment formed to charge, Colonel Donnelly released him from arrest. Armed with a cudgel, Bush joined the advance. Major Elliott W. Cook went forward eccentrically armed as well, carrying a

12 OR 12, pt. 2, 146-147; Andrews, "Cedar Mountain," 432-433; Quint, *2nd Massachusetts*, 108-109; Gordon, *Brook Farm*, 294, 302-303; Brown, *Twenty-Seventh Indiana*, 201.

13 "An Historic Flag," undated newspaper clipping from the *Dayton Journal*, James Garver Collection, USA; Andrews, "Cedar Mountain," 424-425; Julian Wisner Hinkley, "Memorial Day Speech," Julian Wisner Hinkley Papers, WHS; *National Tribune*, February 28, 1895, and April 29, 1886. Neither Hinkley nor Colonel Andrews were in Crawford's brigade. Hinkley made this charge even though he was out of sight of Crawford's command. Both men, however, wrote conscientious postwar accounts and they likely corresponded with members of Crawford's brigade before asserting that Donnelly led the charge. "An Historic Flag" was written by a member of the 28th New York.

Adjutant Charles P. Sprout, 28th New York
William Buckley, Buckley's History of the Great Reunion

Maynard breech-loading rifle that he had used for hunting before the war. He coolly retrieved each casing from the breech, dropping it into a satchel. After the 28th New York reformed in the field, the order to charge resounded. The regiment's tough and fearless adjutant, Charles P. Sprout, flung himself ahead of the line and fortified the men with his chivalrous spirit.[14]

Garnett's 42nd and 48th Virginia regiments delivered a crashing volley at Gordon's men. The 5th Connecticut, on the left of the line, absorbed this blow after advancing a short distance across the Wheatfield. Private Charles E. Thompson of Company B was killed and several others were wounded. The Virginians coolly maintained a rapid fire on the Connecticut men.[15]

The Rebel fire took a heavy toll on the 5th Connecticut's color bearers. The national flag changed hands at least four times. Its initial bearer, Color Sgt. Elijah B. Jones, was killed instantly. Captain George W. Corliss, commanding Company C, then carried the flag until a minié ball went through his leg as the regiment reached the depression formed by the creek. Corliss kept the flag aloft with its staff planted in the ground until Sgt. Luzern A. Palmer relieved him. After Palmer was wounded, he passed it to Color Cpl. Daniel L. Smith, who was soon killed. Sergeant Major William. P. Smith bore the Stars and Stripes next until he was shot in the leg. Color Sergeant Hewison was hit early but went on until he received a more serious wound during the regiment's ascent from the depression to the western woods. By then,

---

14 Boyce, *Twenty-eighth New York*, 12-13; Boyce, "28th Regiment," 124-127; John C. Walsh General Court-Martial Proceedings, October 9, 1862, Record Group 153, NA.

15 OR 12, pt. 2, 203, 205; Marvin, *Fifth Connecticut*, 158. The 5th Connecticut historian wrote that the first volley occurred before the regiment covered 50 feet, while Captain Dobyns's report for the 42nd Virginia suggests his regiment waited until the Federals were mid-field prior to delivering its first volley. The Connecticut version is supported by Hicks's account from the 28th New York. The 42nd Virginia account is seconded by one from the 1st Virginia Infantry Battalion.

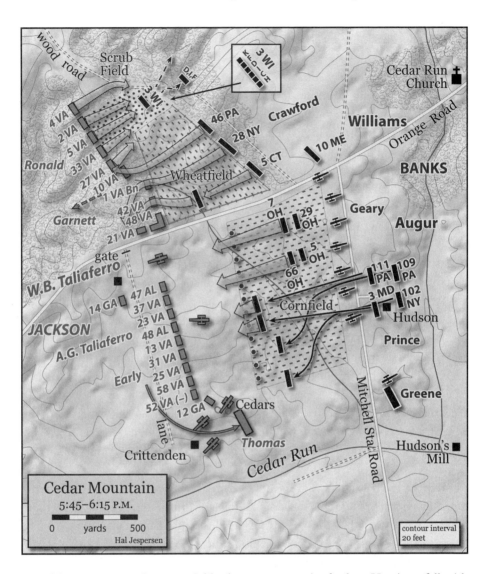

Cedar Mountain
5:45–6:15 P.M.

0   yards   500
Hal Jespersen

contour interval
20 feet

casualties were mounting so quickly that no one noticed when Hewison fell with the regimental colors. To save them, Hewison tore the flag from its staff and stuffed it under his uniform before crawling back to the eastern woods. After descending into the rivulet, the 5th faced a significant climb to Garnett's position. The Virginians' fire became increasingly lethal, and the Nutmeggers faced the most severe frontal fire in all of Crawford's brigade.[16]

16 Marvin, *Fifth Connecticut*, 159-160.

To the 5th Connecticut's right, the 28th New York faced the 1st Virginia Battalion. The 28th received its first volley shortly after moving from the fence, but Major Seddon reported that his Virginians had shot high and achieved "very little execution." Lieutenant William P. Warren, commanding the 28th's Company G, did not think a man was "touched in the brigade" by this initial fire. As he started forward, Warren spotted Confederate colors in the woods; he resolved to capture them and stirred his men to do so. Before reaching mid-field, Corporal Gillam of Company F saw two men next to him killed instantly within arm's reach of each other. Some New Yorkers took cover behind the wheat shocks. Captain Bush of Company B drove one of his soldiers away from a shock, then yelled to the file closers to keep the men up. He soon found 1st Lt. John Walsh behind a shock of wheat to the right of the regiment in a gap between the 28th and the 46th Pennsylvania. Walsh, who reportedly fired his pistol wildly while the regiment waited to charge, remained concealed as the regiment fought in the woods ahead.[17]

With Donnelly's men rapidly closing in on his position, Major Seddon urgently needed a successful volley. His Virginians fired twice more, which he described as "scattering" and having "little effect." The second volley came as Donnelly's men crossed the depression, exacerbating the Virginians' elevation issue. Though Seddon believed their third volley was ineffective, Lieutenant Warren, on the receiving end, recalled that many of his men fell wounded. Corporal Charles L. Pickard of Company K, shot through the head during the charge, was among them. Seddon's last volley proved too little, too late. Now within 100 feet, the New Yorkers delivered one volley and surged into the woods without waiting to reload.[18]

Reports from as far away as the 5th Connecticut described a crossfire from the right. Given Major Seddon's self-doubt about the effectiveness of his volleys and the fact that his men had their hands full dealing with the 28th New York, it is not likely that this crossfire came from Seddon's men. Corporal Frederick A. Camann of Company K soon discovered the cause. As the rest of the 28th dashed into the woods, Camann reloaded. When he finished, the regiment was gone. He moved

17 OR 12, pt. 2, 205; "An Historic Flag," USA; Chandler Gillam to Parents, August 16, 1862, LC; John B. Walsh Court-Martial Proceeding. Seddon placed his unit's first volley at 150 yards from his men, which suggests the New Yorkers covered half the field before being fired upon.

18 OR 12, pt. 2, 205; "An Historic Flag," USA; Boyce, "28th Regiment," 120; Edmund Stoney to "Dear Friend," August 17, 1862, Charles L. Pickard Letters, FNMP.

Colonel Joseph Knipe, 46th Pennsulvania
Library of Congress

forward at a right oblique and discovered the right of the Stonewall Brigade at the wood line to the right.[19]

The 46th Pennsylvania trailed the New Yorkers. On reaching the fence, Sgt. Charles Barrett of Company H climbed it and looked left at the brigade's progress. He called to his men to stop firing and to not let the other regiments get ahead of them. As it crossed the fence, the left half of the regiment had no enemy in its front; the right faced the 10th Virginia, which stalled the Pennsylvanians' advance. The 46th then wheeled right, driving off the 10th Virginia and flanking the Stonewall Brigade, which had just come onto the field.[20]

* * *

Just before Crawford's brigade stepped from the Wheatfield's eastern fence line, Colonel Ronald's Stonewall Brigade reached the fence at the western edge of the Scrub Field. The 4th Virginia anchored the brigade's left, followed to the right by the 2nd, 5th, 33rd, and 27th Virginia. Though not yet tied into the left of any Confederate unit, Ronald sent an aide to notify Taliaferro of his position. This seems to suggest that Ronald may have been flummoxed regarding his own position. As minutes ticked away, his men heard the opening action in the Wheatfield. Taliaferro tersely ordered the brigade to keep advancing. Ronald relayed these instructions and rode forward a quarter of a mile to see what was ahead. When Ronald reached the low ridge that formed the border between the Scrub Field and the Wheatfield and cleared the corner of woods, the view south,

19 C. Lewis to "Editors," August 18, 1862, Yale University, copy at FNMP; Boyce, *Twenty-eighth New York,* 91-92.

20 *National Tribune,* April 29, 1886, and June 21, 1888.

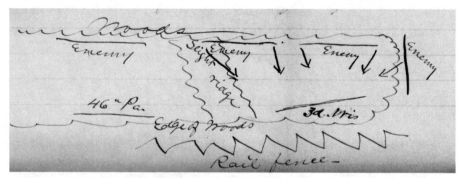

Drawing, previously unpublished, from Col. Ruger's Official Report depicting the fighting in the Scrub Field. Notice the location of the ridge that divided the Wheatfield and the Scrub field, as well as the relative position of the 46th Pennsylvania and the Stonewall Brigade to Ruger's detachment. *National Archives Records Administration, Union Battle Reports 1861-1865 (Trifolded Segment) Unpublished, Vols. 11-13*

down the Wheatfield, opened before him. Ronald hurried back to his troops and commanded, "1st Brigade, prepare for a charge bayonet!"[21]

By the time the Stonewall Brigade advanced across the Scrub Field, the six Wisconsin companies arrived in its front; the two sides became engaged in moments. Neither the 3rd Wisconsin nor the Virginians had deployed skirmishers, and they stumbled into each other. The left of the 3rd Wisconsin arrived before the right. Colonel Ruger rode behind the left on a nervous horse, which would trouble him throughout the battle. Lieutenant Colonel Crane and Major Scott were to the right. All three jumped their horses over the fence after the men crossed. The companies (from left to right: H, C, I, D, F, and K) totaled about 267 soldiers, or between 44 and 45 men each.[22]

The 3rd Wisconsin's advanced battalion stood its ground against three Stonewall Brigade regiments for less than five minutes. Ronald's troops extended beyond the right of the 3rd Wisconsin and created extra havoc on that side of the line with an oblique fire from the woods. Company K of the 3rd, on the right flank, lost a third of its men in the first volley. Captain Hawley received a severe ankle wound and was helped back to the fence, followed in short order by most of the company. First Lieutenant Emanuel J. Bentley, commanding Company F, crawled to the fence. Presumed injured at the time, Bentley was unharmed. While much of

---

21 OR 12, pt. 2, 192; Michael Shuler, Diary, August 9, 1862, LC.

22 OR 51, pt. 1, 124, 192; Hinkley, "Handwritten Essay," 21; Bryant, *Third Wisconsin*, 83.

Lt. Col. Louis H. D. Crane, 3rd Wisconsin
Bryant, Third Wisconsin

the detachment understandably streamed rearward, following the departing right wing, many others loaded and fired frantically. Second Lieutenant Julian Hinkley commanded Company D on August 9 thanks to illness among the company's officers. He watched Captain O'Brien and resolved to hold as long as O'Brien remained. The Irish captain soon called to Hinkley, saying that the colonel, whose horse was still giving him fits, had ordered them back to the woods. By then, the two companies to the left of O'Brien had withdrawn; Hinkley and O'Brien followed them off the field.[23]

As its advance started, the 2nd Virginia, under Lt. Col. Lawson Botts, spotted the 3rd Wisconsin directly across its path. After loosing a volley, the Virginians charged toward the woods. All the while, the 4th and 5th Virginia, on either side of the 2nd, fired while closing in on the 3rd Wisconsin's flanks. The 3rd's lieutenant colonel, Louis Crane, called on the men to rally behind the fence, but several balls struck him as he followed them through one of its gaps.[24]

According to two 3rd Wisconsin accounts, the whole affair lasted between two and three minutes. In that brief time, the Virginians badly mauled the battalion, inflicting 80 casualties, or 30 percent of the total engaged. Fifty-one of them were in the three right companies that were struck by oblique fire from the 4th Virginia, which was partly concealed in the heavy brush and trees about 20 yards from the

23 *OR* 51, pt. 1, 124; Bryant, *Third Wisconsin*, 84; Hinkley, Diary, August 9, 1862; Hinkley, "Handwritten Essay," 21-23; *National Tribune*, February 28, 1895. After the war, Colonel Ruger told Hinkley that he never ordered a withdrawal.

24 *OR* 12, pt. 2, 194-196; Samuel Moore to D. R. Kownslar, August 13, 1862, Samuel J. C. Moore Papers, SHC; Bryant, *Third Wisconsin*, 82-83; Casler, *Four Years in the Stonewall Brigade*, 104. Hinkley (*Third Wisconsin*, 34) asserted that Crane was killed in the first Confederate volley, while Bryant and Casler described him falling as the companies retired.

right of Company K. None of those who chronicled this action thought that more than three rounds had been fired.[25]

Hinkley's Company D and O'Brien's Company I, joined by a portion of Company F, followed an old forest road to a ravine 75 to 100 yards east of the Wheatfield, where they rallied. O'Brien was badly wounded in the thigh, and his boot filled with blood. He cut open his pant leg with a knife and tied a handkerchief around the wound. Colonel Ruger soon arrived with other men he had rallied. They would join another attack into the Wheatfield in short order.[26]

The Stonewall Brigade turned its attention to what remained of Crawford's brigade in the Wheatfield. Ronald ordered his three left regiments—4th, 2nd, and 5th Virginia—to wheel right and face south, forming a right angle with the 33rd Virginia, which fronted the Wheatfield facing east. Half of the 33rd was concealed in the woods. Lieutenant Colonel Lawson Botts left Company I of the 2nd Virginia at the eastern edge of the woods to protect the regiment's rear and to scout for the Federals now hunkering in the ravine below them. The 5th Virginia's Capt. Hugh White described what he saw after he and his men reached the high ground at the northern edge of the Wheatfield:

> As we, on the left, moved forward and gained the top of a ridge before us, we could see the line of battle extending around to the extreme right, all along which the smoke rolled up in great clouds, and fire from the two sides flashed fiercely at each other. I did not have time to look long at this scene, for a little smoke, and some fire too, nearer at hand engaged my attention.[27]

Ronald's right wing included the 27th Virginia, wholly in the forest south of the Scrub Field, and the 33rd Virginia, half of which was in the woods. Reaching the edge of the Wheatfield, both regiments accosted what remained of Crawford's brigade in their front. Lieutenant Colonel Edwin Lee, commander of the 33rd, soon detected portions of the 46th Pennsylvania within 40 feet of his right flank. His adjutant, sent to inquire after the 27th Virginia, found no sign of that regiment, and discovered that the 33rd's flank was in the air. Lee directed his right—Companies A, D, and F—to fire on the Pennsylvanians, who were

25 OR 51, pt. 1, 124; Bryant, *Third Wisconsin*, 83; Hinkley, *Third Wisconsin*, 36; *National Tribune*, February 28, 1895.

26 Hinkley, "Handwritten Essay," 23; *National Tribune*, February 28, 1895.

27 OR 12, pt. 2, 194-196; William S. White, *Sketches of the Life of Captain Hugh A. White, of the Stonewall Brigade* (Columbia, SC, 1864), 113-114.

enfilading them. Colonel Ronald directed Lee to hold fast, for a brigade was inbound. Lee then pushed forward his center and left, which were getting the best of the contest in their front.[28]

The 27th Virginia, on Lee's right, also took enfilading fire from Crawford's brigade. Seeing the Pennsylvanians moving toward their rear, the Virginians fell back and lost cohesion. Crossing paths with Brig. Gen. Lawrence O'Bryan Branch's brigade 150 yards to the rear, the 27th's commander, Capt. Charles Haynes, tried to rally his troops. With the portion of the regiment still under his control, Haynes moved south toward the Orange Road.[29]

* * *

While Crawford's men penetrated the woods beyond the Wheatfield, Brig. Gen. Christopher Augur's division advanced against the Confederate center, which was commanded by Brigadier General Early and Colonel Taliaferro. After Geary's one-hour halt in the Cornfield, the Union artillery paused. Augur ordered an assault, which Geary initiated by advancing his first line, the 66th and 7th Ohio, from their low spot in the Cornfield. The 7th's right was near the Orange Road and the 66th was on its left. Geary's regiments, particularly the 7th, absorbed a heavy fire from the 21st and 48th Virginia on their right front, as well as from Taliaferro's brigade.[30]

The experiences of two members of the 7th attested to the heavy fighting that their regiment faced. A correspondent reported seeing a private, Wallace W. Lapham, come off the field missing two fingers, with a third "dreadfully lacerated." While the correspondent helped him dress the wound, Lapham offered, "I don't care a darn for that third finger, for it warn't of no account, no how; but the 'pinter,' and t'other one, were right good 'uns, and I hate to lose 'em. I shouldn't have come to the rear, if I had been able to load my gun." The private then stood and looked toward the firing and asked the newspaperman to, "Load up my shooting-iron for me; I want to have a little satisfaction out of them cusses for spiling my fore paw." With one round in his rifle and no ready prospects to reload, Lapham returned to

28 *OR* 12, pt. 2, 197-199.

29 *OR* 12, pt. 2, 197.

30 *OR* 12, pt. 2, 158, 160, 163-164.

Col. Charles Candy, 66th Ohio
Library of Congress

his unit at the double-quick. Shortly afterward, he was shot through the lungs, and died at Culpeper on August 13th.[31]

Private James Miller Guinn of Company C had dropped out of the ranks from sunstroke as the fighting started. He rested in the shade while the 7th Ohio was engaged, but crawled away when Confederate artillery shelled his canopy, making it "rather uncomfortable." Guinn considered himself lucky to have missed the fight for, "The first corporal in front of my place was wounded twice. The man on my left was killed, the sergeant behind me was killed and the Lieut. in front was killed." Guinn went on to write that after the battle, the 7th's flag had 57 bullet holes and its staff was hit twice by cannon balls.[32]

The 66th Ohio advanced and fought to the left of the 7th. Its commanding officer, Col. Charles Candy, kept his ranks closing to the right in order to stay connected with the 7th. Other than a pair of orders to advance, he perceived that his men were forward "on their own hook" and without guidance from the brigade. Taking the initiative, Candy attempted to confuse the Confederate artillery with a series of maneuvers. The regiment fell back 10–15 yards, then advanced beyond its original position. Doing this several times allowed the 66th to advance a substantial distance.[33]

---

31 George Wood, *The Seventh Regiment: A Record* (New York, 1865), 129-130; Lawrence Wilson, *Itinerary of the Seventh Ohio Volunteer Infantry, 1861-1864, with Roster, Portraits and Biographies* (New York, 1907), 568.

32 James Guinn to brother, September 7, 1862, James Miller Guinn Papers, HL.

33 *OR* 12, pt. 2, 165; Charles Candy to Harrison Tripp, June 29, 1887, Gould Papers, DU.

Brig. Gen. John White Geary
Library of Congress

Colonel Candy, who had no definitive orders, withdrew as night approached. His men, like all those on the field, were exhausted from the extreme heat and the scarcity of water. Candy, a veteran of the pre-war army, described that day as the hottest he ever experienced in the field. He remembered that any water they could scrounge was "strained through our handkerchiefs into our mouths so as to wet [our] parched lips." Candy's adjutant, Lt. Robert Murdoch, faced other troubles. Some thought Murdoch was angst-ridden about being in the army. An Ohioan wrote that Murdoch made himself "unnecessarily conspicuous on a gray horse all afternoon." Despite this excessive exposure, Murdoch passed through the battle unscathed. But, after being sent to an Alexandria hospital, he ended his life with a pistol on August 25.[34]

As the 7th and 66th Ohio took heavy losses, Geary ordered the 5th and 29th Ohio forward. During the advance, Geary was wounded in the ankle and the left arm. He left the field and command of the brigade passed to Candy, who did not learn of his new duties until between 8:00 and 9:00 p.m. In sardonic fashion, Candy later wrote that had he been sent for, he would have been found with his regiment.[35]

As Geary's second line reached the skirmishers, a single blemish marred the otherwise spotless performance of Capt. Thomas Pitcher's battalion of Regulars. A youthful captain in command of Pitcher's reserve line placed his men in a ditch. As the 5th Ohio passed, the Buckeye volunteers urged this reserve line forward. The captain refused, and the volunteers cast aspersions of cowardice on the Regulars.

34 Candy to Tripp, June 29, 1887, DU; Hunt and Brown, *Brevet Brigadier Generals in Blue*, 98; *Cleveland Morning Leader*, August 27, 1862; William H. H. Tallman, "Memoirs," USA, 21; Evan P. Middleton, *History of Champaign County Ohio: Its People, Industries and Institutions: Volume I* (Indianapolis, 1917), 771.

35 *OR* 12, pt. 2, 160; Candy to Tripp, June 29, 1887, DU.

First Lieutenant Joseph Molyneaux, 7th Ohio
Library of Congress

The captain then left for orders and was not seen again that day. The Regulars, free from this dubious leadership, emerged and joined the left of the firing line.[36]

Approaching the edge of the Cornfield, the 29th Ohio, on the right, moved to support the 7th Ohio, which suffered greatly from its proximity to Garnett's brigade and the batteries at the Crittenden Gate. Colonel William R. Creighton of the 7th, wounded in the arm and side, left the field, as did Maj. Orrin Crane, who was shot in the foot. First Lieutenant J. B. Molyneaux took command. When the 29th marched up, Molyneaux led the 7th to the right and then rear in column, and it reformed on an elevation behind the north branch of Cedar Run. Molyneaux had two horses shot from under him, one of which was hit four times. The 29th, which was led by a captain, took the 7th's place in the line.[37]

To the left, the 5th Ohio faced an open front. The 66th Ohio's numbers had thinned rapidly, and the closing of its ranks created a clearing, into which it advanced. Colonel John Halliday Patrick, a tailor of Scottish extraction, commanded the 5th Ohio. As soon as Patrick's men emerged from the Cornfield, they were hit by a blast of canister. They pressed forward to a small mound, where they found that they were the only troops beyond the Cornfield. The 5th arrived just as Prince's first line began its withdrawal.[38]

As Geary's first line advanced toward Taliaferro, General Prince warily advanced the 3rd Maryland and 111th Pennsylvania against Jubal Early's brigade.

36 OR 12, pt. 2, 163; Anderson, "Twelfth Infantry," 386.

37 OR 12, pt. 2, 161, 164; Wood, *Seventh Regiment*, 127, 218.

38 OR 12, pt. 2, 161, 163; Roger Hunt, *Colonels in Blue: Michigan, Ohio, and West Virginia* (Jefferson, NC, 2011), 101.

Colonel D. P. De Witt led the Marylanders on the left. He and Lt. Col. Joseph M. Sudsburg were both on foot. Later, when they returned to the rear of the Mitchell Station Road, De Witt and Sudsburg found the man with whom they had entrusted their horses lying dead from Confederate artillery fire, still holding the reins. Prince's first line advanced over a small ridge, a ditch, fences, and the Mitchell Station Road before entering the tall corn. Prince kept the second line, the 102nd New York and 109th Pennsylvania, in reserve in case he needed to counter a flank movement against his left. Crossing the road, Prince's staff informed all the battalion commanders that it would be their rallying point if necessary. The two regiments lost their alignment when crossing various obstacles on the way to the Cornfield. The fences disturbed the advance of the 3rd Maryland more than that of the Pennsylvanians. While moving downhill, the units started taking fire and lost sight of one another while passing through the high corn. The Pennsylvanians, who were leading, paused briefly after making it halfway across the Cornfield.[39]

After the short halt, Major Walker ordered the 111th to advance. His men now had their shot at outfighting Pitcher's Regulars. In about three minutes, the two regiments reached the edge of the Cornfield, where Walker and De Witt discovered that the 111th overlapped the 3rd Maryland. To uncover the 3rd, the two regiments maneuvered under rifle fire from Early's brigade and canister fire from Pegram's and Hardy's guns.[40]

Walker's men faced hot fighting while at the edge of the Cornfield. After the initial Confederate volley, Cpl. James S. Newcombe of Company D defiantly yelled, "I'll have one shot at them before they kill me." The moment he fired, Newcombe fell, shot through the head. Corporal Blanchard, also in Company D, was luckier. He was shot in the leg, but the ball hit his pocketbook and the wound was slight. In Company B, a man two feet from Pvt. James Miller was shot through the face. Miller was surprised by how cool he remained. He felt no fear but wanted revenge for those falling around him. A Marylander remembered the men "reeled and staggered," with entire ranks seeming to wither away. Behind the main line, the 111th Pennsylvania's Pvt. John C. Ellis was on provost guard. He found "stout big healthy men" taken with fright, running to the rear. Though "there was not one of

---

39 *OR* 12, pt. 2, 168; Henry Prince to Christopher Augur, August 16, 1862, C. C. Augur Papers, NL; Boyle, *Soldiers True*, 44; James Gillette to parents, August 12, 1862, LC; James Miller to brother, August 13, 1862, James T. Miller Letters, UM.

40 *OR* 12, pt. 2, 168; Miller to brother, August 13, 1862, UM; William B. Matchett, *Maryland and the Glorious Old Third in the War for the Union: Reminiscences in the Life of her "Militant," chaplain and Major Samuel Kramer* (Washington, DC, 1882), 18.

them but what pretended to be sick," Ellis and his guard "encouraged" the pleading men forward at the point of the bayonet.[41]

As De Witt's and Walker's regiments neared the edge of the Cornfield, an aide arrived from Augur, ordering Prince to advance his entire command. Still concerned about his flank, Prince hurried back to deploy his second line, while his first line untangled its alignment. Behind the Mitchell Station Road, the order to advance was a great relief to "A. H." of the 102nd New York. He wrote that he was so full of fear from the ordeal of lying under the Confederate artillery fire that "sweat poured off of me in streams." Liberated from the strain of lying still, A. H. sprung to his feet, dropped his coat, and advanced in his shirt.[42]

When the second line crested the ridge behind the Mitchell Station Road, Confederate artillery fire swept through its ranks. The 102nd New York demolished three fences and right-obliqued to pass to the right of Robinson's battery. In the plowed area before the Cornfield, Pvt. Albert Baur of the 102nd New York could see minié balls striking the dirt in front of his regiment. Passing into the range of Confederate small arms, the New Yorkers turned to the left to reach the location where Prince ultimately deployed them. The New Yorkers advanced with their left out of the field. The descending nature of the terrain to the left, however, obscured their advance from the Confederates. The 109th Pennsylvania and the right of the 102nd New York were fully in the Cornfield. Continuing down the slope through the corn, the tense New Yorkers began firing at will. They soon discovered men ascending the slope toward them. A few New Yorkers fired into them before realizing they were Pitcher's skirmishers, withdrawing from their post at the base of the slope. Private Baur spotted a bearded soldier who lamented, "My God, it is hard to be shot by your own men." Baur described the disorienting scene as a, "Seething, burning, hell-ridden cornfield, where the screech of shells, the ping of the bullets and shouts of the men, together with the fearful havoc in our ranks, made it possible to imagine oneself in a

41 *The Warren* [PA] *Ledger*, August 27, 1862; Miller to brother, August 13, 1862, UM; Matchett, *Maryland and the Glorious Old Third*, 18; Boyle, *Soldiers True*, 44; John C. Ellis to sister, August 15, 1862, USA.

42 OR 12, pt. 2, 168; Henry Prince to Christopher Augur, August 16, 1862, Augur Papers, NL; *New Paltz* [NY] *Times*, September 10, 1862. Though it would make sense that Geary and Prince advanced into the Cornfield and halted before going forward, that does not appear to have been the case. All extant sources from Geary's brigade agree that it advanced and then paused for about an hour; conversely, all of the sources from Prince's brigade describe a single advance that included negotiating fences, the road, and the Cornfield in one movement. This suggests that Prince left them behind the Hudson house when he moved his first line forward. This was a long supporting distance, given Prince's concern for his left flank.

veritable hell with the concomitant devil and all his imps." The stress and confusion of this situation soon led to a Federal blunder.[43]

Reaching the rear of the first line, Prince deployed the second line *en echelon* 100 paces to the left and rear in order to protect the vulnerable left of his first line. He also directed fire against the heavy Confederate crossfire coming from the second line's front left quarter, which he estimated as about 30 degrees to the left. Much of his second line had to shoot past the left of the 3rd Maryland, and Prince explicitly directed his men where to aim in order to miss their comrades. On the subsequent volley, however, a portion of the second line fired in their direction. The Marylanders insisted the 109th Pennsylvania shot into their backs. Colonel De Witt rode to Prince and announced that his regiment was withdrawing in disorder. The fire from their rear completely dispirited the Marylanders, and they streamed past the right of the second line. Major Walker saw them go and also lost contact with the 66th Ohio on the right. The Ohioans had been closing their ranks to the right to fill gaps. These circumstances were enough for Walker, who soon led his regiment off the field after the Marylanders. Both regiments reformed on the Mitchell Station Road. As Prince's second line settled into a more sustained engagement with Early, Prince moved to the left to investigate a change in the Confederate position.[44]

*   *   *

Jubal Early had been concerned about his flanks for some time. During the early part of the Confederate deployment, he suspected a Federal move toward the army's left. The aide he sent to forewarn Winder arrived after that general's death, and told Jackson instead. This resulted in Boswell's trip to the left and a caution

43 2nd Annual Report, 102, 112.

44 *OR* 12, pt. 2, 168; Prince to Augur, August 16, 1862, NL; James Gillette to parents, August 12, 1862, LC; Marks, Diary, August 9, 1862, FSNMP; Boyle, *Soldiers True*, 44. Colonel Patrick reported that the regiment to his left, from Prince's brigade, fired one shot after it arrived and then departed. Prince's second line reportedly stood in line until dark. So he likely meant the 111th, especially since it followed the 3rd Maryland's premature departure from the field, and Prince's first line was nearer to Geary than the second line. The suggestion that the 111th fired one volley and left, however, begs explanation. The regiment was in line long enough for Prince to return to his second line and guide it forward about a half mile. This was ample time for the 111th to fire multiple volleys and accumulate 90 casualties. It seems most likely that the 5th Ohio, in Geary's second line, arrived at about the time that Prince's first line took flight, which would mean that Patrick was confused about whether the regiment to his left was arriving or merely closing up, since the 111th had lost contact with the 66th Ohio.

from Jackson to Garnett to look to his left. These actions ultimately proved insufficient.[45]

Early's concern with the right flank was more immediate. After observing Geary approach the edge of the corn, Early watched Prince's brigade advance and overlap his right. Making matters worse, the ground beyond Early's right dropped sharply, leaving him blind to any Federal advance from that direction. Early positioned the 12th Georgia along the ridgeline that extended at an angle from his main line in order to support the batteries at the cedars and secure his flank. This regiment was responsible for the initial fire 30 degrees to Prince's left. Early also requested an additional brigade to extend his right, and Jackson promised to send one.[46]

Brigadier General Edward Thomas commanded A. P. Hill's lead brigade, which had not yet reached the field. When it did, a courier from Jackson directed it to the rear of Taliaferro's brigade to bolster that part of the line. Jackson soon ordered Thomas to move right to support Early, but at that moment, Geary was pushing Taliaferro. Thomas therefore detached the 14th Georgia, which remained behind Taliaferro's brigade.[47]

Thomas's arrival markedly worsened the situation for Prince's second line of New Yorkers. First Lieutenant Aaron Bates remembered, "The balls came in perfect sheets around us, besides this, flank batteries played us with heavy shell." The Rebels lined a stone wall seemingly beside the New Yorkers, and sharpshooters climbed trees for better vantage points, shooting down onto their flank. They picked off officers down the line as far as the third company from the right, one short of Bates's company. A member of the 49th Georgia recalled nearly incessant volleys into the Northerners' ranks until ammunition ran low. The 49th's officers scoured the dead and wounded, collecting cartridge boxes. Thomas's and Early's fire hit the 102nd New York color guard hard. A. H., who had been so relieved to advance, was the only member of the eight-man color guard to leave the field uninjured. When the color sergeant fell, A. H. dropped his rifle and picked up the banner, carrying it the rest of the day. A ball hit the man next to him in the head, killing him instantly.[48]

45 OR 12, pt. 2, 230; Early, *Autobiographical Sketch*, 97.

46 OR 12, pt. 2, 230-231; Early, *Autobiographical Sketch*, 98.

47 OR 12, pt. 2, 215, 219.

48 *2nd Annual Report*, 102-103; James M. Folsom, *Heroes and Martyrs of Georgia: Georgia's Record in the Revolution of 1861* (Macon, GA, 1864), 129; *New Paltz Times*, September 10, 1862.

The Southern artillery wreaked havoc on Augur's men. After his initial run-in with Pitcher's skirmishers, Willie Pegram began using double canister on Geary's and Prince's brigades on either side of him with terrible effect. To the right, a member of Dement's battery at the cedars wrote that the Federals made nine charges and were repulsed each time with "great slaughter." A gunner in Dement's forward section heard, "A rumbled roar and crackling like the noise of a mighty wind-storm, smashing and breaking through the woods." An officer galloped up and ordered the battery to limber to the rear. This threat to the cedars originated when Crawford's brigade plunged into the woods beyond the Wheatfield.[49]

*   *   *

Around this time, Col. Thomas Garnett approached Major Seddon's 1st Virginia battalion and discovered Federals 50 yards away, moving quickly and delivering a "most galling fire." Under the weight of this pressure, Seddon's men fled in disorder, despite the battalion officers' exertions. The 10th Virginia, whose flanks were in the air as the regiment neared its objective, lost its chance to connect with Garnett's left. Suddenly, Federals swarmed from the forest on the front and right. Discovering that the 1st Virginia battalion was breaking to the right and that enemy infantry was streaming toward its right flank, the 10th fell back as well. Its three leftmost companies held for a short time but, unable to find their regiment, they eventually joined the 33rd Virginia. Meanwhile, Donnelly's 28th New Yorkers swept through the yawning gap in the Confederate line left by the 1st Virginia Battalion and wheeled left onto the flank and rear of unsuspecting units down Garnett's line.[50]

The 42nd Virginia stood south of Seddon's fleeing battalion, still confronting the 5th Connecticut. Its left flank had never connected with Seddon's right. Rising from that gap in the line was a small ridge that put the two units out of each other's view. As a result, they were unaware that their neighbors were gone and that the

---

49 Mammie Yeary, ed., *Reminiscences of the Boys in Gray*, 1861-1865 (Dallas, 1912), 197; Kelley, *Scharf Memoirs*, 34; Hatton, "Memoir," 310.

50 *OR* 12, pt. 2, 200, 205, 210; George Hamman, Diary, August 9, 1862, typescript at FNMP. The men of the 28th New York, like those in several of the other regiments, carried saber bayonets. These two-foot-long weapons appeared fearsome. Indeed, a member of the 27th Indiana, half of which also carried them, wrote, "We were elated by them at first. . . . A command armed with them seemed ready for very bloody work . . . [but] experience proved that the short swords had no other or higher use than to cut tent stakes and kindling wood." (Boyce, *Twenty-eighth New York*, 135; Brown, *Twenty-Seventh Indiana*, 173.)

Lt. Col. Richard H. Cunningham, 21st Virginia
Worsham, One of Jackson's Foot Cavalry

New Yorkers were surging around their left and rear. Attempting to avert further disaster, Garnett rode to Major Lane, commanding the 42nd Virginia, and directed him to change front to face the threat on his left. Lane fell before he could execute the order. With the 5th Connecticut attacking the 42nd's front, the task was likely unrealistic.[51]

As the threat to the left and rear grew, the 42nd Virginia continued to fight the 5th Connecticut in its front, its fire increasing in intensity as the Yankees approached the high log fence at the wood line. In some spots, it appeared that the Virginians were in three ranks—prone, kneeling, and standing. The final yards of the 5th Connecticut's approach were markedly uphill, and the regiment stalled for a few minutes. The 5th's adjutant, Heber S. Smith, fell at the edge of the woods with nine bullet wounds. The Federals took heavy losses but they were now close enough to see their targets. After the New Yorkers swept onto the 42nd Virginia's flank within the woods, the 5th Connecticut then leapt over or knocked down the fence and were suddenly within the cover of the woods, where they used bayonets and gun butts.[52]

Smoke hanging low amid the trees hastened the forest's thickening darkness. Robert L. Dabney of Jackson's staff wrote, "The whole angle of forest was now filled with clamor and horrid rout," and "the terrific din of the musketry, the smoke, and the dense foliage" hid the contending lines until they were almost on top of each other. For the moment, the regiments maintained some cohesion, but

---

51 OR 12, pt. 2, 200-201, 203; Turner, "Major Charles A. Davidson," 29.

52 Marvin, *Fifth Connecticut*, 160-162.

the heightened passion of the men was palpable. Soldiers in the 5th Connecticut shouted feverishly as they fired.[53]

Turmoil descended on Garnett's unsuspecting right. While the 21st Virginia and the right of the 48th Virginia faced Geary's Ohioans, Crawford's men came within 30 paces of their rear and fired. Due to the shock of a point-blank volley into their backs, their orders to reposition beyond the Orange Road were not executed swiftly enough to avoid hand-to-hand fighting and unravelling order in the corner of the darkening woods. The 21st Virginia was particularly hobbled. Its commander, Lt. Col. Richard H. Cunningham, was quite ill, his voice faint. He walked his horse along the line, attempting to extract his regiment. Reaching Capt. William A. Witcher, Cunningham inaudibly called to him. He repeatedly motioned toward the fence, and Witcher began moving his troops. Cohesion collapsed as men slowed to shoot. Cunningham appealed to John Worsham of the 21st, "John, help me get the men out of this, I can't talk loudly." Worsham organized a handful of men to move south. But, as he started, he found a Federal sergeant entering the road, followed by a private. The sergeant advanced on Worsham's group, grabbed one man, and started rearward with his prisoner. Another of Worsham's party shot the sergeant.[54]

Cunningham entered the road himself and dismantled a section of fence to aid his regiment's withdrawal. After passing into the field beyond the fence, he placed a foot in one of his mount's stirrups. In an instant, rifle fire killed rider and horse. Cunningham fell to the ground as Crawford's men filled the road. The Virginians began to realize they were nearly surrounded, and the battle descended into what Worsham described as, "Such a fight as was not witnessed during the war; guns, bayonets, swords, pistols, fence rails, rocks, etc., were used all along the line."[55]

The fighting in the smoke-filled forest was horrific. Corporal Chandler Gillam of the 28th New York wrote that men in his regiment were "fighting like devils." Private Roswell Lindsay of the 21st Virginia bayoneted a Yankee and immediately fell from multiple gunshots. The first came from a Federal captain, who in turn was bayoneted by several of Lindsay's comrades. A Confederate was about to strike Lt. William C. Rockwell of the 5th Connecticut when he was shot dead, falling with his

---

53 Robert L. Dabney, *Life and Campaigns of Lieutenant General Thomas J. Jackson* (Richmond, 1866), 500; Gillam to parents, August 16, 1862, LC; Marvin, *Fifth Connecticut*, 162-163.

54 OR 12, pt. 2, 202; *Grand Army Scout and Soldiers Mail*, September 4, 1886; Worsham, *One of Jackson's Foot Cavalry*, 112-113.

55 OR 12, pt. 2, 202; Worsham, *One of Jackson's Foot Cavalry*, 113; Marvin, *Fifth Connecticut*, 162.

raised weapon swinging before him. Spared at the last moment, Rockwell unloaded his pistol on six separate Rebels. First Lieutenant Alfred A. Chinery also felled six victims with his pistol as he and several of other members of Company E were surrounded in the woods. The Confederates took him prisoner. To continue the fight through the obscuring smoke, the 28th New York's Lieutenant Warren ordered Company G to kneel and aim above any legs they could see beneath the haze.[56]

The Confederates also may have used the tactic of firing beneath the smoke. Several members of the 28th New York were shot through both legs, including 1st Sgt. Lucien R. Bailey, leader of Company F. Bailey coolly executed his command duties before he fell, and his troops carried him from the field. Lieutenants Lafayette Chaffee and Orson Southworth, similarly wounded, were not as fortunate as Bailey; their men carried them in the opposite direction. Sergeant William Lewis of Company D's color guard was shot through the legs, and passed the colors to a comrade. After dark, he crawled to the woods on the Federal side and cut tree limbs for crutches.[57]

Though the Union advance cut an irresistible swath across Garnett's brigade, pockets of resistance remained on its flanks. Portions of Confederate regiments reached relative safety south of the Orange Road. Other bands cut through the Union line and gathered on a height in the woods to the Federals' right rear. In its push to drive through the trees and into the field beyond the road, Crawford's brigade bypassed much of the 48th Virginia, which remained in the corner of the woods. The rest of the 48th joined remnants of the 21st Virginia, effecting a narrow escape. Oscar White, an officer in the 48th Virginia, pulled the seriously wounded Lt. Charles Alexander of the 1st Virginia Battalion onto his horse, which was soon shot in the head. Fortunately for the riders, their mount carried on until beyond immediate danger, then collapsed.[58]

The turmoil that reigned in the woods quickly spilled into the open country to the south. Jackson posted Capt. Charles Blackford at the Crittenden Gate to wait for A. P. Hill and to direct him to push his brigades to the right to support Early.

56 Gillam to parents, August 16, 1862, LC; Worsham, *One of Jackson's Foot Cavalry*, 113; *Richmond Daily Dispatch*, August 14, 1862; Marvin, *Fifth Connecticut*, 162-163; *National Tribune*, March 29, 1894; "An Historic Flag," USA.

57 Boyce, "28th Regiment," 127-128, 130-131.

58 OR 12, pt. 2, 202, 204; Marvin, *Fifth Connecticut*, 162; *Grand Army Scout and Soldiers Mail*, September 4, 1886; *Richmond Times Dispatch*, July 17, 1904.

Blackford saw at least one Confederate regiment emerge from the woods, disordered, with Northerners intermingled. He could not determine whether the Federals were prisoners or pursuers. The Union troops flooded the road and the area east of the gate. From there, they immediately threatened Taliaferro's guns and his exposed left flank. At that moment, the guns were of no use to their crews. With Confederate fugitives streaming away from the woods, Captain Poague could not safely fire. For the moment, Poague and his men attempted to rally the broken infantry. Lieutenant Carpenter repositioned his rifled piece 200 yards south as the Federals approached to within 150 to 200 yards. After firing, Carpenter ordered his men to limber to the rear. They broke the harness pole and had to leave the limber on the field, but successfully removed the gun. Jackson arrived at the gate at this time and ordered the batteries there to head for the rear. All Confederate reports either suggest that this was successfully accomplished, or are mute on the subject. The New Yorkers later asserted that they reached the batteries and captured two of the guns, but the Rebel crews carried off the remaining cannons and the limbers of the captured pieces. Since Confederate reports did not mention a temporary Federal seizure of their guns, this point remains an open question. Any such capture, however, would have been very brief.[59]

Farther south, Taliaferro's brigade had been holding Geary's Ohioans in check for approximately 20 minutes when they saw the intermingled Confederates and Yankees streaming from the woods on Garnett's right. Federals advancing into the road and the field beyond bore down on Taliaferro's flank, which was occupied by one of his brigade's two green regiments. A volley at 40 paces alerted the 47th Alabama to the Federal presence on its left. The 47th's commander, Lt. Col. James Jackson, ordered his men to face about, which the companies on the right began to execute. Those on the left immediately fled, and the right companies did the same. Jackson followed the regiment to the crest of a hill to the rear, where he was able to reform his green troops out of the way of flying rounds.[60]

The balance of Taliaferro's brigade soon headed for the rear. The 48th Alabama, another green regiment, departed with the 47th Alabama, even though it was on the right of the brigade and farthest from danger. The 37th Virginia, to the 47th's right, also fell back shortly after the 47th's withdrawal exposed it. According

---

59 OR 12, pt. 2, 213; Charles Blackford, Letters from Lee's Army (New York, 1947), 103-104; Cockrell, ed., *Gunner with Stonewall*, 33; Hicks, Diary, 11, LC; *Grand Army Scout and Soldiers Mail*, September 4, 1886.

60 OR 12, pt. 2, 208-209.

to Colonel Taliaferro, a portion of the 37th was "thrown into confusion," compelling the rest of the regiment to retreat. Major H. C. Wood, in command of the 37th after its commanding officer was wounded, suggested that most of the companies withdrew in "tolerably good order." A few of them became "a little confused," however. The 23rd Virginia, to the right of the 37th, left the field under orders, somewhat disorganized. Each regiment of the brigade, except for the detached 10th Virginia, individually rallied in the rear.[61]

To the left of Crawford's brigade, Colonel Patrick of the 5th Ohio discovered that Taliaferro's brigade, in his regiment's front, was retiring. Patrick reported that he did not pursue this opportunity because of a lack of support. While it is valid that a single, roughly handled regiment could not expect much success pursuing a beaten enemy, Crawford's regiments might have benefitted from support themselves. Nevertheless, with the collapse of command and control on the Union left, it is understandable that individual units did not press on alone. While Geary's second line and the 109th Pennsylvania in Prince's brigade failed to pursue Taliaferro, they did take the opportunity to give Captain Pegram's battery the most intense infantry pressure it would face all day.[62]

With Southern infantry support departing, the Federals still in front of the Cornfield made a final surge for Pegram's and Hardy's guns. The only remaining support was Early's leftmost regiment, the 13th Virginia, which was beginning to take fire from its left. Pegram ordered his men to load double canister. With vigor spurred by the grave situation, Pegram took up a Confederate flag and waved it in the faces of his crews, yelling, "Don't let the enemy have these guns or this flag; Jackson is looking at you. Go on, men; give it to them." One of Pegram's cannoneers reported that Geary's men fell back but came on again, "in grand style." As the Federals neared canister range, orders reached Pegram to withdraw. As his men prepared to move, a limber horse fell. In that desperate moment, with the Ohioans nearly at his battery, he yelled, "Action front!" and used double canister again. The horse was replaced, and the battery escaped; Geary's men were about 100 yards away.[63]

---

61 *OR* 12, pt. 2, 206, 211-212.

62 *OR* 12, pt. 2, 163.

63 *OR* 12, pt. 2, 226; John H. Se Cheverell, *Journal History of the Twenty-ninth Ohio Veteran Volunteers, 1861-1865* (Cleveland, 1883), 52; Yeary, *Reminiscences of the Boys in Gray*, 198; *Richmond Times Dispatch*, October 19, 1902.

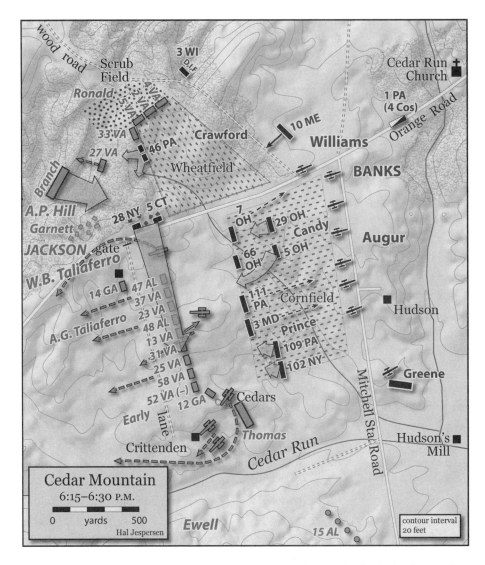

Cedar Mountain
6:15–6:30 P.M.

0   yards   500

Hal Jespersen

contour interval
20 feet

Casualties mounted among the remnants of Crawford's brigade as they proceeded south and engaged Taliaferro's brigade. The daring adjutant Charles Sprout was still at the front of the 28th New York. Just after reaching the guns east of the Crittenden Gate, he fell with at least a half dozen balls in his body. Members of the 5th Connecticut found Sgt. Alex S. Avery nearby after the battle. He still grasped his rifle, which was topped by a bloody bayonet; around him lay five Confederates with bayonet wounds.[64]

64 Boyce, "28th Regiment," 126; Marvin, *Fifth Connecticut*, 163.

Crawford's men had other problems. The farther they advanced, the more isolated they became, losing cohesion and momentum with every yard. Casualties during the advance were relatively light, but many soldiers left to escort prisoners to the rear. These departures, the confused fighting in the woods, and the frenzied advance beyond the road all contributed to retarding the brigade's momentum.[65]

The panic that started in Taliaferro's brigade spread to Early's center regiments. As Crawford's men continued south, the 25th Virginia and parts of the 31st and 58th Virginia instinctively withdrew in a disorderly fashion. But Early's left resisted. Seeing the danger to a single piece of artillery that had recently moved to the 13th Virginia's right front, Col. James Walker ordered that regiment and the remaining portion of the 31st Virginia to advance 30 yards to the gun. They fired into what was likely the 109th Pennsylvania until the cannon withdrew. Walker held his position briefly until Crawford's men, who had fired into his left flank, began moving to his rear. The 13th and the truncated 31st Virginia were the only Confederate infantry within Walker's sight, and he withdrew 200 yards to the southwest, where he rallied his men. En route, he noticed that some of Prince's troops had placed what looked like Maryland's distinctive state flag at the 13th's previous position and harassed its retreat.[66]

Jubal Early, meanwhile, placed Thomas's brigade on the 12th Georgia's right, downhill from the growing emergency. When Early started for his left, he realized the damage that had been done. All that remained of his brigade was the 12th Georgia, four 52nd Virginia companies, and a few companies from the 58th Virginia. Dispatching his assistant adjutant general to rally the fleeing regiments, he tried to prevent further departures, directing the regimental commanders to "hold onto their positions at all hazards." This order elicited a game response from Capt. William Brown of the 12th Georgia. With his men running out of ammunition, Brown asked Early whether they should charge. That vitality was what Early needed at the moment, but the Georgians remained in their position fronting Prince's attack. Using his few remaining regiments and Thomas's brigade, Early prevented the collapse of Jackson's center right. The Stonewall Brigade did the

---

65 Boyce, "28th Regiment," 121.

66 OR 12, pt. 2, 234. Whether this was the 3rd Maryland is questionable. No sources from that brigade suggest a return to the firing line by the 3rd from the Mitchell Station Road. The gun that the 13th Virginia advanced to support was either Carpenter's rifled gun or one of Pegram's guns.

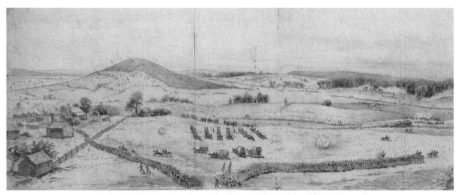

"The Battle of Cedar Mountain (Slaughters Mountain), by Edwin Forbes. *Library of Congress*

same for Jackson's left. It would fall to A. P. Hill and a few returning bands of Jackson's original line to secure the massive gap in between.[67]

A portion of Crawford's brigade now pursued Early's left, shooting Confederates fleeing in the open. A color bearer fell in a field less than 50 yards ahead of Confederate Capt. William Bush, who had replaced his cudgel with a pistol from a fallen comrade. He raced a 5th Connecticut private for the flag and narrowly beat the private to the colors. Any semblance of unit cohesion was lost. At that moment, Crawford's scattered and exhausted troops received volleys from their right.[68]

---

67 Early, *Autobiographical Sketch*, 99.

68 Marvin, *Fifth Connecticut*, 164, Hicks, Diary, 11, LC.

Chapter 4

"We Had to Fight Our Way Out"

— Chandler Gillam, 28th New York

Ambrose Powell Hill Counterattacks

6:15 p.m. to Midnight, August 9, 1862

Alpheus Williams had not yet waved his handkerchief. At a few minutes before 6:00 p.m., Brig. Gen. George Gordon still peered through his field glasses, awaiting the signal to advance. A member of Banks's staff appeared with orders to send the 2nd Massachusetts "up the pike" toward Banks. These orders betrayed Banks's misapprehension about Gordon's location. Colonel Andrews started his 2nd Massachusetts marching left to find Banks. The regiment had barely begun when Captain Pittman of Williams's staff arrived, calling on Gordon to join Crawford's attack with his entire brigade. In an instant, the dormant potential energy of Gordon's brigade uncoiled. Gordon bellowed, "Double Quick!" and the brigade raced down the hillside, the 2nd Massachusetts bearing right to intercept it. Gordon's soldiers were over half a mile from the Wheatfield.[1]

As Crawford's ebbing fortunes became apparent, Banks initiated a series of sacrificial jabs in the twilight, trying to stem the rising Confederate tide. Southern reinforcements arriving on the field created longer odds for these units than those that Crawford's men faced. These moves achieved little beyond decimating the units involved. Gordon's advance was the second such incursion into the

---

1 Gordon, *Brook Farm*, 303; *OR* 12, pt. 2, 144.

2nd Lieutenant John Mead Gould, 10th Maine
Nicholas Picerno Collection

Confederate lines, and the last to make contact. The 10th Maine, guarding Lieutenant Muhlenberg's guns north of the road, was the first to clash with the Rebels.[2]

The 10th Maine shifted to the right twice in discomfort over its proximity to Muhlenberg's guns, its men blanching as Confederate shell fragments fell among them. After getting the worst of the artillery duel, the battery repositioned, leaving the 10th Maine as a de facto bodyguard for Banks. Colonel George L. Beal of the 10th Maine sent 2nd Lieutenant John M. Gould forward to scout. Reaching the far side of the woods, Gould saw the Ohioans advancing near the road and heard firing in his front. Returning through the woods, Gould met the regiment advancing in line of battle. Banks had ordered Beal to advance at 6:00 p.m. Across the battlefield, Crawford's brigade was fighting its way out against the rallying, and growing, Rebel host. Meanwhile, the usually taciturn Stonewall Jackson dramatically inspired a small portion of this rally.[3]

*   *   *

When the battle started, Jackson initially watched the action from just south of the Orange Road, near the Crittenden Gate batteries. The fire on those guns unsettled the staff and couriers who were collected near Jackson, so he soon moved a short distance to the right and allowed his entourage to pass behind the ridge. As the fighting in Early's front intensified, Jackson moved farther right, behind Early's left, often looking to the rear for the lead elements of A. P. Hill's division. Despite his calm demeanor, his relief was apparent to those around him when Thomas's

2 Gould, *10th Maine*, 171.

3 Ibid., 171-173.

brigade emerged from the woods in the rear moving in open order. After sending these troops to secure his right, Jackson returned to his original post near the road.[4]

As the sound of the action in the Wheatfield grew louder, it increasingly drew Jackson's attention. Listening intently to the rising crescendo of musketry and occasionally turning his head to the left, Jackson said, "There is some hard work being done over there." A courier rode up and announced that the left was being pressed hard and would not hold without reinforcements. Without a word, Jackson removed his right leg from across his pommel, straightened in the saddle, secured the strap of his cover across his chin, wheeled left, and raced for the left. After jumping the partially dismantled fence, he halted in the roadway, ordered the artillery to the rear, and leapt the fence north of the road, riding 50 yards into the chaotic woodland scene as Garnett's regiments fled.[5]

In the midst of what a member of Jackson's entourage described as a "full grown tornado" in the woods, the commanding general shed his reserved demeanor and exhibited a personal magnetism that rallied scattered clutches of soldiers around him. Jackson attempted to draw his sword for the only time in the war. Not only had he never drawn his sword in battle, but he apparently had never even removed it from the scabbard for any purpose: the weapon was rusted in place. Undeterred, he unbuckled the scabbard from his belt, raised the sheathed sword, and bludgeoned the heads of those who continued rearward. Then he reportedly seized a battle flag and called, "Rally, men! Remember Winder! Where's my Stonewall Brigade? Forward, men Forward!" While his personal courage rallied small bands of Confederates, he was by that time largely in the wake of the ebbing Federal advance. Other efforts to restore Confederate fortunes were more consequential.[6]

---

4 Blue, *Reminiscences*, 55.

5 Ibid.; Jedediah Hotchkiss to G. F. R. Henderson, July 30, 1896, FNMP. An unattributed account in the *Richmond Times Dispatch*, November 8, 1903, suggested that Jackson, after observing the situation in the woods, cantered to the rear, found Hill, announced that he was "behind time," ordered him to deploy his division, and finally returned. Jackson's cartographer, Jed Hotchkiss, asserted in a postwar letter that Jackson made no forays to the rear to issue orders. Hotchkiss's recollection aligned with John Blue's detailed account of Jackson's actions on August 9.

6 Blue, *Reminiscences*, 55; Hotchkiss to Henderson, July 30, 1896, FNMP; Blackford, *Letters*, 104-105. The Stonewall Brigade, to which Jackson purportedly called, was several hundred yards to his left, at the north end of the Wheatfield.

Major General A. P. Hill, in shirtsleeves and with sword drawn, energetically threw his brigades forward and rebuked fugitives from Jackson's division. He questioned one lieutenant, who replied that he was accompanying his wounded friend to the rear. Hill ripped off the man's rank insignia, censuring him with, "You are a pretty fellow to hold a commission—deserting your colors in the presence of the enemy, and going to the rear with a man who is scarcely badly enough wounded to go himself. I reduce you to the ranks, sir, and if you do not go to the front and do your duty, I'll have you shot as soon as I can spare a file of men for the purpose." For the moment, Hill could spare no such men, and he sent forward Brig. Gen. Lawrence O'Bryan Branch's brigade, followed by those under Brig. Gens. James Archer and William Pender. These brigades deployed into the woods from right to left, with Branch's right near the Orange Road.[7]

Farther to the Confederate right, two other rallying forces kept themselves together and served as focal points where smaller bands of troops gathered. The 14th Georgia, under Lt. Col. James Folsom, stood behind Taliaferro's former position. Left behind when Thomas advanced to the far right, this regiment was still unemployed. As the Alabamans and Virginians of Taliaferro's brigade fell back into the 14th, its line waivered. Lieutenant Colonel Folsom grabbed the battle flag and called on his men to stand "for the sake of old Georgia!" Folsom led the 14th into Crawford's flank until he fell from exhaustion. He returned to his feet and pressed on, supported by two of his men. Beyond Folsom's right, the 13th Virginia, which had withdrawn from the front in relatively good order, was joined by a contingent of the 31st Virginia. After falling back, Colonel Walker reformed his men on the colors and retraced the regiment's path directly at the Federal colors that marked his earlier location. After another 10 minutes of heavy firing, the last of Geary's men fell back from the Cornfield as Branch's brigade arrived to the north.[8]

*   *   *

With Confederate units arriving or resurgent to the west, Crawford's regiments, strung out and spent, needed to run a gauntlet of Rebels to reach safety beyond the Wheatfield. Corporal Chandler Gillam discovered the turn of events

---

7 OR 12, pt. 2, 215; J. William Jones, "Cedar Run (Slaughter's Mountain)," *Southern Historical Society Papers*, 10:89.

8 OR 12, pt. 2, 234; Folsom, *Heroes and Martyrs of Georgia*, 148-149; Account of "Dixie," *Southern Confederacy*, August 21, 1862, M. J. Solomon Scrapbook, DU, 337-338.

when a volley came from the flank as Hill's units reached the field, writing to his parents that "[w]e had to fight our way out." Units were intermingled. Lieutenant William Warren of the 28th New York was standing next to Colonel Chapman of the 5th Connecticut when he first discovered the peril. Chapman turned and said, "Warren, order your men to fall back, they are taking us in the flank." With whatever organization he had left, Warren tried to avert panic by starting the retreat slowly, keeping his men firing as they went.[9]

Casualties accumulated during the retreat. As it started, the 28th New York's Captain Bush led a party of seven to eight men from each regiment; all were killed but one, and Bush was wounded in the arm and taken prisoner. Shortly after the order to retreat, the ailing Captain Bowen collapsed from exhaustion. He and several of his men became prisoners while they tried to help him from the field. Within Bowen's company, three pairs of brothers served together. One of each pair was killed, and the survivors either captured or wounded. Corporal Riley P. Butrick had just fired a shot. Before he could reload, several Confederates ran up, looking to capture him. He swung his rifle, breaking its stock over the head of one man. After another Rebel knocked the weapon from his hands, Butrick continued with his fists. After thrashing four or five men, he succumbed.[10]

Lieutenant William Warren's experience characterized the brigade's suffering. His first wound occurred as the 28th New York was about to begin its charge across the Wheatfield. As he held up his sword, a ball took off the tip of his index finger. He calmly wrapped a handkerchief around the injured hand. Near the far edge of the Wheatfield, while attempting to reach the 1st Virginia Battalion's colors, Warren was hit below the left elbow by the third volley from Seddon's Virginians. The wound nearly knocked him to the ground and surgeons eventually removed 13 pieces of bone from it. He kept on and, in a few minutes, was hit in the head. The ball exited the side of his head, and he lost a piece of his skull when it exited. Briefly knocked senseless, blind in one eye and with one side of his face covered in blood, Lieutenant Warren continued forward with his men. Before long, a fourth ball hit him in the neck, between his windpipe and carotid artery. Fortunately, neither was damaged; the ball lodged at the base of his skull. He remembered that his head seemed to "swell as big as a basket." He somehow kept on, but a final ball struck him above the knee in the center of his left leg. By then,

9 Gillam to Parents, August 16, 1862, LC; "An Historic Flag," USA.

10 Hicks Diary, 13-14, LC; John Walsh Court Martial Proceeding, NA; Boyce, *Twenty-eighth New York*, 39.

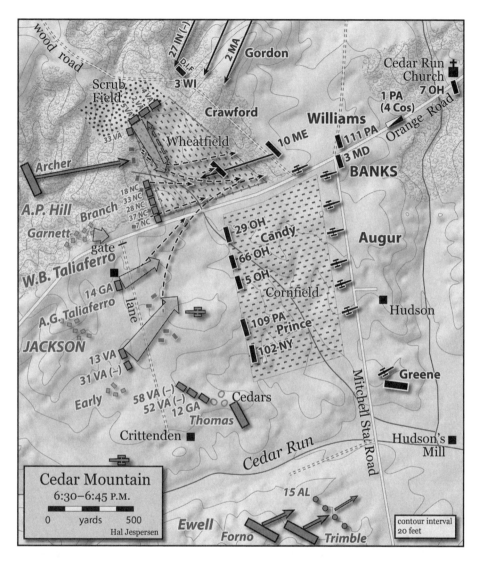

wood road
27 IN (-)
D.I.F
2 MA
Gordon
3 WI
Scrub
Field
Crawford
Williams
Cedar Run
Church
1 PA
(4 Cos)
7 OH
Orange Road
33 VA
Wheatfield
10 ME
111 PA
3 MD
BANKS
Archer
18 NC
33 NC
28 NC
37 NC
7 NC
A. P. Hill
Branch
29 OH
Candy
Augur
Garnett
66 OH
gate
W.B. Taliaferro
5 OH
Cornfield
Hudson
14 GA
lane
A.G. Taliaferro
109 PA
Prince
JACKSON
102 NY
13 VA
31 VA (-)
Greene
Early
58 VA (-)
52 VA (-)
12 GA
Cedars
Thomas
Crittenden
Cedar Run
Hudson's
Mill
Mitchell Sta. Road

Cedar Mountain
6:30–6:45 P.M.
0   yards   500
Hal Jespersen
15 AL
contour interval
20 feet
Ewell
Forno
Trimble

the retreat was underway. Warren fell into a wheat shock, where he remained while
Confederates rushed past him. His suffering, similar to that of many of Banks's
men, would continue for two days.[11]

A member of the 28th New York described the situation upon returning to the
edge of the Wheatfield: "Every man could see plainly the terrible chances he would
have to run by attempting to reach the woods. Exposed to a galling fire from the

11 "An Historic Flag," USA.

rear, both flanks and from the straggling parties in front, but there was no hesitation the determination though unspoken seemed to be unanimous to cross the wheat field or perish in the attempt." As the brigade streamed back across the Wheatfield, the soldiers discovered that erstwhile Confederate prisoners had overpowered and disarmed their guards, creating sporadic obstacles in the Federals' line of retreat. Moreover, Charles Ronald's Virginians maintained a steady fire from the bushes to the north. Colonel Donnelly was convinced that the fire from that direction was friendly, no doubt assuming that Gordon's brigade was there. As he rode in that direction to rectify the situation, a volley exploded from the Scrub Field that wounded Donnelly in the groin. The assistant regimental surgeon, Dr. Robert T. Paine, came to Donnelly's aid, and Donnelly told him that he thought the wound mortal. Wishing to keep it from the men, Donnelly rode off the field with Paine by his side, supporting him.[12]

Command of the 28th New York fell to Lieutenant Colonel Edwin Brown. A ball soon shattered his left arm above the elbow near where Donnelly had been mortally wounded. His fine black horse was hit as well. Horse and rider crashed to the ground, and a group of Confederates reached him before Brown could remove himself from under the animal. With one man for a guard, he headed for the Confederate lines. He soon became light-headed and said that he had to rest. His surly captor suggested that he would give him his rest if he stopped moving, and also ordered a nearby 5th Connecticut corporal who was lying on the ground to join them. This was not possible, since the man was shot through both legs. After Brown and his captor passed, he felt a shot pass by. The corporal's rifle had a broken stock but a loaded muzzle, the wounded man sat up and shot the guard. Brown provided what comfort he could for his rescuer and headed back toward the Union lines. By this time, the 2nd Massachusetts had arrived to the north, and Colonel Andrews detailed a corporal to recover Brown. He made it to a field hospital, and his arm was amputated in Culpeper on August 11.[13]

Major Cook now commanded the 28th New York. He attempted to organize the scattered and intermingled parties in the rear of the retreat but was taken prisoner. His horse had more success. Private Lafayette Van Duzer of Company H stood amongst a group of his captors when he spotted Cook's horse. The animal frustrated the attempts of several Confederates to capture it. In doing so, it moved

12 Boyce, "28th Regiment," 122-123.

13 Hicks Diary, 12, LC; Boyce, *Twenty-eighth New York*, 37.

toward Van Duzer. Seizing the horse's reins, Van Duzer leapt into the saddle and raced away at a gallop.[14]

Corporal Chandler Gillam and five or six others became prisoners twice, but each time escaped in the confusion. Heading back across the Wheatfield, Gillam trailed Corporal Gillett by about 10 yards when they encountered half a dozen Confederates, who called on them to halt and throw down their guns. Gillam and Gillett raised their rifles, and each shot a Rebel. They then bolted across the Wheatfield. Gillam recalled, "balls flying in all directions. I never was so near used up in all my life as I was when I came off the field it was very warm, my blood seemed almost to boil." Gillam's Company F went into the battle with 28 men and sustained casualties of five killed, six wounded, and seven missing.[15]

The fighting was ferocious. Survivors described instances of treachery and ill-treatment of prisoners, which were still considered aberrant episodes at this stage of the war. That behavior, combined with the hand-to-hand fighting that occurred in the woods, made Cedar Mountain exceptional for the war in August 1862. Crawford's men may have resorted to the base expedient of killing prisoners after being hit by the Confederate counterattack. Lieutenant Brown of the 21st Virginia reported that, although he was lying wounded on the field, Federals clubbed and bayonetted him. Lieutenant Davidson of the 1st Virginia battalion heard stories from escaped Confederate prisoners that retreating Yankees tried to shoot or bayonet them. Some were responding brutally to a Confederate ruse that had seemingly dead or wounded men suddenly returning to life. Rising, the once-dead Rebels fired into retreating Northerners. Private George Bower of the 28th's Company I discovered the apparent treachery and calmly bayoneted every Confederate in his path. He exacted this brutal insurance policy on at least six Confederates, living or dead.[16]

Another harrowing episode involved three men in Company G of the 5th Connecticut. Sergeant J. A. Bowen and Cpls. George W. Briggs and Charles H. Corey had advanced as far as the Orange Road and then veered to the west, looking for Confederates in the woods. They continued, but found no enemy. They got no orders to withdraw, and eventually headed back to where the spring exited the Wheatfield and discovered a throng of Confederates blocking their path. Hastened

14 Hicks Diary, 12, 14, LC.

15 Gillam to Parents, August 16, 1862, LC.

16 *Richmond Daily Dispatch*, August 13, 1862; Turner, "Major Charles A. Davidson," 30; Hicks Diary, 14, LC.

by a volley, they ran back into the woods, dodged more Rebels, and again tried crossing where the Wheatfield bordered the Scrub Field. After being chased into the woods yet again, their odyssey ended when they were waylaid by their pursuers.[17]

The 5th Connecticut's Colonel Chapman escaped from imprisonment during the retreat but was recaptured while attempting to rally his men before reaching the Wheatfield near the spring. One of his Nutmeggers shouted, "Let's recapture him,—there's but few rebs around him." A faithful collection of men surged toward him. Nearly all were killed, wounded, or taken prisoner in the failed rescue attempt. At about this moment, the 5th Virginia briefly attacked into the Wheatfield from the Scrub Field.[18]

The 5th Virginia's lunge into the retreating column's flank netted three Union colors, from the 28th New York and 5th Connecticut, and a large quarry of prisoners. Virginians seized the 28th New York's national colors in spite of desperate exertions to save it. Private Narcissus Finch Quarles of the 5th Virginia's Company E reportedly captured all three of the bullet-torn flags and 19 prisoners. Quarles caught Stonewall Jackson's attention while walking his various trophies to the rear. In recognition, Jackson gave the young private a recently captured Union officer's sword. The 28th New York's beautiful silk regimental flag, presented by the ladies of Batavia, survived the battle inviolate; the color sergeant carrying it had never entered the Wheatfield during the initial advance.[19]

* * *

Before the dispersed remnants of Crawford's brigade fully withdrew into the Wheatfield, a fresh brigade of North Carolinians arrived. Brigadier General Lawrence O'Bryan Branch's troops swept into the woods, brushing aside any pockets of resistance. Due to the situation's exigency, Branch moved his brigade forward before it fully deployed. As a result, the 7th North Carolina never achieved its intended position on the left. It meandered through the woods behind the brigade, eventually joining on the right. The 37th North Carolina was already on

17 Marvin, *Fifth Connecticut*, 167-168.

18 Ibid., 166-167.

19 Ibid., 167; Hicks Diary, 14, LC; Anonymous newspaper account, Hotchkiss Papers, Roll 58, Frame 793, LC, copy at FNMP.

Col. George L. Beal, 10th Maine
Nicholas Picerno Collection

the right, guiding its right flank on the Orange Road. To the 37th's left were the 28th, 33rd, and 18th North Carolina.[20]

After marching 100 yards through the woods, Branch's troops came upon fugitives from the first Confederate line. They permitted the stragglers to pass and continued forward. Some retreating Virginians joined the North Carolinians. Branch's men delivered volleys into the exhausted and disorganized remnants of Crawford's brigade, which "broke and fled precipitously through the woods and across the field." Branch wrote as though he had achieved a stunning conquest, yet the only orderly (though severely outnumbered) resistance in his path just arrived at the eastern side of the Wheatfield. When Branch's brigade got to the western edge of the field, with a portion of the 37th North Carolina now in the road, Branch discovered "large bodies of the enemy."[21]

* * *

As it advanced through the woods, the 10th Maine was subjected to Confederate artillery fire. One round dropped a branch, briefly delaying Companies B and D. From the edge of the Wheatfield, the Mainers saw an Ohio regiment to their left, likely the 7th, slowly retreating by the flank while under no apparent compulsion to do so. Farther forward, Lieutenant Gould saw Federals in close quarters, "using their saber bayonets freely" and "fighting like devils."[22]

20 *OR* 12, pt. 2, 220-221.

21 *OR* 12, pt. 2, 221, 223; Thomas Hickerson, ed., *Echoes of Happy Valley* (Chapel Hill, NC, 1962), 84.

22 Gould, *10th Maine*, 173. Gould implied that it was Ohio troops involved in the hand-to-hand fighting, but it seems more likely that these men were the rear of Crawford's retreating brigade.

As the 10th entered the Wheatfield, Crawford's brigade retreated past its right. Colonel Beal called from his horse, "Give them three down-east cheers!" Hurrahs from the Mainers reverberated about the woods. Retreating officers yelled that there were too many Confederates to handle. Colonel Beal realized he was too far forward and ordered his men to face about in order to get to the protection of the wood line.[23]

This retrograde movement proved difficult. While the regiment was halted, allowing Crawford's men to pass, General Banks asked his staff why they had stopped. Major Louis Pelouze, Banks's assistant adjutant general, rode over to them. Arriving behind the regimental colors just as Beal ordered the about face, Pelouze announced that Banks had forbade the redeployment. Beal ignored him and continued issuing orders. This did not sit well with the major, who energetically continued to make his point. Gould recalled that the "gesticulations" of the two officers made it appear that they were having a fistfight right there on the battlefield. After some "unnecessary comments," including an "offer" by Pelouze to lead the regiment, Beal declared he would do so himself.[24]

Beal deployed the regiment to the ridge that rose one-third of the distance across the field and ordered the men to lie down. Before he finished aligning Company E, Capt. Andrew C. Cloudman fell with a bullet in his head. With casualties mounting, the regiment held fast and endured heavy fire in the open field while Crawford's men cleared its front. The sun was nearly down, yet still in the Mainers' faces. While waiting, flashes from Branch's brigade, which had arrived at the Wheatfield's western edge, burst through the evening shade of the western trees. With Crawford's soldiers clear, the 10th Mainers, most kneeling or lying, frantically loaded and fired at will. Gould remembered that the soldiers began to "swear at and gibe" the Confederates. Within a few minutes, the lopsided contest became markedly worse.[25]

Brigadier General James Archer deployed to Branch's left. Before Archer's brigade formed, Branch's men stepped off through the woods. Archer soon followed, obliquing right so as to find Branch's left. Passing Branch's wayward 7th North Carolina, Archer's line became broken, causing Archer to halt and reform. In the meantime, the 14th Tennessee, which had lost contact with Archer, caught up to and rejoined his brigade, which contained, from the right, the 7th Tennessee,

23 Ibid.

24 Ibid., 174, 184.

25 Ibid., 174-175.

the 5th Alabama battalion, the 19th Georgia, the 1st Tennessee, and now the 14th Tennessee. These five regiments sidled up to Branch's left at the edge of the Wheatfield, firing from 45 degrees to the Mainers' right. Besides these nine regiments, much of the Stonewall Brigade was still at the northern edge of the Wheatfield, laying down a crossfire.[26]

The combined fire of three Confederate brigades disinclined Colonel Beal's regiment from further exposure in the Wheatfield. The regimental history described men falling so rapidly and with such movements that it appeared to those in the line, "As if we had a crowd of howling dervishes dancing and kicking around in our ranks. . . . Some reeled round and round, others threw up their arms and fell over backward, others went plunging backward trying to regain their balance; a few fell to the front, but the force of the bullet generally prevented this except where it struck low down and apparently knocked the soldier's feet from under him. Many dropped their musket and seized the wounded part with both hands, and a very few fell dead." Having seen enough, men withdrew individually, creating inviting targets for their foes. A member of the 19th Georgia remembered that the Federals fired one volley with "no effect," and then began breaking rearward individually. Archer's soldiers targeted these fugitives, bringing down many. In the 37th North Carolina, Pvt. Noah Collins fired seven "well directed rounds" into the 10th Maine. His company was in the Orange Road, and he rested his firearm on the fence bordering it.[27]

Colonel Beal did not wait long to withdraw; the 46th Pennsylvania's Sgt. Charles N. Barrett sealed Beal's decision. Barrett sat behind a wheat shock to the right of and in line with the 10th Maine. He announced to Colonel Beal that there were Confederates to the right "in the chincapin bushes." With his men already heading rearward in ones and twos on their own initiative and with the unwelcome news about his right, Beal ordered a retreat. Gould wrote that they "went out disorganized." Private Harrison A. Tripp estimated they had fought for about 30 minutes, but it was likely less. Tripp remembered firing 23 quick-loading patent cartridge rounds. Like everyone else, he would have loaded and fired frenetically. Gould estimated that the Mainers were "peddling out" fire with more speed than

26 OR 12, pt. 2, 218-219; *Gould, 10th Maine*, 176.

27 Gould, *10th Maine*, 175-176; "Participant," Southern Confederacy, August 15, 1862, M. J. Solomon Scrapbook, DU, 338; Noah Collins, Diary, typescript, FNMP.

accuracy. Before Beal ordered the retreat, another Union detachment emerged from the woods, about 300 yards to the Mainers' right.[28]

*   *   *

After Gordon received Alpheus Williams's order to advance, the brigade raced down the hill. Colonel Colgrove's two picket companies posted in the woods to the north were not recalled; whether this was intentional or just haste-induced oversight is unclear. In any event, the Hoosiers were down two companies. After reaching the bottom of the hill, the brigade cut across open fields to the creek bed, the banks of which were as tall as a man and almost vertical. The 27th Indiana's soldiers "jumped, slid or tumbled recklessly down to the water," according to the regimental history. On the other side, they pulled each other up, halting briefly to realign and catch their breath. Gordon rode up, reapplying his spurs to Colgrove in order to get the Indianans to double-quick up the hillside. Gordon's right reached the woods sooner, and the Hoosiers "parted bushes, pushed aside limbs, crawled under or broke through vines and briars, steadied or pulled themselves up acclivities by seizing hold of roots and twigs, dodged around trees, leaped the washouts and stumbled over stones." The left half of the 27th faced a steeper hillside, which slowed its advance.[29]

As Gordon's brigade swept forward, it passed remnants of Col. Thomas Ruger's battalion of skirmishers. O'Brien and Hinkley, after their repulse, reformed approximately 75 men from Companies D, I, and a portion of Company F in the ravine below the Wheatfield. Ruger soon joined these companies, and the detachment followed the brigade and filed onto the right of the fresh 3rd Wisconsin companies moving up the hill. The remains of the two rightmost companies, F and K, which had received the worst abuse, followed the 27th Indiana, rejoining the regiment after it reached the Wheatfield. Some stalwarts from Crawford's brigade also joined Gordon's advance. [30]

The 2nd Massachusetts, on Gordon's left, moved up the hill, entering the tangled wood line near its top. The climb was brutal, and though several officers complained to Gordon that the men could not bear the pace, they kept on.

28 Harrison Tripp to John M. Gould, February 14, 1893, John Mead Gould Papers, DU; Gould, *10th Maine*, 176.

29 OR 12, pt. 2, 156; *Brown, Twenty-Seventh Indiana*, 199, 202.

30 Hinkley, "Handwritten Essay," 23-24; Bryant, *Third Wisconsin*, 88.

Captain Edward Abbott,
2nd Massachusetts, Company A
U.S. Army Heritage and Education Center

Reaching the edge of the woods, Colonel Andrews discovered Crawford's soldiers, disorganized and heading rearward. At the same moment, Major Perkins of Banks's staff decamped from the woods. Perkins warned Andrews of Confederates in the woods: "[G]o in and you will find them." Andrews then took the precaution of sending Capt. Edward Abbott's Company A forward as skirmishers.[31]

On the right, the 27th Indiana crossed paths with a handful of Confederates from Ronald's Stonewall Brigade near the edge of the Wheatfield. John Bresnahan identified them as members of the 4th Virginia. The 2nd Virginia's Company I, which had been left behind at the edge of the woods to guard the Stonewall Brigade's left rear, was likely still in Gordon's path. Owing to the undergrowth, the two sides did not discover each other until they were a mere five yards apart. The Confederates reacted with a mixture of running, surrendering, and fighting. One Rebel grabbed a member of Company A and promptly had his brains strewn across his captive's face by another Hoosier.[32]

As Gordon reached the high ground, he discovered Crawford, alone in the woods, with a musket across the saddle. Meanwhile, the 10th Maine suffered from three brigades' fire, and Colonel Beal from the calumny of Banks's staff. Crawford withdrew from this position when firing started on Gordon's line. General Williams's official report offhandedly suggested that Crawford was absent during the initial assault. After enumerating the losses among the leadership of those three regiments, which included every field officer, every adjutant, and all but 13

31 Andrews, "Battle of Cedar Mountain," 434; Gordon, *Brook Farm*, 304.

32 John Bresnahan, "Battle of Cedar Mountain," the *Sun* (unknown city), August 26, 1902, FNMP; Brown, *Twenty-Seventh Indiana*, 203.

company officers, Williams praised the fortitude of his soldiers, "especially when left without the encouragement and direction of officers."[33]

Captain Edward Abbott's skirmishers, followed by the rest of the brigade, red-faced and breathless, reached the edge of the Wheatfield and pushed into it. Abbott was one of several Harvard graduates in the 2nd Massachusetts. Like Captains Shaw and Russell, he was a member of the class of 1860. He was upright, agile, and strong, with a slender build. Though possessing a countenance of stern gravity and shunning undue familiarity, Abbott was inflexibly assiduous to his men's needs. Through iterative advances, the skirmishers crossed two-thirds of the Wheatfield. Abbott ordered them to lie down after firing and after each advance; he remained standing. When the rest of the brigade arrived, he ordered a slow retrograde.[34]

The brigade's movement over the steep, broken ground thoroughly unraveled its alignment. This was especially true on the right of the line. At the top of the hill, a portion of the 27th Indiana's center briefly followed the road in the woods, which resulted in the center reaching the Wheatfield ahead of the flanks. The right also arrived ahead of the left, thanks to easier terrain. Some of the disorganized Hoosiers entered the Wheatfield before discovering their error and returned to the fence line. After reforming, the 27th Indiana stood with its right near the Scrub Field and fired on Confederate skirmishers, who retreated to the opposite woods or sought shelter amongst wheat shocks. The 3rd Wisconsin stood a short distance to the left of the Indianans. As its skirmish battalion arrived, approximately 300 yards to the left of its original position, it filled some of the interval between the two regiments. The 2nd Massachusetts was next, with the Zouave company on its left.[35]

As Gordon's brigade arrived, the 10th Maine withdrew under the combined fire of Branch, Archer, and Ronald. Some Mainers broke away to help the wounded, while others remained at the wood line, exchanging shots with Branch's brigade. It did, however, maintain some unit cohesion, bearing toward the Union

33 OR 12, pt. 2, 147; Gordon, *Brook Farm*, 305.

34 *Harvard Memorial Biographies*, 2:92-93, 95.

35 OR 12, pt. 2, 156; Andrews, "Battle of Cedar Mountain," 439; Brown, *Twenty-Seventh Indiana*, 203; Josiah C. Williams to "Parrents," August 9, 1862, Williams Family Papers, 1812 to 1926, M302, Box 1 Folder 11, IHS; Bresnahan, "Battle of Cedar Mountain," the *Sun*, August 26, 1902, FNMP; *National Tribune*, June 17, 1886, and February 28, 1895.

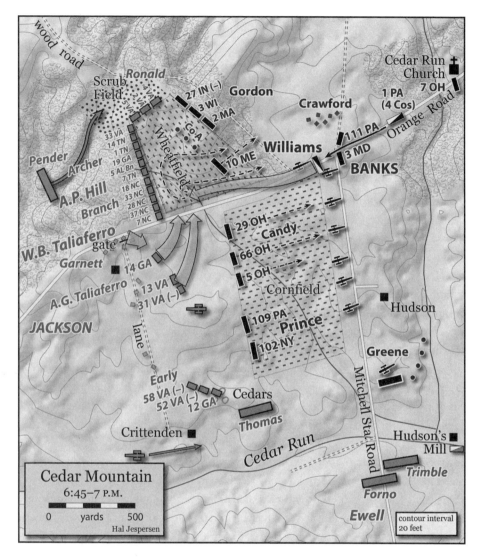

right near the Brown cottage. Colonel Beal reformed his line in the woods near the house and behind Cedar Run before ordering his men to withdraw.[36]

While the 37th North Carolina fired on Beal's retreating troops, Private Collins spotted the 13th Virginia, the 14th Georgia, and the scattered bands that had collected around them. These Confederate stalwarts had advanced toward the Cornfield and pushed out the last remnants of Geary's brigade south of the Orange

36 OR 51, pt. 1, 122; Gould, *10th Maine*, 178.

Road. They now wheeled left toward both the road and the left of Colonel Beal's abandoned position. Despite missing a chance to strike Beal's retreating troops, the effort would still bear fruit. With the 10th Maine's sacrificial advance winding down on the south end of the Wheatfield, Banks now set another in motion.[37]

*   *   *

Through mounting tactical pressure, Banks never lost composure. He became convinced, however, that his batteries were vulnerable, expecting that the guns would have to withdraw through the bottleneck where the Orange Road crossed Cedar Run. There, Confederate infantry might pounce on them. But Captain Knap, whose battery was closest to the resurgent Rebels, did not report any pressure or sense of urgency in withdrawing. Banks was unsure what to do. Colonel John Clark directed Banks's attention to two squadrons of the 1st Pennsylvania Cavalry stationed nearby, saying, "There is cavalry, General." Banks reflexively ordered its commander, Maj. Richard Falls, to charge the Southern line.[38]

Forming in column of fours, the four mounted companies attacked into the southern edge of the Wheatfield, roughly parallel with the road. Falls led his column of 164 mounts to within 50 yards of the Confederates. From there, the riders bore down on Branch's brigade "charging and yelling like demons," wrote Thompson Snyder of Company C. Unfortunately for these Pennsylvanians, Walker's and Folsom's men lined the fence on the south side of the road and fired into the riders' flank at point-blank range. Captain Washington L. Goldsmith of the 14th Georgia spotted the approaching cavalry several hundred yards away and ordered his men to reload and await his order to fire. He gave the order at 50–60 yards, causing riders to go down with their horses in a "conglomerated tangle." A member of the 13th Virginia wrote that the initial volley caused horses and riders to roll over each other, jumbling the path of those bringing up the rear. The Pennsylvanians, of which about 70 remained, turned, scattered, and went back to their starting point. As his horse fell, Snyder braced himself in the stirrups to prevent flying over the animal's head. He hit the ground and, fully aware that he might be trampled at any moment, got as close as he could to his horse and what

37 OR 12, pt. 2, 216, 234; Collins Diary, FNMP, 27; Buck, *With the Old Confeds*, 45; Folsom, *Heroes and Martyrs of Georgia*, 149; "Dixie," *Southern Confederacy*, August 21, 1862, 337-338, DU.

38 OR 12, pt. 2, 134; Wood, *Seventh Regiment*, 129; Thomas Church Haskell Smith, Papers, MSS 158, 83, OHC.

little protection it offered. After the riders behind him passed, Snyder dodged Confederate fire back to the Union lines. With this effort ended, Gordon's brigade became the only Federal force north of the road. Its men faced Archer's and Ronald's brigades, and a third brigade was en route.[39]

* * *

General Gordon reciprocated the 2nd Massachusetts's affinity for its first colonel. One way that he demonstrated this was through staff selection, drawing all of his "military family" from his former regiment. One of these captains, Robert Gould Shaw, would fall at the head of the 54th Massachusetts the following year on a South Carolina rampart. When the advance began, Gordon sent Shaw to guide the disconnected 2nd Massachusetts back to the brigade. As he arrived on the field, Shaw immediately noticed dead and wounded covering the ground. The Bay Staters were ordered to lie down, but the officers mostly remained standing.[40]

As the brigade arrived, Archer's skirmishers fired directly across the Wheatfield. Forest, smoke, and dim light veiled the combatants; flashes from discharging firearms betrayed their positions. While Capt. Edward Abbott's skirmishers withdrew, Archer's men spurned the cover of the woods and fence and moved into the field. Much of Ronald's brigade was still in the Scrub Field, at a right angle to both Archer and Gordon. The 27th Indiana and 3rd Wisconsin instantly responded, keeping up a steady fire.[41]

The 2nd Massachusetts was temporarily preoccupied. Shortly after it reached the field, Major Perkins of Banks's staff ordered Colonel Andrews to charge across it. Andrews replied, "Why, it will be the destruction of the regiment and will do no good." The reticent Perkins shrugged his shoulders. The order turned out to be a mistake. Banks thought the regiment was at the center of the corps, in a position to directly support the 10th Maine. Given its actual position, the order would have disastrously paralleled the 10th Maine's experience. Andrews sought Gordon and related the instructions he had received, and Gordon asked what he thought of

39 OR 12, pt. 2, 141, 223; C. R. Graham, ed., *Under Both Flags* (Richmond, 1896), 219; Buck, *With the Old Confeds*, 45; Early, *Autobiographical Sketch*, 100; Thompson A. Snyder, "Recollections of Four Years with the Union Cavalry, 1861-1865," (typescript, 1927), 12, FNMP.

40 Gordon, *Brook Farm*, 273; Russell Duncan, ed. *Blue-Eyed Child of Fortune: The Civil War Letters of Colonel Robert Gould Shaw* (Athens, GA, 1992), 230.

41 Gordon, *Brook Farm*, 308, 305; Andrews, "Battle of Cedar Mountain," 434-435.

Col. Silas Colgrove, 27th Indiana
U.S. Army Heritage and Education Center

them. Both agreed it was futile, and Gordon, who had already dodged an ill-considered order meant for the whole brigade, told his former lieutenant colonel that he need not obey it.[42]

Earlier, while Major Pelouze and Colonel Beal conducted their mid-field altercation, another of Banks's staffers rode up to the 10th Maine with orders for Gordon's brigade, which appeared on the northern Wheatfield shortly afterward. The aide then ordered a charge across the field. Gordon, stunned, asked which field. Unsure, the staffer said, "I suppose this field." Gordon replied, "Well, sir, 'suppose' won't do at such a time as this. Go back to Banks and get explicit instructions as to what field he wishes me to charge over." According to Gordon, the Rebels made the question moot by "doing all the charging" themselves.[43]

Though only its right half was initially on the line, the 27th Indiana fired briskly. Its left soon joined, but apprehension spread along the line that the regiment was firing into Union troops in the Scrub Field, which ran perpendicular to the Federals' right. The dim light and the look of their own dust-covered uniforms apparently made the Hoosiers think their targets were friendly. Gordon was then at the right of the brigade. When the alarm reached Colonel Colgrove, he explained to Gordon why his men were not firing. Gordon said no friendly troops were there, and ordered the firing renewed. Colgrove hesitated, still unsure. To convince Colgrove, Gordon rode into the Wheatfield ahead of the Federal line and advanced toward the edge of the Scrub Field where Donnelly, Crane, and Brown were killed or wounded. A volley burst from the bushes. Several Northern

---

42 Andrews, "Battle of Cedar Mountain," 435-436; Gordon, *Brook Farm*, 316.

43 Gordon, *Brook Farm*, 316; Gould, *10th Maine*, 184.

witnesses were astonished that Gordon was untouched. Satisfied, the Hoosiers returned fire.[44]

Unfortunately, only Colgrove's right observed Gordon's imprudent boldness; the left continued to hold its fire. At this moment Colgrove began to discover "symptoms of disorder" in his regiment. Gordon described them as "signs of panic." The men did not want to fire and lacked interest in standing around waiting to be shot at. The line began to fade into the woods. Amid the confusion, Colgrove withdrew approximately 200 yards rearward to open ground before he was able to rectify his line. Once reformed, he returned the regiment to the brigade at roughly the same time Archer's brigade advanced across the field. The darkness likely saved Gordon's right from a swift assault by Ronald's brigade at this juncture.[45]

The 2nd Massachusetts was still disconnected a short distance to the left of the 3rd Wisconsin. Gordon, returning to his left, found Colonel Andrews on the left of the 2nd. When asked why his men were not firing, Andrews said he saw no Confederates. Gordon shouted, "Move by the right flank . . . and you will soon find enough to fire at." Just then, Archer's brigade began its advance across the field. With targets suddenly plentiful, Andrews ordered the regiment to fire by files, which occurred with "perfect coolness and great effect."[46]

The Southerners delivered an effective fire against the 2nd Massachusetts. As Captain Abbott returned his company to the regiment, a ball tore through his neck. Private Page ran to him and asked whether he was wounded. Abbott managed to utter, "Yes." Page then asked whether he could do anything for him. Unable to reply, Abbott died in a few moments. As Sgt. Henry Newton Comey aimed, a ball fragment broke his rifle into three pieces. The percussion lock and barrel flew through the air, landing in the brush. Still holding the stock, Comey fell to the ground, thinking he was shot through the neck, but he was only bloody and bruised. As Comey reached for a dead soldier's rifle, he saw a corporal with a severe hip wound. He helped the corporal behind the line and then found a new weapon. A ball went through the head of Company I's acting first sergeant, who fell back

---

44 OR 12, pt. 2, 156; Brown, *Twenty-Seventh Indiana*, 205-206; Gordon, *Brook Farm*, 308-309; *National Tribune*, June 17, 1886. Colgrove described a Confederate regiment drawn up in line almost perpendicular to his line and facing his left, but he did not specify on which side of his regiment he found these Rebels. This was either a portion of Ronald's brigade, on his right and facing his left, or the advance of Archer's brigade, which Wilder Dwight described as advancing across the field diagonally.

45 OR 12, pt. 2, 156; Brown, *Twenty-Seventh Indiana*, 205-206; Gordon, *Brook Farm*, 308.

46 OR 12, pt. 2, 154; Gordon, *Brook Farm*, 306; Dwight to mother, August 17, 1862, MHS.

Col. George L. Andrews,
2nd Massachusetts
Library of Congress

into the arms of Capt. Charles Fessenden Morse, crying, "Lieutenant, I'm killed!" Morse wrote that the man died "with a beautifully calm expression." He was laying the sergeant on the ground when a corporal, within arm's reach to his left, was also shot in the head. He survived, however. Morse, who later found two bullet holes in his trousers, escaped unharmed. During this heavy fire, Colonel Andrews rode along the line, coolly giving orders to the men.[47]

Archer's brigade, which started across the Wheatfield with a yell, "lost quite heavily" during its advance, according to one Tennessean. A. P. Hill reported that the brigade faced a "very heavy" fire, which stalled Archer's men in the middle of the field. Archer's line was oriented diagonally, with its left ahead of its right. The temporary absence of the 27th Indiana from the firing line may explain this orientation, as it resulted in lighter resistance from Gordon's right at the start of Archer's advance. Also, Archer's left would have started from a more advanced position due to the taper of the field. The 19th Georgia lost two color bearers while stalled in the field. A soldier in the 7th Tennessee wrote that the Federals' resistance was, "Obstinate . . . [and] for a few minutes the battle seemed doubtful," but Pender's brigade "changed the aspect at once."[48]

---

47 *Harvard Memorial Biographies*, 2:93; Richard Lyman Comey, ed., *A Legacy of Valor: The Memoirs and Letters of Captain Henry Newton Comey, 2nd Massachusetts Infantry* (Knoxville, TN, 2004), 61; Charles Fessenden Morse, *Letters Written During the Civil War, 1861-1865* (Boston, 1898), 78. Morse had been promoted to captain the month before the battle (Quint, *2nd Massachusetts*, 491).

48 OR 12, pt. 2, 215; "Participant," August 15, 1862; R. T. Mockbee, "Historical Sketch of the 14th Tennessee Regiment," CLSC, 24; Quint, *2nd Massachusetts*, 110; John Berrien Lindsley, ed., *The Military Annals of Tennessee* (Nashville, 1886), 234; Dwight to mother, August 17, 1862, MHS.

From the Orange Road, Brig. Gen. William Pender's North Carolina brigade had advanced through the woods behind Archer's left, eventually appearing at the edge of the Scrub Field. Ronald sent a captain to direct Pender to Gordon's right flank. Moving east behind Ronald's brigade, Pender arrived opposite the 27th Indiana's right shortly after the Hoosiers returned to the firing line. As he approached his objective, he detached the 22nd North Carolina far to the left to secure his flank. Moving through the dark forest in column by companies, Pender's men remained unobserved until it was too late.[49]

After the 27th Indiana fired two volleys, Lieutenant Van Arsdol of Company A spotted the calamity brewing beyond his right flank. He instructed his men to fire in that direction and notified Colonel Colgrove, who rode to the right and discovered the Confederate column 20 paces away. Colgrove ordered his two right companies to change front to the right. Company A executed the maneuver at the same time as Pender's men deployed into line. As Company D attempted to change front, the Rebels' first volley raked the Hoosiers, grazing Colgrove's scalp and hitting his horse. Many Indianans broke at the point of the bayonet, while others fired from two yards at the advancing Confederates. One by one, the 27th's companies headed rearward. John Bresnahan recalled that Pender's men used "ungentlemanly language" when calling for them to halt. Finding themselves ignored, the North Carolinians loosed another volley at the retreating Hoosiers. The 3rd Wisconsin promptly departed as well. The dense woods prevented Colonel Andrews of the 2nd Massachusetts from noticing that the regiments to his right had withdrawn.[50]

Soon after his brigade arrived at the Wheatfield, Gordon gave Captain Shaw the quixotic and ultimately unexecuted task of advancing Cothran's artillery over the difficult terrain from the Brown cottage. En route to the artillery, Shaw discovered Capt. Richard Goodwin, who had written that he would rather die of his chronic illness than resign. Earlier that afternoon, as the regiment prepared to advance, Goodwin hauled himself out of his ambulance. Chaplain Quint asked Goodwin whether he was strong enough to fight. Buckling on his sword, Goodwin replied, "I cannot stay when my men go!" Shaw found Goodwin struggling up the

---

49 OR 12, pt. 2, 215, 225, 193.

50 OR 12, pt. 2, 156-157; Brown, *Twenty-Seventh Indiana*, 207; Gordon, *Brook Farm*, 310; Bryant, *Third Wisconsin*, 89; Andrews, "Battle of Cedar Mountain," 437; *National Tribune*, June 17, 1886. Bresnahan claimed Gordon ordered Lieutenant Colonel Morrison to withdraw after learning from Morrison of Pender's flank attack. He claimed that Gordon made a scapegoat of the 27th by remaining silent on this point and also sacrificed the 2nd Massachusetts by leaving it in place.

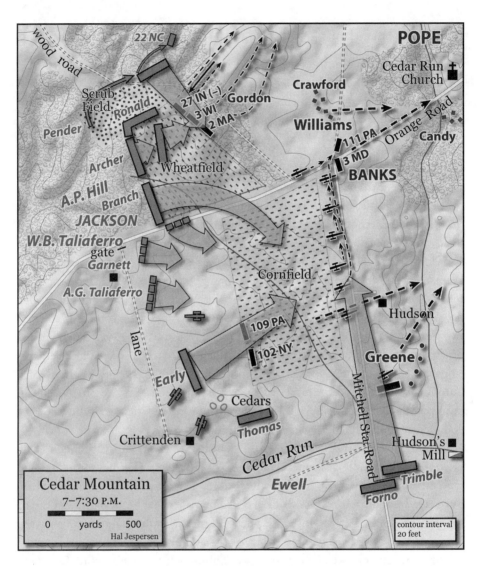

slope well behind his troops, assisted by his personal attendant. Just after he reached Company K on the regiment's right, Pender's first volley erupted from the woods on the regiment's flank, and Goodwin fell dead along with half of his company. Some of his men began to waver. Colonel Andrews was behind Company A and rode forward to rally the right when bullets tore through his horse's neck and shoulder, causing the animal to thrash amongst the trees. By the

Capt. Richard Goodwin,
2nd Massachusetts, Company K
U.S. Army Heritage and Education Center

time Andrews regained control, Pender's men were on his right flank, and he ordered the right companies to retreat.[51]

Gordon wrote that Pender's converging fire "came like a whirlwind." The action soon came into close quarters. The Confederates' first volley hit Major Savage and his horse after he dismounted. Captain Henry Russell placed himself between Savage and the North Carolinians' fire. Both were taken prisoner, and Savage died a few weeks later in Charlottesville. Unaware of Savage's capture, Color Cpl. Leavitt C. Durgin was searching the woods for Savage when he stumbled upon three Confederates. Durgin called out, "Adjutant, bring that squad here. I have three prisoners." His would-be captives hesitated, but then one struck him with a rifle butt. Durgin recovered, doubled the man with a rifle thrust, shot the second, and ran from the third, who also ran from him.[52]

By this point, Gordon was absent. The initial volley on Andrews's right spooked Gordon's horse, which bolted through the undergrowth to the brigade's left rear. Colonel Andrews now rode toward his still-stalwart left. Captain Morse approached Andrews, asking whether he had ordered the retreat on his right. Andrews then led the left off the field. Archer's and Pender's troops became entangled, creating a delay that allowed Andrews's left to disengage cleanly.[53]

After Pender started to unravel Gordon's line, Archer's stalled advance lurched forward. A man in the 1st Tennessee recalled that the regiment surged with

51 Dwight to mother, August 17, 1862, MHS; Alonzo Quint, *The Potomac and the Rapidan: Army Notes from the Failure at Winchester to the Reënforcement of Rosecrans, 1861-1863* (Boston, 1864), 193; Duncan, *Blue-Eyed Child of Fortune*, 231; Andrews, "Battle of Cedar Mountain," 438.

52 Gordon, *Brook Farm*, 311-312; Dwight to mother, August 17, 1862, MHS.

53 Gordon, *Brook Farm*, 312; Andrews, "Battle of Cedar Mountain," 439.

a "wild Rebel yell," making a "terrific dash" for the fence. The Federals were gone, and all Archer's men found was Pender's brigade. Archer's two leftmost regiments, the 1st and 14th Tennessee, became mixed with Pender's men. The brigadiers halted briefly to untangle the knot and agreed to command their two brigades jointly to keep them moving. Though the Confederates swept forward and collected numerous stragglers, they missed an opportunity to inflict greater damage by moving generally south while Gordon's men returned to the Brown cottage to the east. This was likely due to the darkening forest.[54]

Colonels Colgrove and Ruger rallied their regiments at the creek bed with the help of General Gordon and Captain Wilkins of Williams's staff. Gordon began to fear that the 2nd Massachusetts had not gotten away, but the regiment soon emerged from the woods, farther south than it had entered. The brigade moved to the Brown cottage, where the soldiers found a much-altered landscape. Surgeons had established a field hospital there, and dead and dying from Crawford's and Gordon's brigades covered the ground.[55]

* * *

Farther south, Stonewall Jackson's center strengthened and advanced. After repulsing the cavalry charge, the 13th Virginia, 14th Georgia, and other survivors turned from the Wheatfield. Some moved toward the intersection of the Culpeper and Mitchell Station roads, and others went south into the Cornfield. After it had advanced into the Wheatfield, Branch halted his brigade, unsure where to go. Jackson ordered Branch to wheel right into the Cornfield. This hodgepodge of units, heading east and south from the vicinity of the Crittenden Gate, turned Prince's right.[56]

Federal casualties escalated in the Cornfield. Earlier, when Augur called for a section of Napoleons to respond to Pegram's and Hardy's batteries, a ball had hit his horse and another hit Augur's right hip. Geary had already left the field with a shattered left elbow, so Augur sent his adjutant general, Captain Halsted, to notify

---

54 *OR* 12, pt. 2, 219, 225; H. T. Childs, "Cedar Run As I Saw It," *Confederate Veteran*, 28:24.

55 *OR* 12, pt. 2, 157; Gordon, *Brook Farm*, 313.

56 *OR* 12, pt. 2, 235, 223; Graham, *Under Both Flags*, 219.

Prince that he (Prince) now commanded the division. Halsted was captured before he could deliver the message.[57]

Confederate fire decimated Prince's staff as well. One captain was mortally wounded. A wounded lieutenant's languid appearance matched his claimed inability to ride much longer, and a captain led him to the rear. Suddenly Prince was the only mounted officer in the brigade. Uncertain about the slackening firing to his right, he notified the 109th Pennsylvania's major that he would ride to division headquarters for instructions. It was nearly 7:45 p.m. when Prince headed for the ridge where he supposed Augur would be. Daylight had nearly vanished. As Prince neared the edge of the Cornfield, to the right and rear of his second line, someone in the corn suddenly grabbed his horse's bridle. A group of voices yelled, "Surrender!" Momentarily dumbstruck, Prince twice announced that he was their commander. Just then, a mounted Confederate major dashed forward, pushing aside the raised rifles. He ordered Prince to identify himself and demanded his pistol and field glasses. Prince raised his coat, revealing his sword, which the major also demanded. Prince said the major could take it himself.

With these trophies collected, the major escorted Prince about 400 yards rearward until he reached A. P. Hill, who returned the major to his regiment and sent Prince off with a staff major. The pair rode on until Brig. Gen. Beverly Robertson crossed their path. Robertson did Prince the kindness of taking custody of his horse, promising to return it later. He loaned Prince another horse, which he rode under guard to Orange. From there, he took a train to Richmond and captivity.[58]

In the Cornfield, half of Prince's brigade kept contact with Brig. Gen. Edward Thomas's Georgia brigade and with the right of Early's brigade. To these Federal regiments' right rear, the 3rd Maryland and 111th Pennsylvania held the intersection of the Orange and Mitchell Station roads. The Northerners would not hold it long; the threat to Banks's center soon became overwhelming. Most of the advancing Confederate units channeled along the road to Culpeper, driving these regiments back after Banks's artillery retreated behind the intersection.[59]

At dusk, a volley from the Cornfield whistled through the air toward Robinson's battery, causing it to limber up for the rear. Its departure was delayed, however, when a wounded horse had to be replaced. Privates Abiel Chandler, Jr.,

57 OR 12, pt. 2, 158; Jack D. Welsh, *Medical Histories of Union Generals* (Kent, OH, 1996), 9, 127.

58 OR 12, pt. 2, 168-169; Henry Prince to Christopher Augur, August 16, 1862, NL.

59 OR 12, pt. 2, 169; Boyle, *Soldiers True*, 44-45.

Brig. Gen. Henry Prince
National Archives Records Administration

and James Patterson spotted an infantryman, shot through the body, crawling east. They lifted him and started rearward. Suddenly, Confederates charged from the Cornfield in two lines. Patterson and Chandler left their man and darted after the retiring battery. The chaotic scene of men fleeing across the creek resembled a rout until Ricketts's division appeared in line, and Robinson's battery deployed behind it.[60]

The Confederate thrust turned the right flanks of both the 109th Pennsylvania and the 102nd New York. At about 8:00 p.m., Colonel Stainrook discovered this and withdrew his Pennsylvanians as the New Yorkers retreated. First Lieutenant Aaron Bates, a New Yorker who had been a heat casualty earlier in the day, fell behind after crossing the third fence on the retreat. One of his men ran back to get him when a company of Confederates, 100 yards away, fired on them. Officers and men helped him off the field, and a lieutenant colonel of another regiment dismounted and gave Bates his horse. The Yankees headed east, keeping clear of the Rebels along the road to the north and those of Trimble's brigade, advancing from the south.[61]

Major General Richard Ewell had ordered Isaac Trimble's brigade to descend from the mountain against the left flank of McGilvery's battery and Greene's brigade. Fire from Latimer's battery on the mountain delayed Trimble for a time, and a mill pond prevented him from advancing farther east, beyond Latimer's fire. When the mountaintop cannonading finally ceased, Trimble, followed by Col. Henry Forno's brigade of Louisianans, advanced en echelon with Trimble farther to the east. As these Confederates moved north along the Mitchell Station Road,

60 *History of the Fourth Maine Battery*, 20; *National Tribune*, November 11, 1897.

61 *OR* 51, pt. 1, 123; 2nd Annual Report, 103.

Early's brigade converged with and followed them, heading northeast toward the Orange and Mitchell Station intersection.[62]

Private Albert Baur of the 102nd New York barely avoided capture between Early's and Trimble's converging lines. When Baur rose from firing in a kneeling position to follow the regiment from the field, a comrade lying a few feet behind him, shot through the groin, begged him, "For God's sake, Al do not leave me, take me along." Baur wrote that he was afraid they were being surrounded and that he could not get them both out, but that he would come back if he could. They said their goodbyes, and Baur ran off with Confederates yelling a few feet away in the corn. He then stumbled across a dead color corporal. Baur turned the man over and grabbed the flag. Dense smoke and dim light aided his escape. Three Confederates crossed his path and yelled, "Surrender, throw down your gun, G—d d—n you." He kept moving despite musketry discharging close enough that he thought he felt its heat. Leaving the Cornfield, he crossed one of Trimble's regiments coming from the south. Its volley lit the darkening sky to his right. He angled northeast and ran toward the Hudson house, where he handed the flag to Capt. Robert Avery, a member of the regiment who was pausing from what Baur called a "lively" double-quick march to the rear. He lost the regiment again as he headed downhill from the house, bearing northeast toward Cedar Run. Another party of Confederates crossed Baur's path, again yelling at him to surrender. Evading these potential captors, he crossed the creek "like a racehorse" and kept running. He found the rest of his brigade and Brigadier General Greene, who now commanded the division.[63]

Greene's 362-man brigade had taken little part in this battle. It supported Captain McGilvery's battery, which exchanged fire with three Confederate batteries while Trimble's and Forno's brigades threatened its flank. A signal officer on a slave quarters roof south of the Hudson house spotted for Greene and McGilvery until it was too dark. Near dusk, Greene saw Trimble's men in the woods opposite his left flank, and McGilvery turned his Napoleons on them. Greene sent pickets into the Cornfield behind the battery, extending his left, and

62 OR 12, pt. 2, 184, 227, 232, 236.

63 *2nd Annual Report*, 113-116; *Annual Report of the Adjutant-General of the State of New York For the Year 1902* (Albany, 1903), 445.

found Confederate cavalry moving in that direction. He soon learned of Prince's withdrawal and discovered Confederate infantry heading around his left.[64]

Finding his position untenable, Greene withdrew the brigade and guns, forded the run, and headed east to open ground, where he joined Prince's brigade. Learning that Prince was missing, Greene took command of both brigades. This combined command countermarched about the countryside, unsuccessfully seeking General Banks, until it reached the Orange Road and discovered reinforcements. Greene then bivouacked the exhausted soldiers. His brigade had lost one officer and 22 men as prisoners while fleeing Trimble, and three wounded during the actual fighting.[65]

When Charles Candy withdrew the 66th Ohio from the Cornfield, he found that only 60 of the 250 men he had taken into it remained. Scattered soldiers from the other three Ohio regiments, meanwhile, were waiting for orders. Candy took charge of the brigade and reported to Banks, who directed it forward to form on Greene's right, at the edge of the woods behind Cedar Run. By then, Greene had already withdrawn behind that position. It is unlikely that Banks clearly apprehended Greene's location, since Greene had been moving about in search of Banks for some time.[66]

By approximately 9:00 p.m., darkness had fully enveloped the countryside, and Candy's men marched along a path bordered with dense brush. The 66th Ohio, now commanded by Lt. Col. Eugene Powell, led the column. Captain Van Deman advanced with 10 skirmishers. At the edge of the woods, voices from behind the brush called on them to halt and put down their weapons. A volley then erupted from the woods. One Confederate reached from the bushes and grabbed a captain by the collar, pulling him into the Rebel lines. After an exchange of fire in which one captain, three lieutenants, and a handful of enlisted men were wounded, the brigade withdrew. Candy reported to Pope, who was now on the field, and the commanding general directed the Ohioans to the rear to bivouac.[67]

*   *   *

64 Greene, "Official Reports, August 14, 1862"; George Sears Greene, *U. S. Army Generals' Reports of Civil War Service, 1864-1887*, Record Group 94, NA, 7.

65 *OR* 12, pt. 2, 138; Greene, "Official Reports, August 14, 1862."

66 *OR* 12, pt. 2, 166.

67 *OR* 12, pt. 2, 164, 166; Eugene Powell, Memoir, United States Army, Ohio Infantry Regiment 66th (1861-1865), 1862-1878, MSS 842, ch. 5, OHC.

Earlier in the day, after setting his army in motion, John Pope had resumed reading and smoking at his temporary headquarters in Culpeper. When he finally heard the echoes of artillery concussions between 4:00 and 5:00 that afternoon, Pope took to the saddle and ordered McDowell to move Ricketts's division forward from its post at Colvin's Tavern. He also instructed Sigel to march to the battlefield as soon as possible. Due to Sigel's late arrival in Culpeper without prepared rations, his movement would be delayed. Pope, riding with McDowell ahead of Ricketts's division, prudently scouted a fallback position, which was curious given his repeated boasts to the army, and to Banks in particular.[68]

When he reached the field, Pope was surprised to find Banks's corps beyond Cedar Run; he had expected it to be repelling Jackson's assaults from behind the run. Again, this expectation was out of step with his order to "attack him immediately as soon as he approaches." It is also contrary, in part, to General Roberts's direction that morning regarding which ground to hold. Roberts had told Banks to take up the line in front of the creek that Crawford occupied. In his testimony before the Joint Committee on the Conduct of the War, Banks said he considered this a tacit direction to attack, since the better defensive position would have been behind the run. Thomas Church Haskell Smith of Pope's staff saw Crawford's men streaming from the woods and believed that Banks "was evidently already beaten." Lieutenant Colonel David Strother of Pope's staff, often biased regarding which side was successful, was more solicitous. He claimed that he saw "no cowed or stampeded men."[69]

At this point, a short lull in the fighting occurred. Banks and several of his lieutenants met with the commanding general on a spot of high ground. Pope, who saw that Banks was not attacking, demanded, "What does this mean, General Banks? Those troops are in retreat!" Not waiting for an answer, Pope turned to his staff and sent them to rally stragglers and form a line in the nearby woods. After Banks made a futile effort to explain, Pope directed him to pull back his right and concentrate it in the center. Ricketts's division and his batteries would occupy the right.[70]

---

68 OR 12, pt. 2, 134; Gordon, *Brook Farm*, 314; Eby, *Virginia Yankee*, 76; Smith, Papers, 74, OHC.

69 Smith, Papers, 74, OHC; Gordon, *Brook Farm*, 282; *Joint Committee on the Conduct of the War, 38th Congress*, 3: Miscellaneous, 45; Eby, *Virginia Yankee*, 76.

70 OR 12, pt. 2, 134; Eby, *Virginia Yankee*, 76; Smith, Papers, 75, OHC.

Amidst the confusion of disorganized units and the care for the wounded at the Brown cottage, General Gordon received orders from division commander Alpheus Williams to withdraw and reform in the center. Unwilling to abandon the field hospital, Gordon headed for the center to inform Banks of the situation. He found Banks with Pope behind Cedar Run. Pope asked Gordon about the condition of his brigade, and Gordon said he could gather no more than 300 or 400 men. Pope ordered Gordon to move, once relieved, to the right of the Orange Road, and assured him that he would not be relied upon for much the following day, as 20,000 fresh men would be on the field in the morning. Gordon, who thought the reinforcements should have been there sooner, bristled: "General Pope, this battle should not have been fought, sir." Pope replied that he had not ordered it. Banks stood by, mute. Gordon's blood was up. Never tactful, he turned to Banks and announced that he had disobeyed Banks's order to charge across the Wheatfield. Banks denied giving such an order. Gordon then guided Brig. Gen. Zealous B. Tower's brigade to the Brown cottage, near which Tower placed his right, and ordered his brigade to the center, behind Ricketts's left.[71]

Colonel Joseph Knipe left the field with two wounds, including one to his head. As he passed Pope and Banks, accompanied by the 46th Pennsylvania's colors, Knipe bemoaned the results of the charge that he had recently advocated. He told Pope that only six men remained to follow those colors. Though Knipe was exaggerating, the 46th Pennsylvania had been roughly handled, with 244 total casualties, the highest loss in the corps. Ricketts's men cheered the 46th's colors.[72]

As Banks's regiments moved rearward under various levels of control, Rickett's division and its guns deployed on an open ridge behind the woods in which Crawford's men had bivouacked on August 8. General Tower deployed on the right with Brig. Gen. George L. Hartsuff's brigade in his rear. Colonel Samuel S. Carroll's brigade was to Tower's left, with Brig. Gen. Abram Duryée behind Carroll. The 5th Battery, Maine Light Artillery, and Battery F, 1st Pennsylvania Light Artillery, commanded by Captains George Leppien and Ezra Matthews, respectively, were among Tower's brigade, in the direction of the Brown cottage. Captain James Hall's 2nd Battery, Maine Light Artillery was to the right of the road in the space between Carroll's and Duryée's brigades.[73]

71 Gordon, *Brook Farm*, 313-315, 319.

72 *OR* 12, pt. 2, 152; Eby, *Virginia Yankee*, 76.

73 *OR* 12, pt. 2, 170-171.

Jackson continued his pursuit along the Orange Road, still intending to reach Culpeper during the night. He pressed his last two fresh brigades, Field's and Stafford's, into the vanguard. They halted on either side of the road, behind batteries that shelled the woods in front of Ricketts's position. The batteries ceased firing, and A. P. Hill ordered Stafford to advance into the woods. His brigade formed behind a fence on the right of the road at the far edge of the tree line. Field deployed on the left of the road. Pegram's battery moved forward and took a position on the high ground along the road.[74]

* * *

Gordon, Williams, and their staffs returned to the Orange Road. Gordon, not finding his brigade immediately, moved toward the position to which Pope had assigned him, the strip of woods behind Cedar Run that Hill's infantry had recently occupied. A brisk fire raked the party, killing an orderly. The riders quickly broke left, pushing rearward until Gordon found the 2nd Massachusetts and 27th Indiana, but not the 3rd Wisconsin.[75]

The 27th Indiana's Companies C and F also were absent. When Gordon's brigade withdrew from the Brown cottage, no one recalled these units, which were isolated well beyond the right of the corps. Late that night, 1st Sgt. John Bloss became convinced that his two-company detachment had been forgotten. The detachment headed toward the rear, walking along wood roads and across fields by the light of the moon until it located Ricketts's right flank.[76]

Crawford's brigade had a similar experience. After withdrawing from the Wheatfield, Crawford reported to Banks, who directed him to reposition to the rear of the same woods to which Banks had sent Gordon's brigade, with the same result. Confederate cavalry killed two of Crawford's attendants. He then reformed his brigade near Colvin's Tavern, two to three miles north.[77]

Separated from the rest of Crawford's brigade, the 10th Maine's rearward move was also frustrating. Crossing woods and open fields, it encountered a series of commanders, each ordering it to clear out of the way. Meandering from one

---

74 *OR* 12, pt. 2, 216, 218, 224, 226.

75 Gordon, *Brook Farm*, 320, 322; Quaife, *From the Cannon's Mouth*, 101.

76 Brown, *Twenty-Seventh Indiana*, 199.

77 *OR* 12, pt. 2, 152.

direction to another, the men, out of rations, spewed angry utterances. When they reached the rear of Ricketts's division, Colonel Beal learned the location of the wagons, and the men halted in a low clover field with ground rising on every side. Most lay in the clover while some went off to search for desperately needed water.[78]

From high ground to the south, a cannon suddenly discharged, sending a shell to the left of Beal's men. Another soon sailed overhead. Flashes from the guns revealed the outlines of the men, horses, and guns of Willie Pegram's battery. Pegram had discovered indiscrete fires lit amongst Ricketts's division and opened fire. Another round landed in front of the regiment and ricocheted over it. Gould recalled that nearby stragglers ran for the rear, joined by "servants, cooks, and the innumerable horde of skulks, camp followers." Wagons turned around with celerity in "true Bull Run style." Fortunately for the 10th Maine, its wagons avoided a full stampede and only went another mile toward Culpeper. The soldiers returned to their feet and trudged onward. After catching up with their wagons at about midnight, the Mainers finally rested.[79]

Three of Ricketts's batteries responded in kind. Battery C, 1st Pennsylvania Light Artillery, a mixture of rifled Parrotts and 12-pound smoothbore howitzers commanded by Captain James Thompson, was supposed to deploy to the left of Hartsuff's brigade. But once Thompson saw Pegram's battery sending canister and case shot into Ricketts's division, he decided to unlimber to the left of Hall's battery. From this position, Thompson, with help from James Hall's and George Leppien's batteries, silenced Pegram's guns for the night. A rise in the ground between the lines prevented effective counter-battery fire from either side's Parrotts. But Thompson's 12-pound guns quickly got Pegram's range, killing one lieutenant, several men, and over a dozen horses. They also destroyed several caissons.[80]

Pegram created havoc in the Federal ranks, but it was not worth his heavy losses. Two of General Hartsuff's regiments "became temporarily separated" amid the confusion, but soon returned to the brigade. General Robert Milroy, whose brigade led Sigel's corps, described "a general stampede, artillery, cavalry, and infantry retreating in the greatest disorder." After assigning two regiments and

78 OR 12, pt. 2, 122; Gould, *10th Maine*, 179; Townsend, *Campaigns of a Non-Combatant*, 259-260.

79 OR 12, pt. 2, 142; Gould, *10th Maine*, 179; Townsend, *Campaigns*, 260.

80 OR 12, pt. 2, 171-172, 216, 226; OR 51, pt. 1, 121; *Richmond Times Dispatch*, October 19, 1902; Quaife, *From the Cannon's Mouth*, 102.

some cavalry to halt the rearward movement, Milroy deployed his brigade to the left of Ricketts's division, east of the road, near where the 7th Virginia Cavalry had recently ambushed Pope.[81]

*   *   *

While the Confederate infantry renewed its advance, the 7th Virginia Cavalry arrived on the field after a feint toward Madison. When the horsemen crossed A. P. Hill's path, the general suggested to Grumble Jones, commanding the 7th, that he move right. The regiment passed between Stafford's and Early's brigades, then moved beyond the right of the woods that the Rebel artillery had shelled. After watching Ricketts's infantry take position, Jones discovered Pope's party sheltering to the rear of an outcropping that grew to a slight hill.[82]

Pope, Banks, and their staffs had withdrawn to low ground near the other Hudson house to the left of the Orange Road, which at that point ran nearly north–south. They remained there during the artillery duel, sitting on the ground and watching shells arc across the dark sky. The officers heard trampling hooves in the nearby woods, quickly followed by a charge with commingled screams and pistol shots.[83]

When Jones's Virginians charged, the combined general staffs hastily mounted in confusion within 50 yards of their attackers. A cavalryman's horse struck Banks in the hip, wounding him badly enough to hinder his active command of the corps over the coming weeks. Colonel George D. Ruggles, Pope's adjutant general, and a signal corps officer both lost horses to the Confederate fire. As the Federals crossed a hollow in retreat, the 12th Massachusetts fired a volley at the riders approaching in the dark. Riding at full tilt, half a dozen staffers crashed into a high rail fence. Apprehension spread when the entourage halted in a few hundred yards and discovered that Pope was missing. The commanding general was later found sitting under a tree atop a pile of fence rails with Banks, McDowell, and Sigel.[84]

81 *OR* 12, pt. 2, 175, 142.

82 *OR* 12, pt. 2, 239; McDonald, *Laurel Brigade*, 81; *National Tribune*, September 5, 1901; Gordon, *Brook Farm*, 321.

83 Eby, *Virginia Yankee*, 77. This is not the same Hudson house near which Robinson's and McGilvery's batteries and Greene's and Prince's brigades deployed.

84 Eby, *Virginia Yankee*, 76, 78; Gordon, *Brook Farm*, 321-322.

The men of the 7th Virginia, thinking they had merely scuffled with some enemy cavalry, did not realize how near they had come to bagging the one man hated by all of Virginia. The charge nevertheless resulted in the acquisition of valuable intelligence. Jones's men captured a servant who divulged the arrival of Sigel's corps. This information would end Jackson's pursuit of Pope.[85]

*   *   *

While the artillery dueled, Gordon suggested to Williams a move farther to the rear, reasoning that a reserve line would be required. The 2nd Massachusetts led the column rearward. After moving a short distance, Gordon heard a Teutonic voice reprimanding his men for retreating. The man demanded the regiment stop and threatened to report it. In short order, Colonel Andrews and then Gordon arrived to discover Maj. Gen. Franz Sigel. Gordon explained the fighting his men had done and told Sigel what he thought of the way he had addressed them. Recognizing that the troops were moving under orders, Sigel acquiesced. Gordon's men then bivouacked.[86]

Banks's survivors rested. Behind the Confederate lines, the dead and wounded littered the ground, the latter's groans mingling with the sounds of a typical summer night.

85 OR 12, pt. 2, 184, 239.

86 Gordon, *Brook Farm*, 323-324.

Chapter 5

"We Have Had a Very Serious Time"

— William Shimp, 46th Pennsylvania

Lee Shifts Theaters during
Pope's Intermission

August 10 to 17, 1862

In a letter to his wife, Col. George Andrews of the 2nd Massachusetts called the fight at Cedar Mountain, "About as great a piece of folly as I have ever witnessed on the part of an incompetent general." Andrews's critical views of both the battle and Nathaniel Banks were widespread amongst the 2nd's officers. The battle frustrated just about everyone's expectations.[1]

Pope wanted to concentrate prior to fighting a general engagement, but Sigel's delays and Banks's pugnacity crippled that effort. Moreover, Banks neither requested reinforcements nor notified Pope of his intentions and progress, which contributed to Ricketts's division's staying mostly idle during the battle.

Stonewall Jackson's designs were frustrated as well. Though Jackson met his objective of engaging an isolated element of Pope's army, the bungled march on August 8 kept his own force spread along the road and too far from his geographic objective at Culpeper. Further, the Federals' unexpected tenacity against Jackson's poorly disposed left resulted in a pyrrhic Southern victory. While Jackson inflicted far more casualties on Banks than he lost, the result was heavier fighting than was necessary to meet Robert E. Lee's desire for conservation of effort. Lee needed

---

1 George Andrews to wife, August 12, 1862, Andrews Collection, USA.

victories through maneuvering. In order to achieve this, his army would soon disengage from the York-James peninsula and shift to central Virginia. For now, Pope and Jackson gathered their scattered armies and tended to their casualties.

When Gordon's brigade withdrew to the Brown cottage late on August 9, the soldiers discovered hundreds of wounded from Williams's division there. Regimental bands brought off what wounded they could carry until Confederates began capturing their members. The 2nd Massachusetts's surgeon cared for the wounded in spite of a head wound of his own. When the brigade withdrew from the cottage, Colonel Andrews left its chaplain, Alonzo Quint, to stay with those men who were too injured to walk. Pender's and Archer's brigades advanced to within a few hundred yards of the Brown yard, where surgeons worked through the night by moon and candlelight. At 3:00 a.m. on August 10, General McDowell warned Quint that the location was untenable. The Confederates held the road nearest to the Brown cottage, but the chaplain learned of a winding path through the woods to the rear. By 6:00 a.m., all the wounded were removed to another field hospital using this path.[2]

A resumption of the fighting seemed likely on August 10. At 5:30 a.m., a Federal battery fired at Jackson's artillery but got no response. Then, as Jackson's lines fell back, Union pickets advanced to near the location of Banks's original line of battle. Pickets exchanged fire sporadically throughout the morning, but nothing more substantial materialized. Pope offered fatigue from the heat and long marches as his justification for not renewing hostilities. Jackson wrote, more truthfully, that Pope's growing numbers made another attack too risky. Instead of advancing, Jackson set his army to burying the dead, tending the wounded, and gathering the copious rifles that Banks's soldiers had abandoned on the field.[3]

The intense heat returned on August 10, exacerbating the suffering of those wounded men still on the field. Some relief came late that afternoon when a downpour temporarily cut the heat and quenched parched lips. During the downpour, Lieutenant Colonel Strother found Gordon and Crawford in the woods among Sigel's corps. They appeared "worn and sad." Gordon directed Strother's attention to the 300 or 400 hundred men present in his brigade. Banks was also openly discouraged and temporarily turned command over to Williams because of his wound. Strother found Pope and McDowell at the Nalle house, behind

---

2 Quint, *2nd Massachusetts*, 114-115.

3 *OR* 12, pt. 2, 134, 184; Eby, *Virginia Yankee*, 78.

Ricketts's division. The two generals sat on boxes under an apple tree as surgeons transformed the fine home into a "butcher's shambles."[4]

Makeshift hospitals dotted the landscape. General John Geary was one of the first cases to reach the Ward house during the battle. This house sat north of Colvin's Tavern on the east side of the road. The 109th Pennsylvania's chaplain left his wife at the Ward home and told her that he would send friends and any of the wounded officers of his regiment there for treatment. When Geary discovered what appeared to be a white thread hanging from a piece of shirt sleeve that penetrated his elbow wound, he told her to give it a "sudden jerk." She did, revealing that the thread was part of his arm. The tug hurt him so much that he leapt from the bed, bellowing horrendous exclamations. Other wounded streamed into this house and others, where the surgeons' bloody work continued for days.[5]

*   *   *

Jackson's only activity on August 10 involved scouting by Maj. Gen. J. E. B. Stuart's cavalry. Stuart arrived on the field early that morning and, at Jackson's request, took command of his cavalry. Stuart's horsemen passed Pope's left along the Orange and Alexandria Railroad nearly to the Stevensburg Road, southeast of Culpeper. From Union prisoners, Stuart discovered that McDowell's last division, under Rufus King, was en route from Falmouth. Ambrose Burnside's command had arrived from operations in North Carolina, relieving King opposite Lee's vulnerable center. The intelligence that King would soon be on the field with Pope was sufficient to seal Jackson's decision to withdraw beyond the Rapidan. While wagons removed discarded rifles and Confederate wounded, word spread that Union cavalry was advancing, causing the Southern teamsters to stampede their wagons. By that evening, Jackson's army was to the rear of the battlefield. [6]

*   *   *

4 Eby, *Virginia Yankee*, 79; Gould, *10th Maine*, 180.

5 Eby, *Virginia Yankee*, 79; Mrs. John McMillan, Dictation, April 8, 1913, Geary Family Papers, HSP.

6 *National Tribune*, September 5, 1901; Harsh, *Confederate Tide Rising*, 116; Early, *Autobiographical Sketch*, 101; McDonald, *Make Me a Map*, 67.

Several miles away, the 28th Pennsylvania faced uncertainty regarding the battle's outcome and threats real and perceived in its front. On August 9, the 28th, unable to assist its new brigade or the commander its soldiers liked so well, marched to Thoroughfare Mountain. Reaching open country, bursting artillery shells from the raging battle to the south came into view. When the 28th arrived at James City, at the foot of the mountain, it found the 27th Pennsylvania and 54th New York returning to Sigel's command from detached duty at Madison. Thoroughfare Mountain was free of Confederates when the regiment arrived at 9:00 p.m. Lieutenant Colonel Tyndale posted pickets and spent the night assessing the landscape and deploying the regiment for defense. The troops could see the sprawling campfires of Jackson's army from their position.[7]

Out of food early on August 10, Tyndale sent orderlies to find division headquarters and secure supply wagons. They were captured. A few hours later, signalmen established communications with Banks. Between 7:00 and 8:00 a.m., orders came to withdraw. Tyndale moved north then east, avoiding the road from Colvin's Tavern, and at midday reached temporary corps headquarters between Culpeper and the battlefield.[8]

* * *

By nightfall, word spread among Gordon's men that their wounded were still unattended on the field and that Confederate pickets had withdrawn beyond the Wheatfield. With Gordon's consent, Colonel Andrews sent a detail of Massachusetts and Wisconsin men, under the command of a lieutenant, to the battlefield. After the men trekked about three miles to within a half mile of the Wheatfield, pickets detained them. The group slept at the picket line that night. At first light, the lieutenant applied for permission to proceed. Chaplain Quint, meanwhile, escaped notice of the pickets and headed for the Wheatfield. After crossing Cedar Run, he found a wounded soldier. Quint promised the man that help was coming and continued to the Wheatfield, where he waved a handkerchief

---

7 Ambrose Henry Hayward to sister, August 17, 1862, GC; McLaughlin, *Memoir of Hector Tyndale*, 65; Foering Diary, August 9, 1862, HSP.

8 Hayward to Sister, August 17, 1862, GC; McLaughlin, *Memoir of Hector Tyndale*, 65; Foering Diary, August 10, 1862, HSP.

at the Confederate sentry on the opposite side. The sentry waved his cap and nodded implicit permission to enter.[9]

Jackson granted a truce to attend to the Union dead and wounded until 2:00 p.m., and later extended it by three hours. Though the truce request is generally attributed to Pope, David Strother asserted that Jackson had requested it in order to bury his own dead. English correspondent George Townsend reported that Lt. Elliot Johnston of Baltimore claimed he had ridden into the Federal lines that morning with a white flag, thus "opening" the truce.[10]

Contrary to Strothers's assertion, Jackson had no need to apply for a truce to bury his dead, as he held the field. It is likely, however, that Jackson offered a truce in order to occupy Pope's army and to facilitate the care of the Federal dead and wounded, which would have encumbered his own withdrawal. From that perspective, Gen. Robert Milroy's account of the events leading to the truce is convincing. That morning, he sent 400 unarmed men forward with ambulances to bury the dead and collect the wounded. His brigade followed. On reaching the field, Confederates approached under a flag of truce, announcing that the Federals could enter the area and would not be molested while they worked. Then Milroy and Brig. Gen. George Bayard met Stuart, who formally offered the truce so long as Pope agreed. Milroy sent his brigade to the rear and found Pope, who assented to the agreement.[11]

When they reached the battlefield, the Federals found examples of gross neglect, of compassion, and of pilfering. They were horrified at the lack of medical attention for their wounded, who had lain on the field for a day and a half. When Jed Hotchkiss crossed the battlefield on August 10, he heard "the most agonizing shrieks and groans" from the Northerners lying under the burning sun. On August 11, a man in the 28th Pennsylvania found one of his comrades alive but with both arms missing. The 3rd Wisconsin's surgeon recorded his impressions of the battle's aftermath: "O, my God! How the ground did look. Dead bodies with swollen and distorted faces, lay thickly upon the ground in all directions while mingling in and close around, we found the wounded that had been left." Captain Moses O'Brien, the indefatigable leader of Company I who had suffered a severe thigh wound during the 3rd's initial engagement, went back into the fight and fell with a body

9 Quint, *2nd Massachusetts*, 116-117.

10 OR 12, pt. 2, 184; Eby, *Virginia Yankee*, 80; Townsend, *Campaigns of a Non-Combatant*, 273-274.

11 Margaret Paulus, ed., *Papers of General Robert Huston Milroy*, 4 vols (1965), 1:69.

wound during the regiment's second assault. During the August 11 truce, he asked the unit's surgeon, Dr. George E. Conant, about the wound. Conant told him it was fatal. Because he was too badly wounded for the ambulance, O'Brien's men carried him by stretcher to Culpeper, where he died on a hotel porch that the surgeons had commandeered.[12]

Some Confederates had helped the Union wounded cope with exposure and lack of water. On Sunday morning, a sergeant from the 27th Virginia aided the 28th New York's Lieutenant Warren, who had been wounded in the hand, arm, head, throat, and leg. The sergeant filled several canteens for Warren and draped a rubber blanket over him to block the sun. When the downpour came that afternoon, Warren was able to collect more water from the top of the blanket into the canteens. The Federals, who brought Warren off the field on Monday August 11, saw the blood that he had lost and thought he would not survive. Warren refused to have his leg amputated, yet somehow recovered.[13]

Confederate surgeons had earlier passed by Sergeant MacAlpine, who was shot through the back, above his hips, and through the thigh. Two Rebels found him on the 10th and offered to put him in the shade. They carried him to a bed of wheat that they prepared under a tree. He pleaded with them to leave him where he was because of the pain. David Strother wrote of another Yankee who made a shelter of green cornstalks and crawled inside to die. He ignored the possibility that Confederates had built the shelter.[14]

When General Gordon entered the field, Captain Shaw joined him. They discovered the bodies of Captains Abbott and Goodwin of the 2nd Massachusetts, along with Richard Cary, William Williams, and 1st Lt. Stephen Perkins of that same regiment. Like most of the dead, all of them except Cary were blackened and disfigured by the heat. Strother wrote of "hideously blackened and swelled" corpses, and George Townsend described the "blistering and burdening" corruption of the soldiers' bodies. The disfiguration was troubling, but it created practical difficulties as well. Members of the 28th New York's burial party thought they found and buried the body of 1st Lt. William M. Kenyon from their company,

12 McDonald, *Make Me a Map*, 67; Robert Davis to father, August 14, 1862, LV; Dr. Conant, Letter, August 13, 1862, Quiner Scrapbook, 3:49, 54, WHS; Bryant, *Third Wisconsin*, 94-95, 412.

13 "An Historic Flag," USA.

14 Comey, *A Legacy of Valor*, 61-62; Eby, *Virginia Yankee*, 80.

Capt. Robert Gould Shaw, Gordon's Staff,
formerly 2nd Massachusetts
Library of Congress

but Kenyon soon turned up among the paroled prisoners. They learned that they had buried an officer from the 5th Connecticut.[15]

Captain Richard Cary clung to life until late on August 10. First Sergeant Roland S. Williston, shot through the leg, remained by Cary, his company commander, the entire time. When Shaw and Gordon found Cary beneath an oak tree along the fence, he appeared to be sleeping peacefully. Some Rebels had left him a dipper of water. They took his valuables but returned his ring and a locket with a likeness of his wife when Williston pleaded with them to do so.[16]

Shaw's grief at the loss of his comrades soon gave way to a desire for vengeance. He wrote four days later, "I long for the day when we shall attack the Rebels with an overwhelming force and annihilate them. May I live long enough to see them running before us hacked to little pieces." Captain Charles F. Morse arrived with the regimental ambulances from which some of the slain officers had alighted before going into battle. Morse and Shaw had their bodies loaded onto those same ambulances. At Culpeper, Shaw and Lieutenant Francis had them packed in charcoal and shipped to Alexandria, where they were placed in metal coffins and sent to Massachusetts. Shaw took a lock of hair from each to send to their friends. For the rank and file, burial parties dug large trenches, interring the dead in mass graves. In the 2nd Massachusetts's trench,

15 Robert Shaw to cousin, August 13, 1862, Robert Gould Shaw Letters to His Family and Other Papers (MS Am 1910, Box 1 (26)), HLHU; Harvard Memorial Biographies, 2:198; Eby, *Virginia Yankee*, 80; Townsend, *Campaigns of a Non-Combatant*, 276; Boyce, *Twenty-eighth New York*, 39.

16 Shaw to cousin, August 13, 1862, HLHU; Harvard Memorial Biographies, 2:198; Wilder Dwight to mother, August 17, 1862, Dwight Papers, MHS.

soldiers placed green boughs over the bodies before covering them with Old Dominion soil.[17]

The Federals reported widespread thievery. The 28th New York's history considered these offenders "more ghouls than human." The 3rd Wisconsin's surgeon recalled that, "The dead were almost all of them robbed. All of their money, some of their shoes, some of their pants, coats, and generally of their guns." Soldiers from the 5th Connecticut found their dead major had been stripped of "boots, shoulder straps, watch, ring etc." The 10th Maine's Sgt. Robert M. Weeks heard Confederate officers order their men to guard and care for the wounded. Nevertheless, thieves victimized those too seriously wounded to move. Captains George H. Nye and Charles S. Emerson of the 10th described dead and wounded men as having been stripped of their valuables, including the new shoes and trousers that the Mainers had hurriedly donned on the 8th. Before Capt. Moses O'Brien died, he claimed a Confederate doctor told him that he did not have long to live. Due to the captain's evanescence, the doctor took his watch and $280.[18]

The Rebels otherwise occupied themselves with gathering discarded weapons. Since capturing abundant supplies after the battle of Winchester that spring, Jackson's men had derisively called Banks their commissary. The only trophies at Cedar Mountain, however, were a large quantity of small arms, an empty caisson, and a single artillery piece, which the crew had spiked after miring it in the mud. Jubal Early, besides stewarding the truce, was on the field at Ewell's direction, attending to 98 unburied Confederates north of the road. While there, he found a large cache of neglected arms. Union troops were removing them, and Early demanded they stop and return those already taken. They eventually did so, but only after a Federal officer rebuked a member of Franz Sigel's staff for removing the Confederates' spoils. Early's action secured six wagons full of discarded rifles.[19]

The Southerners also sent prisoners to the rear. A member of Poague's battery observed Yankee prisoners on August 9 carrying themselves "as if they had done their best and had nothing of which to be ashamed." Many of the Federals, including Private David A. Starr of the 5th Connecticut and Captain Bowen of the

17 Shaw to cousin, August 13, 1862, HLHU; Morse, *Letters*, 80; Harvard Memorial Biographies, 2:198; Quint, *2nd Massachusetts*, 118.

18 Boyce, *Twenty-eighth New York*, 39; Quint, *2nd Massachusetts*, 177; Quiner Scrapbook, 3:49, 54, WHS; Oscar B. Lane, Diary, August 11, 1862, Lane Family Papers, DU; Gould, *10th Maine*, 182; *Lewisburg* [ME] *Chronicle*, August 22, 1862.

19 OR 51, pt. 1, 120; OR 12, pt. 2, 227; Early, *Autobiographical Sketch*, 101-102; McDonald, *Make Me a Map*, 68.

28th New York, fell into captivity after collapsing from fatigue. Captivity, however, did not rejuvenate them. The prisoners began marching south at 9:00 p.m. on the 9th and continued until they reached Orange at 10:00 the next morning. From there, they boarded trains for Libby and Belle Isle prisons near Richmond. Captors told the 3rd Wisconsin's Lt. Theodore J. Widvey that their treatment, presumably worse than normal, was in retaliation for Pope's proclamations regarding the treatment of Southern civilians.[20]

Bands of Northern burial parties, between 10 and 20 men each, scoured the field. Jubal Early considered the Union details on the field "very large." Nevertheless, the task was not always done thoroughly. Mass graves were so poorly covered that arms and legs protruded from the ground. To George Townsend, the only organization to the burial operation was the gully that served as a dividing line between the two sides' efforts. Some of the erstwhile combatants met on the field, satisfying curiosity about an unfamiliar foe and trading newspapers, tobacco, and other goods. Townsend wrote that enlisted Federals abandoned shovels and "strolled across the boundary, to chaff and loiter with the Butternuts." General Milroy wrote, "our boys and theirs roughed together and joked and talked about their battles as freely as old friends."[21]

The truce also became convivial for some of the general officers. Generals Roberts and Hartsuff arrived as official representatives of the Union Army. As the truce began, they sat on a fallen tree trunk near the rivulet in the Cornfield, awaiting Early and Stuart, who superintended the truce for the Confederates. Two junior Rebel officers sat near them. These youths were there to receive the Federal generals, but were too junior in rank for propriety. The Confederates chatted with correspondent Townsend. Early arrived on horseback from the rise in their front and nodded to the party. Townsend wrote that Early resembled "a homely farmer." He remained taciturn throughout the truce. Stuart, on the other hand, largely abandoned formal duties, and jovially held court amid the macabre sights. En route to the group of officers assembling on the field, however, Stuart halted his horse next to Townsend, who was sketching the battlefield for his paper. Upon interrogation, the Englishman assured Stuart that it was for no military purpose. Stuart responded with an "Umph!" tinged with either disinterest or disdain, and

20 Moore, *The Story of a Cannoneer*, 96; *New London* [CT] *Daily Chronicle*, September 20, 1862; Quiner Scrapbook, 3:55-56, WHS.

21 Townsend, *Campaigns of a Non-Combatant*, 273, 276; Early, *Autobiographical Sketch*, 102; Marvin, *Fifth Connecticut*, 226; Worsham, *One of Jackson's Foot Cavalry*, 117; Paulus, ed., *Milroy Papers*, 1:70.

rode on. The cavalier's initial suspicion was accurate. Townsend's banter with the two junior Confederates was nonchalant by design. He was hoping to secure what details he could without appearing suspicious. He felt that he "got along very well" until someone else arrived and questioned them too pointedly, nearly ruining his surreptitious endeavor.[22]

The generals joked near the rivulet, oblivious to the scattered corpses, which choked the stream in places. West Point classmates Stuart and Hartsuff took a walk, reminiscing about the old days. When they returned, a surgeon produced a whisky bottle. The officers started wishing each other an early end to the war through capture. Stuart entertained the party with a loquaciousness that Townsend described as "airiness." Stuart won over the warier members of his audience, including Crawford, whom Townsend described as initially "gray and mistrustful," eyeing Stuart with a comportment that suggested a forthcoming challenge. But Crawford and Bayard, soon joined the party, bearing a basket of delicacies on which they all lunched.[23]

Crawford's mood lightened, and he initiated a famous episode of Pope's Virginia campaign. Talk turned to the press, and Stuart asserted that Northern papers professed every battle a Union victory. He then bet Crawford a new hat that they soon would declare Pope's army triumphant. Crawford, under no delusion about the battle's results, declared that not even the *New York Herald* would describe Cedar Mountain as a Northern victory. Stuart's hat arrived days later. He was not destined to keep it long.[24]

Eventually, Stuart grew dissatisfied with the Union ambulances' presence and threatened to confiscate them. Yet in spite of their wariness regarding Union intelligence-gathering, the Confederates permitted the enemy to enter their lines on several occasions. Townsend entered their outer lines, accompanied by a Confederate lieutenant, to look for wounded. Captains Morse and Shaw gained access for the same reason. Morse found the Confederate officers "gentlemanly and kind." These officers told them about prisoners from their regiment and accepted money for two of their captured officers. Apprehension about prying

22 Townsend, *Campaigns of a Non-Combatant*, 273-275.

23 Townsend, *Campaigns of a Non-Combatant*, 275; Blackford, Letters, 111.

24 Blackford, *Letters*, 111.

Union eyes was grounded in a cause beyond normal military prudence, for Jackson's army had begun moving to the Rapidan.[25]

Their fears might have come to fruition if not for the propriety of a Massachusetts chaplain. An unidentified Southern general allowed Chaplain Quint to look for missing men from his regiment. With a smile, the general offered entry farther than previously allowed, "on honor." Passing through the line and the woods in its rear, Quint discovered the unmistakable signs of a Confederate army already in motion. The general reminded him, "You are on your honor, you know." Quint was true to his word, and it took a reconnaissance by Milroy's brigade the next morning for this intelligence to reach Pope.[26]

The truce occupied Pope's larger army while Jackson slipped away. He began marching at about 2:00 p.m., when the Federals requested an extension of the cease-fire. His reserve units withdrew first, heading for Orange. Early left immediately after sundown. At that time, members of a Virginia battery built campfires to give the impression that the army remained in place. Hill's infantry marched last, covered by Stuart's cavalry. By August 12, Jackson's army was south of the Rapidan, encamped near Liberty Mills, Toddsburg, and Orange.[27]

Pope's cavalry followed. After Jackson crossed the river, Federal horsemen resumed their earlier positions and duties on the north side of the Rapidan from Raccoon Ford to the Blue Ridge as though there had never been a battle. One critical Southerner, cavalryman Charles Blackford, wrote, "Pope should be cashiered for letting Jackson escape him." Indeed, though Pope bemoaned Banks's initiation of a general engagement before he could concentrate his forces, Pope showed little aggression once his other units reached the field. This belied his self-proclaimed reputation and cost him an irreplaceable opportunity. The renewed troop dispositions circa August 7 continued from the 12th until the 14th, when Brig. Gen. Jesse Reno's division of Burnside's IX Corps arrived from Falmouth. Suddenly feeling secure, Pope marched toward the Rapidan. Sigel commanded the right wing, and kept his right on the intersection of the Orange Road and Robertson's River. Milroy's brigade of Sigel's corps briefly advanced beyond

25 "An English Combatant," *Battlefields of the South, from Bull Run to Fredericksburg* (New York: 1864), 432; McDonald, *Make Me a Map*, 68; Townsend, *Campaigns of a Non-Combatant*, 276; Morse, *Letters*, 80-81.

26 OR 12, pt. 2, 143; Quint, *Potomac and Rapidan*, 193.

27 OR 12, pt. 2, 185; McDonald, *Make Me a Map*, 68; Early, *Autobiographical Sketch*, 102; William Ellis Jones, Diary, August 11, 1862, UM.

Robertson's River on August 13 before being recalled. McDowell commanded the center, straddling Cedar Mountain. Reno commanded the left near Raccoon Ford, covering the approach to Stevensburg and Culpeper. Pope held Banks's corps in reserve at Culpeper.[28]

Pope reported that Banks's troops were not "capable of rendering efficient service for several days." The men held the same opinion. Some considered their units nearly ruined. One 46th Pennsylvanian wrote, "We have had a very serious time. . . . They say they are going to send us to Harrisburg to recruit up our Regt. I hope they will." Many soldiers mentioned this possibility, which was more of an expectation than a desire, following Cedar Mountain. Another member of the 46th thought his regiment had been "almost exterminated." Though earned with heavy cost, the corps' reputation improved among its Confederate rivals. A member of Crenshaw's Virginia battery who had only secondhand knowledge of the battle wrote that, "The Yanks fought with more bravery on this occasion than they have ever done."[29]

Reviving the regiments' fitness for service involved more than time off and gathering stragglers. Cedar Mountain had taken a heavy toll on staff officers at all levels, from the corps down to the brigades. This resulted in temporary disorder. Meanwhile, supplies had to be requisitioned. One hundred enlisted men in the 28th New York lacked rifles. Its losses hobbled the coordination required for resupply. A captain led the regiment, which was consolidated into four companies, commanded by sergeants and corporals. Lieutenant Henry Brinkman, who was now the only officer in the 5th Ohio's Company B, wrote on August 11, "I have my hands full." To make matters worse, the corps commander was not yet fit for service.[30]

Due to the lingering aftereffects of the injury he suffered at Cedar Mountain, Banks could not perform his duties. Consequently, Pope ordered Alpheus Williams to assume command of the corps on August 12. Any enthusiasm Williams might have felt regarding his elevation soon cooled. He had only one lieutenant to help administer the corps, and the two of them were "incessantly and vexatiously

28 OR 12, pt. 2, 28, 143; Blackford, *Letters*, 111.

29 OR 12, pt. 2, 27; Shimp to Anna, August 13, 1862, USA; Matthew Taylor, Memoir, PSA; Jones Diary, August 9, 1862, UM.

30 Quaife, *From the Cannon's Mouth*, 103; Hicks Diary, 15-16, LC; Boyce, *Twenty-eighth New York*, 44; Henry Brinkman to John Brinkman, August 11, 1862, Henry C. Brinkman Papers (Mss 1075), CHA.

Brig. Gen. Alpheus Williams
Library of Congress

occupied." On August 17, Williams wrote that he prayed Banks would be well soon.[31]

Pope's August 12 order also directed Williams to situate the corps at Culpeper and send a "sufficient force" to secure the railroad bridge over the Rappahannock. For this task, Williams detailed six companies of the oversized and still untested 28th Pennsylvania. Colonel Gabriel De Korponay, who recently returned to the regiment, led it for a few days. On August 21, Col. Charles Candy, formerly of the 66th Ohio, took sick and De Korponay relieved him of brigade command for 10 days before he, too, fell ill. Hector Tyndale replaced De Korponay in each of these instances.[32]

When the corps returned to Culpeper, its tents stood as the men had left them. The numerous vacant spaces were striking. Alonzo Quint remembered, "How touchingly our empty tents reminded us of our loss!" While the tents stood inviolate, the town was much altered. Churches, hotels, and shops were now hospitals, filled with many of the soldiers' friends. On August 15, Col. Dudley Donnelly died in one of these hospitals after clinging to life with an excruciating groin wound for six days. The 28th New York's chaplain accompanied his body to Lockport, New York, for burial. The 64 remaining members of the command escorted his body to the train. Donnelly's dying wish was that the regiment be allowed to return to New York to recruit. Lieutenant Colonel Edwin Brown's arm was amputated on August 10. Many Union wounded, including Brown and William Warren, fell into Confederate hands in a few days, when the Union army abruptly evacuated Culpeper. For now, however, the corps kept busy with reviews. After

31 OR 12, pt. 3, 568; Quaife, *From the Cannon's Mouth*, 105.

32 Pope, order to Williams, August 12, 1862, Banks Papers, LC; Hector Tyndale, *U.S. Army Generals' Reports of Civil War Service, 1864-1887*, Record Group 94, NA, 5-6; Foering Diary, August 13, 21, 1862.

one such event on August 13, General Crawford spoke, shedding tears when the topic turned to fallen comrades:[33]

Soldiers of the 1st Brigade,

I stand before your shattered ranks today with feelings not to be expressed in words. The vacant places in your lines these crowded hospitals those wounds on yonder battlefield, speak in loudness not to be misunderstood of what you have done + suffered.

I dare not enumerate your loss. My heart bleeds as I think of it. Your loss did I say. Alas, my loss + the country's as much as yours. I need not say that I am proud of you.

You have just earned the reputation of the brigade at fearful sacrifice, + you had exhorted from the enemy himself a tribute to your bravery.

I look among you to find those who placed themselves before you led most of you into action. I ask for them in vain—"killed" "wounded" or "prisoners" is the only response I get.

But soldiers our duty is not yet done. We live & our country still calls upon us for help. The enemy you met & whose overwhelming numbers you resisted so gallantly is in retreat before us. "Onward" must be our only thought, our only desire. I know [you are] despondent. I ask no more than to lead you to the end, & let us [illegible] to those whose hearts are fallen in, whose eyes are upon us our reputation & our perseverance.[34]

For the moment, the rest of Pope's army operated near the Rapidan amid vacillating guidance from Union leadership. On August 11, the new general-in-chief Henry W. Halleck, telegraphed Pope to keep Jackson "in check" until reinforcements arrived. Beginning the next day, Halleck made it clear that Pope's only means of occupying Jackson's force was to sit still and watch him, and he warned him to be aware of the Confederate proclivity for feigned retreats. In a second telegram on August 12, he advised Pope to send all rolling stock behind the Rappahannock and to guard the railroad bridge. This resulted in the 28th Pennsylvania detachment being shifted to the railroad bridge. These orders

---

33 Quint, *Potomac and Rapidan*, 185; Quint, *2nd Massachusetts*, 119; Boyce, "28th Regiment," 135-136; *Maine Bugle*, 84, 87-88; Gould, *10th Maine*, 198.

34 Samuel Crawford, "Address to 1st Brigade," Union Battle Reports, 1861-1865 (Trifolded Segment) Unpublished, vols. 11-13 (Box 4), Record Group 94, NA. It is easy to imagine this speech being poorly received, given Crawford's reported involvement, or lack thereof, on the field.

betrayed Halleck's angst over potential calamity. On August 13, Halleck forbade a Rapidan crossing and again cautioned Pope to beware of an attack on his flank. With confidence springing from Reno's arrival, Pope moved his force, less Banks's corps, near the Rapidan as previously described. Pope advanced within an evolving strategic environment that extended to the York-James peninsula.[35]

*   *   *

Major General George Brinton McClellan and the Army of the Potomac had landed on the York-James peninsula in March 1862. Moving deliberately up the peninsula, the army finally stood outside Richmond in May. By June, McClellan planned a shift away from his supply line on the York River toward one on the James. Beginning in late June, Lee's Confederate army accelerated McClellan's movement with a string of attacks over the space of a week. Though the Southerners did not always succeed tactically, occasionally executing costly frontal assaults that Lee hoped to avoid, their pugnacity caused McClellan to back away from Richmond. Though the movement ended with McClellan on the James, a position that was more threatening to Richmond than where he had started the week prior, the attacks confirmed for the Union general his incorrect opinion that he faced an overwhelming Rebel army and needed substantial reinforcements before he could again advance.[36]

Following the "Seven Days" battles, Halleck and President Lincoln told McClellan he could expect no further reinforcements. McClellan spent July consolidating his position near Harrison's Landing. He continued requesting men, and made a specific appeal on July 17 for two divisions under Maj. Gen. Ambrose Burnside that had been operating in eastern North Carolina. Instead, on July 30, Halleck ordered McClellan to evacuate his 12,500 sick and wounded. This order heightened McClellan's suspicions. Over the next few days he repeatedly asked Halleck and Lincoln what they intended for his troops. Finally, on August 3, Halleck ordered McClellan to move the army toward Aquia Creek near Fredericksburg. McClellan received the order the next day.[37]

---

35 OR 12, pt. 3, 560, 564-565, 569.

36 Harsh, *Confederate Tide Rising*, 89-97.

37 OR 11, pt. 1, 75-76, 78, 80-81.

The evacuation fell short of Halleck's expectations. McClellan began withdrawing two corps from the front on August 14, the same day Pope advanced his infantry to the Rapidan. McClellan wired Halleck on August 17 that he planned to have his whole force behind the Chickahominy River by the next morning. He continued, "Thus far all is quiet, and not a shot that I know of since we began the march." Indeed, there were barely any Confederates left to engage. Much of Lee's army was already on the Rapidan.[38]

Lee was unaware of Halleck's August 3 order to evacuate the Peninsula for days. On August 7, Lee, wary of an advance by McClellan, thought it "too hazardous" to divert forces from Richmond to Jackson. He did, however, suggest that recent moves by McClellan were likely an effort to divert attention from a thrust at his center by Burnside from the direction of Fredericksburg. Halleck planned no such move. In any event, Lee did not yet suspect McClellan's impending withdrawal. On August 8, in a second letter to Jackson in which he conditionally blessed Jackson's advance toward Culpeper, Lee betrayed no knowledge regarding what was afoot on the Peninsula.[39]

This began to change on August 13, when Lee directed Maj. Gen. Daniel Harvey Hill to send his "most reliable and intelligent men" down the right bank of the James River to judge the correctness of a deserter's claim that a portion of McClellan's force was embarking. This appears to be Lee's first indication of McClellan's retrograde movement. Lee had received reports a few days after Cedar Mountain that Burnside's corps had shifted west, away from strategic coordination with McClellan. Burnside had constituted a troubling threat to the soft center between Jackson's force near Gordonsville and Lee's on the east side of Richmond. His movement west shifted the strategic center of gravity toward Pope.[40]

As early as August 9, General Longstreet's assistant adjutant general, Maj. Moxley Sorrel, issued orders for a westward movement. With a hint at the type of warfare that Lee intended upon reaching Orange County, Sorrel's orders directed the men to pile entrenching tools in camp before boarding the trains. Longstreet followed on August 12, taking command of the entire force in Orange County. On August 13, learning that Burnside's command was marching toward Pope, Lee ordered Brig. Gen. John Bell Hood's two brigades to join Longstreet from their post fronting Fredericksburg. In reality, this Federal movement involved only Jesse

38 OR 11, pt. 1, 89, 91.

39 OR 12, pt. 3, 925-926.

40 OR 11, pt. 3, 673-675; OR 12, pt. 2, 551; Harsh, *Confederate Tide Rising*, 115-124.

Reno's division of Burnside's command. In an August 14 letter to Secretary of War George Randolph, Lee expressed confidence that McClellan had withdrawn to reinforce Pope's army. His official report cogently summarized the strategic situation: "It seemed active operations on the James were no longer contemplated, and the most effectual way to relieve Richmond from any danger of attack from that quarter would be to reenforce General Jackson and advance upon General Pope." Lee ordered an additional division westward on August 14 and headed west himself on the 15th.[41]

Lee needed to cross the Rapidan and engage the Army of Virginia before McClellan's army joined it. While Lee worked to ascertain the Army of the Potomac's movements on August 13, Jackson's chief engineer, Capt. James Boswell, climbed Clark Mountain, three miles east of the Rapidan railroad bridge. Boswell reported Pope's dispositions, and Jackson told him to return on August 14 to determine the best way around the Northerners' flank. Boswell proposed moving the army east, through Orange, to cross the Rapidan at Somerville Ford. It would then advance through Stevensburg and Brandy Station, cross the Rappahannock at Beverly Ford, and march to Warrenton. Though Longstreet preferred a move around Pope's right, Lee favored turning Pope's left to get between Pope and McClellan. The army headed for Somerville Ford on August 16, and Lee expected to cross the river on the 18th. Longstreet would cross at Raccoon Ford, Jackson at Somerville Ford, and Stuart at Mitchell's Ford. The problem with this plan was that, with Pope's left posted as far east as Raccoon Ford, both Longstreet and Jackson would have run into Federal infantry when crossing the river. This was not the campaign of maneuver that Lee had extolled to Jackson on August 7.[42]

This problem proved ephemeral. Delays shifted Lee's planned advance from August 18 to 20. After deciding to delay, Lee and Longstreet rode up Clark's Mountain on the 18th to view Federal positions. They saw Union camps from the Rapidan to Culpeper rapidly transform from calm repose to bustling activity. The frustrated Southern commanders watched their adversaries' wagons roll toward the Rappahannock and out of immediate reach.[43]

41 OR 51, pt. 2, 604-606; OR 11, pt. 3, 674-675, 677; OR 12, pt. 2, 551-552.

42 OR 12, pt. 2, 552, 648-649; OR 11, pt. 3, 676; OR 12, pt. 3, 926; Harsh, Confederate Tide Rising, 125-126.

43 OR 12, pt. 2, 552; James Longstreet, From Manassas to Appomattox: Memoirs of the Civil War in America (Philadelphia: 1896), 161-162.

Chapter 6

"How well do I remember those fearful days, days of gloom and sadness, days of hardship and suffering, and days of hunger and almost of nakedness."[1]

— Lewis King, 27th Indiana

Pope's Campaign from the Rapidan to the Potomac without Regard for Supply Lines

August 18 to September 3, 1862

As first light broke over the eastern horizon on August 18, "Jeb" Stuart slept on a front porch in Verdiersville, a little hamlet situated along the Plank Road, south of Raccoon Ford. Rising to the sound of approaching horses, Stuart walked bareheaded to the fence at the front of the yard, expecting to see Brig. Gen. Fitz Lee's cavalry, which was late in joining him. Shots rang out, disabusing the flamboyant cavalier of any preconceived notions. After a close pursuit, Stuart and most of his companions narrowly escaped. But he lost the hat he had won from Brig. Gen. Samuel Crawford days earlier. More consequentially, the Federals also captured Stuart's adjutant general, Maj. Norman Fitzhugh, who had ridden overnight searching for Lee's cavalry. He would prove a useful haul.[2]

As Pope gradually moved nearer the Rapidan between August 12 and 18, he continued to receive reports that Confederate reinforcements were arriving from the east. During that same period, general-in-chief Henry Halleck cautioned Pope against overexposing himself far beyond the Rappahannock until his own

---

1 Lewis King, Manuscript, Lewis King Papers, 39, ISL.

2 *OR* 12, pt. 2, 726.

reinforcements showed up. He urged Pope to maintain contact with Fredericksburg, from which McClellan's men would march. On the 16th, Halleck announced to Pope that "it would be far better if you were in rear of the Rappahannock." On the morning of the 17th, one day before Federal cavalry rousted Stuart from his porch, Pope telegraphed Halleck that, "Our position [on the Rapidan] is strong, and it will be very difficult to drive us from it."[3]

Pope dispatched John Buford's cavalry across the Rapidan on August 17 to watch for indications of a turning movement against the Federal left from Louisa or Hanover Junction. Though Pope apparently had anticipated Lee's intentions, he expected the thrust to occur farther east, through Germanna Ford and Ely's Ford. When Buford's men captured Major Fitzhugh of Stuart's staff, he carried a map from Lee for Stuart that depicted roads and farmhouse names at every crossroad between Gordonsville and Hagerstown, Maryland. Buford, with his valuable bird in hand, wasted little time. Riding weary horses and expecting they had kicked a hornet's nest that would precipitate a harried withdrawal, Buford's men beat a quick retreat cross country to Germanna Mills.[4]

Fitzhugh's papers satisfied Pope that the majority of Lee's army was arrayed against him. Lee's strategic intention was apparent from the detailed portion of Fitzhugh's map, and Pope decided he was sufficiently exposed to require a withdrawal behind the Rappahannock to ensure contact with his reinforcements. That same day, Halleck notified Pope that indications from around Richmond suggested that reinforcements were heading to Jackson in order to attack Pope before McClellan arrived. These developments elicited the move to the Rappahannock that left Lee and Longstreet atop Clark Mountain watching their quarry hasten out of reach. Pope notified Halleck of his intent to withdraw around midday.[5]

At 3:30 p.m. on August 18, Colonel John S. Clark sent a dispatch to Banks from the Rapidan. Based on "a number of circumstances," Clark assessed that Jackson was about to cross Raccoon Ford "in force" to isolate Pope's army from Washington and the reinforcements arriving near Fredericksburg. Clark advised

3 OR 12, pt. 2, 28-29, and pt. 3, 576, 589.

4 OR 12, pt. 3, 589; Washington Roebling to John Roebling, August 24, 1862, Roebling Family Papers, RU.

5 OR 12, pt. 2, 726; OR 12, pt. 3, 591; Smith Papers, 90, OHC.

Banks that "the movement is practicable—and if successful—fatal." Fortunately for Pope, he had already come to the same conclusion.[6]

Pope's midday orders directed his army rearward in three columns, each preceded by its wagon trains. Reno's command would move through Stevensburg and cross at Kelly's Ford. McDowell would follow Banks's corps through Culpeper and cross at the railroad bridge. Sigel was to head through Jeffersonton and cross at Fauquier White Sulphur Springs, where the 60th New York was convalescing. After reaching the left bank, Sigel's men were to turn east until they linked with McDowell's right. The cavalry would cover the retreat. Pope's chief of staff, Col. George Ruggles, directed Reno to keep Buford at Raccoon Ford until the "gray dawn begins to appear" on August 19.[7]

*　　*　　*

On August 18, as Pope moved north, Quartermaster General Montgomery Meigs wrote to General Halleck. He made two points that portended future woes. Pope's cavalry horses were broken down from overuse, and Meigs pointed out that the units spent too much time riding faster than a walk when it was not necessary. Additionally, Pope had already expected much of his cavalry, pulling it from point to point and spurring it to continuous activity. This continued over the next two weeks. His cavalry degraded accordingly.[8]

Meigs's second concern, which soon involved the whole army, centered on Pope's wagons. Meigs did not like the size of regimental trains, which required protection. He quoted Sigel's quartermaster: "Regiments average 550 to 600 men; brigades, four regiments, one battery, and one to three companies of cavalry. Each regiment has 15 wagons, drawn by four or six mules. Each brigade has a supply train in addition of 40 wagons, making an average of about 23 wagons to a regiment of 600 men. With this, I understand, they carry ten days' provisions. . . . Napoleon

---

6 Clark to Banks, August 18, 1862, Banks Papers, LC.

7 OR 12, pt. 2, 29, and pt. 3, 592. Reno's orders were to cross at Barnett's Ford. There was a "Barnett's Ford" on the Rapidan but not on the Rappahannock. Pope presumably meant Kelly's Ford. Going by way of Stevensburg as ordered, Reno would have found Kelly's Ford the most direct crossing. Pope's aide, T. C. H. Smith, interchanged the two names in a single sentence of his memoir. John J. Hennessy, *Return to Bull Run: The Campaign and Battle of Second Manassas* (New York, 1993), 483.

8 OR 12, pt. 3, 596.

asserted that 500 wagons were enough for 40,000 men. We are using at the rate of three times this number. . . . If the army is to move with efficiency, rigorous measures must reduce this luxury of transportation." It is unclear whether Meigs's message to Halleck influenced Pope's decision to remove the Army of Virginia's wagons from the front. That decision would come back to haunt Pope.[9]

*   *   *

Pope's marching orders reached Brig. Gen. Alpheus Williams, temporarily commanding Banks's corps, about 2:00 p.m. on August 18. He got the corps's trains out of town quickly. Before the trains left, the infantrymen deposited their knapsacks into the wagons. In the 10th Maine and 3rd Wisconsin, men also packed tents and blankets in the wagons. No member of Banks's corps would see whatever he had put in a wagon on the 18th until early September. With Banks's wagons gone, McDowell's and Sigel's trains plodded on overnight, creating a bottleneck in and around Culpeper. As the infantry waited, the citizens' exuberance convinced Lt. Col. Eugene Powell that the Rebels would soon be after them. General Williams's orders were to follow the trains starting at 1:00 a.m. Some units executed a roughly two-mile march under a clear, moonlit night, only to halt behind the traffic jam and remained "under arms" until morning. The men spent the night awake, listening to teamsters' profanities toward their mules.[10]

Dissatisfied with the state of affairs, Pope arrived in Culpeper at 9:00 that night. He sent staff officers to clear the two blocked roads. Pope, McDowell, and Banks reportedly worked the same task in person, though Banks's role seems questionable, given his convalescence. Their efforts avoided the extremity of abandoning or destroying wagon trains in order to extract the army. Banks's wagons crossed the river early on August 19, about the time the last trains left Culpeper, 12 miles away.[11]

While General Williams waited, he discovered a companion for the coming day. Major Fitzhugh of Stuart's staff, whose capture precipitated this movement, arrived in Culpeper early on the 19th. He and Williams took coffee before riding to the Rappahannock together. The march northeast behind the wagons was slow.

9 OR 12, pt. 3, 597.

10 OR 12, pt. 3, 598; Quaife, *From the Cannon's Mouth*, 105; Gould, *10th Maine*, 198-199: Hinkley Diary, August 18-19, 1862, WHS; Eugene Powell, Memoir, chap. 5, OHC.

11 Smith Papers, 91, OHC; James Guinn to "Dear Folks at Home," September 3, 1862, HL.

John Gould of the 10th Maine remembered "halting frequently to see the mule-menagerie exhibit." Though the heat was not oppressive, water was scarce. The path into the Rappahannock region was, according to Charles Boyce of the 28th New York:

> Through a barren and almost uninhabited country . . . war had ransacked and pillaged these homes; war had laid waste their fields, war had brought a weight of misery and woe upon the land, requiring the length of years to remove. . . . As we approached the Rapahannock river the devastation was more complete desolation seemed to reign supreme. The land produced nothing but weeds; timber had all been cut off and not a fence or wall could be seen. Several fortifications had been built along the river showing where the timber had gone to. Three or four forts or breastworks were visible from one point, abandoned and looking as destitute as the dwellings in the vicinity.[12]

This was the environment through which the corps had briefly passed in early July en route to Little Washington, and in which it would have to subsist for the next two weeks with little help from its own supply chain. That night, the 28th New York found it difficult to prepare food; the only fuel for fire was dry weeds that required a great deal of effort to collect. The only water the men could find for coffee came from the river, and it was so muddy that horses and mules coming off the bridge would barely drink it. This was the troops' first experience in the war in which basic necessities were scarce. Some of them grumbled, but Sergeant Hicks wrote that, within a week, they would think themselves fortunate to return to those spartan conditions. The men in Robinson's battery were told not to drink from the river, so they headed for the rear and gathered water from a marshy puddle in the dark. This water source was short-lived. The next morning some of the Federals returned and discovered a partially decomposed hog on the other side of the pool.[13]

A 28th Pennsylvanian guarding the bridge, John P. Nicholson, noted the "continuous stream of wagons" crossing throughout the day. At 5:00 p.m., he saw Banks and his staff cross the river and noted the corps's arrival an hour later, though by then it was probably his own division that he recognized, in the rear of the corps. The 60th New York's historian reported Banks's arrival well up the river at White Sulphur Springs before dawn on August 19. To cross later in the day at Rappahannock Station, Banks would have had to recross to the south bank at the

---

12 Quaife, *From the Cannon's Mouth*, 105; Gould, *10th Maine*, 199; Hinkley Diary, August 19, 1862, WHS; Boyce, "28th Regiment," 137.

13 Hicks Diary, 16, LC; *4th Maine*, 24.

springs before reaching the railroad crossing. This peripatetic movement could have happened, but it would have been impressive for someone who was then recovering from a hip injury. In any event, Banks was not exercising command of the corps, and he sought medical treatment at a farmhouse behind the lines on August 20 for his badly swollen and discolored wound.[14]

Banks's corps reached the Rappahannock at 2:00 p.m. on August 19, when Gordon's brigade crossed. Greene's division got across after sunset. Once over the river, the majority of Banks's corps turned right, forming a line about a half mile south of the railroad. The 10th Maine and the 28th New York sheltered in a field of weeds. The 28th's Corporal Gillam fixed their location as within a quarter mile of the bridge and within sight of a number of batteries. The 5th Connecticut bivouacked farther back in the woods. General Williams wrote that since the regiment's tents were gone, the men found that "their best shelter was the woods." The 3rd Wisconsin, and presumably the 2nd Massachusetts, bivouacked a half mile from the river. The 27th Indiana continued northeast along the railroad to the north side of Bealeton and guarded the wagon train. It remained there until noon on August 20, when it returned to the corps.[15]

In the 2nd Division, now under Brig. Gen. George Greene, the detachment of the 28th Pennsylvania rejoined the regiment as it crossed the river at about 6:00 p.m. That night, while crossing a swamp, a portion of the regiment became separated and had to march an extra three miles before reuniting. When it halted for the night, it was on the corps's extreme left. The Purnell Legion remained scattered along the railroad as far as Catlett's Station, 12 miles northeast of Rappahannock Station. The 60th New York continued to convalesce at White Sulphur Springs, about 10 miles northwest of Rappahannock Station. Its quiet stay was interrupted on August 17, when word of an impending Confederate guerilla attack caused nurses and those who could bear arms to turn out to repel the attack. It never came.[16]

Pope's army lined the north bank of the river, extending southeast from just above Rappahannock Station. By morning on August 20, McDowell's corps

14 Nicholson, "Diary in the War," August 19, 1862, HL; Eddy, *Sixtieth New York*, 159; Welsh, *Medical Histories*, 14.

15 Hinkley Diary, August 19, 1862, WHS; Foering Diary, August 19, 1862, HSP; Quaife, *From the Cannon's Mouth*, 105, Gould, *10th Maine*, 199; Gillam to Wife, September 8, 1862, LC; Marvin, *Fifth Connecticut*, 229; Brown, *Twenty-Seventh Indiana*, 216.

16 Tyndale, *Generals' Reports*, 5-6; Guinn to "Dear Folks at Home," September 3, 1862, HL; Eddy, *Sixtieth New York*, 159.

"Fauquier Sulphur Springs, Virginia. Officers of the 60th New York Volunteers," August 1862, Timothy O'Sullivan. Colonel Goodrich is standing in the center. Major James stands on his left. *Library of Congress*

covered the vicinity of the railroad bridge at Rappahannock Station. One regiment of Hartsuff's brigade, plus one battery, advanced to the south side of the river and occupied two hills and a fortification protecting the southern end of the bridge. When Williams sent a portion of the 28th Pennsylvania to secure the bridge on August 12, the construction corps had built this blockhouse and another like it on the north bank. The hills were 150 and 600 yards from the river, north of the railroad. Sigel moved down the left bank, approaching McDowell's right. His rear brigade under Robert Milroy, however, was still only four miles beyond Culpeper. Milroy's men crossed the river at Sulphur Springs at 5:00 p.m. on August 20. Banks's corps stood in reserve, slightly left of McDowell. Reno was left of Banks, downriver at Kelly's Ford. Major General John Reynolds's division, the first troops to arrive from the Peninsula, marched toward Reno's position from Fredericksburg. Bayard's cavalry stood beyond Hartsuff's infantry, centered on Brandy Station. When Lieutenant Colonel Strother rode to Rappahannock Station early on August 20, he was impressed by the "exciting" scene. He found artillery on all the heights with infantry massed in support. Pope and McDowell sat on a hill looking south. They would have seen dust clouds roiling in the distance. At noon, firing erupted south of the river.[17]

*   *   *

At dawn on August 20, the Army of Northern Virginia marched over the Rapidan. Jackson's Corps crossed at Somerville Ford with A. P. Hill in the lead. Once again, the early morning march did not meet Jackson's demands. Aggravated that most of his troops were not prepared, he pushed forward the only brigade ready to march shortly after 3:00 a.m. It bivouacked that night two miles beyond Stevensburg on the road to Brandy Station. James Longstreet's corps crossed Raccoon Ford and followed Fitzhugh Lee's cavalry to Kelly's Ford. After the Rebel horsemen skirmished with the Union rearguard, Longstreet bivouacked near the ford. The remainder of Stuart's cavalry, including the newly incorporated brigade under Beverly Robertson, pressed ahead of Jackson.[18]

That morning, Brig. Gen. George Bayard sent scouting parties along each of the roads from Brandy Station. A squadron of the 1st Maine Cavalry discovered Robertson's horsemen, less the 2nd Virginia and the brigade artillery, which Stuart had left along the upper Rapidan with instructions to keep pace with Jackson's left. Robertson and Stuart advanced with the 6th, 7th, and 12th Virginia Cavalry and the 17th Virginia Cavalry Battalion along the road from Raccoon Ford south of Stevensburg. The Mainers fell back through Stevensburg to the edge of a large wood, where Col. Judson Kilpatrick and the 5th New York Cavalry delayed Robertson long enough for all of Bayard's detachments to withdraw through Brandy Station toward the railroad bridge. Kilpatrick's dismounted line held the Confederates at a distance using carbines, while several mounted detachments operated near the flanks of the advancing Rebel line. One audacious half squadron was nearly cut off by Robertson's men. His task accomplished, Kilpatrick fell back, northeast of Brandy Station.[19]

17 OR 12, pt. 2, 330; Pope, order to Williams, August 12, 1862, Banks Papers, LC; Smith Papers, 94, OHC; Eby, *Virginia Yankee*, 84; Hicks Diary, 16, LC; Gould, *10th Maine*, 199.

18 OR 12, pt. 2, 552, 649; McDonald, *Make Me a Map*, 69.

19 OR 12, pt. 2, 89, 726; Smith Papers, 92-93, OHC; McDonald, *Laurel Brigade*, 81; Heros von Borcke, *Memoirs of the Confederate War for Independence* (Philadelphia, 1867), 75-76.

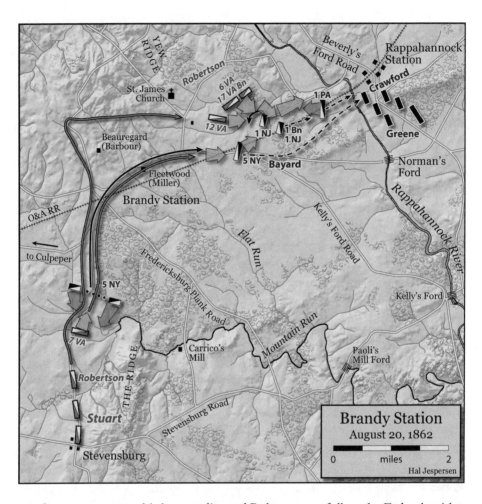

Stuart, to preserve his horses, directed Robertson to follow the Federals with a single regiment, while the rest trailed at a trot. Colonel Grumble Jones's 7th Virginia Cavalry was in the van, and Robertson took the 6th and 12th Virginia Cavalry, and 17th Virginia Cavalry Battalion to the left "to sweep across the open country toward "Barboursville," toward Bayard's right. As a result, for a time the 7th was the only unit engaged between the two railroad stations. East of Brandy Station, an open plain two to three miles long and interspersed with small wooded patches, stretched before Jones's regiment. Jones advanced along the road because abundant ditches crisscrossed the plain. The field was within sight of Federal infantrymen and batteries beyond the river.[20]

20 OR 12, pt. 2, 89, 726-727; Von Borcke, *Memoirs*, 76; McDonald, *Laurel Brigade*, 81-82.

Ordered to avoid a general engagement, Bayard did not commit his entire force. He deployed Kilpatrick's New Yorkers beyond the woods that partitioned the plain from the river. This was on a ridge about midway between Brandy Station and Rappahannock Station. Colonel Joseph Karge and the 1st New Jersey Cavalry were 600 yards behind and to the right of the New Yorkers with orders to support Kilpatrick, if necessary. Colonel Owen Jones's 1st Pennsylvania Cavalry stood behind the woods in reserve. Bayard's two remaining regiments, the 1st Maine and 1st Rhode Island, were farther back. Given his orders, he did not intend to employ them.[21]

Shortly after the 7th Virginia Cavalry appeared in front of Kilpatrick, the Virginians formed and charged with clamorous shouts. Kilpatrick's men were maneuvering and facing away from the Virginians as the charge began. The New Yorkers broke rearward, but Kilpatrick and a member of Bayard's staff soon reorganized them. Colonel Karge attempted to change the 1st New Jersey's front with a half wheel to his left in order to meet the 7th Virginia as it pursued the 5th New York past his left. This move was sluggishly executed. Meanwhile, the rest of the Confederate cavalry descended on Karge's front and right.[22]

Beverly Robertson had taken the wrong road and headed too far to the left. When he arrived, the 12th Virginia charged the Federal center in columns of four while the 6th Virginia and 17th Virginia Battalion charged Bayard's flank, held by the 1st New Jersey. Karge's skirmishers stalled the Confederate attacks in front. Before Karge could complete the 1st's left wheel toward the 7th Virginia, Confederate attacks threatened both of his flanks. Karge emptied his pistol and ordered a charge. Unfortunately, his men either did not hear the order or had seen enough. He dashed toward the 7th Virginia with a few staffers behind him and rode into the Virginians, who were scattered from charging Kilpatrick's New Yorkers. He extricated himself after receiving a serious leg wound. The Garden Staters broke and retreated through the woods along the railroad. Bayard ordered Capt. Virgil Broderick, commanding the 1st New Jersey's reserve battalion, to form at the edge of the tree line and use carbines. This briefly held off the Virginians, who soon moved around the woods. Seeing this, Bayard rode through the trees and ordered Maj. R. J. Falls's Pennsylvanians to charge the Southerners. This blunted the Confederate advance, and Bayard's men withdrew, fording the Rappahannock near

21 OR 12, pt. 2, 89-90; 727.

22 OR 12, pt. 2, 90; Henry R. Pyne, *The History of the First New Jersey Cavalry* (Trenton, NJ, 1871), 96.

the bridge. Before leaving, bands of Union horsemen turned and charged back into the woods only to return and cross the river.[23]

As cavalry battled across the river, the long roll brought Federal infantry to arms. Crawford's brigade deployed behind a stone wall less than half a mile from the bridge. The soldiers waited an hour, listening to shouts and crackling pistol and carbine shots. Pope appeared with his staff and inquired which regiment stood before him. Learning that it was the 1st Brigade, 1st Division, of Banks's corps, Pope responded, "What business have you here in front? Who ordered you here?" No one answered, though Crawford, then in command of the division, had led the brigade there. Pope, who considered Banks's corps unfit for active operations, ordered the brigade back, saying it should not be called upon unless "absolutely necessary." It withdrew into the woods for the night. A company from each regiment picketed downriver.[24]

*   *   *

Pope sought to preserve contact with reinforcements from Fredericksburg. This hindered his options, especially after Lee started edging upriver on August 21. To address this difficulty, Pope entertained several courses of action. Writing to Halleck at 8:30 a.m., he suggested keeping most of his force massed behind Marsh Run, which entered the Rappahannock southeast of Kelly's Ford. Advanced elements of his left and center would occupy both Kelly's Ford and the railroad bridge, with his right refused along the railroad to Bealeton Station. Pope demonstrated a sound appreciation for what would develop in his front in two days' time. Suggesting that Lee might cross at Sulphur Springs and advance on

23 OR 12, pt. 2, 90, 727; Pyne, *First New Jersey*, 96-97; William P. Lloyd, *History of the First Regiment Pennsylvania Reserve Cavalry* (Philadelphia, 1864), 29; George H. Gordon, *History of the Campaign of the Army of Virginia Under John Pope, Brigadier-General U. S. A; late Major-General U. S. Volunteers; from Cedar Mountain to Alexandria, 1862* (Boston, 1880), 13. Stuart claimed in his official report that the Federals fled thanks to the "incentives and aspirations" of the Confederate cavalrymen before the "clash of their sabers could make havoc in his ranks." Heros von Borcke, however, gave a contradictory account. Von Borcke described multiple mêlées, one of which involved his nearly separating a Northern horseman's head from his body with a saber blow as the man fired at him (Von Borcke, *Memoirs*, 78). At least one of these men embellished his story. Participant accounts conflict on how this action ended; both sides claimed they scattered their opponents. Confederate reports, though self-aggrandizing, were likely more accurate. General Gordon wrote that Bayard's withdrawal was made "in confusion." Washington Roebling wrote that the Union cavalry had been "whipped" (W. Roebling to J. Roebling, August 24, 1862, RU).

24 Hicks Diary, 17, LC; Hinkley Diary, August 20, 1862, WHS.

Warrenton, Pope announced his intention to cross the river and fall on Lee's exposed right and rear.[25]

Late on August 20, Pope sent the 3rd Maryland upriver to a spot of high ground near a cornfield overlooking Beverly Ford to screen the river upstream from the railroad bridge. Brigadier General Zealous Tower's brigade and Capt. James Hall's 2nd Battery, Maine Light Artillery, both from the III Corps, were also positioned in the direction of the ford that night. Two miles upriver from the railroad bridge, Beverly Ford did not concern Pope on the 20th. His plan and this detachment's strategic purpose would change overnight.[26]

By the morning of August 21, Pope decided to defend the Rappahannock rather than refuse his right. The river was a strong defensive line, but his lines became thinly stretched. He considered the railroad bridge and Kelly's Ford the best crossing points, and he needed to defend them in order to preserve the option of crossing himself and maintaining contact with Fredericksburg, while covering any move upriver by Lee. Exacerbating Pope's apprehensions about these conflicting requirements, Halleck regularly telegraphed his concerns. That day, as the general-in-chief cautioned Pope to position scouts well to his right, reports of Lee's movements began arriving at Pope's headquarters. McDowell's corps observed dust rising from behind woodlots and ridges on the south bank that morning. McDowell passed this information to Pope after noon. Additionally, Colonel John Clark of Banks's staff went to Pope's headquarters on August 21 and reported Confederates shifting upriver. Pope felt prepared. At 7:30 a.m., in the same message in which he declared to Halleck that he intended to maintain his line on the Rappahannock, Pope stated, "I have masked the fords above and below me with infantry, cavalry, and artillery, and have no concern about any attack in the front." Now that Pope had decided to defend the river, the Marylanders sent to Beverly Ford needed to prevent a crossing, whether they knew it or not. They proved unequal to that task.[27]

---

25 *OR* 12, pt. 2, 56.

26 *OR* 12, pt. 2, 330, 385; [Montpelier] *Vermont Watchman and State Journal*, August 29, 1862; Marks Diary, August 20, 1862, FNMP. According to this newspaper account, the 88th Pennsylvania and Hall's battery were at the ford that night. Ricketts's report, which placed Tower's brigade, containing the 88th, and Hall's rifles upriver on the night of August 20-21, did not mention any fighting at the ford on August 21. Marks's account described the 3rd Maryland as supporting a four-gun Parrott battery on August 21. It is not certain whether this was Hall's battery.

27 *OR* 12, pt. 2, 56, 331, and pt. 3, 611; Eby, *Virginia Yankee*, 85.

As Pope's telegraphed messages conveyed confidence to Henry Halleck, the 3rd Marylanders at Beverly Ford collected breakfast from the nearby cornfield. It was the first corn of the year for Abraham Marks. A member of his company killed a pig, which was cooked with corn shaved off the cob in an old pot discovered in the field. Shortly after breakfast, the 3rd's officers called the men forward toward a battery. Cavalry arrived across the ford, initiating Lee's first move to feel for Pope's right. Taliaferro's division soon emerged from the woods a quarter mile from the ford. Taliaferro deployed four batteries: Brockenbrough's, Wooding's, Poague's, and Carpenter's. The first unlimbered on a hill south of where the Hazel River empties into the Rappahannock. A Confederate scouting party on the south bank spied Federals gathered around a card game near the battery. Marks sat nearby, reading a letter. The indolent morning ended abruptly.[28]

Within minutes, Rebel artillery opened fire, sending the Marylanders to the ground. Marks wrote that these shots, which were from a single two-gun section, "came thick and fast." An engineering officer attached to McDowell's command wrote that the Confederates fired so accurately that they silenced the six-gun Union battery in 15 minutes. A few Marylanders were killed and wounded, and the rest abandoned their prone positions. Marks could not tell which way to go. The regiment had bolted in every direction. He entered a cornfield to the left, then an open field, before reaching a woodlot, which provided little help. At about 9:00 a.m., a man yelled, "[H]alt you Yankee S— B— or I'll shoot you." Marks looked up and found that he was confronted by three members of the 5th Virginia Cavalry.[29]

In order to avoid hard fighting, Lee sought a crossing that was not heavily defended. Toward this end, Col. Thomas Rosser took two guns over Beverly Ford, while General Robertson crossed Freeman's Ford and descended the north bank toward Rosser. When word of these movements reached Pope, McDowell and Sigel hurried forward brigades under Brig. Gens. Marsena Patrick and John Milroy, respectively. Milroy's brigade had just reached Rappahannock Station at noon. Two hours later, Milroy moved toward the ford, west of Patrick and the rest of Brig. Gen. Rufus King's division. After marching half a mile, Sigel ordered Milroy to split his brigade. Two regiments accompanied their brigadier across fields while Sigel led the other two along the road to the ford. Milroy's two regiments flushed a

28 OR 12, pt. 2, 649, 654; Marks Diary, August 20, 1862, FNMP; Blackford, *Letters*, 118-119.

29 OR 12, pt. 2, 730; Marks Diary, August 20, 1862, FNMP; W. Roebling to J. Roebling, August 24, 1862, RU. Roebling wrote that he was at Freeman's Ford, but elements of his account, Marks's account, and Stuarts's description of Rosser's action, which took place at Beverly Ford, match.

squad of Confederate horsemen from the woods in their front. Once Milroy reached the forest, which was 400 yards deep, he deployed sharpshooters and skirmishers and gave them a five-minute head start before following. After crossing the woods, Milroy's regiments joined the right of the 21st New York, which General Patrick had thrown forward on his right in skirmish formation. Sigel brought Milroy's other two regiments and his battery up on the right, along the road. Farther to the left, Patrick's three other regiments deployed behind a battery. Brigadier General John Gibbon's brigade, also from King's division of McDowell's corps, supported him. Patrick claimed that McDowell, Pope, and King each "took a hand in" the operation, which "fizzled." At 5:00 p.m., the three generals turned the effort over to Patrick, who advanced batteries and infantry. On the right, Milroy maintained his position for two hours. Rosser's Virginian's did not move against him.[30]

Around that time, Robertson reported a "heavy force" moving toward the ford. With no Confederate infantry crossing the river and with growing resistance in his front, Stuart recalled Rosser. Both cavalry detachments returned to the south bank. Taliaferro deployed sharpshooters from his former brigade, and they engaged Federal troops until late afternoon, when his four division batteries commenced a lively artillery duel with the guns Patrick had deployed. According to Patrick, the Confederate fire was so well directed that "the wonder is we weren't destroyed." This fight continued until dark. Taliaferro's division remained at Beverly Ford, while Ewell's division bivouacked at St. James Church, about two and a half miles northwest of Brandy Station.[31]

Colonel Rosser collected approximately 70 prisoners and 50 stacked rifles during the day's action. Abraham Marks saw Marylanders captured with rifles still on their shoulders. Once across the Rappahannock, the prisoners moved south, through Stevensburg. The Confederates determined that one of them, William Johnson, was a deserter and hanged him. The unfortunate column received its first food when it reached Rapidan Station. The captives were told they had to pay $15 for their meals, but got away with giving the Rebels only $9.50.[32]

Jackson's infantry never followed Rosser because Lee abandoned the effort after establishing the foothold. Either Robertson's report of advancing Federals or

30 OR 12, pt. 2, 730, 655, 316; David S. Sparks, ed., *Inside Lincoln's Army: The Diary of Marsena Rudolph Patrick, Provost Marshal General, Army of the Potomac* (New York, 1964), 126.

31 OR 12, pt. 2, 642, 655, 704, 730.

32 Marks Diary, August 22, 1862, FNMP.

the Union presence at the ford likely informed this decision. Since Federals commanded all the fords at which his army rested, Lee determined, "To seek a more favorable place to cross higher up the river, and thus gain the enemy's right." Before the day ended, he directed Longstreet to move toward Rappahannock Station. This was the first of many upriver shuffles. As replacements from Longstreet's Corps arrived from the right, Jackson's relieved units moved left behind ridges and tree lines, preventing gaps in the line. Jackson's cartographer, Jed Hotchkiss, cogently described the Confederate program that commenced on the 21st. "Our troops are rapidly concentrating and we are engaging the enemy's attention, at every ford on the river, as we progress, so they cannot divine where we intend to attempt to cross. The cannonading from both sides was quite heavy."[33]

*   *   *

Pope still fixed his attention down the river. At 4:00 p.m. on August 21, he telegraphed Halleck that he would need to abandon the railroad and fight lower on the Rappahannock to maintain contact with Maj. Gen. Fitz John Porter. This view developed thanks to demonstrations from Longstreet near Kelly's Ford and a subsequent cavalry skirmish south of the river. An hour later Pope notified Reno that he had sent Banks's corps to within two miles of Kelly's Ford. From there, midway between the ford and the railroad bridge, it would support Reno or McDowell as needed.[34]

Much of Banks's corps spent August 21 idling. Its supply wagons left early that morning, and the 10th Mainers futilely scavenged for food. John Gould reported finding only "the leavings of other regiments." At noon, the 10th entered a woodlot and built pine bough huts. The 28th New York countermarched so much that it doubled its mileage downriver. The regiment was almost out of rations but found cows to slaughter. The men were not yet hungry enough to eat meat without salt or bread, and ate green corn instead. They had been without clean water since crossing the river and readily drank from "stagnant pools and muddy ditches," according to one New Yorker. They spent the night under arms.[35]

33 OR 12, pt. 2, 552; McDonald, *Make Me a Map of the Valley*, 70.

34 OR 12, pt. 2, 610-611.

35 OR 12, pt. 2, 325; Gould, *10th Maine*, 200; Hicks Diary, 16, LC.

In Greene's division, the 28th Pennsylvania also spent the day moving about with no apparent aim. The 3rd Delaware rejoined its depleted 3rd Brigade from garrison duty at Front Royal. Another detached regiment, the 60th New York, ended its convalescence on August 21. At 2:00 a.m., the regiment loaded 525 sick onto wagons and evacuated Sulphur Springs. The men of the 60th had not imagined such a quick return to service after enduring widespread illness, and were startled at the order to return to the corps. The 60th New York and the Purnell Legion rejoined Greene's 3rd Brigade, which got back to something like full strength over the next few days. At 8:00 p.m. on the 21st, the corps moved downriver per Pope's orders and bivouacked under pine trees near Norman's Ford in a heavy downpour. Skirmishing occurred along the Rappahannock throughout the night, and cavalry continually patrolled the lines.[36]

At 6:30 on the morning of August 22, as Gordon's brigade was enduring an artillery duel at Norman's Ford, Alpheus Williams, still commanding the corps, arrived with questions from Pope. Gordon was about to trip over his untiring recalcitrance. Two days earlier, Halleck had cautioned Pope that his staff was "decidedly leaky." His telegrams to Pope were appearing, nearly verbatim, in the papers. He encouraged Pope to "clean out" his headquarters. That same day, Pope barred his staff from sending outbound letters. On August 21, he had countered Halleck's charge, suggesting that he had control of both the telegraph and the distribution of Halleck's orders. He did, however, bemoan the "laxity about all official business" within the army, drawing particular attention to Banks's corps. "I observe in the newspapers official reports from the senior aide-de-camp of General Banks and at least one of his general officers about the battle of Cedar Mountain." Pope learned of the general officer, rumored to be Gordon, when a Northern newspaper arrived containing an account that was contrary in tone to the optimistic portrayals that had earned Jeb Stuart his hat. This aggravated Pope's primed sensitivity. Williams asked Gordon whether he was responsible for the leaks. Gordon replied that he had delivered an account to an Associated Press reporter. One of Pope's staff rode up and told Gordon to consider himself under arrest and to pass his command to the ranking officer, Col. Thomas Ruger.[37]

*   *   *

36 Foering Diary, August 21, 1862, HSP; *Danbury* [CT] *Times*, August 21, 1862; Eddy, *Sixtieth New York*, 159, 161; Quint, *2nd Massachusetts*, 121.

37 *OR* 12, pt. 3, 602, 608, 620; Eby, *Virginia Yankee*, 84; Gordon, *Army of Virginia*, 38-39.

Persuaded by persistent reports of Confederates passing by his right, Pope now sent Banks's corps back upriver. This movement occurred shortly after Gordon's arrest. As the corps prepared to move, messengers dispersed to recall the various pickets. The man sent from Crawford's brigade missed Company F of the 28th New York. Commanded by 2nd Lt. George M. Elliott, the company did not discover that the regiment had moved on for about an hour. Elliott marched his company to the woodlot where the regiment had bivouacked and allowed the men to prepare coffee and cook breakfast before continuing. As they finished their repast, a furious artillery barrage hit the woods, devastating the trees and churning the ground. Elliott and a few others headed away from the river at a run and at a right angle from the regiment's course. One of the New Yorkers had sufficient forethought to grab the coffee kettle. Unable to keep pace with the lieutenant, the man stopped running. Those that remained behind finished breakfast, periodically sprayed with sandy soil cast in the air by falling shells. They then continued upriver, catching up with their regiment after dark.[38]

Before making breakfast, the men of the 10th Maine completed the first leg of their march, arriving at the bough huts near Rappahannock Station. They disappointedly discovered that a shoddy-looking regiment occupied their huts. As his brigade passed Pope's headquarters above Rappahannock Station, orders directed Gordon to present himself to Pope for "explicit instructions." By that time, Gordon's arrest was terminated thanks to entreaties by Ruger and other brigade officers. When Gordon arrived at headquarters, Pope made no mention of the infraction or the arrest. Instead, he directed Gordon in what the latter described as a "bombastic tone" to "move with his brigade to Beverly ford," to position Cothran's battery there, to support the battery with the brigade, and to "hold that crossing till the last extremity." Given the previous day's Confederate lodgment, Pope might be forgiven his misapprehension and some melodrama regarding Lee's intentions at Beverly Ford. With this move, Banks's corps now stood with Sigel to its right and McDowell to its left.[39]

When he reached Beverly Ford at about 3:00 p.m., Gordon placed Cothran's Parrott guns on his left. They were concealed by the crest of the hill above the ford and commanded the open field and wood line across the river. To his right, Gordon deployed his infantry in the large woods where Abraham Marks had been captured the day before. He arranged the brigade, from right to left, as follows: 2nd

---

38 Hicks Diary, 17, LC.

39 Gould, *10th Maine*, 200; Gordon, *Army of Virginia*, 40.

Massachusetts, 3rd Wisconsin, and 27th Indiana. It rested from early afternoon until the next morning. At about 8:00 p.m., Second Lieutenant Hinkley "turned out" the 3rd Wisconsin's Companies D and H in the midst of a heavy storm that started at dusk. After some difficulty finding their destination under torrential rain and a blackening sky, Hinkley placed pickets at the ford. Before dark, Gordon's men observed a desperate struggle involving one of Sigel's brigades on its right near Freeman's Ford.[40]

* * *

Dissatisfied with developments on August 21, Lee continued sidling his army upriver, seeking a vacant ford. Shifting from Kelly's Ford, Longstreet maintained contact at the railroad bridge, while his lead brigades arrived at Beverly Ford. Thus relieved, Jackson's Corps, with Ewell's division leading, followed Stuart across the Hazel River, a Rappahannock tributary, at Welford's Ford. At Freeman's Ford, Stuart discovered artillery and Milroy's brigade of Sigel's corps, which he engaged using four guns of Pelham's horse artillery. A Confederate cavalry detachment had picketed the ford overnight. Stuart and Milroy arrived almost simultaneously. As Milroy reconnoitered with his cavalry in advance of his infantry, he drew Confederate artillery fire. He deployed a battery in response. The artillery fight continued until mid-afternoon, with Jackson's guns eventually relieving Stuart's.[41]

Given the inauspicious situation at Freeman's Ford, Stuart proposed a movement around Pope's right to disrupt his line of communication along the Orange and Alexandria Railroad. About mid-morning, while Ewell's infantry passed farther upriver behind the artillery duel, Stuart received a note from Lee approving the plan. By 10:00 a.m., Stuart departed with all of Robertson's and Fitzhugh Lee's brigades, less the 7th and 3rd Virginia. Ewell, meanwhile, continued westward through fields and woods so as to remain concealed. Ewell's command arrived at Sulphur Springs in the early afternoon, finding the place unguarded. Meanwhile, a gap formed between Jackson's rear brigade, under Brig. Gen. Isaac Trimble, and Longstreet's van, two brigades commanded by Brig. Gen. John Bell Hood.[42]

40 Gordon, *Army of Virginia*, 41; Hinkley Diary, August 22, 1862, WHS.

41 *OR* 12, pt. 2, 316, 552, 642, 649-650, 655, 730.

42 Ibid., 642, 650, 730, 704.

As Jackson's Corps moved toward Sulphur Springs at 10:00 a.m., Ewell directed Trimble's brigade to remain near Welford's Ford on the Hazel River to guard the passing wagon train's flank. It halted about a mile from the ford, near Welford's Mill. That afternoon Trimble learned that a small Union force had crossed the river. He maintained a defensive posture, guarding the trains, until Hood's brigades arrived. The Federals threatening Jackson's trains were a brigade under Brig. Gen. Henry Bohlen of Sigel's corps.[43]

*   *   *

The balance of Sigel's corps joined Milroy's brigade at Freeman's Ford on the morning of August 22. The artillery contest across the ford with Pelham's guns continued until 3:00 p.m. The lull precipitated probing across the river by elements of Sigel's command to ascertain, "The enemy's strength and the movements on the other side of the river, and to disturb those movements if possible." Milroy crossed the ford with 150 cavalrymen. After occupying a hill that had recently contained Confederate artillery with a company of sharpshooters, Milroy discovered and harassed the trains with his cavalry, skirmishing briefly. He soon returned to the left bank. Before doing so, he heard heavy firing downriver to his left. This commotion also drew the attention of Gordon's men, farther downriver at Beverly Ford.[44]

Sigel ordered Brig. Gen. Carl Schurz to send a regiment across the Rappahannock below the ford. Colonel Alexander Schimmelfennig led the 74th Pennsylvania across the river, wading through waist-high water. After climbing a sloping open field on the south side, it crossed a strip of woods at the top of the rise. Emerging from the woods, it ran into a Confederate wagon train, which Schimmelfennig harassed, capturing 11 pack mules and some infantry. He sent the prisoners rearward and ordered the rest of the brigade up. Brigadier General Henry Bohlen led the 8th Virginia (Union) and 61st Ohio to join Schimmelfennig.[45]

Around 4:00 p.m., Hood arrived with two brigades. Trimble had turned and sprung on the Federals. With skirmishers well in front, he made contact with Bohlen in a cornfield. Hood's Texas Brigade moved to the right of Trimble, while Col. Evander Law's brigade joined on Trimble's left. As Trimble advanced, he

---

43 Ibid., 642, 704, 719.

44 Ibid., 317.

45 Carl Schurz, *The Reminiscences of Carl Schurz*, 2 vols. (London, 1909), 2:356-357.

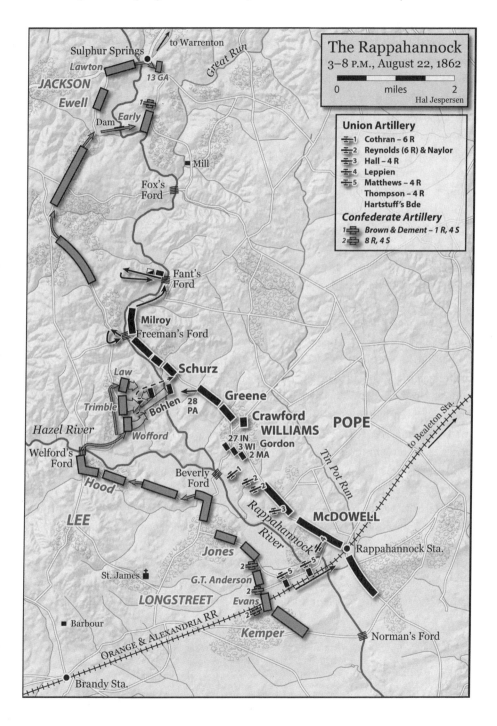

The Rappahannock
3–8 P.M., August 22, 1862

0   miles   2

Hal Jespersen

Union Artillery
1 Cothran – 6 R
2 Reynolds (6 R) & Naylor
3 Hall – 4 R
4 Leppien
5 Matthews – 4 R
   Thompson – 4 R
   Hartstuff's Bde

Confederate Artillery
1 Brown & Dement – 1 R, 4 S
2 8 R, 4 S

discovered that the terrain facilitated a concealed flanking movement. The 15th Alabama and 21st Georgia moved to hit Bohlen's flanks while Trimble led the 21st North Carolina against Bohlen's front. The Federals fell back to the belt of woods near the river. Attempting a stand, Schurz ordered a bayonet charge, which was accompanied by drums and cheering. After their charge was repulsed, Bohlen's troops left the woods and moved downhill toward the river "at a somewhat accelerated pace," according to Schurz. The Confederates lining the woods directed a heavy fire into the fleeing Northerners, killing Bohlen. In a scene reminiscent of the Ball's Bluff debacle on the Potomac in October 1861, the Federals splashed into the river. A member of the Texas Brigade wrote that they were, "Pouring a dreadful fire into their crowds of confused and broken lines, as they were huddling together to cross, many were shot in the back, and others drowned by the crushing crowd which pressed for the other shore." Dead and wounded Federals floated downstream.[46]

Although Gordon's brigade could see the nearby battle, it was in no position to assist. The 28th Pennsylvania was nearer the action and double-quicked toward Bohlen's crossing, but it arrived too late to take part in the action. Though heavy timber shrouded the 10th Mainers' view, they heard the musketry directly in their front, which placed Crawford's brigade to the right rear of Gordon's brigade. While rain fell on the river valley that evening, the Mainers marched to within a quarter mile of the Rappahannock. Gould, who was unclear of his course, recalled that the men "floundered" for an hour in the concealing darkness, "During which, rain water, profanity, thunder, hogs, lightning and mud were 'mixed.'" Pope's staffer T. C. H. Smith called Bohlen's crossing a disaster, and blamed Sigel. Smith wrote that the brigade had gathered all the intelligence to be gained by crossing the river well before it was attacked and should have been withdrawn or reinforced. He added, "As the affair was conducted, it indicates a want of clear instructions to the officer in command."[47]

Meanwhile, on the right of Sigel's line, a cavalry troop and an infantry regiment, accompanied by a section of mountain howitzers, crossed the Rappahannock at Fant's Ford. The detachment set fire to a stone house on the right bank to prevent

---

46 OR 12, pt. 2, 719, 605; Henry W. Thomas, *History of the Doles-Cook Brigade, Army of Northern Virginia, C. S. A.* (Atlanta, 1903), 351; Schurz, *Reminiscences*, 2:358; Nicholas A. Davis, *Campaign from Texas to Maryland* (Richmond, 1863), 73.

47 OR 12, pt. 2, 251; Bryant, *Third Wisconsin*, 100; Foering Diary, August 22, 1862, HSP; McLaughlin, *Memoir of Hector Tyndale*, 54; Gould, *10th Maine*, 201; Smith Papers, 102A-102B, OHC; Schurz, *Reminiscences*, 2:358.

its use by Confederates, then continued a mile beyond the river. It met Rebel infantry and cavalry and retired across the Rappahannock to the sound of Bohlen's fight downriver. As Sigel's men withdrew from the right bank and the guns went silent, a heavy downpour from the west drenched the living and the dead.[48]

*   *   *

Under blackening skies, Jackson and Ewell waited at Sulphur Springs. The 13th Georgia, part of Brig. Gen. Alexander R. Lawton's brigade and commanded by Col. Marcellus Douglass, crossed at the springs. One mile downriver, Early's brigade marched across on a decrepit dam. Brigadier General Harry Hay's brigade, under Col. Henry Forno, had orders to follow Early but did not, due to darkness and the dam's worsening condition.[49]

Early had orders to occupy the pine woods across the river and establish communications with Lawton's brigade at the springs. After entering the woods, Early found the Foxville Road, which ran from the springs toward Rappahannock Station. He anchored his left at this road, positioning it parallel with the river, and extended his right into a field just below the dam. He sent a major to find Lawton, but the officer stumbled into a party of Federal cavalry in the dark and was nearly captured. Early abandoned further attempts to establish communications for the night but set pickets beyond his front and flanks. To his front was a stream called Great Run. Captain Charles Blackford, who carried dispatches for Jackson that evening, noted how black the storm made that night. He managed to make his way thanks only to the effulgent, temporarily blinding streaks of lightning. The storm's intermittent light, however, did not immediately reveal the problem growing in Early's rear.[50]

The threat of rising water soon became apparent to everyone. Brown's and Dement's batteries crossed with the 13th Georgia. One of Dement's cannoneers wrote that "everyone thought we would be captured." The artillerymen were frustrated because the artillery major who had led them across the river made his escape on a log after the flood waters destroyed the dam. The Confederate detachment was isolated in a perilous situation, and the shooting of a Federal

---

48 OR 12, pt. 2, 276; Gordon, *Army of Virginia*, 30

49 OR 12, pt. 2, 705; Early, *Autobiographical Sketch*, 107.

50 OR 12, pt. 2, 650, 705; Early, *Autobiographical Sketch*, 107; Blackford, *Letters*, 122-123.

Brig. Gen. Jubal Early, CSA
Library of Congress

cavalryman within 50 yards of Dement's battery heightened their anxiety. The best that Early's men could do that night was to use the exceptionally dark night and rain to their best advantage and attempt to remain concealed in the woods.[51]

*   *   *

Twelve miles to the east, a Federal detachment waited out the storm under its tents. Five Purnell Legion companies, detached from Greene's brigade before Cedar Mountain for railroad duty, were at Catlett's Station. Nearby these Marylanders, a spattering of detachments from various Army of Virginia brigades camped in order to guard the wagon trains. In some instances, these guards consisted of the brigade's invalids.[52]

Jeb Stuart's force had moved west, passing through Jeffersonton before crossing the Rappahannock at Waterloo Bridge and Hart's Mill. That afternoon it reached Warrenton, where it was greeted by jubilant residents, and continued through Auburn to the north bank of Cedar Creek at Catlett's Station. The column arrived north of Catlett's after dark as a furious thunderstorm erupted. Stuart sent Capt. W. W. Blackford forward to scout the area. At a crossroads a few hundred yards from the camp, Blackford found a small guard, but no other pickets. He also observed a "vast assemblage of wagons and a city of tents, laid out in regular order." These were Pope's trains, which had withdrawn to Catlett's per his August 20 order. Banks's wagons had moved past Catlett's to Bull Run.[53]

---

51 *OR* 12, pt. 2, 705; Kelley, *Scharf Memoirs*, 36.

52 *National Tribune*, July 28, 1887, and October 11, 1888.

53 *OR* 12, pt. 2, 730-731; W. W. Blackford, *War Years with Jeb Stuart* (New York, 1946), 100; Nicholson, "Diary in the War," August 22, 1862, HL.

After Blackford's quick scout around the camp's perimeter, a bugler's signal sent the column forward. The regiments fanned out with various assignments. One set out for the depot, and another headed for Pope's headquarters, guided by a former slave who knew Stuart and was familiar with the surrounding country. The rest of the force spread through the various tents and wagons, wreaking havoc and taking prisoners.[54]

While the sudden attack befuddled the poorly prepared Northern infantry, quartermasters, and teamsters, the storm mired Stuart's raid in futility. Thanks to the drenching rain, the campfires and lamplit tents that had made the camp quite bright were now black under the storm clouds. Flashes of lightning would reveal bands of fugitive Northerners scurrying across the cavalrymen's paths, while the next strike would show an empty road. Balls randomly flew from all sides. All of this resulted in a scene of intense confusion. As one column approached the railroad bridge, a force of Federals startlingly though ineffectively volleyed from the edge of the woods bordering the road. Soon afterward, a burst of fire erupted from a company across the river.[55]

The most determined resistance came from a battalion of the 13th Pennsylvania Reserve, known as the "Bucktails" for the furry accoutrement attached to their caps. But even in this case, only a portion of the force resisted. Many of the Bucktails were scattered and separated from the command in the initial confusion and, in small bands, did their best to evade the Rebel cavalry that the lightning flashes revealed. Despite the confusion, about 70 men from the 13th rallied in nearby thickets and harassed Stuart's horsemen. Their commander, Lt. Col. Thomas Leiper Kane, vigorously led his band at a wood line, volleying, moving by the flank, and volleying again. Though this small party by no means drove off the Confederates, as one of Pope's staff suggested, it annoyed them, adding to Stuart's rain-induced frustration.[56]

In addition to sowing confusion, the rain thwarted Stuart's plans to destroy property and disrupt the rail line. It fell so heavily that the saturated wagons, their contents, and the bridge were incombustible. The men sent to destroy the bridge

54 OR 12, pt. 2, 731; H. B. McClellan, *I Rode with Jeb Stuart* (New York, 1969), 94; Blackford, *War Years*, 100-101.

55 OR 12, pt. 2, 731; Blackford, *War Years*, 102, 106; McClellan, *I Rode with Stuart*, 94; Von Borcke, *Memoirs*, 85-86.

56 *Philadelphia Weekly Press*, April 7, 1886; Blackford, *War Years*, 106; Warner, *Generals in Blue*, 257; Smith Papers, 97-98, 100, OHC.

scrounged axes, which also proved ineffective against the wet timbers. A party under Captain Blackford managed to cut and disable a length of telegraph wire while under fire. By 3:00 a.m., Stuart made off with Pope's money chest, uniforms, and dispatch book, as well as approximately 300 prisoners.[57]

Lieutenant Colonel Benjamin Simpson of the Purnell Legion scrawled a message to Pope on the morning of August 23, informing him that "a dash was made on this place." Simpson announced that the Legion's colonel, a captain, three lieutenants, and 40 to 50 men had been taken. The official returns for the enlisted men in the regiment during this campaign listed three killed, seven wounded, and 59 missing or captured. Simpson explained that his force was "inadequate" owing to its being spread between Bealeton Station and Catlett's Station, and closed by declaring that his men had not been issued rations in five days. The message did not indicate the time, but presumably it was written very early. At 2:20 a.m., Pope notified Halleck that "considerable damage" had been done to the wagon trains "through the gross carelessness of the guard, which was amply sufficient to protect them." Pope underestimated the roughly 1,500-strong cavalry force as totaling no more than 300 men.[58]

Colonel T. C. H. Smith colorfully described Stuart's raid. He first delivered a barb at General Bayard, commander of the cavalry upriver from Sigel, writing that the Confederate column passed within three miles of Bayard's troops. Though notified that Rebel cavalry had crossed the river, Bayard sent no scouts or other reconnaissance to develop the movement, but instead reported the crossing to Col. Edwin Schrivner, McDowell's chief of staff. Reserving some vitriol for the Maryland infantrymen guarding Catlett's Station, Smith charged that they were "in no shape" to handle that assignment. Besides the implicit charge of drunkenness, Smith recalled a conclave of the regiment's officers, sitting on a veranda at the station with "feet on the rail, enjoying themselves." For his part, Lieutenant Colonel Kane reported with acidulous decorum, "I cannot ascertain that the Purnell Legion or the other troops reported to be in the vicinity posted any pickets last evening or rendered any service in effecting the enemy's repulse."[59]

Colonel Smith's final denunciation echoed Kane's views. It presupposed sufficient pickets had not been placed, suggesting that foiling Stuart's advance

57 OR 12, pt. 2, 732; Blackford, *War Years*, 103-104.

58 OR 12, pt. 2, 31, 60, 253; Benjamin Simpson to John Pope, August 23, 1862, Banks Papers, LC.

59 OR 12, pt. 3, 626, 400; Smith, Papers, 95-96, OHC.

would have been an easy matter by using pickets, since the wagons were only accessible by a single narrow road through the woods. On examination of a map from 1863, it appears that several paths, from both the north and west, led to the location of the camp. While none of the Purnell Legion's officers published a report on this action, 22 men from the 13th Pennsylvania Reserve had marched at dusk for picket duty. Stuart's cavalry captured them en route to their post.[60]

*   *   *

Even before Pope learned about Stuart's horsemen in his rear, he became increasingly apprehensive about his right. At 10:50 a.m. on August 22, he wired Halleck, "everything is tending up the river." Pope once again stated his presumption that Lee would cross at Sulphur Springs and head for Warrenton, and repeated that assertion throughout the day. The letter that Buford's men captured at Verdiersville on August 18 substantiated this assessment. While he still needed to maintain contact with Fredericksburg, Pope had become more sanguine about the situation downriver. "I think there is little danger whatever on the lower fords of the Rappahannock." Presumably, he meant the crossings below Kelly's Ford.[61]

On the evening of August 22, Pope was in the throes of decision-making. Though confident about the lower fords, he still felt constrained. He did not think he could attack toward Sulphur Springs and Warrenton because of the need to remain connected to the troops downriver. As a result, he told Halleck at 5:00 p.m. that he did not intend to prevent a crossing; instead, he would mass his forces near Fayetteville, about five miles southeast of the springs. At 9:15 p.m., he reported that the Rebels had crossed at Sulphur Springs and farther upriver. Pope determined that remaining in his current state, with his right exposed, would soon become untenable. Wishing to act aggressively, he dusted off his August 20 plan to cross the Rappahannock at both the railroad bridge and at Kelly's Ford to attack the exposed Confederate right and rear. This time, he pushed the decision up to Halleck, who endorsed the plan later that night. But by that time, the weather interceded, making Pope's planned move inadvisable. Rising waters washed out the fords and freed a temporary bridge from its moorings, lodging it against the

60 Smith Papers, 96, OHC; United States Army, Corps of Topographical Engineers, and J. Schedler, *Map of Culpeper County with parts of Madison, Rappahannock, and Fauquier counties, Virginia* (Washington, DC: U.S. Bureau of Topographical Engineers, 1863); *Philadelphia Weekly Press*, April 7, 1886.

61 *OR* 12, pt. 2, 57-58.

railroad bridge, which was also threatened. As a result, he withdrew Hartsuff and the batteries from across the river. While the rain dashed his flanking plan, it also created another, smaller opportunity on Pope's side of the Rappahannock. Since the high water temporarily freed Pope from the threat of a Confederate crossing downriver, he could advance on Early's north bank lodgment without worrying about a threat to his rear. But while Pope prepared to move on Sulphur Springs and Waterloo Bridge, James Longstreet drew Pope's attention downstream.[62]

*   *   *

Before dawn on August 23, a thick fog blanketed the Rappahannock Valley at Beverly Ford. Taking heed of Pope's warning en route to the ford on the 22nd, Gordon and Ruger had a wakeful night. They sat behind a rail fence that ran along the crest of a wooded hill, alert for a Confederate attempt to ford the river. Though the fog obscured movements in their front, it conducted noise quite well. Shortly before daylight, they heard the sound of artillery wheels and crawled toward the riverbank. Careful to keep out of sight of Confederate sharpshooters, they discovered Confederate guns on the opposite bank. Gordon sped word to Capt. George W. Cothran to prepare his Battery M, 1st New York Light Artillery. A breeze accompanied the rising sun and swept aside the fog, revealing two Confederate batteries. At this time, Hinkley's two companies of pickets withdrew from the bank and found a position from which the Midwesterners could "pour a heavy fire on the ford." Irvin McDowell's corps occupied the space from Gordon's left to Rappahannock Station.[63]

Despite Pope's warning about a crossing, Longstreet had no intention of doing so at either Beverly Ford or Rappahannock Station. Rather, he directed his artillery chief, Col. J. B. Walton, to drive the Federals from the river at those two points to protect the Confederate rear from the sort of move Pope had planned the night before. By putting the Federals at those fords on their heels, Longstreet could move upriver unmolested. Opposite the blockhouse at Rappahannock Station, the Rebels deployed six three-inch rifles, four 12-pound Napoleons, and two Blakely rifles. Behind these guns stood two brigades under Brig. Gen. Nathan G. "Shanks" Evans and Col. George "Tige" Anderson. Across the river, McDowell's artillery

---

62 OR 12, pt. 2, 58-59, and pt. 3, 623.

63 Gordon, *Army of Virginia*, 42-43; Bryant, *Third Wisconsin*, 101; Hinkley Diary, August 23, 1862, WHS.

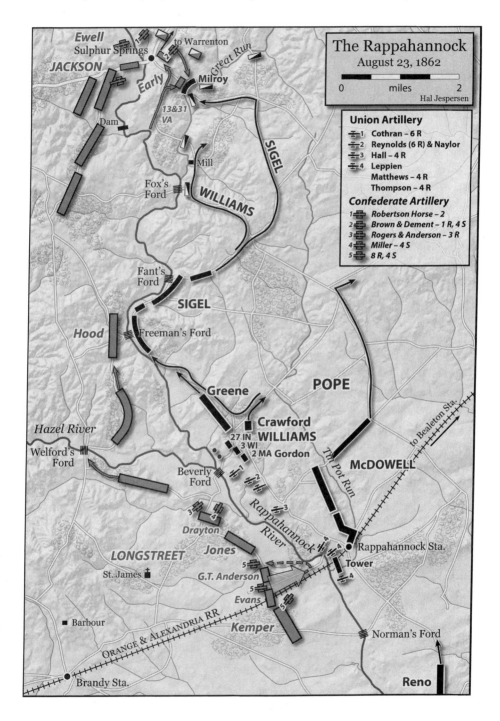

The Rappahannock
August 23, 1862

0   miles   2

Hal Jespersen

Union Artillery
1 Cothran – 6 R
2 Reynolds (6 R) & Naylor
3 Hall – 4 R
4 Leppien
   Matthews – 4 R
   Thompson – 4 R

Confederate Artillery
1 Robertson Horse – 2
2 Brown & Dement – 1 R, 4 S
3 Rogers & Anderson – 3 R
4 Miller – 4 S
5 8 R, 4 S

Ewell
Sulphur Springs
JACKSON
to Warrenton
Great Run
Early
Milroy
13&31 VA
Dam
Mill
Fox's Ford
WILLIAMS
SIGEL
Fant's Ford
SIGEL
Hood
Freeman's Ford
Greene
POPE
Crawford
WILLIAMS
27 IN
3 WI
2 MA Gordon
to Bealeton Sta.
McDOWELL
Hazel River
Welford's Ford
Beverly Ford
Rappahannock River
Tin Pot Run
Drayton
LONGSTREET
Jones
St. James
G.T. Anderson
Rappahannock Sta.
Tower
Evans
Kemper
Norman's Ford
Barbour
ORANGE & ALEXANDRIA RR
Brandy Sta.
Reno

included George Leppien's, Ezra Matthews's, and James Thompson's batteries, and Hall's guns stood farther upstream. McDowell's two remaining batteries, Battery L, 1st New York Light Artillery, and the 16th Battery, Indiana Light Artillery, commanded by Captains John A. Reynolds and Charles Naylor, stood between Hall's battery and Gordon's brigade.[64]

Across from Gordon, Walton placed seven guns on the face of the slope that dropped to the river, at a spot just forward of the wood line that extended to the edge of the ridge and within 1,000 yards of the river. Three rifled Parrott guns under Captains Rogers and Anderson were behind a partially constructed fieldwork to the northwest of the road that climbed away from the river. Farther right, four Napoleons commanded by Capt. Merritt B. Miller of the Washington Artillery of New Orleans stood southeast of the road. Brigadier General Thomas Drayton's brigade of Longstreet's Corps supported these guns at Beverly Ford.[65]

At 6:30 a.m., as the fog lifted, Miller opened fire with spherical case, which was the signal for all 19 Confederate guns to fire. The Federal guns' fearsome response came before Miller got off his third shot. A member of his battery remembered that, "Every shot they fired tore through our ranks, killing and wounding the men, and smashing the pieces." Miller's guns initially drew the attention of one of McDowell's rightmost batteries directly across the river and from Hall's battery of rifled guns. The latter enfiladed Miller from his right, making him "considerably annoyed." This was especially so since Hall's guns were out of range of Miller's Napoleons. After about an hour, the guns in Miller's front slowed their fire considerably, but Miller was unable to press his advantage. At the same time, the Parrotts to his left abandoned the field without orders. This freed Cothran's 1st New York Artillery Parrotts to turn to their left and enfilade the Louisianans. Miller reported that these rifles, "having our exact range, fired with terrible precision and effect." He kept up what he described as an unequal conflict "for some time" before nearly expending his ammunition and withdrawing. Up to the point when the batteries on his left drew off, precipitating Cothran's enfilade fire, Miller had suffered only one man wounded and two horses killed. After the engagement, he

---

64 OR 12, pt. 2, 564, 569, 331.

65 OR 12, pt. 2, 569, 578; William Miller Owen, *In Camp and Battle with the Washington Artillery of New Orleans: A Narrative of Events During the Late Civil War from Bull Run to Appomattox and Spanish Fort* (Boston, 1885), 103; Gordon, *Army of Virginia*, 43-44.

reported four killed, 10 wounded, and 21 horses killed. On his departure, a Confederate regiment appeared, but retired rapidly once Cothran fired on it.[66]

While the artillery dueled, Gordon's infantry sheltered in the woods. Shot raked the trees. After a round shot passed over an "impromptu breakfast table" used by Alpheus Williams and his staff, they mounted and moved out of range. Lieutenant Colonel Wilder Dwight remembered eating with Colonel Andrews under a tree, "with shell and round shot moving merrily about us." A Confederate shell destroyed a portion of the fence where the 2nd Massachusetts lay. In the midst of this, Gordon paused in front of a drenched and filthy Bay State private. The man had moved a few feet behind the line and quixotically cooked breakfast over a fire, hampered by renewed rainfall. He faced away from the river with his back to a large tree. Gordon asked the private how he liked his tree and whether he thought it was a safe place to cook. He answered, "Gin'ral, I've made a little calc'lation abeout this place, and I've found that the rebels has two batteries a-firin' on us, and that their fire crosses jest abeout three feet behind my tree. Gin'ral, you ain't in the safe angle; jest step up your hoss a little, and you'll be out of range." Gordon's satisfaction with the man's pluck is clear from his narrative. As the shelling ended, the brigade moved west. Hinkley was then recalled and had to catch up to his regiment.[67]

Downstream, McDowell was locked in a severe artillery exchange with Longstreet around the railroad bridge while evacuating his corps, which was to march by way of Warrenton and join on Sigel's right to support an attack on the trapped Confederates. Banks and Reno would follow Sigel up the river toward Waterloo Bridge, supporting as needed.[68]

As the morning artillery duel at Beverly Ford and Rappahannock Station raged, "Shanks" Evans's and "Tige" Anderson's brigades moved against the evacuated hills near the Rappahannock. The Confederates occupied one of the hills briefly before McDowell's guns convinced them the position was too hot. By this time, McDowell's rearguard under General Tower was all that remained. Tower kept the

66 OR 12, pt. 2, 576; Napier Bartlett, *A Soldier's Story of the War Including the Marches and Battles of the Washington Artillery and Other Louisiana Troops* (New Orleans, 1874), 111; Owen, *In Camp and Battle*, 104; Gordon, *Army of Virginia*, 46.

67 Hinkley Diary, August 22, 1862, WHS; Quaife, *From the Cannon's Mouth*, 106; Dwight to mother, September 5, 1862, MHS; Quint, *2nd Massachusetts*, 122; Gordon, *Army of Virginia*, 47.

68 OR 12, pt. 2, 331.

Rebels at bay until he destroyed the railroad bridge and turned to follow the corps.[69]

*   *   *

Approximately 10 miles upriver from Rappahannock Station, daylight on August 23 revealed the extent of Jubal Early's problems at Great Run. The river had risen enough to prevent a crossing. A messenger from Sulphur Springs informed Early that only one regiment, the 13th Georgia, and two batteries had crossed upstream, and not Lawton's entire brigade. He quickly scrawled a note to be carried across the Rappahannock by a swimmer and given to whichever of his superiors, Ewell or Jackson, the messenger could find first. It expressed Early's belief that he would be captured if a large Federal force attacked and suggested that his brigade and the 13th Georgia move upriver to Waterloo Bridge. A message from Jackson arrived first, directing Early to head to the springs and place his left on the river and his right on Great Run. Early positioned the 13th and 31st Virginia regiments on his right, across the road, facing Great Run and Sigel's approaching corps. The rest of his command, including the 13th Georgia and the two Maryland batteries, were across the crest of a hill three-quarters of a mile away, fronting Warrenton and McDowell's advance. All these units used woodlots for concealment. Under normal circumstances, Early's right would be considered open, but both Jackson and Pope considered Great Run unfordable. Colonel Smith of Pope's staff, however, contended that it was easily fordable at several locations and should not be an impediment. In any event, the 13th Georgia destroyed a partially flooded bridge, and Early posted a few companies along the run to prevent a crossing[70]

Though Jackson thought Great Run was not fordable and that the land between it and the Rappahannock was free of Northerners, he started arranging Early's extrication. That morning, A. P. Hill's engineers started building a temporary bridge using the pilings of the Sulphur Springs Bridge, which had washed away in the night. Infantrymen dismantled a barn and other outbuildings to supply boards for the makeshift structure. Throughout the day, Jackson sat on his horse in the river next to the construction site, watching the opposite shore and barely speaking a word. The single aide that joined him sensed a rare though

69 OR 12, pt. 2, 331-332, 564.

70 OR 12, pt. 2, 650, 705-706; Smith Papers, 103, OHC; Early, *Autobiographical Sketch*, 108-109.

restrained angst in the severely stoic general. Jackson sent word to Early to head for Waterloo Bridge if pressed, keeping along the river, across which Jackson's whole force would mirror his movement and attempt to support him.[71]

By the afternoon, Early thought Great Run fordable. Union cavalry lingered across the run, facing the right of his main body, and he discovered McDowell's large infantry force advancing toward Warrenton. Sigel's vanguard soon came into view on the hills across from Early's right flank, proceeding "with great caution" toward the run. Early changed front to face Sigel, masking his movement within the woods. His batteries encouraged Federal timidity by engaging in firefights at several different points, giving the impression of a larger force than he actually had. Two of Beverly Robertson's regiments and two pieces of artillery returned from the Catlett's Station raid. These forces conducted a similar ruse as the Maryland artillery, showing themselves during a series of countermarches. Robertson placed his two guns on a hill to the north of the springs and fired on the Federal infantry. One of Robertson's regiments stood behind this artillery on low ground near the springs. A Federal battery opened on Robertson's guns, and Early sent two of Brown's Parrotts in support. This artillery fight ended shortly before sunset, when the bridge could support infantry, and the 60th Georgia moved to Early's side. At this time, Robert Milroy's brigade arrived at Great Run.[72]

After a volley from Milroy's brigade landed harmlessly in the dark woods opposite the run, Early moved two of Dement's smoothbore Napoleons forward to the left of the line. Canister from these guns fired obliquely at Milroy's brigade, killing or wounding eight to 10 men and causing Milroy to withdraw for the night.[73]

*   *   *

For Banks's men, August 23 was another day of frustrating, halting marches. Greene's division walked a short distance at 7:00 a.m. before halting until 3:00 that afternoon. It then marched until 10:00 p.m. A heavy downpour fell for two hours during this march. From 10:00 to 11:00 p.m. the division stood in line of battle, expecting action. It then stacked arms and lay down, but soon marched again briefly at midnight before bivouacking for the rest of the night. Crawford's brigade

71 Early, *Autobiographical Sketch*, 108-110; Blackford, *Letters*, 125.

72 *OR* 12, pt. 2, 732; Early, *Autobiographical Sketch*, 108-111; Kelley, *Scharf Memoirs*, 36.

73 *OR* 12, pt. 2, 317-318; Early, *Autobiographical Sketch*, 111-112; Paulus, *Milroy Papers*, 1:75.

had marched at 9:30 a.m., moving a short distance before retracing its path to take another road. The roads were poor that day. Crawford's men soon halted in a field for hours under a scorching sun.[74]

Near sunset, while plodding quietly on the muddy road near the river, Banks's troops heard the robust cannonade ahead between Early and Sigel. Officers ordered rifles loaded. Lieutenant Gould remembered that the men executed several moves and halts in the dark with "much expectation and fear." The artillery concussions stopped and all became quiet. The soldiers marched uphill by torchlight from the signal corpsmen, filed right, headed back downhill, and traversed a ravine. Gould's 10th Mainers, after meandering in the dark through wet grass, thoroughly aggravated, "swearing and tumbling, damning everybody from Pope down to our cooks," who did not seem as well supplied as Sigel's, finally bivouacked. In wet uniforms, on wet ground, and without fires, they "miseried away till morning."[75]

Banks's Generals likewise endured a "soggy and comfortless" night, Gordon remembered, and they had concerns that extended beyond mere discomfort. They crowded into a small clearing that was surrounded by wooded hills and bordered a raging stream, likely a tributary of Great Run. The position of this low-lying camp, half a mile from the Rappahannock, prevented them from making observations that could alert them to an enemy advance. According to Gordon, any unusual sounds that night, including some unanswered volleys at dusk, created "unusual anxiety." Williams left to locate Sigel and found him in a farmhouse with generals Milroy, Schurz, and Robert C. Schenk. Williams reached camp at 2:00 a.m. on August 24 over a "horrid" road, his way lit by a mounted orderly carrying a lamp.[76]

* * *

Though Early passed the night unmolested, he heard a large force gathering around him. He informed Ewell, who crossed the river at 3:00 a.m. on August 24 shortly after the balance of Lawton's brigade joined Early. Convinced that the situation on the left bank was unsustainable, Ewell ordered Early back to the Confederate side. The whole force crossed shortly after dawn. Cannoneers

---

74 Foering Diary, August 23, 1862, HSP; Gould, *10th Maine*, 202.

75 Gould, *10th Maine*, 202-203.

76 Gordon, *Army of Virginia*, 57; Quaife, *From the Cannon's Mouth*, 106.

dismantled their guns and carried them across the makeshift bridge. As Early's men returned to relative safety, a Union pioneer detachment completed a bridge across Great Run. Milroy's infantry pushed into the abandoned Sulphur Springs, only to be greeted by shots from Confederate artillery across the river.[77]

Pope failed to destroy an isolated and overwhelmingly outnumbered brigade because he poorly understood the size of Early's force. An earlier and more thorough attempt to develop the enemy's strength, regardless of the state of Great Run, probably would have served Pope well.

A. P. Hill's guns maintained an intense duel with Sigel's guns across the river throughout the day. Sigel's infantry, meanwhile, moved toward what he thought was a Confederate force still trapped between the springs and Waterloo Bridge. It relieved John Buford's cavalry, which Sigel expected had destroyed the bridge. The bridge was still standing. Milroy arrived at the head of Sigel's column at 5:00 p.m. and deployed sharpshooters along the north bank. The rest of the corps, followed by Banks and Reno, stretched along the road toward Waterloo Bridge.[78]

* * *

Two divergent perspectives on the August 24 operations demonstrate differing experiences during this campaign. For Franz Sigel and other officers perhaps down to the brigade level, the 24th was the second day of chasing a phantom Confederate force on the left bank of the Rappahannock. According to 1st Lt. John Gould of the 10th Maine, a rumor began spreading on the 24th that a Confederate force was on the north bank. Indeed, the scope of the campaign for the rank and file was generally confined to excessive countermarching with no apparent purpose, and they rarely encountered civilians in the essentially abandoned countryside. As a result, they mostly had no idea where they were, except when they passed a road sign.[79]

The soldiers' other concern was food. They largely failed to get it. Gould recalled that their diet for the past two days had consisted of a little green corn and "the crumbs, bones and coffee-grounds" that Sigel's men had discarded. They salvaged what meat they could from castoff bones. Gould found some pieces of

77 *OR* 12, pt. 2, 317-318; Early, *Autobiographical Sketch*, 111-112.

78 *OR* 12, pt. 2, 263, 318.

79 *OR* 12, pt. 2, 64; Gould, *10th Maine*, 203.

hard tack in the mud. They had been stuffed in the haversack of one of Sigel's men, and flavors of tobacco, pork, and matches came through. Gould gave a clean but "buggy" piece to a gratified Mainer. On August 23, an unnamed general had procured three-quarters of a barrel of bread for the men. Each received a small portion plus one spoonful of molasses and two to three spoonfuls of coffee. Trade in such items was brisk, and a few enterprising souls still had hard bread on the 24th. Pieces sold for 50 cents, and the price inflated swiftly. Despite the rains that turned the roads to mud, a 28th New Yorker wrote that the only water available was no better "than could be obtained from a stagnant swamp hole."[80]

Laboring in the mud early on August 24, the soldiers heard cannonading ahead at Sulphur Springs. With Banks returned to corps command, Alpheus Williams led his division off road to the right, behind a wooded hill on which Sigel's and Banks's batteries were engaged in what Williams described as the fiercest artillery duel of the war. His column passed up and down hills in the woods, crossing streams on logs, as shells burst in the treetops and solid shot tore branches. The cross-country trek degraded the soldiers' limited sense of direction. Eventually, a hollow opened before them, and the resort buildings at White Sulphur Springs came into view. They halted in the hollow for about an hour while the artillery battle continued. After a pioneer detachment charged and fired the bridge, the column turned away from the pounding guns and followed Sigel toward Waterloo Bridge. The 28th Pennsylvania of Greene's division stayed behind the hill to the rear of Knap's and Hampton's batteries, and remained there under the barrage until it ended at 8:00 p.m. It followed the corps to Waterloo Bridge an hour later.[81]

After marching two or three miles along the Warrenton Turnpike, the corps halted at a crossroad to wait for orders. Turning left late in the afternoon, it continued toward Waterloo Bridge and bivouacked after dark in an abandoned hayfield. Rations briefly improved for part of the corps. The 2nd Massachusetts discovered sheep that put up futile resistance. At 9:00 p.m., an ambulance full of rations reached the 10th Maine. That evening small fires were permitted for the first time in days. The soldiers overstepped the privilege, remembering it as the sole happy moment during the two weeks of Pope's retreat. Supply wagons for Col. Gabriel De Korponay's brigade left Warrenton at 3:00 p.m. and reached the Ohio regiments at dusk, delivering three days' rations. These men had gone four days

80 Gould, *10th Maine*, 202-203; Quint, *2nd Massachusetts*, 122; Hicks Diary, 19, LC.

81 Quaife, *From the Cannon's Mouth*, 107; Quint, *2nd Massachusetts*, 122; Gould, *10th Maine*, 204-205; Foering Diary, August 24, 1862, HSP.

without being resupplied. The 28th Pennsylvania, left behind supporting Sigel's and Banks's artillery, could not be found. When the wagons reached the regiment one and a half miles from the springs the next morning, its soldiers looked starved.[82]

For days, shelling had been severe and nearly incessant. Infantry on each side had little to do but wait. A Virginian in the Stonewall Brigade wrote on August 24, "We have had their shells to awake us in the morning, keep us uneasy during the day, and scarcely to allow us to sleep at night. They have sometimes split the trees under which we were lying, but we have thus far escaped without injury." For many, the nature of events was about to change markedly. The transformation affected the armies in stages. The men under Sigel, Banks, and Reno and in Longstreet's five divisions maintained this status quo the longest. For those in Ewell's, Hill's, and Taliaferro's divisions, the campaign altered at dawn on August 25.[83]

* * *

Robert E. Lee's opportunities to turn John Pope's right via a Rappahannock ford while keeping east of the Bull Run mountains ended when the Federals took Waterloo Bridge. Lee knew from dispatches taken by Stuart at Catlett's Station that the first of McClellan's corps had landed. Needing to cross the river and come to grips with Pope before the Army of the Potomac arrived, Lee decided on August 24 to act boldly. Jackson would detach from the Rappahannock line, swing to the west, and fall on Pope's rear while Longstreet fixed the Union commander's attention on the Rappahannock.[84]

Jackson's command, less Hill's artillery, withdrew to Jeffersonton on August 24 and prepared to march the next morning. Chief engineer J. K. Boswell, a Fauquier County native, recommended a route that would conceal Jackson's movement. The march that Jackson stole on Pope, described by the understated Stonewall as "severe," went through Amissville, across the Hedgeman River tributary at Hinson's Mill Ford, through Orlean, to near Salem. On August 26, the forced turned east at Salem, crossed the Bull Run Mountains at Thoroughfare Gap,

82 Quaife, *From the Cannon's Mouth*, 107; Gould, *10th Maine*, 205; Nicholson "Diary in the War," August 24, 1862, HL.

83 White, *Sketches*, 114-115.

84 *OR* 12, pt. 3, 603; Harsh, *Confederate Tide Rising*, 132-133.

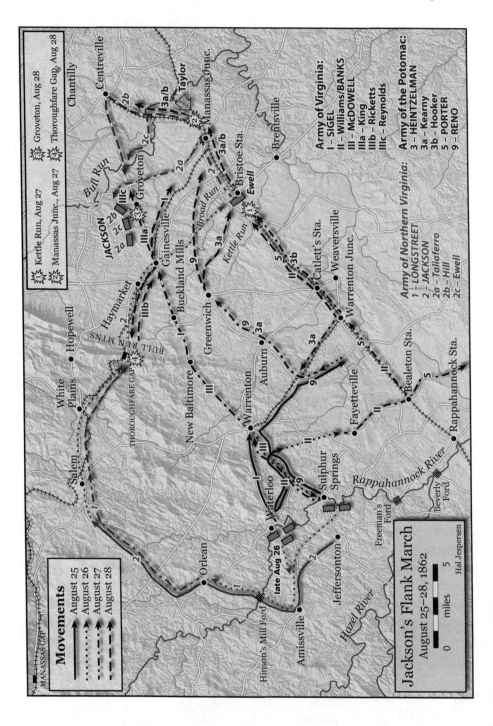

Jackson's Flank March
August 25–28, 1862

Hal Jespersen

and marched through Gainesville to the Orange and Alexandria Railroad at Bristoe Station. Jackson appeared with three divisions in Pope's rear, astride the rail artery by which supplies and reinforcements reached the Army of Virginia. He nearly caught the Union commander entirely by surprise. On August 26, Pope still had no idea of Jackson's menacing position, but by the 25th he knew something was afoot.[85]

* * *

As Jackson marched on August 25, Pope planned to draw his right away from the Rappahannock and, inexplicably, extend his left to Kelly's Ford, from which Longstreet had long departed. His new line would stretch from Warrenton to Kelly's Ford. For the men in each corps, this meant more superfluous marching. McDowell would hold the right at Warrenton and Sigel would countermarch eastward to Fayetteville. Banks's assignment was even farther east. He was to post his right at Bealeton Station and his left at the north end of Marsh Creek. Reno would return to Kelly's Ford. Pope made additional arrangements for units arriving from the Army of the Potomac. Sigel remained in place at Waterloo Bridge, under verbal orders from Pope's staffer Brigadier General Roberts, to hold his position "at all circumstances" against Longstreet, whose corps stood across the river. Sigel was anxious after discovering that Banks and McDowell had marched away from his flanks. At sunset, he ordered General Milroy to destroy the bridge, and the corps headed toward its assigned position, which Pope amended to Warrenton. Sometimes muddled, Pope's planned movements for August 25 proceeded, despite his learning that the Confederates were on the march as well, rendering his assumptions outdated.[86]

Banks's corps began the day marching toward Waterloo. Its marching orders for Bealeton Station had not yet arrived. The march ended abruptly when Crawford's brigade surged into Sigel's ranks, which Williams referred to as "confused." Crawford's indelicate intrusion elicited a verbal explosion from Sigel that included a healthy dose of German expletives. Williams termed it a "tremendous cursing." Banks was in Warrenton, and Williams, leading the corps, helped cool Sigel's rage. He found the whole affair amusing, given Sigel's broken English, long cloak, and broadbrim hat. Several other accounts described Sigel

---

85 OR 12, pt. 2, 642-643, 650; McDonald, *Make Me a Map*, 72; Robert Krick, *Staff Officers in Gray* (Chapel Hill, NC, 2003), 78.

86 OR 12, pt. 2, 263-264, and pt. 3, 641.

dressing down Crawford after he had crowded Sigel's column on multiple occasions. Gould wrote that Sigel called the Pennsylvania brigadier "a very hard name." Sigel suggested that he thought Banks's corps had done enough fighting, that it was unfair to expect it to do anything else so soon, and that he considered it a reserve that could be called upon if necessary. The men left the road for the trees and fields. A New Yorker recalled that Crawford's men were "mortified" by their commander's "forwardness" since they had left Rappahannock Station.[87]

After uncovering Sigel's corps, Williams's men waited around eating green corn until 4:00 p.m., when they were ordered to march to Bealeton Station. Retracing their steps to the Warrenton Pike junction, they turned left toward Warrenton. Two to three miles prior to that town, the column turned right and marched two miles on a dirt road and bivouacked in what Williams called a "fine camping ground." According to Lieutenant Gould, this meant the spot had ample hay for horses and beds and fences for fires. Many blankets were still in the wagons and the night was unusually chilly for August.[88]

Meanwhile, new information arrived at Pope's headquarters. At 11:25 a.m. on August 25, Banks sent the commanding general a dispatch with intelligence of Jackson's flank movement. From atop a Union signal station, Col. John Clark observed Jackson's column on the road between Jeffersonton and Amissville. He sent Banks three dispatches between 8:45 and 10:30 that morning, reporting a well-closed column of infantry, accompanied by cavalry and artillery, with colors flying. Banks forwarded Clark's opinion, which Pope adopted, that the Confederates were headed for Front Royal and into the Shenandoah Valley. Pope responded by ordering Reno, McDowell, and Sigel to cross the Rappahannock at Kelly's Ford, Sulphur Springs, and Waterloo Bridge, respectively, and determine whether the Rebels had evacuated his front. As Pope issued the order at 9:30 p.m., Sigel's corps left the burning bridge for Warrenton. It was 2:00 a.m. before the order to cross the river reached Sigel, whose men were entering Warrenton. Sigel begged off and ultimately stayed where he was. After McDowell left Warrenton for

87 Quaife, *From the Cannon's Mouth*, 107; Gould, *10th Maine*, 205-206; Boyce, "28th Regiment," 147. Boyce suggested that the Bohlen crossing on the 22nd was a ruse by Sigel to lure the Confederates across the river, and that Crawford scuttled the deception by marching into a clearing without orders. Sigel then dressed Crawford down in a mixture of German and broken English, including, "You no gentleman, no general, no fighting man, fight better on paper, make coot Fourt July general, coot for noting else." (Boyce, 146.) This was more likely due to the flareup on the 25th near Waterloo. The dates in the Hicks and Boyce accounts appear to go astray from actual events during late August.

88 Quaife, *From the Cannon's Mouth*, 108; Gould, *10th Maine*, 206.

Sulphur Springs, Pope permitted him to use his discretion, given Sigel's inactivity. Reno, who had marched to Warrenton Junction and was miles away from Kelly's Ford, also was unable to execute Pope's design.[89]

*　　*　　*

Beginning on August 25, and increasingly over the next four days, Pope was nonplussed by the movements of both the Confederates and his own units. The various marches by Pope's army and arriving reinforcements, beginning on August 26, are outside the scope of this narrative. Beginning with the movement away from the Rappahannock on the 25th, Banks's corps became increasingly isolated from the rest of the army. Pope indicated the cause in a dispatch to Halleck late that day. He wrote that, for various reasons, McDowell's corps was the only reliable one of the three corps he had. He lacked confidence in Banks's corps because of its condition after Cedar Mountain, writing that it was "very weak, not amounting to more than 5,000 men, and is much demoralized. . . . Banks's corps must be left somewhere in the rear to be set up again." The activities of Banks's corps *vis-à-vis* those of the rest of the army had little impact on or relation to each other until after the battle of Second Manassas.[90]

On August 26, Banks's corps continued countermarching, moving southerly and then southeasterly toward Bealeton Station. Lieutenant John Gould wrote, "The men are terribly jaded, literally half starved and in great want of meat. We are dirty and becoming lousy again. This constant marching and countermarching to no apparent purpose is aggravating in the extreme." While passing north of Sulphur Springs, the soldiers saw its hotel, which was aflame. Banks returned from Warrenton and ordered Williams to halt and fill the division's ammunition chests. As Crawford's brigade camped in the woods, Banks's and Williams's tents were at one end of the brigade and Crawford bivouacked under a fly at the other. The 10th Maine provided a guard for Crawford, who offered those men breakfast the next morning.[91]

Early on August 27, ambulances delivered meager rations to the campground near Fayetteville. Though gratefully received, the resupply was barely sufficient for

---

89 OR 12, pt. 2, 67, 333, 359, and pt. 3, 653-655.

90 OR 12, pt. 3, 653.

91 Gould, *10th Maine*, 207; Quint, *2nd Massachusetts*, 123; Nathaniel Banks, Order to Alpheus Williams, August 26, 1862, 7:30 a.m., Banks Papers, LC.

a single meal per soldier. Two 27th Indiana companies returned, exhausted, from accompanying ordnance wagons on an 11 or 12-mile round trip to Bealeton Station. Orders arrived and the men had the pleasure of returning to their feet and retracing their path with the corps. The rest of the army marched to concentrate at Gainesville and Greenwich, west of where Jackson had struck the day before. Banks headed for Warrenton Junction to relieve Fitz John Porter's V Corps from guarding wagon trains. Banks's corps was ordered to get the wagons going from Warrenton Junction and guard their move toward Manassas Junction. After passing Warrenton Junction, Banks was to position his troops behind Cedar Run, near Catlett's Station, guarding its crossings and also railroad trains. To Gordon, the orders had an "undefined air of nervous apprehension."[92]

On August 26, Jackson's men destroyed bridges across Kettle Run and Broad Run and two locomotives. The next day, they raided and destroyed an immense supply depot at Manassas Junction before disappearing in the direction of Centreville. Near Bristoe Station, Joseph Hooker's division assaulted Stonewall's rearguard under Richard Ewell. Banks's men heard that fighting while marching northeast along the railroad. Bridge demolitions had stranded five steam engines and 148 cars loaded with supplies and ammunition. Banks stayed on Pope's right flank for a day to guard this property while the rest of the army chased a specter northeast toward Manassas Junction and Centreville. Jackson's Corps turned west and eventually halted August 28 near Groveton. From that day and through the end of the coming battle, Banks would be beyond Pope's left flank as the army attacked Jackson near the old Bull Run battlefield. Lee completed the concentration of the Army of Northern Virginia when Longstreet sidled up to Jackson's right on August 29.[93]

After reaching Bealeton Station by road on August 27, Banks's column turned northeast and marched along the Orange and Alexandria Railroad. Its route through the desolate countryside was crowded with stragglers from the V Corps. The men heard fighting from the direction of Washington, and rumors spread that Confederates were behind their army. Gould acerbically referred to this as "a pleasant theme for consideration." He then described that night's bivouac, a mile south of Warrenton Junction, as "reeking with the filth from other troops, the air thick with the stench from a hundred carcasses, and no water to be found."

92 OR 12, pt. 2, 70-71; Hicks Diary, 21, LC; Brown, *Twenty-Seventh Indiana*, 219; Gordon, *Army of Virginia*, 192.

93 OR 12, pt. 2, 35, 72, 556, 643-644; Foering Diary, August 31, 1862, HSP.

Lieutenant James Gillette of the 3rd Maryland wrote on August 27, "Events are fast approaching a crisis in this neighborhood." As acting brigade commissary officer and quartermaster, Gillette ranged across the countryside to obtain rations. He was able to gauge the accuracy of the rumors.[94]

The situation had indeed changed markedly for Banks's men since August 20, when one of the regiments passed up fresh meat because there was no salt or bread. Near the end of the month, the 28th Pennsylvania ate an uncooked steer. They had no salt, either. The lack of food became serious and caused inflated prices in the burgeoning market. The 27th Indiana's Cpl. Edmund Brown recalled that men refused a dollar for a single cracker. The regiment had been without meat for five days. James Stewart of Knap's Battery saw men offer five dollars for as many crackers. Someone offered Stewart 50 cents, but he gave up his surplus free of charge. While still on the Rappahannock, a 27th Indianan desperately sought food. He finally discovered a haversack in an abandoned wagon that contained "two bites of the grossest, fattest pork I ever saw, and also a small handful of moist, dirty cracker crumbs." But it was "the sweetest morsel I ever ate."[95]

The weather affected the men as much as the poor rations did. One Hoosier recounted the previous week on the Rappahannock: "Much of the time we were wet to the skin, our feet were almost always wet and sleeping habitually on wet ground, with wet blankets, we chilled with cold and were bedraggled with mud." The 111th Pennsylvania's history summarized the campaign conditions after leaving the Rappahannock:

> The weather . . . was oppressively hot. The roads were deep with powdered dust. Water was scarce and foul, and at times unobtainable. The tongues of the men in some instances swelled, and their parched lips cracked from thirst. They chewed bullets when their tobacco was gone, to excite the salivary secretions. They were well-nigh choked with the dust clouds raised by the marching troops, the artillery, and the wagon trains. They were marched by day and night. . . . Many of them were ill with dysentery and low fevers. And so worn did they become that on the night marches, as momentary halts were made, they

94 Gould, *10th Maine*, 207; Quaife, *From the Cannon's Mouth*, 108; Gillette to father, August 27, 1862, LC.

95 Joseph Addison Moore, "A Rough Sketch of the War," 5, FNMP; Brown, *Twenty-Seventh Indiana*, 218; James P. Stewart to mother, September 7, 1862, USA; King, Manuscript, 39, ISL.

dropped in their tracks as one man, overcome with weariness and loss of sleep. The officers were obliged to rouse them man by man as the column moved again.[96]

Problems with heat and dampness affected more than soldiers. Captain Charles F. Morse of the 2nd Massachusetts noted the "wretched condition" of the horses. The animals had remained harnessed almost constantly for 10 days in oppressive late August heat and suffered the effects of sweat under equipage that was unable to dry. The men suffered similarly. A cannoneer in Knap's Battery wrote on September 7, "So we done 3 weeks without any clean shirt or drawers to our backs so you can judge the plight we were in."[97]

At 10:40 a.m. on August 28, the corps was ordered to march to Kettle Run, a small stream five miles from Manassas Junction, where it would continue to safeguard property loaded in freight cars. The first of two bridges that Jackson's men destroyed spanned Kettle Run, and Banks's men were stalled there for a time. Charles J. Mills, a freshly arrived lieutenant in the 2nd Massachusetts, wrote, "We are crossing today the plains of Manassas, the most barren, dusty, God-forsaken spot imaginable with very little water. Water, by the way is very scarce and abominably bad everywhere in this part of Virginia, and about the color of coffee." Crawford's brigade arrived at 5:00 p.m. Gordon, with Williams, arrived next, followed by Greene's division at about 6:00 p.m. Wagons blocked the nearby ford. Williams halted Crawford's brigade as it began crossing to form a guard. Around 8:15 that night, Banks assigned guard duty to one of Greene's brigades and a cavalry regiment. The corps bivouacked south of Kettle Run, within 300 yards of the bridge. Just past midnight, Banks received orders to forward two batteries to Heintzelman's corps. It became apparent that Pope planned to exclude Banks's corps from the upcoming fight.[98]

96 Boyle, *Soldiers True*, 50; Adjutant Boyle, whose passage recounted the conditions in the 111th during late August, was in a Confederate prison in Richmond at that time; he had been captured at Cedar Mountain.

97 Stewart to mother, September 7, 1862, USA; Brown, *Twenty-Seventh Indiana*, 219; Charles Fessenden Morse, "From Second Bull Run to Antietam," *Sketches of War History, 1861-1865. War Papers and Personal Reminiscences 1861-1865. Read before the Commandery of the State of Missouri, Military Order of the Loyal Legion of the United States* (St. Louis, 1892), 1:269.

98 OR 12, pt. 2, 73, and pt. 3, 716; Gregory Coco, ed., "Through Blood and Fire: The Civil War Letters of Major Charles J. Mills, 1862-1865," 17, Copy at USA; Foering Diary, August 28, 1862, HSP; Captain Piper to Nathaniel Banks and Banks to Piper, August 28, 1862, Banks Papers, LC.

August 29 was a restful day for much of Banks's corps. The first supplies of pork and coffee in a week arrived. At leisure to write for the first time in days, a 102nd New Yorker summed up the past week simply: "Boys most tuckered out." Early that morning, the 28th New York buried dead from Hooker's nearby fight on August 27. Federals had individual graves, while Confederates were dumped into trenches. The 10th Maine spent the day bathing in the run, picking lice from uniforms, and sunning atop a small hill northwest of the bridge. The construction corps showed little progress. Captain Knowlton led a work party of 50 Mainers all night helping to repair the bridge. With the structure complete early on August 30, both the trains and Banks's corps advanced to Broad Run and its disabled bridge, just beyond Bristoe Station. The men welcomed the inactivity, but found it disconcerting.[99]

By August 30, many soldiers wondered why they were guarding government property instead of joining the battle they had heard raging the day before. At 1:50 a.m., Banks requested clarity from Pope's chief of staff, Col. George Ruggles: "How important is the ammunition train to this day's work?" Banks was then waiting for 200 wagons that he had requested the previous evening to remove the sick and various supplies. Though he expected the bridge over Kettle Run to be complete within the next two hours, the work did not progress quickly enough.[100] A message from Halleck, dated August 30 without a timestamp, instructed Banks to forward as many troops as possible to Pope, unless Pope had ordered otherwise. Ruggles, however, sent Banks a firm answer at 8:45 a.m., suggesting that Banks seemed to misunderstand his instructions and that he was not to move his command "from its present station until the very last extremity." Frustration at Pope's headquarters over a recent string of corps commanders failing to arrive where expected may have precipitated Ruggles's surliness. In any event, Banks's mission was clear; but, the "last extremity" was fast approaching.[101]

99 Brown, *Twenty-Seventh Indiana*, 219; Sullivan McArthur, Diary, August 29, 1862, BHM; Hicks Diary, 22, LC; Gould, *10th Maine*, 208-209.

100 Nathaniel Banks to George Ruggles, 1:50 a.m. and 1:50 p.m., August 30, 1862, Banks Papers, LC. In what appears to be a second version of the 1:50 a.m. message, timestamped 1:50 p.m., Banks asked more directly, "Shall my command remain until this is done, or move on to the battle ground. I cannot decide how important the ammunition may be for the army + cannot therefore decide what to do."

101 OR 12, pt. 2, 77; Banks to Ruggles, 1:50 a.m. and 1:50 p.m.; Ruggles to Banks, 8:45 a.m., Banks to Alpheus Williams, 11:15 a.m., August 30, 1862, all in Banks Papers, LC.

At Bristoe Station, the 28th Pennsylvania heard heavy cannonading. False reports of approaching Confederates occasionally arrived, and at one point, the 28th formed rapidly. Companies D and K deployed as skirmishers, while the balance of the regiment supported Knap's Battery. It remained in line for an hour before recognizing the false alarm. Williams's division, and possibly the balance of Greene's, had crossed Broad Run that morning and moved to near Manassas Junction, where Williams's men witnessed the fighting. At 3:00 p.m., Williams perceived the Northern line was "receding." Orders arrived to return to the trains, and the concussions of heavy cannonading accompanied the division's march. After covering the four miles to Broad Run, Williams could not find Banks. He bivouacked his troops in the woods east of the run. Williams went to sleep, despite thoughts full of "uncertainty and doubt and anxiety."[102]

As a precaution against the unknown results of the day's battle, the 10th Maine and 5th Connecticut crossed to the south bank of Broad Run at midnight and turned northwest on the Gainesville Road. The 5th Connecticut stood guard in a swamp where, the regimental history reported, "No rebel could have found us with a deer hound. It was dismally wet and muggy, and mosquitoes and all kinds of vermin tortured us fearfully." Banks was in the swamp just behind the line. He was without a tent, had few staff, and looked "sick and discouraged." Banks had been away from the corps at intervals thanks to the injury he suffered at Cedar Mountain. When with his command, he was largely confined to an ambulance for transportation. Posted toward the Confederate position at Groveton during the battle, both regiments sent companies a half mile farther, into woods, to pass the rest of the night in the rain.[103]

Lieutenant Julian Hinkley and three 3rd Wisconsin companies spent that night picketing the woods on the north bank. As Hinkley and his men returned to the regiment after breakfast, he saw smoke billowing over the treetops. At the same time, about 7:00 a.m., Lieutenant Gould saw a few large fires on the rails. Continuing toward the tracks, a loud explosion issued from an ammunition car. Exploding rounds made sharp pops along the line, and more ammunition cars blew up. Gould saw "flames red, green, white and blue" radiating from medical cars. The

102 Foering Diary, August 30, 1862, HSP; Quaife, *From the Cannon's Mouth*, 108-109; Gould, *10th Maine*, 210; Marvin, *Fifth Connecticut*, 231. Gould reported that when they returned from Manassas, none of the other regiments at Broad Run had heard the battle.

103 Hinkley Diary, August 30, 1862, WHS; Gould, *10th Maine*, 210, 213; Marvin, *Fifth Connecticut*, 232; Gordon, *Army of Virginia*, 453.

whole corps suddenly understood that Pope's fighting to the northwest had not gone as planned.[104]

* * *

On the previous afternoon, Samuel Heintzelman and Jesse Reno attacked, expecting that Jackson was withdrawing. Meanwhile, Fitz John Porter moved from Pope's left up the Warrenton Turnpike with Rufus King in support. They discovered that Jackson's Corps was still at the unfinished railroad that it had defended on August 29. To their further surprise, Longstreet's infantry and artillery fell upon the open Federal left flank. As both Confederate corps advanced, Pope's army buckled and poured eastward. The retreat was much more controlled than the rout on the same ground the previous summer. Indeed, some troops effected pockets of stiff resistance, and the army eventually congealed around Centreville. At 6:30 p.m., Pope's chief of staff ordered Banks to, "Destroy the public property at Bristoe and fall back upon Centreville at once. Destroy all the railroad property. Your troops at Bristoe will withdraw through Brentsville." Brentsville was four miles southeast of Bristoe Station, while Centreville was north by east. Banks's small corps, which Pope thought unready to return to battle, was now isolated beyond the army's left flank and facing the prospect of being cut off by the Confederate army. The wide swing south and east made it clear that Pope thought it was in peril. Worse still, the rider carrying the order to withdraw lost his way in the dark, delaying him until daylight on August 31. The intervening 11 hours added to Banks's potential vulnerability. Gordon characteristically thought Banks received the order with some "apprehension." Banks showed it to Williams before ordering Tyndale's 28th Pennsylvania, which was then on the south bank near the smoldering cars, to destroy the locomotives and nearly 150 freight cars still full of supplies. The Pennsylvanians stuffed hay and forage under the cars as kindling.[105]

Banks and Crawford were the only commanders to follow Pope's directives, issued prior to their hasty departure. Ambulances and regimental wagons were to be destroyed. Gordon's brigade, Greene's division, and Alpheus Williams's headquarters all retained wagons with the assurance that they would not allow the

---

104 Hinkley Diary, August 31, 1862, WHS; Gould, *10th Maine*, 213-214.

105 OR 12, pt. 2, 42-43, 78, 340, 557; Hicks Diary, 22, LC; Gordon, *Army of Virginia*, 424; Tyndale, *Generals' Reports*, 6; McLaughlin, *Memoir of Hector Tyndale*, 54; Foering Diary, August 31, 1862, HSP; Marvin, *Fifth Connecticut*, 233.

encumbrances to hinder a fast march. Guards were placed in Crawford's brigade to prevent enlisted men from pilfering supplies from the cars. In the 28th New York, those able to snatch a handful of crackers were considered fortunate. This restriction caused much bitterness in the 10th Maine. Before the men's eyes, flames consumed millions of dollars of property, including supplies they had sorely needed for weeks. Other brigades pilfered more freely. In some cases, the looting was superfluous. Some Wisconsin soldiers liberated overcoats, which were on sale the next two days for 25 cents. This bargain was undoubtedly driven by low demand in the August heat and the burden of carrying such an item on what proved to be three days of discouraging marching.[106]

Everyone knew what this destruction meant. According to Gordon, the men had merely been "dismal and hungry." Now that orders spread to fly in retreat after destroying the property to save it from capture, dejection gripped the men. Lieutenant Colonel Eugene Powell, commanding the 66th Ohio, realized the gravity of their situation and felt downcast. With demolition well underway, much of the command began a hurried march by 9:00 a.m. The 28th Pennsylvania stayed behind until noon, completing the destruction before following as a rearguard. Men moved without panic, but they all understood the seriousness of the situation and the need to march rapidly. Many expected either a desperate fight or to be taken prisoner. There were no halts except to cross streams. The lead regiment, the 2nd Massachusetts, set a grueling pace. Before the day's march ended, men fell from exhaustion only to rise and press on from necessity, expecting to discover Confederates, flush with victory, around every corner. Overtaxed horses that fell were unharnessed and left to die.[107]

After marching four miles and traversing Kettle Run, the column passed through Brentsville, where locals, understanding the significance of the fast pace, jeered the men. On the other side of Brentsville, the overnight rain caused Broad Run to rise rapidly, and there was no bridge. The waters in Kettle and Broad runs rose to a horse's breast, and the men now raced to get across the two stream crossings near Brentsville before they were too high. At 1:15 p.m., the head of the column reached Manassas Junction and the road to Centreville, with five miles to go. It eventually crossed Bull Run at Blackburn's Ford and bivouacked on the high

106 Gordon, *Army of Virginia*, 425; Quaife, *From the Cannon's Mouth*, 109; Hicks Diary, 22, LC; Gould, *10th Maine*, 214; Bryant, *Third Wisconsin*, 113.

107 Gordon, *Army of Virginia*, 425; Powell, *Memoir*, chap. 5, OHC; Foering Diary, August 31, 1862, HSP; Gould, *10th Maine*, 214; James Guinn to brother, September 7, 1862, HL; Quint, *2nd Massachusetts*, 125; Bryant, *Third Wisconsin*, 113.

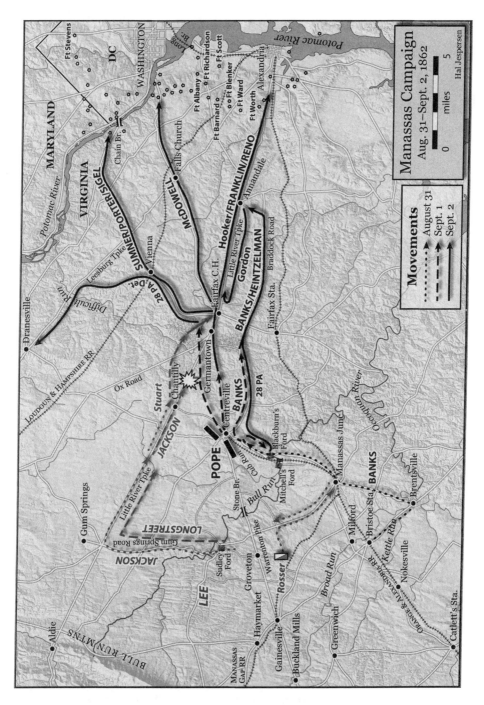

ground between the ford and Centreville. The rearguard under Lieutenant Colonel
Tyndale crossed at 6:00 p.m. Confederate cavalry reportedly harassed the 28th and

its Ohio brigade mates en route, with a few Ohioans taken prisoner. The men had marched 20 miles to go about 12 miles as the crow flies. That night, details of the previous day's battle reached them, causing a gloomy bivouac. Adding to their misery, they had neither dry wood nor drinkable water. Teamsters and stragglers had made the few pools filthy. Gould recalled, "Dead mules and the offal of slaughtered cattle lay around within good smelling distance."[108]

Banks's men were not the only ones who felt dismal on August 31. At 10:45 a.m., about the time Banks's men hustled through Brentsville, Pope made what must have been an unsettling inquiry of the general-in-chief. Pope asked whether Halleck felt that Washington would be secure "should this army be destroyed." If Lincoln and Halleck had any confidence left in John Pope, it must have been spent with that statement. Its tone suggested that Pope was preoccupied with defending the force about him and did not feel capable of interceding if Banks's marching column got into trouble.[109]

As it happened, the potential for danger never materialized into anything beyond a dash by the Confederate cavalry. On August 31, Jackson crossed Bull Run at Sudley Ford and made a swing around Pope's right along the Little River Turnpike, to the side of Pope's army that was away from Banks's line of march. After spending the morning tending to dead and wounded, Longstreet followed Jackson, with a brigade moving between Bull Run and Cub Run, never going far enough east to block Banks's path. Rebel cavalry under Col. Thomas Rosser, however, struck at Manassas Junction and captured some Federals before Stuart recalled him for the move around Pope's right. Rosser's short occupation of Manassas Junction was along Banks's path and preceded the column's arrival there. After arriving north of Bull Run, the 28th Pennsylvania, a section of Knap's Battery, and a squadron of Pennsylvania cavalry marched south to defend the bridge over the run.[110]

After idling until about 3:00 p.m. on September 1, the command marched north to Centreville. An enormous collection of soldiery, the disorganized corps of Pope's army, appeared to the left of the road ahead of it. Moving regiments and

108 Marvin, *Fifth Connecticut*, 233; Henry Perkins to Nathaniel Banks, August 31, 1862, Banks Papers, LC; Quaife, *From the Cannon's Mouth*, 109; Bryant, *Third Wisconsin*, 113; Gould, *10th Maine*, 214.

109 *OR* 12, pt. 2, 80.

110 *OR* 12, pt. 2, 566, 647, 743; George Ruggles to Banks, August 31, 1862, Banks Papers, LC; McLaughlin, *Memoir of Hector Tyndale*, 54; Foering Diary, August 31, 1862, HSP; Hicks Diary, 23, LC.

supply trains filled open fields, stretching into the distance. The 5th Connecticut's historian wrote cheekily that, "For the first time in two months [Pope] had been in command, his army was finally pretty well in hand." The men in the 10th Maine begged other units for breadcrumbs and bones, and received some. The army moved east toward Fairfax and Fairfax Station on parallel roads. Banks's corps was on the route farthest south, a road that had been constructed by British general Edward Braddock in the 1750s on his way to a disastrous ambush in a Pennsylvania forest. One mile beyond Centreville on the Braddock Road, Banks ordered the 28th Pennsylvania and a section of Knap's Battery to return to the Bull Run bridge south of Centreville. A detail of 12 men destroyed it after reaching it about 8:00 that night. At 4:00 a.m. on September 2, the 28th left the bridge and hustled after the corps, with Rebel horse artillery harassing it. The regiment made it to the ring of forts near Alexandria at midnight after marching 27 miles.[111]

As the corps moved east along the Braddock Road in the late afternoon of September 1, ominous storm clouds approached from the southwest. As the column neared some woods and a crossroad leading to Fairfax, the concussion of a cannon shot reverberated from its left. Others soon followed, indicating that a sharp engagement was taking place. Jackson had advanced along the Little River Turnpike, intending to cut off Pope's retreat. But Jackson's column and two Federal divisions on his right stumbled into each other. In a brief engagement at Ox Hill, near a plantation named "Chantilly," two of Jackson's divisions, Hill's and Ewell's, beat back Union divisions under the one-armed, tenacious Maj. Gen. Phil Kearny and Brig. Gen. Isaac Stevens. Brigadier General Alexander Lawton had replaced Ewell, who lost a leg at Groveton on August 28. Both Federal commanders were killed. As the battle raged, a violent thunderstorm burst over the combatants.[112]

When the fighting began, Banks's corps halted. Crawford's brigade filed into the timber south of the road while Gordon's brigade stood in it. Both faced the fighting to the north. Lightning struck nearby trees, and flashes from gunfire lit the black clouds. A request that appears to be in Crawford's handwriting was made to swing right and land on Jackson's left flank. The partial, unsigned note also indicated that Best's battery had been called up. Another unsigned note, time

111 OR 12, pt. 2, 558; *4th Maine*, 27; Marvin, *Fifth Connecticut*, 233; Gould, *10th Maine*, 215; McLaughlin, *Memoir of Hector Tyndale*, 54; Foering Diary, September 1, 1862, HSP.

112 OR 12, pt. 2, 45, 647; Hicks Diary, 24, LC; Quaife, *From the Cannon's Mouth*, 109; Harsh, *Confederate Tide Rising*, 171.

stamped 5:00 p.m. with a header reading "2nd Corps Headquarters," included a map depicting a northbound road to the right that could be used, and suggested that a request had been made to execute this movement. Awaiting orders, the corps remained there all night.[113]

Banks's men well remembered the misery of that night. After the storm and the battle ceased, they remained in the road, soaked, for over an hour. After dark, they entered the woods. The temperature dropped significantly, exacerbating their discomfort. The men still had neither tents nor any necessities from the supply wagons. The 3rd Wisconsin's Lieutenant Bryant wrote, "We were drenched and benumbed, supperless, hungry, and our bivouac was one of the most cheerless and comfortless that falls to the lot of soldiers in the field." A 28th New Yorker remembered, "a more uncomfortable night we scarcely ever experienced." In a letter to his mother, Lt. Col. Wilder Dwight of the 2nd Massachusetts wrote, "We were all night under arms wet through and without fires. The worst night I ever spent." Lieutenant Hinkley lay down to sleep but was soon awake. Too cold to fall asleep again, he sought a fire at 2:00 a.m. Soon after he found one, a staff officer ordered it put out. A game of kindling new fires and having them ordered out went on through the night. Some in the 10th Maine had better accommodations after finding a haystack that provided dry bedding. Banks and Williams spent the night in ambulances.[114]

The dawn broke on a corps grateful for the sun's comfort. It marched at 8:00 a.m. for the safety of the Alexandria forts. The men had gone two days without rations but anticipated that the end of their ordeal was near. Greene's division led, but his wagons stalled Williams's division until noon. Williams's men halted again at Annandale, where the Braddock Road joined the Little River Turnpike, waiting for other corps to pass.[115]

Gordon's men lounged near a stream, taking comfort in talk of the campaign's imminent end. After a few hours, Major Perkins arrived from Banks's headquarters seeking Gordon. Perkins ordered the brigade to remain until the road cleared and then march west to Fairfax to load government supplies into wagons. He did not

113 Hicks Diary, 24, LC; Hinkley, *Third Wisconsin*, 44; Unmarked note, September 1, 1862, Banks Papers, LC; Harsh, *Confederate Tide Rising*, 171; Gould, *10th Maine*, 215.

114 Hicks Diary, 25, LC; Hinkley Diary, September 1, 1862, WHS; Bryant, *Third Wisconsin*, 116; Dwight to mother, September 5, 1862, MHS; Hinkley, *Third Wisconsin*, 45; Gould, *10th Maine*, 216; Quaife, *From the Cannon's Mouth*, 110.

115 Hicks Diary, 25, LC; Bryant, *Third Wisconsin*, 116.

specify whether this meant Fairfax Station or Fairfax. Both locations were about six miles away and four miles from each other. Confederates were thought to be in possession of both. Fitzhugh Lee's Rebel cavalry had in fact occupied Fairfax since the Federal infantry departed, and most of Stuart's command bivouacked near Fairfax that night. It is unclear whether Fairfax Station was similarly occupied. Jackson's infantry stayed near Chantilly until Lee's army departed to the northwest.[116]

Perkins could say neither the correct destination nor who gave Banks the order. Most importantly, he did not know when the order had been given. Gordon found Banks in his ambulance. He, too, had no answers and would not recant the order. Gordon later wrote that Banks eventually replied, "I would go, sir, first to Fairfax Court House [Fairfax], and if I found there were no provisions there to load, I would then go to Fairfax Station." Gordon returned to his command and "blank dismay" on his soldiers' faces. With darkness falling rapidly, Gordon's openly dejected men headed west, alone, toward what they imagined was a substantial mass of Lee's army. Though not as bad as they thought, Stuart's cavalry would have posed a problem for Gordon's three small regiments. Nearing Fairfax, they found the corps's rearguard, which was likely the 28th Pennsylvania, returning from destroying the bridge over Bull Run. When Gordon reported their destination, the commander of the regiment, pointing to Stuart's bivouac east of Fairfax, asked, "Can you whip the whole rebel army?" With this, Gordon put Colonel Ruger in charge and hastened east to Banks's ambulance. Banks refused to bend in spite of this new intelligence, and Gordon returned to his command. He found it on the road heading east. Ruger had taken it upon himself to leave Fairfax, accompanying the rearguard. At this point, Gordon took responsibility for ignoring the order, and the brigade followed the rest of the corps.[117]

Morale throughout the corps was low. Many soldiers had developed diarrhea over the preceding two weeks and were infested with lice. Heavy marches and inadequate diet further debilitated them. Depressed at having been beaten by their own commanders, the men expected to bivouac at any moment. They struggled

---

116 OR 12, pt. 2, 558, 647, 744; Gordon, *Army of Virginia*, 453.

117 Gordon, *Army of Virginia*, 453, 456-458; Bryant, *Third Wisconsin*, 116-117. Major Haller, 7th U.S. Infantry, reported (OR 12, pt. 3, 804-805) that he discovered Confederate cavalry at "Fairfax" on the road leading to Accotink Creek and expected to set up a defense against a raid. He wrote that a portion of Banks's corps arrived and got in his way. This unit's colonel, perhaps Ruger or Tyndale, was not interested in the major's suggestion that they stay and assist his defense. Haller may be the officer who had the exchange with Gordon.

through each step, and darkness brought a cold northerly wind that penetrated uniforms, threadbare from weeks of uninterrupted use. Crawford's brigade pressed on from 9:00 p.m. until midnight without stopping. Reaching the forts outside Washington, they floundered in the darkness until about 2:00 a.m., then bivouacked at a manor near Fort Ward. When told to halt, "the men dropped as if they were shot," wrote Gould. He called it, "*the darkest day and the darkest hour in our regimental history*." [Emphasis in original.] Gordon's brigade followed, bivouacking near Fort Worth.[118]

The next morning, the corps rested for a few hours and scrounged food by scouring green regiments' camps and buying out sutlers near the forts. It then moved north to Fort Albany, almost due west of Washington. After bivouacking in a damp ravine, the corps crossed the Potomac at Chain Bridge, northwest of Georgetown on September 4.[119]

On September 1, Lieutenant Gillette summarized the campaign quite well:

If heavy marches by night and by day, loss of sleep, absence of food, exposure to rains in the most severe of climates without an hours relaxation from arduous duties made necessary by the presence of an active and overpowering enemy—If this can entitle soldiers to an honorable name, the army under Genl Banks, so severely handled at Cedar Mountain have earned by experience, if not by length of service, the title of veterans. . . . Without a days respite we have been ordered from post to post from one flank to the other supporting this column and that column, this battery and that battery, until we are wearied into a condition that involves exhaustion bodily and mental. . . . One by one officers and men are becoming fagged and wearied to that degree that they are compelled to drop . . . to speak of individual hardship or of an officers privation in comparison with those endured by the enlisted men were foolish.[120]

On September 5, Lt. Col. Wilder Dwight began his account of the preceding three weeks with, "It has been so tense and corrosive that I am not yet in tone to write on account of it." He did bring himself to provide a cogent, terse summary of the corps's experience: "Disaster, pitiable, humiliating, contemptible." Though the truth of Dwight's statement was evident, the 7th Ohio's Pvt. James Guinn

---

118 Gould, *10th Maine*, 216-219; Quaife, *From the Cannon's Mouth*, 110; Bryant, *Third Wisconsin*, 118; Hinkley Diary, September 2, 1862, WHS.

119 Marvin, *Fifth Connecticut*, 235; Gould, *10th Maine*, 221-222; Bryant, *Third Wisconsin*, 118.

120 Gillette to Parents, September 1, 1862, LC.

mitigated this sentiment. "We suffered. But we have become inured to hardships." They would soon test their freshly tempered resolve against Lee's veterans.[121]

121 Dwight to mother, September 5, 1862, WHS; Guinn to "Dear Folks at Home," September 3, 1862, HL.

Part II

XII Corps, Army of the Potomac
From Chain Bridge to the Dunker Church
September 4 to 30, 1862

"Sweet are the uses of adversity,
which, like the toad, ugly and venomous,
wears yet a precious jewel in his head"
— As You Like It, Act 2, Scene 1

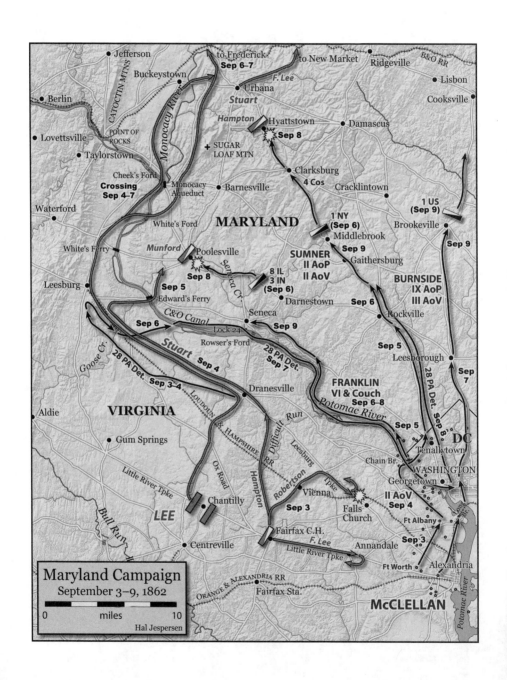

Jefferson •   to Frederick
           Sep 6–7
Buckeystown •

to New Market   Ridgeville •
                        B&O RR
                         Lisbon •

F. Lee
Urbana •
Stuart
Cooksville •

• Berlin

CATOCTIN MTNS

POINT OF
ROCKS

• Lovettsville

• Taylorstown

Hampton   Hyattstown •
            Sep 8

Damascus •

＋ SUGAR
    LOAF MTN

Cheek's Ford
**Crossing
Sep 4–7**
Monocacy
Aqueduct
• Barnesville

Clarksburg •
4 Cos

Cracklintown •

1 US
(Sep 9)

• Waterford

White's Ford
MARYLAND

1 NY
(Sep 6)
Middlebrook •
Sep 9

Brookeville •

Sep 9

White's Ferry

Munford
Poolesville •
Sep 8

SUMNER
II AoP
II AoV

Sep 9
Gaithersburg •

BURNSIDE
IX AoP
III AoV

• Leesburg

Edward's Ferry
Sep 5
8 IL
3 IN
(Sep 6)

Darnestown •

Seneca Cr.

Sep 6

Rockville •

Sep 6
C&O Canal
Lock 24
Rowser's Ford
Seneca
Sep 9

Sep 5
Leesborough •

Sep 7

28 PA Det.
Sep 3–4

Goose Cr.

Stuart   Sep 4

28 PA Det.
Sep 7

28 PA Det.
Sep 8

Sep 7

LOUDOUN & HAMPSHIRE RR

Dranesville •

FRANKLIN
VI & Couch
Sep 6–8
Potomac River

Sep 5

DC

VIRGINIA

• Aldie

Ox Road
Difficult Run

Leesburg

Tenallytown •

Chain Br.

• Gum Springs

Little River Tpke

Hampton
Robertson
Vienna •

Falls
Church

WASHINGTON
Georgetown •

II AoV
Sep 4

LEE
Chantilly •

Sep 3

Fairfax C.H.
F. Lee

Annandale •

Ft Albany •

Sep 3

• Centreville

Little River Tpke

Ft Worth •

Alexandria •

Bull Run

ORANGE & ALEXANDRIA RR
Fairfax Sta.

Potomac River

McCLELLAN

| Maryland Campaign |
| September 3–9, 1862 |
| 0   miles   10 |
| Hal Jespersen |

Chapter 7

"We hope soon to have an opportunity of again advancing."

— Ario Pardee, 28th Pennsylvania

A New Corps, a New Campaign:
Pursuing Lee in Maryland

September 4 to 16, 1862

Private William Wallace of Company E, 3rd Wisconsin, had a close call at Cedar Mountain. While Gordon's brigade was at the edge of the Wheatfield after dark, a ball pierced his hat, "just clearing the crown." Another hit his hand, injuring the two smallest fingers on his right hand, the ring finger badly. He remained on the field until between 9:00 and 10:00 p.m., after Ricketts's men relieved Gordon's brigade. He then moved to Culpeper, which he reached "pretty tired and hungry" a little after midnight. The surgeons were busy removing limbs, so it was another four days before his fingers were dressed. The orderly burned the flesh with "costic," an experience Wallace termed "mortifying." On August 13, he rode with General Geary on one of 15 train cars loaded with wounded, headed for Alexandria. By August 22, Wallace's hand was healing nicely. On that day, he saw new Pennsylvania regiments marching into Virginia.[1]

---

1 William Wallace to Wife, August 10 and 22, and September 1, 1862, William Wallace Papers, WHS.

In July, President Lincoln issued a new call for recruits. Unlike the veteran units in Banks's corps, which had enlisted in the spring of 1861 for three years or for the war's duration in some cases, these new recruits volunteered to serve only nine months and were quite green. The 124th, 125th, and 128th Pennsylvania regiments arrived at Camp Curtin in Harrisburg between August 8 and 10, while the corps fought at Cedar Mountain. These regiments spent a week mustering into service. The 125th Pennsylvania received Springfield rifles on August 16 and boarded freight cars that evening for Baltimore and Washington. Its soldiers slept August 17 in a warehouse near Capitol Hill. All three regiments kept similar schedules. As each arrived, it moved to support the forts in northern Virginia. The 125th marched to Fort Richardson on August 18 and took position near Fort Barnard on August 26. The 124th moved to the vicinity of Forts Albany, Scott, and Richardson. Between August 18 and 21, the men learned squad and company drill and occasionally attempted regimental drill. The 124th repositioned several times before moving to a hill next to Fort Blenker on September 2. During the first week of the month, the three new Pennsylvania regiments, along with the green 13th New Jersey and 107th New York, marched north to join the veteran brigades of Banks's corps and face a newly discovered threat. They were largely unprepared to do so.[2]

*　*　*

On September 1, Nathaniel Banks once again, and for the last time in this campaign, supervised the collection of beneficial intelligence. First, he dispatched four signal officers to eminences near Frederick, Maryland, to observe approaches to the nearby fords. They relayed observations by signal flag and then by wire to Washington. On September 3, Lt. B. N. Miner occupied the most consequential of these positions, on Sugar Loaf Mountain, south of Frederick. From there, he reported Confederates marching through Leesburg and crossing the Potomac just south of the mouth of the Monocacy River until he was captured.[3]

That same day, Banks sent the 28th Pennsylvania on what became an eventful reconnaissance mission. Four sergeants, seven corporals, and two privates were

---

2 *History of the One Hundred Twenty-Fifth Regiment Pennsylvania Volunteers, 1862-1863* (Philadelphia, 1906), 31, 38, 41; Robert M. Green, *History of the One Hundred and Twenty-fourth Regiment Pennsylvania Volunteers in the War of the Rebellion—1862-1863* (Philadelphia, 1907), 19-21.

3 OR 19, pt. 1, 118.

selected to proceed to the Catoctin Mountains near Leesburg to investigate Lee's movements. Sergeant Francis B. M. Bonsall commanded the party. At Banks's headquarters, Col. John Clark gave instructions. He pointed out expected Confederate positions and told his men to avoid contact. Given the option of going on foot or on horseback, they chose to go less conspicuously by foot. Clark instructed them to carry only rifles, haversacks, and canteens, so they could move quickly. Each day, one man would return to the Union lines until only five remained, at which point all would return. Clark issued a pass to enable them to cross Union lines and resupply from any quartermaster they might come across.[4]

The reconnaissance began from the corps's position on Bull Run, south of Centreville, midmorning on September 1. The Pennsylvanians thought they could move through the Confederate lines opposite Centreville, but after discovering that opposing pickets had exchanged fire all day, they continued north two miles, unwittingly toward Jackson's turning movement along the Little River Turnpike. Finding no Federal pickets, Bonsall's men moved carefully through woodlots until they reached a clearing with a small farmhouse. Sergeant Bonsall approached the house in order to find out the way to the Leesburg Turnpike. The residents told him to leave, because Federal cavalry had recently been chased off. As the men lay waiting in a cornfield, a volley passed overhead and they ran for the woods, where Bonsall met them. Returning the way they came, they found skirmishers from Maj. Gen. Philip Kearny's division approaching ahead of a line of battle. The Pennsylvanians told the officer in charge the direction from which they had received fire and continued toward Fairfax.[5]

The next day, September 2, the detachment headed northeast, passing Vienna, when it came close to two Confederate cavalrymen guarding three Federal officers. After waiting for the small party to pass, the first man headed back with a dispatch. The remaining 12 Pennsylvanians moved north through the night, passing Dranesville and observing enemy cavalry pickets. For two days, Bonsall's party continued northwest, keeping to woodlots. By the night of September 4, the men neared Leesburg and their destination in the Catoctin Mountains. Rebel soldiers were visible among various local houses. Exhausted, the detachment descended into a deep gully to conceal a fire for coffee.[6]

---

4 Foering Diary, September 1, 1862, HSP; Hayward to brother, September 28, 1862, GC.

5 Hayward to brother, September 28, 1862, GC.

6 Ibid.

Sunrise on September 5 revealed the looming foothills of the southern Catoctins, south of Leesburg. Confederate wagons and artillery had traveled the road all night, blocking the Pennsylvanians' path. One man crept forward while the rest stayed prone in the grass. Six Rebel cavalrymen emerged from the nearby woods with pistols out, ordering that the Federals halt. Bonsall's men chose to run for a thick patch of woods. They found a place to hide, and the cavalry rushed past them. Carefully whispering among themselves, they remained hidden until dark. At one point during the day, two Southern infantrymen passed, talking about their unfruitful search of the woods. Since September 3, the detachment had been out of food. That night, Bonsall and his men decided that continuing to the mountains was unnecessary, since they had established that Lee's army was heading north through Leesburg. Indeed, the Pennsylvanians had inadvertently run into the Confederates' path repeatedly since September 1.[7]

The detachment headed east and reached Goose Creek early on September 6, where they captured three Confederates sleeping under a tree by the side of the road. After throwing the Southerners' weapons into the creek, they interrogated the prisoners, who spoke freely about moving toward Leesburg. While debating whether to keep or release the Rebels, they heard another squad of gray infantrymen. After nabbing all four of those as well, the Federals hurriedly moved on. Rifle shots rang out as they went. Their new traveling companions explained that the gunfire was from enterprising Southern infantrymen securing breakfast. Bonsall's men soon found evidence of this when they met three more Southerners, plus two slaves preparing food. These five joined the party, which hustled on until reaching the Leesburg Turnpike. Sergeant Bonsall went ahead to scout. The road, filled with stragglers and wagons, could not be crossed, so the detachment returned the way it came. They hid in a thicket, throwing out guards on either side. These sentries brought in more straggling Confederates. The growing throng of prisoners had become a serious concern for the Pennsylvanians. By nightfall, they had 17, plus the two bondsmen; the scouting party itself was down to 11. Bonsall had sent one man back on September 2, and the Confederates captured another while he fled their cavalry.[8]

As the sun set, the Pennsylvanians put their haul of prisoners in line and crept from the undergrowth. As they approached the Leesburg Turnpike, the Confederates' path into Maryland, campfires blazed in all directions.

7 Ibid.

8 Ibid.

Circumventing the sprawling camps was impractical, so a ruse was in order. The Pennsylvanians walked straight through the area, passing within 10 feet of three Rebels around a campfire. The detachment made it across with its quarry intact, astonished that no one ran or called out to them. Clearing the camps, the Northerners still had to make good time. One prisoner had gotten away while they were in the thicket, and the men suffered from the nagging fear that Confederate cavalry was after them.[9]

Reaching a deep spot in the Potomac, two men guarded the sleeping prisoners while the rest hurriedly built a raft before sunrise. Several roundtrips got them to the Maryland side. The relieved Northerners headed southeast on the Chesapeake and Ohio Canal towpath, reaching a Federal picket at Lock 24, near Seneca Creek. After securing breakfast, they boarded a canal boat and reached Georgetown that evening. After a day in Washington, the detachment returned to its regiment near Rockville. Lieutenant Colonel Tyndale was surprised to see the men—by that time, they had been recorded as prisoners. Their daring reconnaissance did not bear intelligence as quickly as the signal station near Frederick, but their journey was most commendable. Banks issued a general order that heaped praise on the men, and the 28th Pennsylvania gave three boisterous cheers after it was read.[10]

* * *

The Confederate army among which the Pennsylvanians tiptoed had started moving toward Leesburg the day after Chantilly. By that time, Lee discovered that any chance of getting between Pope's army and Washington's forts had evaporated. He felt, however, that despite the extraordinary success that his army had achieved since June, an opportunity to inflict further damage on the Federal army and on Northern public opinion had slipped through his fingers. Keen to create a fresh opportunity and to remove the Northern army for as long as possible from Virginia's agricultural areas, Lee turned northward on September 3. General D. H. Hill's division, which had arrived the day before from Richmond's defenses, led the way, bivouacking near Leesburg that night. On September 4, Hill's division

9 Ibid.

10 Foering Diary, September 1, 1862, HSP; Hayward to brother, September 28, 1862, GC.

crossed the Potomac at several points, and attempted to damage the Chesapeake and Ohio Canal, the Monocacy Aqueduct, and the Baltimore and Ohio Railroad.[11]

The next day, Jackson's Corps began crossing at White's Ford, followed by Stuart's cavalry and Longstreet's Corps. By the 6th, Jackson had reached Frederick, Maryland, where the whole army, except Stuart's cavalry, rested from September 7th to 9th. Southern cavalry spread out toward Baltimore and Washington, screening the army and creating confusion regarding Lee's objective. It skirmished with Union cavalry at Hyattstown and Poolesville between September 8 and 12 as the Army of the Potomac, reorganized and reequipped, began its pursuit.[12]

*   *   *

While Pope retreated in the early days of September, Maj. Gen. George Brinton McClellan made himself available in this time of crisis. With his corps transferred to Pope, McClellan had idled at Alexandria since August 27, overseeing a headquarters and a 100-man camp guard, eager to return to his troops. As the corps of the combined armies lumbered toward the forts on September 2, orders directed McClellan to command the fortifications and "all the troops for the defense of the capital." He rode out to meet the men as they arrived. He immediately set into motion proof of the organizational prowess for which he was well known, strengthening garrisons, arranging units to defend the capital, and resupplying an army that had suffered from logistical neglect. With word of his return, the army's confidence immediately improved.[13]

McClellan's return electrified the veterans of his Peninsula campaign. The sentiment largely lifted Banks's corps as well, reenergizing the battered troops within days. Colonel George Andrews wrote on September 4 that McClellan's reassumption of command gave "great satisfaction" to the army. Andrews's lieutenant colonel, Wilder Dwight, wrote on September 7 from the front near Rockville that if the Confederates crossed into Maryland as was rumored, "And if our hearts have not really died within us then we shall be fit to strike them. We want Soldiers, Soldiers and a General in command. . . . For the history of the past fifteen months is the sad record of that want. . . . It has come back to McClellan! I met him

---

11 OR 19, pt. 1, 144-145; Joseph Harsh, *Taken at the Flood*, 66-119.

12 OR 19, pt. 1, 144-145, 814-815, 952-953; Harsh, *Taken at the Flood*, 66-119.

13 OR 19, pt. 1, 24-25.

Maj. Gen. George Brenton McClellan
Library of Congress

as I went into Washington the other day. His manner was gay, confident, elated. His staff were jubilant. Again he takes the reins and what do you expect? I must hope tho' I know not why." The 28th New York's history recounted, "The army was perfectly wild with joy, and the men shouted themselves hoarse when they learned that 'Little Mac' was again in command. . . . A feeling of confidence soon pervaded, order was restored, and needed supplies of all kinds were furnished." The 27th Indiana's historian wrote that, as soon as the corps crossed into Maryland, "As if by magic . . . every one who was the least discouraged or doubtful before, was now buoyant and full of confidence." The Indianans' history, however, was unwilling to ascribe credit to McClellan, since the men had no firsthand experience with the young commander. An observer in the 5th Connecticut recalled the days immediately following the entry into Maryland:

> The disorganized masses of men, which less than a week ago fell back to and through Washington are beginning to have some form, array and connection with each other as an army. Off to the right and also to the left as far as we can see, when we cross the ridges, several parallel lines of troops can be seen advancing in unison and ready in a few minutes' time. . . . A feeling of confidence is coming again. Order is being evolved from disorder . . . every day needed supplies are being pushed forward to us, and we are being, to the extent of our immediate needs, equipped and clothed anew.

On September 4, Maj. Ario Pardee of the 28th Pennsylvania wrote simply, "We hope soon to have an opportunity of again advancing."[14]

14 Andrews to Wife, September 4, 1862, USA; Dwight to mother, September 7, 1862, MHS; Boyce, *Twenty-eighth New York*, 45-46; Brown, *Twenty-Seventh Indiana*, 224; Marvin, *Fifth Connecticut*, 236; Ario Pardee to "Dear Pa," September 4, 1862, Pardee-Robison Collection, USA.

Morale was also strengthened by various instances that proved the maxim that an army marches on its stomach. This began as early as September 4 on the march to Chain Bridge. The column halted briefly in Georgetown, where, Lieutenant Gould wrote, "Women and young ladies opened their doors and windows to give us bread and butter, meat, apples, peaches and preserves!" Bivouacking two miles beyond Tenallytown, the corps reunited with its wagons. The men had been without all the comforts that the wagons provided since leaving Culpepper on August 19. According to Lieutenant Bryant, "The luxury of a tent, a chance for a bath, a change of underclothing we enjoyed to the full." The next day, the corps passed through Rockville, going into camp two miles north of the town. While passing through Rockville, locals provided plentiful lunches. At one spot, citizens furnished the troops with whiskey from buckets. The corps remained at this camp, next to Maj. Gen. Edwin V. Sumner's II Corps, until September 9.[15]

While morale improved, the XII Corps's condition still left something to be desired. It received five new regiments during its stay near Rockville, but the original regiments remained broken-down. On September 9, Crawford wrote a foreboding dispatch to Alpheus Williams. He mentioned that his brigade had been "well nigh destroyed" at Cedar Mountain and that its existence as an organized unit was threatened. Its four regiments contained just 629 soldiers fit for duty. In the wake of Pope's grueling campaign, men who never straggled in the past could no longer keep up on marches. The corps was organizationally degraded as well. Captains led the 28th New York, 5th Connecticut, and 46th Pennsylvania, while corporals commanded companies. To avert what Crawford felt would be the regiments' disintegration, he urged Williams to remove the brigade to reorganize and recruit. Williams forwarded the request, which came to nothing. The 5th Connecticut, however, ultimately remained in Frederick while the rest of the corps fought at Antietam. The command structure of Crawford's brigade is unclear until September 11. He had confined Col. George Beal to camp for disobeying an order to stand the 10th Maine to arms for insulting a member of Banks's staff. Beal returned on the 11th and led the brigade until Colonel Knipe returned from his injuries three days later.[16]

Five days before Crawford's appeal, Col. Henry Stainrook highlighted the condition of his 109th Pennsylvania in a letter to Banks. The degradations that

---

15 Gould, *10th Maine*, 222-223; Hinkley Diary, September 4, 1862, WHS; Bryant, *Third Wisconsin*, 118; Marvin, *Fifth Connecticut*, 236.

16 OR 19, pt. 2, 223-224; Marvin, *Fifth Connecticut*, 237; Gould, *10th Maine*, 221-222, 224.

Stainrook recounted were common throughout the corps, and his request to remove his regiment from active service was approved. But instead of getting rest, Stainrook was placed in command of the brigade for the rest of the campaign.[17]

Another of Crawford's brigade commanders, Maj. Thomas Walker of the 111th Pennsylvania, also advocated for his command. While his regiment was encamped near the capitol, instead of asking for a respite, Walker applied in person to Secretary of War Stanton to rearm his men. Like many regiments in the corps, the 111th still carried outdated weapons that the infantry called "Belgian rifles." The men had no confidence in these guns and were pleased when Major Walker secured Enfield rifled muskets for them. Though they were still not of the same quality of the Springfield rifles that it would receive the following spring, the Enfields were a substantial improvement.[18]

*　　*　　*

For those of Pope's corps that crossed into Maryland (Sigel's stayed behind), McClellan established center, right, and left wings after assuming command of the field army on September 7. Major General Ambrose Burnside commanded the right wing, which included the I and IX Corps under Maj. Gens. Joseph Hooker and Jesse Reno, respectively. (The I Corps had been Irvin McDowell's III Corps in the Army of Virginia.) The center, under Maj. Gen. Edwin Sumner, was comprised of Sumner's II Corps and the XII Corps, then commanded by Alpheus Williams. The left wing consisted of Maj. Gen. William Franklin's VI Corps, supported by Maj. Gen. Darius Couch's division. Fitz John Porter's V Corps would follow in a few days. Nathaniel Banks formally took command of the capital's defenses on September 8. On the 12th, General Order 129 assigned the erstwhile Army of Virginia corps that crossed into Maryland to the Army of the Potomac, formally designating them I and XII Corps.[19]

McClellan had been in his element early that month, taking massive strides September 2 through 6 toward returning morale and wresting order from chaos. While not yet in command of the field army, he pushed its units forward to positions suitable for securing Washington. His progress with reordering,

17 Henry Stainrook to Nathaniel Banks, September 4, 1862, Banks Papers, LC.

18 Boyle, *Soldiers True*, 5

19 OR 19, pt. 1, 25, 38-39, and pt. 2, 214, 279; D. Scott Hartwig, *To Antietam Creek: The Maryland Campaign of September 1862* (Baltimore, 2012), 132; Quaife, *From the Cannon's Mouth*, 111.

resupplying, and subsequently advancing two recently beaten armies significantly outperformed his track record and ultimately outpaced Lee's expectations. On September 8, Little Mac, now in command of the field army, notified Halleck that his intelligence was "still entirely too indefinite to justify definite action." But, two hours later at 10:00 p.m., he announced that he intended to advance.[20]

When the XII Corps moved on September 9, it had a different complement of regiments and a different command structure than when it had crossed the Potomac. New regiments joined their brigades at Rockville that day, but the discipline and utility of these regiments was questionable. The three Pennsylvania regiments—the 124th, 125th, and 128th—joined Crawford's decimated brigade. The 107th New York and the 13th New Jersey became part of Gordon's brigade. The latter regiment's colonel, Ezra Carman, told Colonel Andrews on September 10 that his men had not yet learned to load and fire their weapons. They had spent most of their time performing rudimentary drill and digging rifle pits since forming.[21]

Besides being unprepared, the green regiments had a reputation for slack discipline, likely because most of their officers were green volunteers as well. Complaining about the trespasses of the Union army on the Maryland countryside, First Lieutenant Gillette might have had some of these regiments in mind when he wrote the following on September 13:

> No one can point to a single act of vandalism perpetrated by the rebel soldiery during their occupation of Frederick while even now a countless host of stragglers are crawling after our own army devouring, destroying or wasting all that falls in their devious line of march.[22]

Many in the new Pennsylvania regiments reportedly left the ranks and Crawford stayed busy curbing them. A 124th Pennsylvanian wrote, "Trespasses were committed upon the corn and potato fields and orchards, and bountifully they yielded." On the march to Rockville, Pvt. Edward G. Davis of the 124th came

---

20 OR 19, pt. 1, 39, pt. 2, 145-146, 211; Marion V. Armstrong, Jr., *Unfurl Those Colors! McClellan, Sumner, and the Second Army Corps in the Antietam Campaign* (Tuscaloosa, AL, 2008), 112-113; Harsh, *Taken at the Flood*, 130-131, 213.

21 *Historical Sketch of CO "D" 13th Regiment N.J. Vols.* (New York, 1875), 12; Gregory A. Coco, "Through Blood and Fire: The Civil War Letters of Major Charles J. Mills, 1862-1865," 33, manuscript copy at USA.

22 Gillette to mother, September 13, 1862, LC.

upon an attractive farmhouse. He and several of his comrades ran after chickens. As Davis nabbed one, Crawford rode up, firing expletives and calling Davis a chicken thief. Davis pulled the chicken from his haversack. Crawford then chased another man who had grabbed one of the farmer's geese. Taking advantage of the distraction, Davis made good his escape with the bird. Mischievous characters in the 125th Pennsylvania bought food from sutlers, then distracted them while others stole from the vendors. Someone pulled the linchpin from a wagon, sending it rolling away. The 125th's Cpl. William Homan likewise saw men chasing chickens and geese at a full run as he marched on September 10. The old farmer appealed to Crawford, who arrested some of those involved. Several days later, as Crawford rode past, soldiers in Company F of the 124th Pennsylvania complained that they were hungry. With the memory of the corps's time in Virginia undoubtedly fresh in his mind, Crawford disparagingly called the men "Pennsylvania Cattle." Sergeant William W. Potts of that company remembered that some of them wanted to "get square" with their brigadier. Potts reflected, "If I was aiming at a reb and the General got in the way, I would not stop firing on his account." Potts later tried buying food from a house. After Crawford turned his back, Potts thought he might shoot Crawford if he had been alone. Besides the unruly behavior, Lieutenant Gould noted that the new regiments kept ranks closed better on the march than the veterans, but kept "hurrahing or yelling all the time."[23]

Samuel Crawford was not the only disliked commander on the march north. One day, George Gordon and his staff were at the head of his brigade, following Company B, 125th Pennsylvania, at the tail of Crawford's line. One of the Pennsylvanians had killed a pig, carved off a hind quarter, and continued after his company with the partial carcass suspended from his rifle. Gordon sharply yelled, "Close up! Join your company!" The man maintained a deliberate pace, causing Gordon to repeat the command, adding for good measure, "I am General Gordon." The irreverent Pennsylvanian turned and saluted, adding, "I am happy to make your acquaintance!" Gordon's staff broke into laughter.[24]

The size of Gordon's staff paled in comparison with the pack of erstwhile 2nd Massachusetts junior officers that he had had at Cedar Mountain. As in the rest of

23 Green, *One Hundred and Twenty-fourth Pennsylvania*, 22; George E. Davis, Memoir (typescript), Parry Family Collection, 5, USA; William Homan, "Corporal's Diary" (typescript), September 10, 1862, USA; Gould, *10th Maine*, 223. When donated to the USA, the author of the Davis memoir was listed as George Edward Davis of Company A. A review of the roster in Green's history reveals that Company A contained a Pvt. Edward George Davis.

24 Miles Clayton Huyette, *The Maryland Campaign and the Battle of Antietam* (Buffalo, 1915), 14.

Lt.Col. Hector Tyndale
National Archives Records Administration

the corps, the regiment's heavy losses created gaps that had to be filled. Staffers such as Capt. Robert Gould Shaw returned to company command as a result. The 2nd was fortunate to receive fresh officers and men while on Pope's retreat. Lieutenant Charles Mills became adjutant after arriving in camp. Lieutenant Colonel Wilder Dwight suggested, "I fancy [Mills] finds himself quite as busy as he likes to be. He comes at the moment when we need every officer's service. He will do well I think." Gordon's staff needs, however, remained unresolved. The day after the corps reached Washington's forts, Gordon found a friend in town. Massachusetts Congressman Charles Train had returned to Washington on September 2. On the 4th, he met Gordon and described him, maybe with a bit of hyperbole, as "all worn out, and without a staff officer left." He immediately requested a commission from President Lincoln, who granted one at the rank of captain. Train now offered what services he could, at his own expense, to Gordon.[25]

On September 8, Lt. Col. Hector Tyndale, the senior colonel in Geary's brigade, took command. A string of predecessors had fallen out from sickness during Pope's campaign. That day, an officer from the 28th Pennsylvania wrote, "Officers as a general thing have been subjected to the most overbearing conduct towards them by their commanding officer Col. Tyndale. . . . He has been most fortunate that we were not in a regular engagement as I fear he would if the balls of the enemy had spared him, been injured by his own command. A more disagreeable man I never met."[26]

25 Dwight to mother, August 20, 1862, MHS; Arthur Train, *Puritan's Progress* (New York, 1931), 263-265.

26 Tyndale, *Generals' Reports*, 6; Foering Diary, September 8, 1862, HSP; McLaughlin, *Memoir of Hector Tyndale*, 54; Ario Pardee to "Pa," September 8, 1862, USA.

Brig. Gen. George Sears Greene
U.S. Army Heritage and Education Center

Brigadier General George Greene had commanded Augur's division since it recoiled from the Cornfield at Cedar Mountain. He was no spring chicken. Born in 1801, the 1823 West Point graduate was six years Robert E. Lee's senior. Greene had spent 13 years teaching engineering and serving on garrison duty in New England. He left the army in 1836 and missed the formative Mexican War experience. For the next 26 years, he worked as a civil engineer. He reentered the service early in 1862 as colonel of the 60th New York. After being promoted to brigadier general in April, he briefly supplanted Gordon in command of that brigade until Gordon received a promotion. Gordon's brigade, especially the 2nd Massachusetts, disliked Greene's appointment. The angst toward Greene sprung from causes beyond a mere affinity for Gordon. The soldiers disliked his detached and strict manner and his attempts to protect the property of Southern civilians. Even the members of the 27th Indiana, no fans of Gordon, were unhappy. The regimental history described a "crotchety" commander who implemented methods that "a grannyish old farmer might adopt to get his favorite stall-fed calf to the county fair." The regiment marched only in the cooler parts of the day, and he attempted to regulate the frequency and amount the men ate and drank. Captain Richard Cary, who died at Cedar Mountain, had called Greene, "A finiking old Jackass: takes all day to do nothing & puts guards on all the houses to prevent the soldiers from doing any harm to the property of scoundrelly cut-throats of secessionists." Greene once ordered the 29th Pennsylvania to rebuild a fence it had torn down for firewood. Lieutenant Colonel Eugene Powell, commanding the 66th Ohio, described Greene as "rigid and severe, and our troops had taken a great antipathy to him." The 7th Ohio's Pvt. Charles Tenney described similar sentiments in a letter home. "By his [too] familiar manners, and the supercilious way he treats officers in the Ohio regiments," Tenney wrote, "he has rendered himself completely obnoxious." The soldiers began to greet Greene's approach with, "Here comes Greeney!" and "Hurrah for our green general!"[27]

Under its new leaders, the corps marched at noon on September 9. Sumner's wing advanced north from Rockville along the Frederick Road. French's division of Sumner's corps used the road itself, while Sumner's other two divisions advanced cross country in parallel columns east of it. Williams's division, under Crawford, and Greene's division marched parallel to each other on the west of the road. That evening, both corps were along Seneca Creek at Middlebrook. During these first advances, the army was en echelon, with Burnside's right wing in front. On September 10, McClellan determined that the main Confederate force was still at Frederick and pushed forward to occupy Parr Ridge, on the eastern border of the Monocacy Valley. The XII Corps halted a mile short of Damascus; Sumner's II Corps stopped three miles east of Clarksburg. Both positions fell short of McClellan's objective for the day. The two corps encamped on Parr Ridge on September 11 after marching a mile. The next day, Burnside's lead elements entered Frederick from the east, Sumner advanced to Urbana, nearing the Monocacy River, and Williams was near Ijamsville, on Sumner's right. On September 13, the corps rose at 3:30 a.m. and marched at 7:00. Though most expected a forced crossing as it approached the Monocacy, it forded uncontested.[28]

*   *   *

Following a skirmish in Frederick on September 12, Confederate cavalry left the area prior to Burnside's arrival there. Lee's infantry had left Frederick on September 10 to reduce Harpers Ferry. The Federal garrison there had not withdrawn as Lee supposed it would once he got between it and Washington. Accepting the risk involved in reducing that garrison, Lee split his army into four columns. Jackson crossed the Potomac at Williamsport, captured Martinsburg, and arrived at Harpers Ferry from the west on September 12. Brigadier General John G. Walker took Loudon Heights, across the Shenandoah River from Harpers

27 Warner, *Generals in Blue*, 186-187; Brown, *Twenty-Seventh Indiana*, 173, 176; Richard Cary to Wife, June 13, 1862, MHS; Powell Memoir, chap. 6, OHC; Charles Tenney to "My Darling Addie," September 9, 1862, "Correspondence of Charles Tenney with Adelaide Case [manuscript], 1861-1863," MSS 11616, UVA.

28 OR 19, pt. 2, 233, 241, 255, 271; OR 51, pt. 1, 811; Armstrong, *Unfurl Those Colors*, 91; Gould, *10th Maine*, 224; Hinkley Diary, September 9-13, 1862, WHS; Quaife, *From the Cannon's Mouth*, 122.

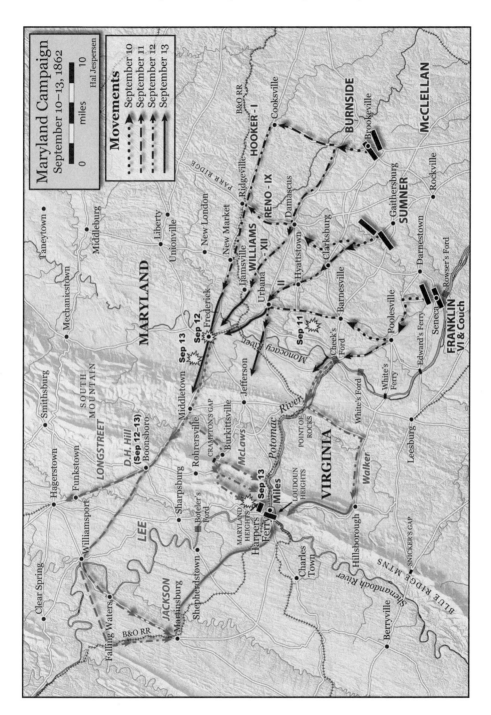

Maryland Campaign
September 10–13, 1862

Movements
········ September 10
– – – September 11
–·–·– September 12
——— September 13

miles   Hal Jespersen
0   10

Ferry. Major General Lafayette McLaws, with his division and Maj. Gen. R. H. Anderson's division, crossed South Mountain into Pleasant Valley. McLaws sent Brig. Gen. Joseph B. Kershaw with his South Carolina brigade and Brig. Gen. William Barksdale's Mississippi brigade to Elk Ridge, west of Pleasant Valley. These brigades advanced south along the mountain to capture Maryland Heights, a commanding position over Harpers Ferry and the key to the operation. D. H. Hill's division and the remainder of Longstreet's command, guarding the army's rear, retired to the vicinity of Boonsboro. Longstreet eventually continued toward Hagerstown. On September 12 and 13, Kershaw and Barksdale attacked a Federal detachment garrisoning Maryland Heights. They secured this critical position by afternoon on the 13th. The remainder of McLaws's command occupied the southern end of Pleasant Valley and South Mountain, blocking the exits from Harpers Ferry.[29]

Special Order 191, the Army of Northern Virginia directive that set these events into motion on September 9, detailed Lee's plan, including the far-flung destinations of each command. A copy of the order, stuffed in an envelope with three cigars and addressed to D. H. Hill, lay in a field on the Best farm, south of Frederick. It was one of two copies that had been written for Hill, one by Lee's staff and one by Jackson himself.[30]

*   *   *

With Confederate infantry gone, Williams's XII Corps uneventfully forded the Monocacy and advanced toward Frederick's clustered spires. After traversing a belt of woods on the east bank, the men discovered smoke billowing west of town from Federal horse artillery firing on Rebels withdrawing over Catoctin Mountain, six miles west of Frederick. A 13th New Jersey recruit recalled that the men took the distant artillery as a sign they were approaching the enemy and burst into cheers. He noted, however, that the veteran regiments displayed no such sentiment. They "moved along in stolid indifference to all these preliminaries to our approaching battle" and appeared to view the green regiment's fervor with "amused yet

---

29 *OR* 19, pt. 1, 145-146, 853-854, 953-954.

30 Harsh, *Taken at the Flood*, 152-153.

seemingly sneering contempt." The 27th Indiana led the corps, wading the knee-deep river before halting in a clover field.[31]

Fredericktonians received the army enthusiastically. With the XII Corps parked southeast of Frederick, some soldiers entered town that afternoon, generally without permission. The corps's original regiments had camped outside Frederick the previous winter, and many of the men now visited acquaintances. The 3rd Wisconsin had been particularly well regarded by the townspeople and made the most of its return. Lieutenant Hinkley recalled, "All had something toothsome" for the callers from the Badger State.[32]

Frederick's citizenry extended generosity to new guests, as well. Private Edward Davis temporarily absconded from the 124th Pennsylvania and solicited a feast of "ham, fried eggs, potatoes, stewed tomatoes, preserves, coffee, bread and butter, and milk and honey," accompanied by a piano recital by the lady of the house. He then returned to his regiment and to picket duty, which he also found pleasant. "I shall never forget the panorama which was spread before me. It seemed as though two heavens had united, the one above with stars shining brightly, the other below caused by the thousands of flickering camp fires spread out over the hills for miles around, casting a weird light over the river as it flowed peacefully by and over the thousands of sleeping soldiers." The entire XII Corps camped closely together and near the rest of the army. The 2nd Massachusetts's Lieutenant Mills enjoyed that night, as well. Someone scrounged a hospital tent, wherein the line officers, some of whom presumably were from Gordon's brigade, gathered and "had quite a jolly evening with songs, brandy, water and peaches."[33]

Meanwhile, George McClellan had plenty of diversion of his own. When the 27th Indiana had halted in the late forenoon, a skirmish line, Companies A and F, advanced. After halting, the men stacked arms. First Sergeant John M. Bloss of Company F noticed a large envelope in the grass, and asked Cpl. Barton W. Mitchell to hand it to him. They divided the cigars contained within but did not readily discover a match. While waiting, Bloss looked over the papers that were

---

31 OR 19, pt. 1, 26; "The Clustered Spires of Frederick" is taken from the poem "Barbara Fritchie" by John Greenleaf Whittier; Gould, *10th Maine*, 225; Quaife, *From the Cannon's Mouth*, 122; Huyette, *Maryland Campaign*, 17; Brown, *Twenty-Seventh Indiana*, 228; James O. Smith, "My First Campaign and Battles: A Jersey Boy at Antietam, Seventeen Days from Home," *Blue and Gray* (April 1893), 281.

32 Hinkley, *Third Wisconsin*, 48.

33 Davis Memoir, 6-7, USA; Gould, *10th Maine*, 225; Coco, "Through Blood and Fire," 35, USA.

wrapped around the cigars. Soon, thoughts of smoking left Bloss's mind and he immediately sought Capt. Peter Kop. After returning Confederate Special Order 191 to its envelope, with the cigars, the three Hoosiers delivered the parcel to Colonel Colgrove, who took it to Williams's headquarters. Williams forwarded it to McClellan with a cover letter. Gordon reportedly saw the package as well and correctly commented that it was "worth a mint of money."[34]

The opportunity that this document provided McClellan to destroy isolated elements of Lee's army was not lost on him. He began issuing preparatory dispatches at 3:00 p.m. Wishing to rule out a ruse, McClellan directed his cavalry chief, Alfred Pleasanton, to verify the movements enumerated in the order. By early evening, McClellan felt sufficiently informed to initiate the plan he had developed in the interim. At 6:20 p.m., he ordered Franklin's VI Corps, supported by Couch's division, beyond Burkittsville and up Crampton's Gap to secure the mountain pass and isolate and destroy McLaws's force. The rest of the army would cross Catoctin Mountain and then South Mountain along the National Road to attack the forces that he expected to be at Boonsboro under Longstreet and D. H. Hill. Much of Reno's IX Corps was already across Catoctin Mountain and en route to Middletown in the Catoctin Valley. Hooker's I Corps, which was two miles east of Frederick, was next to advance, with orders to march at daylight. By the time these two corps reached Fox's and Turner's Gaps on September 14, D. H. Hill had two brigades on the mountain to delay the Federal advance, which Stuart had reported.[35]

In the midst of his planning on September 13, McClellan tried to effect a series of personnel moves. He was not satisfied with Alpheus Williams's position atop the XII Corps. At about 9:00 p.m., as an aide wrote orders for Pleasanton to randomly fire artillery as a sign to the Harpers Ferry garrison that the army was approaching,

34 John Bloss, "The Lost Order," *Paper Read Before Kansas Commandery of Military Order of the Loyal Legions of the United States*, January 6, 1892, copy in NYPL; John Bloss to "Dear Friends," September 25, 1862, typescript, and Richard Datzman, "Who Found Lee's Lost Dispatch," copies at Monocacy National Battlefield; Silas Colgrove, "The Finding of Lee's Lost Order," in *Battles and Leaders of the Civil War: Being for the Most Part Contributions by Union and Confederate Officers*, 4 vols. (Secaucus, NJ, 1982), 2:603; Ezra Carman, *The Maryland Campaign of September 1862: Vol. I: South Mountain*, Thomas Clemens, ed. (El Dorado Hills, CA, 2010), 279-281; Hartwig, *To Antietam Creek*, 111, 282-283. Samuel Pittman, Williams's assistant adjutant general, was on hand when the order arrived. He declared that he was a prewar acquaintance of Lee's staffer, Robert Chilton, and recognized Chilton's signature. According to a note by Thomas Clemens in the Ezra Carman campaign history, the two men were not as well known to each other as Pittman asserted.

35 OR 19, pt. 1, 45, 48, 146; OR 51, pt. 1, 829; Hartwig, *To Antietam Creek*, 284-291.

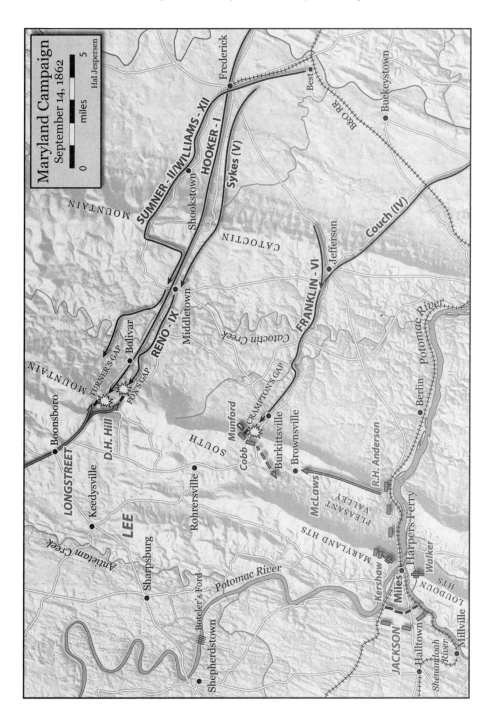

Maryland Campaign
September 14, 1862

0 miles 5

Hal Jespersen

Frederick

Buckeystown

Best

B&O RR

SUMNER - II/WILLIAMS - XII

HOOKER - I

Shookstown

Sykes (V)

CATOCTIN MOUNTAIN

Jefferson

Couch (IV)

Middletown

Bolivar

RENO - IX

Catoctin Creek

FRANKLIN - VI

TURNER'S GAP

FOX'S GAP

Potomac River

MOUNTAIN

D.H. Hill

CRAMPTON'S GAP

Berlin

Boonsboro

Munford

Burkittsville

LONGSTREET

Cobb

Brownsville

SOUTH

R.H. Anderson

Keedysville

McLaws

LEE

Rohrersville

PLEASANT VALLEY

Sharpsburg

MARYLAND HTS

Antietam Creek

Kershaw

Harpers Ferry

Boteler's Ford

Potomac River

Walker

Miles

LOUDOUN HTS

Shepherdstown

JACKSON

Halltown

Shenandoah River

Millville

McClellan announced that someone needed to take command of the XII Corps. He asked one of his aides to read the list of general officers. When Maj. Gen. John Sedgwick was named, McClellan fixated on him. The staffer suggested that Sedgwick would not want to leave his division in Sumner's corps, but McClellan insisted. That same day, Sedgwick was temporarily assigned command of the corps, but the order was never executed. Upon receipt of it, Sedgwick requested to retain his current command.[36]

Sumner's wing, scheduled to march at 7:00 a.m., was to be last on the road, following Hooker's corps, Sykes's V Corps division, and the reserve artillery. Delay was inevitable, since Hooker's corps had to march to and through town before the II and XII Corps could move. Once the route cleared, the corps marched through Frederick. Church bells rang and flags fluttered from windows. The march stalled frequently, amidst incessant cheering. Someone began singing "John Brown's Body." A band picked up the tune, which every regiment in the corps carried rearward. Thousands of voices filled the air.[37]

The high spirits the men experienced while marching through the town wore off during the subsequent grinding march. At 9:00 a.m., McClellan's headquarters ordered Sumner's wing to take the Shookstown Road to Middletown. This road was north of the congested National Road. Williams's men plodded up the primitive road over Catoctin Mountain behind Sumner's corps while artillery rumbled in the distance. They reached the summit about 3:00 p.m. Before them stretched the picturesque Catoctin Valley. Private James Smith of the 13th New Jersey thought it the "beau ideal of pastoral beauty and loveliness." Juxtaposed against his "awesome wonderment" at the bucolic scene was the sight of battle clearly visible on the opposite mountain range. About eight miles across the valley as the crow flies, a fierce struggle raged on the eastern slope of South Mountain. Smoke billowed from artillery in the western valley, and thick clouds of smoke emanated from the infantry fight. Smith saw the Northern army, with bayonets glinting in the sunlight, "Wending and twisting its way toward South Mountain

36 OR 51, pt. 1, 830; OR 19, pt. 2, 283; John Gibbon, *Personal Recollections of the Civil War* (New York, 1928), 72-73; Armstrong, *Unfurl Those Colors*, 109. Precisely what misgiving McClellan had with Williams is unclear, though Scott Hartwig, probably accurately, assigns three causes in his recent history of the campaign (*To Antietam Creek*, 145): Williams was not a West Pointer, did not serve with the Army of the Potomac on the Peninsula, and was an unknown quantity to McClellan.

37 OR 19, pt. 1, 48; OR 51, pt. 1, 826; Marvin, *Fifth Connecticut*, 237; McLaughlin, *Memoirs of Hector Tyndale*, 55; Gould, *10th Maine*, 225; Carman, *Maryland Campaign: South Mountain*, 370-371.

passes, like some great octopus drawing in his tentacles . . . creeping resistlessly onward." The corps, however, did not advance as the crow flies.[38]

Without halting to take in the view, the corps hurried down the western slope of Catoctin Mountain, briefly rested, and then cut a circuitous route through fields before reaching a road that later joined the National Road to Middletown. Supply wagons, three abreast, jammed the National Road. As a result, the men marched alongside the road, through fields and woodlots. Fences, stone walls, and ditches slowed the march considerably. Reaching Middletown after dark, the corps was ordered onto the wrong road and headed back toward Frederick. After a half mile of retrograde movement, it returned to Middletown. The men slept in the streets for about an hour. McClellan arrived from Burnside's headquarters, where he had observed the battle and, with staff in tow, rode carefully through the sleeping infantrymen. At 9:00 p.m., he ordered Sumner to take the XII Corps to the vicinity of Bolivar, at the base of Turner's Gap. General Crawford, the second most senior officer in the corps, received orders that night to report in person to McClellan in Middletown. McClellan's chief of staff, Brig. Gen. Randolph Marcy, directed Crawford to move to Turner's Gap and be prepared to carry it in the morning if the enemy put up a fight.[39]

Alpheus Williams was not with the corps in Middletown when McClellan reached it. He had stopped at a farmhouse for dinner while the corps marched from Catoctin Mountain. En route to find the command, Williams stopped to ensure that a staff officer, whose horse had fallen, received medical attention. Orders then found Williams directing the corps to Middletown to report to McClellan. Williams found neither the corps nor McClellan in Middletown. After some searching, he discovered his corps at 2:00 a.m. where it had bivouacked an hour before, behind Joseph Hooker's I Corps and below Turner's Gap. Sunrise found the corps with a new commander. Brigadier General Joseph King Fenno Mansfield arrived that morning from Washington and reported to McClellan in Middletown. McClellan's perceived problem with the XII Corps's leadership was solved.[40]

38 OR 51, pt. 1, 831; Green, *One Hundred and Twenty-fourth Pennsylvania*, 26; Quaife, *From the Cannon's Mouth*, 122; Smith, "My First Campaign," 282; Hinkley Diary, September 13, 1862, LC.

39 OR 51, pt. 1, 831; Carman, *Maryland Campaign: South Mountain*, 371; Hinkley, *Third Wisconsin*, 49-50; Bryant, *Third Wisconsin*, 121; Gould, *10th Maine*, 226; Crawford, *Generals' Reports*, 12.

40 Quaife, *From the Cannon's Mouth*, 121-122.

Williams's inability to find the corps may have derived from its erratic movements upon leaving Middletown. The march there was tedious, with countermarching up a narrow road and then off road through a hollow. Lieutenant Bryant remembered having a "wearying, hurrying time of it" as the men "groped and stumbled" in the dark across brooks and over outcroppings on the mountainside. A 128th Pennsylvanian found the route, "So steep and rocky that it was almost impossible to get along at some places." The column eventually returned to the National Road and the rear of Hooker's corps, where the men fell to the ground, hungry and exhausted.[41]

The march on the September 14 taxed the entire corps. Lieutenant Hinkley thought it the "hardest march of our experience." Less than half of the 3rd Wisconsin veterans kept up through the entire march. The 10th Maine had less than 100 soldiers when it stacked arms. According to Sgt. Henry Comey, the 2nd Massachusetts, which had trekked for 16 hours over wet fields and through creeks, with no food since breakfast, was "cold, tired and in very bad spirits." For the green troops in the new regiments, entirely unused to hard marching, the day was a miserable one. Sergeant Potts of the 124th Pennsylvania remembered how the full day of marching in wet fields and through streams made shoe soles slippery. By the end of the day, with heavy feet, toes began catching on vines, causing some men, too tired to catch themselves, to fall on their faces. When their halts were over, the new soldiers stood their rifles on end and pulled themselves up onto their feet. Potts wrote that, "Some of our mess were completely played out, and their feet were bleeding. They begged us to fall out as they could not go any further." Only about 60 men in the 125th Pennsylvania and 27 men in the 13th New Jersey initially reached the bivouac. Stragglers continued trickling in until noon on September 15.[42]

When those who kept up dropped to the ground, they were close enough to the scene of the recent fighting to see lamplights floating eerily as men attempted to treat the wounded. Crawford stumbled through the darkness, examining the ground in front in order to execute the orders to carry the pass in the morning.[43]

41 Gould, *10th Maine*, 226-227; Comey, *A Legacy of Valor*, 74; Bryant, *Third Wisconsin*, 121; *Reading* [PA] *Daily Times*, September 27, 1862.

42 Hinkley Diary, September 14, 1862, LC; Comey, *A Legacy of Valor*, 74; Gould, *10th Maine*, 226; Green, *One Hundred and Twenty-fourth Pennsylvania*, 118; *One Hundred Twenty-Fifth Pennsylvania*, 170; *Historical Sketch of Co. D, 13th Regiment*, 13.

43 Huyette, *Maryland Campaign*, 25-26; Crawford, *Generals' Reports*, 12. Crawford wrote that he explored the ground with "Sturgis." This was presumably Brig. Gen. Samuel Sturgis, who led

As they awoke on September 15, the soldiers discovered that there would be no fight. Skirmishers advanced at daylight without opposition. D. H. Hill's division and the portion of Longstreet's Corps that had reinforced Hill, having succeeded in delaying the Northern army, withdrew overnight. The Confederates retreated through Boonsboro and Keedysville to Sharpsburg, where Lee awaited the detachments under Jackson, McLaws, and Walker.[44]

Except for the Ohio regiments in Tyndale's brigade, none of the men had been in a fight where they controlled the field after the battle. First Lieutenant John Gould woke to discover that he was in the midst of about 20 wounded men from both sides. The corps remained until midday, so some of the men went over the battlefield. William Roberts, Jr., of the 28th Pennsylvania, found Federal gravesites along the road, marked with the deceased's name, regiment, and company. Up the mountain, he came upon a ghastly scene:

> I counted 84 dead rebels lying as they fell on a space not over 40 feet square, and on a ploughed field on the summit of the hill were over 600 in a space of 8 acres all unburied and perfectly black, hideous and distorted some with ghastly wounds in the head, bowels, and chest. . . . The stench was fearful and the carrion buzzards in immense flocks were hovering over this scene of blood and woe.

The 13th New Jersey's Private Smith looked with, "Trepidation and unconcealed horror upon the torn and bloody corpses that lined one side of a stone wall." Corporal William Homan of the 125th Pennsylvania helped move wounded men into ambulances. According to a veteran in the 28th New York,

> One man I saw had just had both his legs taken off just below the knee. He lay on the table; his feet lay on the ground; arms and legs lay all around that had been taken off. . . . The ground lay strewn with dead rebels shot in all places. I saw 15 in one heap laying always piled upon one other, all shot through the head. These were behind a stone wall. The ground was covered with blankets, knapsacks, shirts, pants, and everything else that a soldier carries. They lay on the fence as they were shot. One man had the top of his head all taken off.

---

one of Jesse Reno's divisions. This is curious, for the accounts of Williams and Bryant point to a move toward the Confederate left at Turner's Gap and up the mountain defiles. Williams even identified the position as behind Hooker's corps, which was at Turner's Gap. Reno's corps, in which Sturgis had fought, was farther to the Union left, at Fox's Gap. McClellan's report (*OR* 19, pt. 1, 52) put its bivouac near Bolivar, which is on the National Road leading to Turner's Gap.

44 *OR* 19, pt. 1, 147; Crawford, *Generals' Reports*, 12.

In spite of these horrific sights, 1t Lt. Gould was filled with encouragement at the sight of discarded Confederate knapsacks strewn across the field. "From that hour we felt strong, and what is far better we felt that victory and battle were synonymous terms," he wrote. "A wonderful change had come over us in two weeks."[45]

Near midday, the corps in front began clearing the road. As the 125th Pennsylvania of Crawford's brigade waited to march, "A venerable, white-haired officer came galloping along the line, and, noticing this oversight, exclaimed, 'why are these men kept standing in the sun?' Brigadier General Joseph Mansfield had arrived. First Lieutenant Edwin Bryant of the 3rd Wisconsin observed that the corps commander was, "A soldierly, brave, gray-haired old man; but he rode his horse with proud, martial air and was full of military ardor." Gould found Mansfield, "Fresh and vigorous, his face showed that intelligent courage which a soldier admires. . . . There was nothing pretentious about him, though his dress and horse equipments were new and beautiful." Indeed, they had had little opportunity for wear yet. Though Mansfield had been in continuous service since 1822, earning brevets in the Mexican War, he spent the first year of the Civil War unsuccessfully seeking a field command. During much of that time, he worked on constructing the defenses around Washington. Alpheus Williams felt some skepticism with respect to the new commander. Writing to his daughters, he readily highlighted Mansfield's lack of experience with a large command, adding that Mansfield was "very fussy."[46]

Once underway, the column soon reached the summit of South Mountain and descended its western face on the National Road. Just after passing the summit, Capt. Charles Morse of the 2nd Massachusetts heard a low rumble to the rear that grew until it "swelled into a roar." As the men looked rearward, they saw caps flying in the air and men cheering wildly as McClellan rode past on his black horse followed by a large staff. Sergeant Comey remembered, "We all seemed to believe that at last we had a general who could lead us to the victories we deserve." Shortly after passing Comey and Morse, McClellan stopped when he found his West Point classmate Gordon at the head of the brigade. The two friends shook hands and

45 Gould, *10th Maine*, 226-227; Roberts to father, September 21, 1862, HSP; Smith, "My First Campaign," 282; Homan Diary, September 15, 1862, USA; Gillam to Wife, September 15, 1862, LC.

46 *One Hundred Twenty-Fifth Pennsylvania*, 171; Bryant, *Third Wisconsin*, 122; Gould, *10th Maine*, 227-228; Warner, *Generals in Blue*, 309; Jeremiah Taylor, *Memorial of Gen. J. K. F. Mansfield, United States Army, Who Fell in Battle at Sharpsburg, MD. Sept. 17 1862* (Boston, 1862), 48-49; Quaife, *From the Cannon's Mouth*, 123.

Brig. Gen. Joseph King Fenno Mansfield
National Archive Records Administration

rode together for a short distance. Gordon thought McClellan seemed anxious to close with Lee's Confederates. McClellan said he, "Should feel much obliged if they would only stop long enough to let him whip them." Despite the spirit that McClellan exhibited to Gordon, Lee's extreme vulnerability lessened over the next two days.[47]

On the night of September 14-15, after William B. Franklin carried Crampton's Gap, McClellan directed him to detach a portion of his force to Rohrersville in Pleasant Valley to guard against a move by Lee on Franklin's rear. The move pulled men away from the effort to get at McLaws, who drew most of his command into Pleasant Valley that night. He had left a single regiment to support the artillery on Maryland Heights, threatening Harpers Ferry until its surrender the next morning.[48]

McLaws's move proved sufficient to save his command and seal the garrison's fate. After Harpers Ferry capitulated, Jackson immediately marched to join Lee at Sharpsburg, leaving only A. P. Hill's division to manage prisoners and captured arms and supplies. Jackson arrived at Sharpsburg early on September 16. John Walker arrived that afternoon. McLaws, who perceived that he was cornered in Pleasant Valley, took his two-division command across the Potomac to Harpers Ferry and trailed Jackson and Walker south and west of the river to Boteler's Ford at Shepherdstown.[49]

* * *

47 OR 19, pt. 1, 148; Quaife, *From the Cannon's Mouth*, 124; Morse, *Letters*, 86; Comey, *A Legacy of Valor*, 75; George H. Gordon, *A War Diary of Events in the War of the Great Rebellion: 1863-1865* (Boston, 1882), 2.

48 OR 19, pt. 1, 148, 854; Hartwig, *To Antietam Creek*, 287, 441-442, 472-474.

49 OR 19, pt. 1, 148.

While Jackson hurried north, McClellan's advance from South Mountain stalled after his lead divisions halted just short of Antietam Creek, creating a logjam. Mansfield's XII Corps followed Sumner and Hooker to Boonsboro, where Pleasanton's cavalry had skirmished with the Confederate rearguard, and then to Keedysville. The IX Corps, now led by Ambrose Burnside after Jesse Reno's death on September 14, crossed Fox's Gap and headed directly toward Sharpsburg on the Old Sharpsburg Road. The first of Fitz John Porter's V Corps divisions to arrive, under Brig. Gen. George Sykes, followed Burnside. Sykes and Sumner's lead division, under Maj. Gen. Israel Richardson, made it to the eastern bank of Antietam Creek by the end of the day. A portion of Lee's army, D. H. Hill's division and part of Longstreet's Corps, was concealed among the rolling hills and ravines west of the creek, with the Potomac and the ford at Shepherdstown behind it. McClellan, along with many officers at the front, decided that it was too late to attack on September 15. This was prudent, since he had only two divisions on hand.[50]

By the next morning, McClellan had all his corps in the positions that he had initially designated, east of the Antietam. Mansfield's corps had bivouacked on September 15 near Nicodemus Mills, east of Keedysville. On the 16th, it moved to Antietam Creek, north of Pry House. Initially delayed by the need to determine where Confederates lurked under a morning fog, McClellan spent much of the day making observations and repositioning units. He intended to attack Lee's left with Hooker's and Mansfield's corps. Sumner would support as needed, but would remain near the Pry house, east of the creek. William Franklin also would support the right when his VI Corps arrived from Crampton's Gap. When McClellan judged the time was right, Burnside, on the Federal left, would attack across a bridge downstream, pressing toward Sharpsburg from the southeast. When either Confederate flank appeared to give way, McClellan's center would attack across the bridge on the Keedysville-Sharpsburg Road.[51]

At about 2:00 p.m., McClellan ordered Hooker, without Mansfield, to cross the creek using the "Upper Bridge," just upstream from the Pry mill. Hooker's task was to reach a high ridge in the vicinity of the Smoketown Road and the Hagerstown-Sharpsburg Pike and to seek and turn Lee's left. Hooker put his command in motion right away. Well aware of the isolated situation into which his

50 OR 19, pt. 1, 53-54; Hartwig, *To Antietam Creek*, 509-514.

51 OR 19, pt. 1, 54-55; Hartwig, *To Antietam Creek*, 582-588.

corps marched, the capable Massachusetts general soon returned to headquarters, hoping to solicit further instructions. McClellan explained that he would receive reinforcements, to be placed under his command, when needed. Hooker returned to his corps. After a short ride, McClellan arrived with his staff in tow. Hooker spoke plainly. He told McClellan that the idea of crossing the Antietam with one corps of less than 13,000 men to attack the entire Confederate army was ill-considered. He ended by warning that if reinforcements were not forwarded to him rapidly, "the rebels would eat me up." Following this interview, Hooker's lead division under Brig. Gen. George Gordon Meade continued westward from the Hoffman farm and then southwest toward a woodlot on Joseph Poffenberger's farm.[52]

The momentous events that took place south of the Poffenberger farm, beginning at the "North Woods," bestowed a haunting formality on seemingly commonplace terrain features such as "the Cornfield," the "East Woods," and the "West Woods." South of the North Woods stretched four fields. At the time of the battle, the first three fields were, from north to south, a plowed field, a meadow, and a cornfield. The western third of the meadow contained the David R. Miller house and an orchard. A knoll at the center of this field overlooked Miller's Cornfield to the south. This field was approximately 260 yards north to south and double that distance east to west. The three fields were similarly sized and oriented rectangles. East of the Cornfield and the meadow, the East Woods was a roughly "L"-shaped woodlot, through which ran the Smoketown Road. This road coursed nearly north-south as it entered the northern portion of the East Woods. Exiting the southwestern corner of the woods, it headed southwest until it terminated at the north-south Hagerstown Pike. Immediately west of this junction—at the edge of another "L"-Shaped, open woodlot, the West Woods—sat a modest, whitewashed meetinghouse, the Dunker Church. Between the two woods, south of the Cornfield and north of the Smoketown Road, was a large, trapezoidal field, part grass and part clover. This field was hollow in the middle, with a large swale running from the northeast corner to the southwest corner. This low ground extended in both directions, forming important ravines in both the East and West Woods.[53]

---

52 OR 19, pt. 1, 55, 217, 269; Carman, *Maryland Campaign: Antietam*, 32-33.

53 United States War Department atlas of the battlefield of Antietam, prepared under the direction of the Antietam Battlefield Board, George W. Davis, Ezra A. Carman, U. S. V., Henry Heth, surveyed by E. B. Cope, H. W. Mattern, drawn by Charles H. Ourand, position of troops

On the evening of September 16, Brig. Gen. John Bell Hood's two brigades, commanded by Cols. Evander Law and W. T. Wofford, stood south of the Cornfield. A brigade of Pennsylvania reserves, which Meade had detached south of the division, fought briefly in the East Woods with Hood's men before the two sides disengaged for the night. After Hood's brigades fell back to the West Woods, Jackson's two divisions that had arrived from Harpers Ferry became the front line on this part of the field. Two brigades of Ewell's division, commanded by Brig. Gen. Alexander R. Lawton, were to the right. This line ran from the Hagerstown Pike to the east, across the large hollow field, ultimately turning southwest across the Smoketown Road, with its right resting at a white frame farmhouse owned by Samuel Mumma, south of the East Woods. Lawton's other two brigades were detached and positioned west of the Stonewall Division, which was drawn up in two lines west of the pike, facing north. Brigadier General John R. Jones now commanded the division. Behind Jackson's line in an open field south of the Smoketown Road and just east of the Dunker Church ran a plateau on which stood four Confederate batteries, commanded by Col. Stephen D. Lee. The rest of Lee's Confederate line extended southeast from this point. D. H. Hill's division was next. Hill's three closest brigades were under Brig. Gen. Roswell Ripley and Cols. Alfred Holt Colquitt and Duncan McRae. These troops experienced heavy fighting on South Mountain on September 14. Ripley's men bivouacked south of the eastern end of Lawton's line, 150 yards west of the Mumma house. Colquitt's and McRae's brigades spent the night along a sunken farm road about a half mile south of the house. The Confederate line meandered southeast, with significant gaps, until it connected with Antietam Creek on a high bluff above the Lower Bridge.[54]

With the evening's conflict over, Hooker notified McClellan after dark that he intended to attack at dawn. Except for one brigade that remained in the East Woods, Hooker's corps would begin the battle from the North Woods. Hooker planned to advance south, straddling the Hagerstown Pike. His objective was the

---

by Ezra A. Carman, published by authority of the Secretary of War, under the direction of the Chief of Engineers, U.S. Army (Washington, DC, 1908), map, https://www.loc.gov/item/2008621532/. Hereafter referred to as Carman-Cope, *Antietam Atlas*. Based on a post-battle photograph of Knap's Battery by Alexander Gardner (*Antietam, Maryland. Captain J.M. Knap's Penn. Independent Battery "E" Light Artillery*, Sept. 19, 1862, https://www.loc.gov/item/2018671473/), the trapezoidal field may have been bisected by a fence running east to west.

54 OR 19, pt. 1, 923, 955; Carman, *Maryland Campaign: Antietam*, 33-38, 42, 55, 126, 132; Stephen Thruston to William DeRosset, June 18, 1886, APD; Ben Milikin to Ezra Carman, December 20, 1897, NA-AS; Armstrong, *Unfurl Those Colors*, 171.

Dunker Church and the high plateau south of it. That point commanded the rest of the Confederate line. Hooker suggested that the reinforcements McClellan promised should be forwarded "in season to reach me before that moment."[55]

As Hooker's men started fighting late on September 16, his intended reinforcements, the XII Corps, settled down for the night east of the Antietam. No intimation had yet arrived regarding a movement to support Hooker. During the day, some of the men bathed in the creek. Wagons arrived in the camp, which was near the Upper Bridge and the Samuel Cost farm. Each man was issued 60 rounds of ammunition. No food had been available during the day except crackers. That evening, a few head of cattle arrived for each regiment. In the 125th Pennsylvania, the men assigned to slaughter failed with an initial hammer blow and the animal ran wildly through the camp and over some of the men. Mansfield dined in Samuel Cost's home that night.[56]

At about 9:00 p.m., rain began to fall, and soldiers retired to their tents for the night. Private Charles Tenney of the 7th Ohio wrote that "a hush, solemn in its stillness, settled over camp." Around 10:00 p.m., officers moved through camp, stooping into tents to rouse soldiers in low voices. The corps would move at once. Officers passed strict orders against noise, lights, and fire of any kind. Within 10 minutes, Mansfield arrived at the 2nd Massachusetts, asking when it would be ready. He was pleased to learn that Gordon's brigade was prepared to move. The precipitation turned to a drizzle. After crossing the stone Upper Bridge, the column left the road and marched through soupy obscurity, over a course of fields and woodlots that a 102nd New Yorker called "torturous and zigzag." A Hoosier remembered marching quietly with nothing to do but watch the man in front and "meditate upon the situation." While on the march, soldiers heard at least one rifle discharge to the left of their column. The 7th Ohio halted, formed into line, and fired in the direction of the noise, which likely had come from distant skirmishers. Mansfield and a guide led the way, meandering through the countryside. Williams kept losing them in the darkness and had to send someone forward several times to stop them until he regained contact.[57]

---

55 *OR* 19, pt. 1, 218, 970.

56 Joseph Clark to John Gould, March 18, 1892, APD; Comey, *Legacy of Valor*, 75; Matchett, *Maryland and the Glorious Old Third*, 21; Green, *One Hundred and Twenty-fourth Pennsylvania*, 111; Homan Diary, September 16, 1862, USA; John W. Schildt, *Drums Along the Antietam* (Parsons, WV, 1982), 106.

57 *OR* 19, pt. 1, 218; Boyle, *Soldiers True*, 57; Tenney to "My Darling Addie," September 21, 1862, UVA; Matchett, *Maryland and the Glorious Old Third*, 21; Comey, *Legacy of Valor*, 75; Brown,

At around 2:30 a.m., the column halted on the Line and Hoffman farms. Its position—apparently chosen in recognition of the need to stop, though not in the right place—was not conducive to supporting Hooker quickly. It was about a mile and a half north-northeast of Hooker's corps. The XII Corps went to ground as it had marched, in column by companies,[58] ready to move at once. Guards watched nearby wells to preserve water for the wounded. With thoughts of this suggestive order in mind, most of the corps rested in the furrows of plowed fields, wet with the evening's rain. The 125th Pennsylvania lay between cornrows. Mansfield slept in a grass field, west of a fence that ran southward from George Line's garden to a woodlot. The 10th Maine was east of the fence in a plowed field. Some of the Mainers talked too loudly, and Mansfield ordered them to keep it to a whisper. The 111th Pennsylvania and 102nd New York bivouacked in a freshly manured field. Repulsive as this was, Cpl. J. Porter Howard wrote, "we were tired enough to sleep almost anywhere." Private Miles Huyette, a recruit in the 125th Pennsylvania, recalled that evening on the Line farm:

> The night was close, air heavy, some fog and smoke from the skirmish firing of the late evening and picket firing of the night and from stragglers' bivouac fires—to the rear—hung low; the only lights the twinkling flashes of fire-flies. . . . The air smelled a mixture of crushed green cornstalks, rag-weed and clover. . . . The night sounds—the scattered firing and occasional rattle of musketry on the picket lines—to the front; the mingled low-toned conversation of the men, occasional neighing of horses, barking of dogs—at the farm houses, crowing of roosters—disturbed at an unusual hour, and the chirping of crickets; Katy-dids joined in the night chorus with high pitch and speed.

Alpheus Williams wrote, "I shall not . . . soon forget that night; so dark, so obscure, so mysterious, so uncertain."[59]

Twenty-Seventh Indiana, 238; Isaac Van Steenbergh to John Gould, March 27, 1892, and Joseph Clark to Gould, March 18, 1892, APD; Quaife, *From the Cannon's Mouth*, 124. McClellan had issued orders for this movement at 5:50 p.m. Sumner forwarded the orders late that night. (*OR* 51, pt. 1, 839; Carman, *Maryland Campaign: Antietam*, 43.)

58 The "column of companies" formation arrayed one company behind the next, each in line of battle.

59 Carman, *Maryland Campaign: Antietam*, 43; Homan Diary, September 16, 1862, USA; John Mead Gould, *Joseph K. F. Mansfield, Brigadier General of the U. S. Army. A Narrative of Events Connected with His Mortal Wounding at Antietam, Sharpsburg, Maryland, September 17, 1862* (Portland, ME, 1895), 9; J. Porter Howard to John Gould, February 4, 1892, and James Wheeler to Gould, January 22, 1892, APD; Huyette, *Maryland Campaign*, 27-28; Quaife, *From the Cannon's Mouth*, 125; *One Hundred Twenty-Fifth Pennsylvania*, 62.

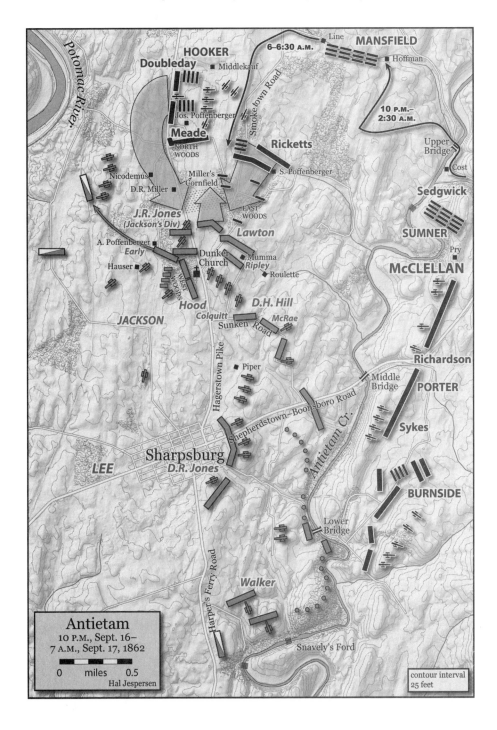

Potomac River

HOOKER
Doubleday
Middlekauf

6–6:30 A.M. Line MANSFIELD
Hoffman

Smoketown Road

Jos. Poffenberger

Meade
NORTH
WOODS

10 P.M.–
2:30 A.M.

Ricketts

Upper
Bridge
Cost

Nicodemus
D.R. Miller
Miller's
Cornfield

S. Poffenberger

Sedgwick

J.R. Jones
(Jackson's Div)

EAST
WOODS

SUMNER

Lawton

A. Poffenberger
Early

Dunker
Church

Mumma
Ripley
Roulette

McCLELLAN

Pry

Hauser

WEST
WOODS

Hood

Colquitt

D.H. Hill

McRae

JACKSON

Sunken Road

Hagerstown Pike

Piper

Richardson

Middle
Bridge

PORTER

Shepherdstown–Boonsboro Road

Sykes

Antietam Cr.

Sharpsburg

LEE

D.R. Jones

BURNSIDE

Lower
Bridge

Harper's Ferry Road

Walker

Snavely's Ford

Antietam
10 P.M., Sept. 16–
7 A.M., Sept. 17, 1862

0   miles   0.5
Hal Jespersen

contour interval
25 feet

Chapter 8

"It was Ugly Work, Unusually Severe, Sharp and Terrible."[1]

— John Mead Gould, 10th Maine

Crawford and Gordon in the East Woods and the Cornfield

7:20 to 8:30 a.m., September 17, 1862

The XII Corps woke before dawn to the sound of gunfire. Despite the looming combat, Pvt. Charles N. Tenney of the 7th Ohio thought, "[t]he morning came fresh and beautiful." Mounting skirmish fire beyond their view and heavy cannonading soon punctuated the early morning's splendor, sounding a foreboding reveille.[2]

When the firing intensified, recalled a corporal with the newly formed 124th Pennsylvania, each man "[s]prang to his feet, rolled up his blanket, seized his gun and awaited command." When "the ball opened" a fellow soldier offered a droll response to one musket shot in particular: "Hello, do you hear that? Some fellow is out shooting squirrels this morning." Though the new regiments, which had joined Brig. Gen. Alpheus S. Williams's division just a week prior, met the impending struggle with eagerness and levity, Williams's veterans also instinctively responded to the unconventional wakeup call, standing to their arms "by a common impulse." Burgeoning battle sounds to the southwest fixed their attention. Sharp rolls of

1 Gould, *10th Maine*, 239.

2 Wood, *The Seventh Regiment*, 137; Eugene Powell, "Lee's First Invasion: Recollections of the Eastern Campaigns of the Fall of 1862," *National Tribune*, June 27, 1901.

small arms soon mingled with the cannon fire. "The day was opened by a fierce volley of musketry, succeeded by another, and yet another," Private Tenney continued, "which were soon so continuous as to be blended in one unremittent roll."[3]

Brigadier General Crawford rode to the front of the XII Corps's column and ordered the 10th Maine's colonel, George L. Beal, to advance. Captain Nehemiah T. Furbish quickly dismantled a few sections of fence, and the 10th Maine poured through the opening and crossed an open field, heading west. The post and rail fence at the other end of the field met the same fate before the column crossed the Smoketown Road and turned south. Temporarily relieved from the stress of idling, the soldiers moved eagerly. The corps marched over woodlots and fields, both plowed and planted with mature corn, paralleling the Smoketown Road's course. Brigadier General Gordon's brigade followed Crawford's. Gordon detached a new regiment, the 13th New Jersey, to a wood line to guard the column's right flank. The 13th's commander, Col. Ezra Carman, used a fence to instruct his green regiment in forming a line of battle. Greene's division trailed Williams.[4]

Shortly before 6:30 a.m., the corps halted for nearly an hour, facing an upward slope to the south. Crawford's men stood west of Samuel Poffenberger's woods, less than a half mile from both the East Woods and the northern border of Miller's cornfield. Officers told the men to rest in formation. Williams ordered Crawford to deploy into line, but Brigadier General Mansfield instructed Crawford to stop. Certain that his green regiments would run if given the opportunity, Mansfield adamantly refused Wiliams's request to continue forming into line. The columns of companies formation, arranged one company after another with only six paces between them, presented a solid mass and an inviting target for Confederate artillery. The regiments remained massed during the halt, and luckily no Confederate shells landed on them.[5]

The men attended to other matters while waiting to go into battle. Lieutenant Colonel Tyndale, commanding Greene's lead brigade, was with his former 28th Pennsylvania. Mansfield arrived and asked whether the men had eaten. Upon learning they had not, he ordered Tyndale to let them make coffee, which they

3 Green, *One Hundred and Twenty-fourth Pennsylvania*, 29, 111; Quaife, ed., *From the Cannon's Mouth*, 125; Wood, *Seventh Regiment*, 137.

4 OR 19, pt. 1, 475; Gould, *10th Maine*, 233; Carman, *The Maryland Campaign: Antietam*, 111, 124.

5 OR 19, pt. 1, 475, 484; Quaife, *From the Cannon's Mouth*, 125; Alpheus S. Williams to Ezra Ayers Carman, May 16, 1877, NYPL.

quickly started to do. Henry Newton Comey of the 2nd Massachusetts, already full of coffee and hardtack from his quick breakfast on the Hoffman farm, brewed some more on this halt. Some 27th Indianans hurriedly prepared coffee and gobbled down raw pork and crackers. Much of the corps, however, got nothing to eat before the battle.[6]

The sound of firing in their front could not be ignored. In Gordon's brigade, Lieutenant Hinkley of the 3rd Wisconsin described "crashing volleys" that became so continuous as to sound like "the roll of distant thunder." Wounded I Corps soldiers filtering to the rear—some assisted by comrades, others on stretchers—clearly showed the effects of battle. Some lightly wounded men stopped to tell Hinkley how they were "driving the Johnnies." Chaos ruled. Ammunition wagons dashed for cover from artillery fire, while horses dragged a dismounted cannon rearward. Occasionally, cheers of combatants carried over the violent storm beyond the ridge. James O. Smith, a new recruit in the 13th New Jersey, followed the battle by ear: "We soon learned to distinguish the 'Ki-yi-yi,' of the 'Rebel yell,' and the three distinctive cheers of the Union troops, thereby distinguishing which side and portion of the line were sensing success.[7]

This bleak, overwhelming sensory experience stirred disquieting feelings in some. Corporal Edmund R. Brown of the 27th Indiana recounted:

> Many arrangements are made, quietly yet openly, which have reference to a possible dire contingency. Valuables and keepsakes are handed to members of the ambulance corps and others, whose duties do not require them to be greatly exposed. Directions are given and requests are made, concerning business matters at home, the care of those dear and dependent, messages to friends, and, in some instances, concerning the final disposition of one's own mortal remains.[8]

Others attempted to divert their thoughts from the fear of what lay in wait for them. The 27th Indiana heckled absconders scurrying to the rear, and Private Smith watched his colonel, future renowned Antietam historian Ezra Carman, force a straggler into the 13th New Jersey's ranks at sword point. Smith's attention

---

6 Carman, *Maryland Campaign: Antietam*, 113; John Foering to John Gould, June 22, 1891, APD; Comey, *A Legacy of Valor*, 75; Joseph L. Cornet, "The 28th Pennsylvania at Antietam," *Grand Army Scout and Soldiers Mail*, September 22, 1883; Brown, *Twenty-Seventh Indiana*, 239; Boyle, *Soldiers True*, 57-58.

7 Hinkley, *Third Wisconsin*, 52-53; Smith, "My First Campaign," 283.

8 Brown, *Twenty-Seventh Indiana*, 239.

was soon drawn elsewhere, for a battery had unlimbered behind him unnoticed. Its first discharge sent him jumping, thinking Confederates had gained their rear. A corporal in the new 125th Pennsylvania saw a ball strike the ground about a hundred yards away and take several long bounces.[9]

Lieutenant Colonel Wilder Dwight of the 2nd Massachusetts, a young, beloved officer, sat on his horse scrawling a quick note to his mother. Dwight maintained a prolific and detailed correspondence. This message had to be brief. Noting the "misty-moisty morning," he said the 2nd supported Hooker, "who is now banging away most briskly." With his love, he wrote that he was well so far. The din of battle grew more menacing. Private Tenney of the 7th Ohio noticed the noise reaching a crescendo. It was about 7:00 a.m.[10]

*   *   *

Brigadier General Truman Seymour's brigade of Meade's division and Brig. Gens. Abner Doubleday's and James Ricketts's divisions had come to blows with Jones's and Lawton's divisions of Jackson's Corps in the Cornfield, the East Woods, and west of the Hagerstown Pike. These divisions had played each other out, and Hooker and Jackson called on their reserves. Jackson directed Hood's two brigades from positions in the West Woods into the open, hollow field north of the Smoketown Road. Evander Law's brigade headed northeast and then north into the eastern half of the Cornfield, and the Texas Brigade under Col. William T. Wofford moved north along the east side of the pike. Hood's division swept the victorious Yankees before it as far as the northern end of the Cornfield. Hooker, however, greeted Hood's men with two fresh brigades of George Meade's Pennsylvania reserves, which stood behind the Cornfield's northern fence. Lieutenant Colonel Robert Anderson's brigade was on the Union right, near the pike, and Col. Albert L. Magilton was on the left, near the East Woods.[11]

Besides Anderson's fresh Pennsylvania reserves in his front, Wofford also contended with a flank attack from elements of Doubleday's division. Half of Brig. Gen. John Gibbon's brigade and half of Brig. Gen. Marsena Patrick's brigade,

9 Brown, *Twenty-Seventh Indiana*, 240; Smith, "My First Campaign," 283; William Homan, "Corporal's Diary" (typescript), September 17, 1862, Civil War Document Collection, USA.

10 Wilder Dwight to Elizabeth Dwight, September 17, 1862, George H. Gordon Papers, MHS; Wood, *Seventh Regiment*, 137.

11 OR 19, pt. 1, 218, 269-270, 923, 956; Carman, *Maryland Campaign: Antietam*, 89-90, 93.

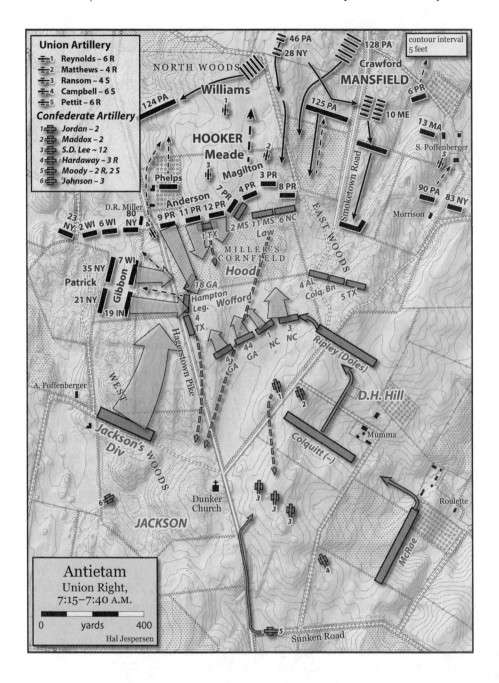

supporting Capt. Joseph Campbell's Battery B, 4th U.S. Artillery, raked Wofford's flank from the western side of the pike. This fire compelled most of Wofford's brigade to change front to the west, while the 1st Texas continued north, well ahead of the rest of the brigade. The 1st Texas eventually gave way before the combined fire from the Pennsylvanians in its front, from Gibbon's men on its flank, and from Capt. Dunbar Ransom's Battery C, 5th U.S. Artillery, situated ahead of and to its right, on the ridge east of D. R. Miller's house. The 1st Texas suffered 82 percent casualties on September 17, the highest rate for any regiment engaged at Antietam.[12]

Meanwhile, Law's men crossed the Cornfield, drove James Rickett's units, and caused serious trouble for Albert Magilton's brigade, striking just as it deployed. Magilton had initially deployed his men southward near the northwest edge of the Cornfield fence. Hooker soon ordered a move toward the East Woods. The brigade marched by the left flank, along the northern edge of the Cornfield. Law's men sprung from the corn into Magilton's flank. The 8th Pennsylvania Reserves, at the front of the column, was able to reach the edge of the woods before turning and stubbornly engaging the Rebels. The 7th Pennsylvania Reserves, on the right of the brigade after facing south, refused its left and managed to hold its ground. The two regiments in the center, the 3rd and 4th Pennsylvania Reserves, fell back, but Hooker rallied them a short distance to the rear. Seeing this, Meade redirected Ransom's battery's fire from the 1st Texas into Law's brigade.[13]

As Law's men flowed over the Cornfield fence, engaging the 7th and 8th Pennsylvania Reserves, the Southerners spotted the advanced elements of the XII Corps deploying on high ground ahead and to the right. The sight of these fresh troops, combined with the Union artillery on the high ground in front, was too much for Law's dwindling numbers and his soldiers' emptying cartridge boxes. Without further support, Law and Wofford could neither advance nor hold their ground without disaster. Wofford rode off to consult with Hood but found only Hood's assistant adjutant general, Capt. William Sellers. By the time Wofford returned, his men were giving way. Both Wofford and Law ordered a withdrawal.[14]

---

12 OR 19, pt. 1, 244, 932-933; Carman, *Maryland Campaign: Antietam*, 90, 93, 616; J. P. George to John Gould, March 4, 1892, and January 21, 1892, APD. Unless otherwise noted, the casualty figures cited will draw from the thorough analysis in appendix 3 of Thomas Clemens's edition of the Carman manuscript.

13 OR 19, pt. 1, 269-270; Carman, *Maryland Campaign: Antietam*, 96-98.

14 OR 19, pt. 1, 923, 928, 938. Hood suggested that the gap between Law and D. H. Hill allowed the Federals to gain Law's flank and rear. This was inaccurate, since the regiments

*   *   *

Two regiments of Hood's division had not accompanied their brigades. The first, the 4th Alabama under Capt. Lawrence Scruggs, on Law's right, advanced along the Smoketown Road due to the limited space in the field. Fences bordering the road forced the 4th to move in column of fours. The regiment drifted right of the brigade and gradually lost contact with it. The long-range artillery fire that it had endured while in the West Woods continued after it crossed the open ground. Nearing the East Woods, remnants of Ricketts's division fired on the Alabamians from inside the wood line. A foot wound from this fire disabled Scruggs and command devolved upon the acting major, Capt. William Robbins. Robbins had taken on a gruesome appearance that morning. While the regiment waited in the West Woods before the advance, his friend, Lt. David King, stood next to him. A Federal artillery shell hit King in the head, spraying Robbins with blood and brains. Upon taking charge, Robbins immediately directed the regiment into line. It rapidly formed while demolishing a portion of fence north of the road.[15]

While the 4th Alabama got into line beside the Smoketown Road, a detachment approached and asked to join Robbins. This was a skirmish battalion consisting of one company from each of the five regiments in Col. Alfred Holt Colquitt's mostly Georgia brigade. These companies drilled together regularly to deploy when required, covering the front of each company's own regiment, and to fall back into line when the regiment moved forward. They acted solely under the orders of the company commander. Captain George Grattan, Colquitt's aide-de-camp, wrote that this method proved "effective and convenient." The battalion sometimes operated independently of the brigade. Colquitt had sent it ahead on September 16, led by Capt. William M. Arnold. Near the East Woods, it fought alongside Hood's skirmish line against Seymour's Pennsylvania reserve brigade before retiring to the Roulette Farm. It went forward again early on the 17th and, from a field southeast of the East Woods, engaged Federals positioned within the wood line. A member of the 27th Georgia, back with the brigade, said, "It is getting pretty warm down there." Another replied, "Yes, Arnold will fight a whole brigade of Yankees with five companies of skirmishers." But Arnold was

---

about to be introduced, under William Robbins, cleared the East Woods and covered Law's right flank.

15 William Robbins to John Gould, March 25, 1891, APD; Jeffrey Stocker, ed., *From Huntsville to Appomattox: R. T. Cole's History of the 4th Regiment, Alabama Volunteer Infantry, C. S. A., Army of Northern Virginia* (Knoxville, 1996), 67-68.

Captain William Robbins, 4th Alabama.
Alabama Department of Archives and History

soon wounded and command of the battalion went to Capt. Marcus R. Ballenger of the 23rd Georgia. Ballenger moved the battalion southeast looking for the rest of the brigade. Discovering that it had moved on, the battalion headed northwest, reaching the Smoketown Road as the 4th Alabama neared the East Woods. The officers explained to Robbins that the detachment was separated from its command but wanted to rejoin the fight. Robbins told the officers to form on his right. Together, these Southerners advanced through the East Woods, clearing out the remnants of Ricketts's division.[16]

16 Carman, *Maryland Campaign: Antietam*, 127; Robbins to Gould, March 25, 1891, George Grattan to Gould, August 15, 1892, Sidney Lewis to Gould, May 7, 1892, and June 4, 1892, and R. V. Cobb to Gould, February 23, 1892, APD; James Cooper Nisbet, *Four Years on the Firing Line*, Bell Irvin Wiley, ed. (Jackson, TN, 1963), 104-105. Postwar uncertainty shrouded the identity of the five "Georgia" companies. Carman concluded that these troops were the 21st Georgia of Trimble's brigade. Carman's evidence for this was that Robbins remembered that the Georgians who joined him carried a flag (Robbins to Gould, March 25, 1891). According to Robbins, the unit he saw consisted of five companies. That is in line with the size of Captain Arnold's skirmish battalion. Though Carman rejected this possibility, Gould, and eventually Robbins (Robbins to Carman, October 9, 1896, NA-AS), felt that the Georgians were Arnold's men. Robbins had concerns because he presumed Colquitt's skirmishers would not have fought before Hood's division. But Arnold's detachment had gone forward well ahead of the rest of the brigade (Robbins to Carman, October 9, 1896, NA-AS). Also, R. T. Cole, in his history of the 4th Alabama, attributed these men to Arnold's detachment, going so far as to call out the 13th Alabama, the sole non-Georgia unit in Colquitt's brigade. The 21st Georgia had fought since dawn and did enter the East Woods. Captain James Nisbet, commanding the 21st Georgia, never mentioned, either in his history or a letter to Gould (April 21, 1891, APD), attaching himself to another unit. He did, however, write that the 21st Georgia advanced through the woods, fighting in open order, and, importantly, notifying Lawton's rightmost regiment before advancing into the woods. Lawton's brigade withdrew as, or shortly before, Hood's division advanced. It is likely that the 21st Georgia entered and departed the woods before Hood's men entered, chasing remnants of Seymour's Pennsylvania Reserves and then facing Federal reinforcements, Col. William Christian's brigade of Rickett's division, not the XII Corps as Nisbet claimed. In any event, several members of Arnold's battalion corresponded with Gould and felt that the battalion had joined Robbins in the East Woods.

Leaving behind a scattering of men at the fence on the northern edge of the East Woods, Captain Robbins moved his command back into the woodlot with his left against its western fence at about the southeast corner of the Cornfield. Robbins deployed his line in open order, concealed behind rocks and trees. There it waited, taking cover during occasional artillery barrages and providing left oblique and enfilading fire when its comrades in the Cornfield fell back. Otherwise, infantry fighting temporarily halted in the East Woods.[17]

Meanwhile, the 5th Texas of Wofford's brigade, under Capt. Ike N. M. Turner, advanced north across the open ground. Hood's assistant adjutant general, Captain Sellers, rode up to Turner and ordered a halt to make way for other units. The men took to the ground for cover. Soon, Hood approached from the direction of the 1st Texas, which was heavily engaged to the north, and said, "The 1st Texas can attend to this: oblique to the right and uncover and drive those people out of that wood," pointing to the East Woods. The 5th changed front to the east and advanced into the trees. It deployed on Robbins's right, initially along the fence at the far edge of the woods. The three captains, leading isolated units from three brigades, regrouped in the East Woods.[18]

The captains' lines cut across the swale that extended northeast from the hollow field. Rock ledges protected much of the 4th Alabama, which was on elevated ground. The 5th Texas's right was on higher ground than its left. The whole line faced open woods with good visibility. Beyond the Texans' and Georgians' section of trees stretched an open field. The Smoketown Road bordered its western side, with rock ledges in the western half of the field and a hill rising toward the center of its slightly wider northern edge. Samuel Poffenberger's stone house stood beyond the northeast corner of the field. Frigid water flowed from a spring under the rear ell of the house. Ahead of the Alabamians, west of the Smoketown Road, the East Woods extended 100 yards farther north than it did in front of Ballenger's and Turner's men, east of the road. North of these woods was the eastern cornfield, a trapezoid with a longer northern edge and an acute northwestern angle. A narrow strip of the East Woods stretched halfway up the western border of this cornfield. This strip was also the eastern boundary of D. R. Miller's meadow and was adjacent to the northeast corner of Miller's Cornfield. It

17 Carman, *Maryland Campaign: Antietam*, 92; Robbins to Gould, March 25, 1891, P. D. Bowles to Gould, February 25, 1891, APD; Nicholas Pomeroy, Memoir (typescript), Confederate Research Center, 35-36, copy at AMP.

18 OR 19, pt. 1, 936; Ezra Carman to John Gould, January 19, 1899, and J. M. Smither to Gould, February 26, 1891, and March 24, 1891, APD.

contained a knoll that overlooked the surrounding ground. Joseph Poffenberger's farm lane separated the western edge of the eastern cornfield from the northwestern reaches of the East Woods. This lane began at the Smoketown Road in the center of the East woods and meandered northwest to the North Woods and to Mr. Poffenberger's house. North of the eastern cornfield was a plowed field. North of that, in a meadow to the west of the Samuel Poffenberger Woods, sat Samuel Crawford's men, waiting to go into battle.[19]

*   *   *

While his corps waited, Mansfield rode to the high ground at the edge of the North Woods to observe the engagement. He returned at a full gallop, his white hair and beard flowing behind him. Mansfield's men leapt from the ground and grabbed their stacked arms. When Tyndale ordered his brigade to fall in, his 28th Pennsylvanians almost had their water boiling. The men of the 66th Ohio, another of Tyndale's units, hurriedly snatched cups off the fire, formed ranks, and blew on their coffee to cool it as they moved. It was their only breakfast. As Mansfield rode past, the 27th Indianans cheered the new commander, who raised his hat and shouted, "That's right, boys; you may well cheer. We are going to whip them to-day." The Hoosiers yelled even louder. An onlooker remembered that Mansfield's words "[e]nthused every man with the old General's spirit. We felt for the first time that we had a corps commander capable of leading us to victory."[20]

Crawford's brigade was massed in two columns. On the right, from front to rear, were the 10th Maine, the 28th New York, and the 46th Pennsylvania, and on the left, the 124th, 125th, and 128th Pennsylvania. Mansfield and Williams initially intended to position the new regiments in front with the veteran units as a reserve.[21]

While the column waited, Williams gathered his commanders under a tree to give instructions for the advance. Williams, Knipe, and Beal, in full view of the brigade, pulled from a canteen, which most of the officers understood to contain

19 Bowles to Gould, February 25, 1891, and Gould to William Robbins, May 5, 1894, APD; Carman-Cope, *Antietam Atlas*. What this narrative calls the "eastern cornfield" was often described as the "10-acre cornfield."

20 John Bresnahan, "Battle of Antietam," *National Tribune*, February 21, 1889; Cornet, "28th Pennsylvania"; D. Cunningham and W. W. Miller, *Report of the Ohio Antietam Battlefield Commission* (Springfield, OH, 1904), 44; Brown, *Twenty-Seventh Indiana*, 241.

21 OR 19, pt. 1, 475, 484; Carman, *Maryland Campaign: Antietam*, 113-115.

something other than water. The optics were not good. Crawford's veterans already lacked confidence in their highest-ranking officers. Gould later wrote that the 28th New York and 46th Pennsylvania were "only a little short of mutiny [due to] the contempt they felt for Crawford." Still, Mansfield was able to inspire his men.[22]

A few minutes after Mansfield returned, Hooker altered the deployment orders. The three new regiments would now move to the right as far as the Hagerstown Pike; the veteran regiments would form on the green regiments' left, in the East Woods. Gordon's brigade would act as a reserve for the new regiments, while Greene's division would come in on the left of the veteran units. When put into motion, this deployment quickly degenerated into a muddle.[23]

At about 7:15, Mansfield personally led the 10th Maine to the left. As the regiment approached the eastern cornfield, Mansfield wanted it to move farther east before advancing into the East Woods. Private Azro C. Hibbard's Company H, on the right of the column, skirted the eastern cornfield, as Southerners in the woods opened fire. At first, the Mainers continued advancing closed in mass, fronting two companies wide and five deep. Gould wrote that the 10th was "almost as good a target as a barn." When the left oblique march that Colonel Beal had directed failed to shift the regiment sufficiently east for Mansfield's liking, Beal ordered a march by the left flank as it reached the Smoketown Road. The men dismantled the fences and advanced into the open field north of the East Woods at 7:30 a.m. The Confederate skirmish line inflicted several casualties there. Just after Capt. George Nye cleared the fence, a ball killed Pvt. James D. Eaton behind him. While crossing the road, Hooker arrived. He told Beal, "The enemy are breaking through my lines, you must hold these woods." Then he was off to another part of the field. At Beal's command, "Right flank," the Mainers faced south toward the East Woods. The regiment was still massed in column and only the front of the two lead companies, G and I, could return fire. With the regiment's turn south, Mansfield rode away to guide another regiment into position. Beal immediately

---

22 Carman, *Maryland Campaign: Antietam*, 115-116; Gould to Carman, January 7, 1898, APD. Gould felt that the meeting was deleterious to morale, at least among the officers. It apparently was not the first public use of the flask. The attendees listed here are according to Gould's memory.

23 Carman, *Maryland Campaign: Antietam*, 115. According to Carman, Williams would deploy the 124th and 125th Pennsylvania to the right, and Mansfield would oversee the veteran regiments and the 128th Pennsylvania. It is unclear how Crawford figured into deploying his own brigade. No other sources, however, suggest the 125th Pennsylvania was assigned to Williams.

deployed his men at the double-quick. Companies G and I continued forward at quick step while the companies behind ran to the left and right, respectively. As each company gained a clear path to the front, its soldiers halted, turned toward the Confederates, and ran until arriving in line with companies G and I. A copse of bushes and a large rock outcropping obstructed the paths of the right and left companies, respectively, but the regiment held together, firing on the move, and closed on the edge of the woods, where it halted behind a fence. Confederate skirmishers withdrew to the main line.[24]

The 10th Maine was then the leftmost Federal unit west of Antietam Creek. Its right abutted the Smoketown Road, and its left was anchored on a substantial rock ledge. The two left companies, F and C, refused the regiment's line, conforming to the ledge and protecting its open left flank. Almost immediately, casualties mounted among the regiment's leaders. Shortly after Colonel Beal reached the fence, a ball hit his horse in the head. It lashed about, becoming untenable and causing Beal to dismount. The moment Beal reached the ground, he was shot through both legs. He was on the right side of the regiment and crawled to a large oak tree directly in its rear. Private Hibbard found him and helped him into a wagon, but feared the jostling ride would kill the colonel. Lieutenant Colonel James Fillebrown also dismounted. Beal's horse continued its frenzied death throes and kicked, planting its hooves in Fillebrown's chest and stomach. Major Charles Walker then assumed command of the regiment. On the far right, next to the Smoketown Road, a ball hit Sgt. George W. True in the forehead. Two companies over, Capt. George Nye saw both Capt. Nehemiah T. Furbish and acting lieutenant William Wade killed within a few feet of him. Wade was sitting on a fence behind his men, sword in hand, when a bullet hit him with a thud heard four companies away. He tumbled backward off the fence. A Confederate ball went through Furbish's front teeth. On the left side of the regiment, another acting lieutenant, 1st Sgt. Edward Brackett, was shot in the bowels. Gould called him "one of the bravest

<hr>

24 OR 19, pt. 1, 489; Carman, *Maryland Campaign: Antietam*, 115; Gould, *10th Maine*, 235, 237; Azro Hibbard to John Gould, October 19, 1893, H. F. Smith to Gould, March 24, 1870, APD; Gould, *Mortal Wounding*, 10-12. Lieutenant Colonel Fillebrown's official report stated that Mansfield personally delivered the order for the 10th Maine to deploy and that he was the only general officer present. Gould noted this "fling" at Crawford in a January 7, 1898, letter to Carman.

and most promising men" in the regiment. Brackett's commission arrived shortly after he died.[25]

The companies on the right leapt the fence to face the Confederates and were hit with an oblique fire. The line disintegrated as men sought cover behind logs and trees. Some soldiers advanced deep into the open woods and fought well ahead of the colors. Robbins's men were clearly visible among the trees. Gould wrote that the Confederates were, "Dodging from tree to tree, aiming at us, yelling, shaking their fists sometimes, and saucy generally." The combatants resembled a pair of skirmish lines, as there were no large volleys. Sergeant Henry F. Smith took position behind a tree. Private Jerome Sanborn, on Smith's right, did the same. A ball hit Sanborn in the leg as he fired, and he fell to the ground with a groan. Another man to Smith's left was hit in the foot. Since he was ahead of the line, shots flew over Smith's head and shoulders from the rear as thickly as from the front. Fire also came from above. Several of the men shot Confederates who had climbed trees. Beal's regiment kept up what Robbins later described as a "lively fusillade." Meanwhile, Crawford's other regiments deployed.[26]

While Mansfield led the 10th Maine to the left, Alpheus Williams took the 124th Pennsylvania to the right. Reaching high ground at the eastern edge of the North Woods, Williams directed Col. Joseph Hawley to deploy one company at a time by the flank along the front edge of the woods to aid the new regiment's alignment. Once in position, the rightmost company lapped over the pike. Before Williams left the regiment, he told Colonel Hawley to advance once the other regiments of the brigade joined him. None came. Soon, an unfamiliar officer ordered Hawley to advance. The regiment headed south, through D. R. Miller's yard and orchard. With only a rudimentary capacity for close-order drill, it slowly passed the spring house and halted about 20 yards north of the Cornfield with its right partially sheltered in a gully. Hawley ordered his men to lie down. While waiting, a Confederate battery fired on the Pennsylvanians from west of the West Woods.[27]

25 Gould, *10th Maine*, 237, 240, 242, 258; Gould, *Mortal Wounding*, 7; George Nye to John Gould, January 25, 1870, and March 15, 1891, Hollis Turner to Gould, April 8, 1891, and Hibbard to Gould, October 19, 1893, APD. Turner's letter confused Nye and Furbish.

26 Gould, *10th Maine*, 237-239; Edwin Fowler to John Gould, January 5, 1891, Smith to Gould, March 24, 1870, Robbins to Gould, March 25, 1891, APD.

27 *OR* 19, pt. 1, 491; Alpheus Williams to Ezra Carman, May 16, 1877, and C. D. M. Broomhall to Carman, March 1, 1899, NYPL; Green, *One Hundred and Twenty-fourth Pennsylvania*, 30-31;

The 125th Pennsylvania deployed in front, under Crawford's personal direction. But it did so farther left than planned; with the shortest distance traveled, it reached its destination before the 124th and the 10th. With some confusion, Colonel Higgins's official report described the deployment: "I was then ordered into the woods and then back again by General Crawford, then to throw out skirmishers and again advance through the woods until I reached the other side of the timber, and then deploy in line of battle and advance through the fields and there halt." The regiment did not reach the East Woods. After passing the Samuel Poffenberger Woods, Colonel Higgins deployed into line. After moving south into the plowed field, Higgins advanced Company G as skirmishers and gave the command, "Forward guide center." This was the first time most of the men had heard that command, and it was the first of several occasions over the next hour where the green regiments' lack of drilling became painfully obvious. After Higgins gave the order, the 125th hastened to shove toward the center, which became so congested that it pressed backward. Seeing this, the left and right hesitated in order to wait for the center. This response was likely aggravated by the converging nature of the J. Poffenberger Lane and the Smoketown Road at that point. Being a new, large regiment, the 125th Pennsylvania nearly filled the distance between the two roads.[28]

When they neared the eastern cornfield, Higgins recalled the skirmishers after receiving fire from the woods. The men then lay down. From the East Woods, Major Robbins first saw a regiment with a "full compact line" that was "helpless, ineffective, and inclined to retire." A handful of Robbins's men fired, and the green Northerners retracted, though not entirely on their own. After returning from leading the 10th Maine to the Smoketown Road, Mansfield saw this new regiment's flailing movements and rode hard to the 28th New York and 46th Pennsylvania, which were on the plowed field north of the small cornfield. He arrived, hat in hand, looking for Williams. With no one knowing his whereabouts, Mansfield asked for Crawford, saying there was "work for us to do up there." The 68 New Yorkers and roughly 150 Pennsylvanians got to their feet. As Mansfield came "dashing down the line," Sgt. Hugh A. Jameson of the 28th New York heard Mansfield command, "Forward with these old troops or this day is lost." Finding

Carman, *Maryland Campaign: Antietam*, 123. Williams claimed that he used a fence at the edge of the North Woods for the deployment of the 124th; Broomhall denied this.

28 OR 19, pt. 1, 491; A. M. LaPorte to John Gould, September 27, 1892, and Milton Lytle to Gould, October 27, 1892, APD.

Crawford, Mansfield ordered him to bring his veteran units forward and "take back these Pennsylvania cattle." Crawford recalled the 125th into the partial safety of a depression north of the eastern cornfield that allowed it to be partially screened. While there, the 125th incurred its first casualty of the war, Pvt. Jason H. Hunter of Company A.[29]

The two diminutive veteran regiments advanced at the double-quick to the eastern cornfield. Colonel Knipe, his head wrapped in a handkerchief covering his Cedar Mountain wound, led the 46th Pennsylvania forward. Passing through the corn, it entered the northwest portion of the East Woods. The quick pace through the woods disordered its alignment, and it halted at a slight ridge as the fog on that part of the field began to lift. Part of the 46th's line was in the East Woods and part was in D. R. Miller's meadow as the men opened fire on the Confederates 500 to 600 feet away. The 28th New York anchored its left on a prominent rock ledge in the woods. The 46th Pennsylvania's right was in the air except for a battery of four three-inch rifles led by Capt. Ezra Matthews. These guns moved forward to the left of Captain Ransom's battery of four 12-pounder Napoleons, and the 124th Pennsylvania, which was deploying much farther right. Matthews's Battery F, 1st Pennsylvania Light Artillery, was in battery behind Crawford's men, 30 yards from the northwest corner of the East Woods. It exchanged fire with Colonel Stephen D. Lee's artillery battalion on the plateau near the Dunker Church.[30]

---

29 OR 19, pt. 1, 491; LaPorte to Gould, September 27, 1892, Robbins to Gould, March 25, 1891, M. J. Hawley to Gould, January 24, 1892, and February 18, 1892, Gillam to Gould, January 17, 1892, Hugh Jameson to Gould, February 5, 1892, APD; Thomas McCamant to Gould, March 20, 1891, NYPL; Carman, *Maryland Campaign: Antietam*, 116-118. Gould was convinced that Robbins described the 10th Maine as wavering (Gould, *Mortal Wounding*, 13), but the 10th did not immediately retreat as the Pennsylvanians had. Moreover, Robbins did not mention these Federals firing shots before retiring, which is true of the 125th Pennsylvania's first deployment. LaPorte thought it was his own 125th Pennsylvania. Gould, writing to J. Fletcher Conrad (March 6, 1897, APD) accepted that it was possible. M. J. Hawley of the 46th Pennsylvania initially claimed that the unit in front of him, about which Mansfield commented, was the 132nd Pennsylvania. He later wrote that he thought it could have been the 125th and "might have been 99th Ireland for I had no time to ask questions." Carman averred that the 125th was the first to deploy, but also that it had been behind the 124th Pennsylvania during the advance. It appears that Williams and Mansfield left first. Crawford then positioned the 125th, which had a shorter distance to cover than the other two and neared the woods before Mansfield left the 10th Maine. The ground over which the 125th deployed was within sight of Mansfield at the Smoketown Road. Mansfield reportedly made his "Pennsylvania cattle" comment to Williams, but the latter would not have been on hand once he left to deploy the 124th.

30 Carman, *Maryland Campaign: Antietam*, 57, 93-94, 118, 583; Gillam to Gould, January 17, 1892, Jameson to Gould, February 5, 1892, Almon Graham to Gould, August 5, 1896, and August 17, 1896, J. R. Wade to Gould, April 3, 1894, APD; Williams to Carman, May 16, 1877,

After putting the veteran regiments in motion, Mansfield rode to the North Woods, where he finally found Alpheus Williams. Both Mansfield and Crawford were at the third company from the right when Mansfield exclaimed to Crawford, "You must hold this wood!" He mentioned being hard-pressed in the center as he looked toward the East Woods, where firing was intensifying. The wizened general then bolted in that direction. Crawford rode up behind Williams and asked what he should do. Williams snapped tersely, "Attend to the deployment of your Brigade at once." In a letter to Carman after the war, Williams contrasted his brigadiers, writing that "Gordon needed no watching." Conversely, he thought little of Crawford and asserted that he, "Had no more knowledge of deployment or handling troops than the green Colonels of the new regiments—fifteen days from home."[31]

Mansfield rode off to bring up the 128th Pennsylvania. He led Col. Samuel Croasdale's command forward to deploy to the right of the veterans. Before moving, Croasdale had given a quick speech. Officers reminded the men not to shoot until ordered to do so, and to fire low when they did. The 128th advanced, still in column, through the 125th Pennsylvania's right. While doing this, the left of Company K broke away from the rest of the command as it traversed the fences bordering the J. Poffenberger Lane. First Lieutenant Frederick Yeager took command of that portion of the company and right-obliqued until rejoining the regiment. As the 128th reached the northwestern strip of the East Woods, the 3rd Pennsylvania Reserve passed to the rear. Perhaps sensing the frangible nature of

---

NYPL; Curt Johnson and Richard C. Anderson, *Artillery Hell: The Employment of Artillery at Antietam* (College Station, TX, 1995), 36, 38. Wade described two companies on the left of the 46th Pennsylvania as being in the woods while the rest were in D. R. Miller's meadow. Some accounts put the 28th New York, which was on the 46th Pennsylvania's left, in the open field, while others placed it straddling the border between the woods and the field.

A note about artillery: About half of the XII Corps's batteries crossed Antietam Creek with the infantry; the rest remained east of it. Even for those batteries that crossed, only two, Knap's and Cothran's, were involved in any coordinated way with the infantry in this corps. Most of the batteries relevant to this narrative at Antietam belonged to the I and II Corps. As a result, only batteries that had an impact on XII Corps infantry are described.

31 Broomhall to Carman, March 1, 1899, and Williams to Carman, May 16, 1877, NYPL. Williams's poor impression of Crawford's ability likely caused Williams to deploy the 124th without telling Crawford what he was doing with one of his regiments. Crawford's official report suggested that the 124th was "detached from my brigade by some superior order unknown to me." Crawford's statement betrayed a lack of knowledge that his three new regiments were ordered to deploy to the right. The 124th, on the Hagerstown Pike, was clearly intended as the rightmost.

the big regiment with new uniforms and undamaged colors waving in the breeze, the 3rd Pennsylvania Reserve's major called, "Keep your regiment well together."[32]

Despite the advice, things quickly fell apart. Mansfield released Colonel Croasdale to deploy the 128th Pennsylvania into the open ground to the west of the woods. These companies crossed behind the veteran regiments, through the woods, and into Miller's meadow. Croasdale was mounted atop a wooded knoll west of the Smoketown Road. A puff of smoke came from a tree 100 yards to the left front and Croasdale was shot in the head. Lieutenant Colonel Hammersly immediately rode to him. As soon as Hammersly arrived, he was shot through the wrist. Major Joel B. Wanner now commanded the regiment.[33]

The 128th Pennsylvania's deployment unraveled amid a leadership vacuum. Much of the regiment crowded just to the right of the 46th Pennsylvania. The first volley from the front hit it as individual shots continued from Robbins's Confederates to its left. The 46th Pennsylvania's Colonel Knipe and a sergeant in the 28th New York both left their commands to help extricate the 128th. Once the regiment was somewhat in line, its right extended well beyond the East Woods toward the Miller house. Recognizing the futility of the new regiment perfecting its line further under fire, Knipe advised Major Joel Wanner to charge into the Cornfield. Wanner did so. After moving a short distance, the green Pennsylvanians halted at a washed-out gully just before the Cornfield and took advantage of the cover it afforded, firing a volley.[34]

The inexperienced Pennsylvanians were loath to abandon the gully's relative safety. With substantial effort, officers induced the men to stop shooting and advance. The raw Pennsylvanians, wearing distinctive white haversacks, advanced nearly to the Cornfield's southern edge. They approached a veteran brigade of Georgians and North Carolinians as well as Robbins's main line, which greeted the Pennsylvanians with enfilade fire. The 128th soon fell back, but inflicted heavy

32 Carman, *Maryland Campaign: Antietam*, 120; Frederic Crouse, "An Account of the Battle of Antietam" (typescript), AMP; McCamant to Gould, March 20, 1891; Frederick M. Yeager to Gould, December 29, 1893, APD. Yeager wrote that the break came when the regiment crossed the Smoketown Road. He appears to be incorrect on this point. The regiment never crossed to the east of the Smoketown Road. Its line of advance would have taken it over the fences on the lane to J. Poffenberger's farm.

33 Carman, *Maryland Campaign: Antietam*, 122; Crouse, "Account," AMP; H. A. Shenton to Gould, May 2, 1894, Jameson to Gould, February 5, 1892, APD; *Reading Daily Times*, September 27, 1862.

34 OR 19, pt. 1, 487, 493; Carman, *Maryland Campaign: Antietam*, 122; Crouse, "Account," AMP.

Colonel Samuel Croasdale, 128th Pennsylvania
Courtesy of Scott Hann

losses on the easternmost Confederate regiment, as will be seen. Major Wanner charitably described the retreat through the corn as occurring "in tolerable order." The regiment's spirit apparently remained high. On the march away from Sharpsburg on September 19, Colonel Knipe said within earshot of the 128th that the men had been "whipped a half dozen times, but they did not know it."[35]

As the 128th started deploying, Mansfield rode downhill from the knoll in the northwest section of the woods and across the Smoketown Road to the 10th Maine. Only a few minutes had intervened since Mansfield left the Mainers and completed a circuit around the brigade. The men had fired only a few rounds. Mansfield galloped down the line, calling to the men, "Cease firing, you are firing into our own men!" He rode until he reached the leftmost companies, F and C, where the line was refused along the rock ledge. At that point, Capt. William Jordon, commanding Company C, ran to the general and stood atop the ledge, next to the fence. Jordon and Sgt. Henry A. Burnham pointed to Confederates 50 yards away who were then aiming at the exposed gaggle of men. Mansfield acceded, "Yes, you are right," and a shot immediately tore through his chest. He rode to the rear and tried to pass through a fence opening, but his wounded horse would not cross the jumble of rails in its path. He dismounted. First Lieutenant Gould met Mansfield at the fence, where he saw the general's coat blow open, revealing blood pouring from his chest. After walking the horse through the fence opening, Mansfield tried to mount, but had little strength and agreed to let his men help him to a surgeon. Gould, Sgt. Joe Merrill of Company F, Pvt. Storer S. Knight of Company B, and Pvt. James Sheridan of Company C carried Mansfield to the rear

35 OR 19, pt. 1, 493; Carman, *Maryland Campaign: Antietam*, 122; Crouse, "Account," AMP; Jameson to Gould, February 5, 1892, Robbins to Gould, March 25, 1891; Yeager to Gould, December 29, 1893, APD; "125th Pennsylvania Retort on the Location of General Mansfield's Wounding," NYPL; Stephen Thruston to Ezra Carman, September 3, 1898, NA-AS.

but could not find a surgeon. They crossed paths with General Gordon at the Sam Poffenberger woods, where he was positioning one of his reserve regiments, the 107th New York. About a dozen members of the 107th's Company F broke ranks to let Gould's detail carry Mansfield through the line. When Gould reached the gate leading southeast to Samuel Poffenberger's house, he ran to Gordon and asked him to send an aide for a surgeon, but Gordon had no staff available. He found an ambulance and two medical officers in the woods. One of the surgeons put a flask to Mansfield's mouth. The alcohol nearly choked him. The party put Mansfield in the ambulance and left him with Lieutenant Witman of Crawford's staff. The ambulance took Mansfield to a field hospital, where he died the next morning.[36]

Some men on the 10th Maine's right, meanwhile, began to notice new Confederate movements. Captain Nye spotted a Confederate column in the field beyond the woods marching past the regiment's flank toward the Cornfield. Private Xaveri Martin of Company H was not satisfied with his position. After several minutes of firing, he complained that he wanted to see the Confederates at whom he fired. He moved to a ridge deeper in the woods. He still did not find many of Robbins's men there, but he and a comrade found a Confederate perched in a tree. Both shot, dropping the Southerner from his roost. Though Martin saw little in the woods, his new position afforded a good view of the field beyond. From beside an oak tree, about 150 feet in front of the regiment, he watched the Confederate column moving past the regiment's flank. Martin took shots at the passing column,

---

36 OR 19, pt. 1, 494; Gould, *Mortal Wounding*, 15-17. Theo G. Smith to Gould, June 17, 1895, APD; Taylor, *Memorial of Gen. J. K. F. Mansfield*, 51-52. Soldiers throughout the corps asserted various locations for Mansfield's wounding, but only one regiment besides the 10th Maine insisted on its version. Members of the 10th Maine and the 125th Pennsylvania engaged in newspaper-based polemics for years. Gould's need to collect facts on this issue precipitated correspondences with members from every regiment, north and south, that fought in the Cornfield and East Woods. Nothing in the 125th Pennsylvania's argument is more convincing than Gould's account. Moreover, a major basis of the 125th's rebuttal ("125th Pennsylvania Retort on the Location of General Mansfield's Wounding," NYPL) was that the 10th Maine was away from the fighting in the Cornfield. This argument was ignorant of Robbins's presence in the East Woods. In any event, the 125th claimed that Mansfield was wounded 140 yards forward and to the right of where the location is marked on the field today. The 125th claimed that Sgt. John Kehoe and Pvts. Samuel Edmunson and E. S. Rudy helped Mansfield from his horse and carried him a short distance to the rear.

Gould later wrote (Gould to Carman, January 7, 1898), "Mansfield was the only man who inspired any of us + when we saw him go down it was pretty blue times." According to Gould, this loss, combined with the ill feelings the brigade's veterans had for most of their leaders, caused many to take the first excuse to withdraw: "The marvel is that we got in or staid in any length of time." He attributed this to individual courage.

which pressed on. Others in Companies A and H then advanced to fire on the distant column.[37]

*   *   *

Stonewall Jackson, without reserves and in the midst of an increasingly critical situation after Hood's assault, began drawing troops from Lee's center. When Wofford's brigade began to withdraw, the 9th, 11th, and 12th Pennsylvania reserves of Anderson's brigade advanced south of the Cornfield after them. The Pennsylvanians saw Roswell Ripley's brigade of D. H. Hill's division approaching from the southeast. Ripley's brigade, consisting of the 1st and 3rd North Carolina and the 4th and 44th Georgia, had bivouacked 150 yards west of the Mumma house on September 16. Ripley, an Ohio native and West Point graduate, won two brevets for gallantry in the Mexican War. He married into a South Carolina family in 1852 and worked in business there until Fort Sumter fell. His northern heritage and recent military record earned Ripley little respect among his men. Near 7:00 a.m., a courier delivered a message, the fourth, from one of Ripley's disenchanted officers.[38]

Colonel William L. DeRosset, commanding the 3rd North Carolina, had an eventful morning. Before the war, DeRosset was a merchant in Wilmington, established an iron works, and served as a state militia captain. Before sunrise, at about 6:00 a.m., he called for volunteers to incinerate the Mumma farmhouse. He was concerned that this structure, which he noted as a "dwelling of some pretentions," might provide good cover for Federal sharpshooters. Two members of Company A volunteered. Union artillery across the Antietam noticed the conflagration and enfiladed DeRosset's soldiers; one of the first shells killed or wounded 16 men. After DeRosset's fourth message, Ripley arrived, and DeRosset let loose a verbal salvo, saying, "In all the engagements I had been in I felt the need of advice from my commander and had never seen him." He explained that the

---

37 Nye to Gould, March 15, 1891, and Turner to Gould, April 8, 1891, APD; Gould, *10th Maine*, 241.

38 Carman, *Maryland Campaign: Antietam*, 42, 107-108; Ezra J. Warner, *Generals in Gray: Lives of the Confederate Commanders* (Baton Rouge, 2008), 257. D. H. Hill, William DeRosset, and Stephen Thruston wrote of Ripley's alleged cowardice and dereliction of duty and noted that his Yankee birth was a source of suspicion. Their opinions were most pointed with respect to South Mountain, suggesting that Ripley purposely kept his brigade out of the fight; see DeRosset to Hill, June 18, 1885, and Hill to DeRosset, June 22, 1885, APD.

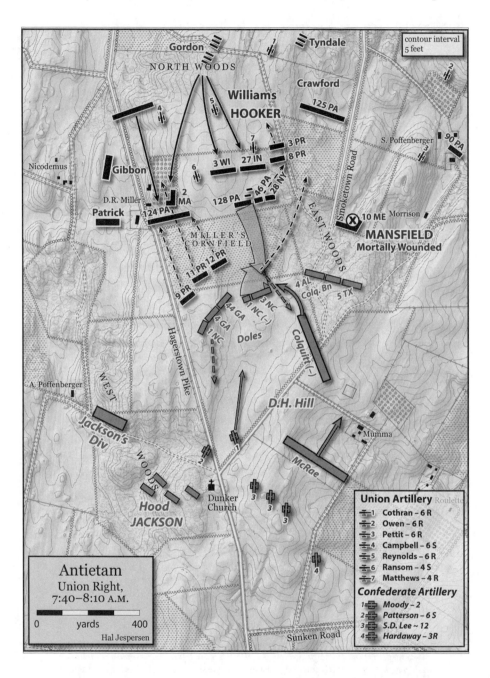

Antietam
Union Right,
7:40–8:10 A.M.

0   yards   400

Hal Jespersen

Union Artillery
1 Cothran – 6 R
2 Owen – 6 R
3 Pettit – 6 R
4 Campbell – 6 S
5 Reynolds – 6 R
6 Ransom – 4 S
7 Matthews – 4 R

Confederate Artillery
1 Moody – 2
2 Patterson – 6 S
3 S.D. Lee ~ 12
4 Hardaway – 3 R

contour interval
5 feet

men had not yet seen Ripley under infantry fire and felt he purposely avoided it. They had in fact been "talking freely of his cowardice." With this, Ripley abandoned decorum and blustered that he would prove he was no coward.[39]

Around this time, each man in the 3rd North Carolina, on the right of the brigade, devoured one biscuit, which had been baked on hot stones. This was the first food issued to them since September 14. To the 3rd's left was the 1st North Carolina, 44th Georgia, and 4th Georgia. The regimental surgeon of the 44th had acquired 90 dozen eggs in Sharpsburg. Finding pots, the doctor had the eggs boiled and sent to the men on the line. When the regiment left, a line of eggshells marked its bivouac.[40]

At about 6:45 a.m., the brigade advanced toward the Mumma house. As it passed, the flames' heat lashed the men's faces and caused the brigade to become disordered. The 3rd North Carolina's left executed a shallow right oblique. The 1st North Carolina, on the 3rd's left, marched by the right flank to clear the burning structure. Both regiments passed east of the house and halted at a rail fence surrounding the Mummas' apple orchard. Here the regiments fixed their alignment and awaited the rest of the brigade, which passed west of the house. The two Georgia regiments had the added difficulty of negotiating the fenced family graveyard, northwest of the house. As the brigade corrected its alignment, a wound removed Ripley from the battle long enough to miss the brigade's advance on the Cornfield. D. H. Hill's official report described the injury as a severe one that would have been fatal had Ripley's cravat not been in the way. Writing so generously as to appear insincere, Hill added that Ripley "heroically" returned after having the wound dressed. Brigade command passed to Col. George Doles of the 4th Georgia.[41]

---

39 Bruce S. Allardice, *Confederate Colonels: A Biographical Register* (Columbia, MO, 2008), 127; Stephen Thruston to John Gould, May 11, 1891, and William DeRosset, *Wilmington Messenger*, April 27, 1890, NA-AS; DeRosset to Hill, June 18, 1885, DeRosset to Thruston, July 12, 1886, APD.

40 Stephen Thruston, Sketch, July 27, 1886, APD; John Key, Memoir, RG 57-1-2, 44th Infantry Unit File, 13, GA.

41 *OR* 19, pt. 1, 1,027; Thruston to Gould, May 11, 1891, Thomas Boone to Ezra Carman, September 27, 1897, and John Key to Carman, June 8, 1898, NA-AS; Key Memoir, 14, GA; Thomas, *Doles-Cook Brigade*, 470; Thruston to DeRosset, June 18, 1886, and July 28, 1886, and Thruston Sketch, APD. Hill wrote after the war that, before Antietam, he had feared Ripley was "either a coward or a traitor." In another postwar letter, one of Ripley's officers sarcastically penned that Ripley was "severely hit in the cravat."

Once realigned and facing north, the brigade advanced a few hundred yards through an open field toward the southern end of the East Woods. The North Carolinians discovered a Federal general officer, with staff, riding into the field. A volley sent the mounted Federals north. D. H. Hill arrived and directed a move by the left flank to put the brigade south of the Cornfield. Hill led the brigade in column of fours at the double-quick across the Smoketown Road, its right grazing the southwest corner of the East Woods, which was still held by Robbins's detachment. Beyond the road, the brigade deployed into line, facing the Cornfield, from which remnants of Anderson's Pennsylvania reserve brigade were pursuing Hood's division. Doles wheeled his Georgia regiments and part of the 1st North Carolina left, facing the 9th Pennsylvania Reserve. The 3rd and part of the 1st North Carolina moved nearly north to confront the 11th and 12th Pennsylvania Reserve regiments. These Southerners drove the Pennsylvanians off, but did not follow them into the corn. Ripley's men then saw a mounted Federal officer dashing between two lines of troops deploying north of the Cornfield. The rider elicited resolute cheers from the Northern regiments, which were elements of Crawford's and Gordon's brigades. The officer was likely Joseph Hooker, whose vigor, daring, and ubiquitous presence that day inspired all those whose paths he crossed. At approximately this time, Mansfield was mortally wounded on the other side of the East Woods.[42]

Ripley's brigade now engaged the 28th New York and 46th Pennsylvania across the Cornfield. Colonel DeRosset of the 3rd North Carolina spotted the 128th Pennsylvania 75 to 100 yards from the 3rd's right. He immediately applied to Doles for direction but found his response unsatisfying. Doles said, "Colonel, I don't know what to do, have just lost my Major, and I wish you would act as you think best." Disgusted, DeRosset sped down the line, yelling to each officer that he passed, "Change front to rear on 10th Co.!" Before reaching all the companies, DeRosset was shot in the hip and thigh. His men carried him off in a blanket.[43]

---

42 Carman, *Maryland Campaign: Antietam*, 119-120; Thruston Sketch and Hamilton Brown to Carman, August 27, 1897, APD. The 9th Pennsylvania Reserve reformed briefly in the gully at the northern edge of the Cornfield before withdrawing further, supplanted in that position by the 124th Pennsylvania (*OR* 51, pt. 1, 151).

43 Carman, *Maryland Campaign: Antietam*, 123, DeRosset to Hill, June 18, 1885; Thruston to Gould, May 11, 1891; Thruston to Carman, September 3, 1898, NA-AS; Allardice, *Confederate Colonels*, 127. According to Carman, the 128th Pennsylvania fired on the 3rd North Carolina as the 3rd changed front to meet Greene's division maneuvering beyond the East Woods. But Greene did not arrive until after Colquitt's brigade had supplanted Ripley's. DeRosset and Thruston both claimed that the Federal unit was a brigade in column of battalion, 75 yards away

Major Stephen D. Thruston now commanded the 3rd North Carolina. Thruston was a physician and part-time teacher who had attended the University of Virginia and graduated from the University of Pennsylvania Medical School. He grabbed DeRosset's dropped pistol and took his place next to the colors. Thruston discovered a color corporal facing rearward. As the man executed Thruston's order to face the enemy, a ball killed him instantly. Thruston grabbed the flag and called on the officers to steady the men, but few officers remained. By the time Thruston accomplished DeRosset's change of front, all the officers in seven companies had been killed or wounded. Once the regiment realigned to face slightly east of north, it drove back the 128th Pennsylvanians; M. P. Boyer of the 128th recalled that his regiment was fighting "by companies and squads" in the Cornfield. Behind the 128th's withdrawal stood the 46th Pennsylvania and the 28th New York, which the 3rd North Carolina and part of the 1st North Carolina engaged as well. Part of the 1st North Carolina had shifted to the brigade's left. The 128th attempted to reform alongside the veteran regiments, but all three were ordered to withdraw and clear the way for another brigade forming to the north. Boyer recounted that many of his comrades then joined other regiments.[44]

*   *   *

Alpheus Williams learned of Mansfield's wounding when he returned from deploying the 124th Pennsylvania. Again commanding the corps, Williams sought Hooker for instructions. Mansfield had not shared details from his earlier meeting with Hooker. Williams found the energetic I Corps commander in the plowed field south of the North Woods. While they talked, balls kicked up dirt in front of them, and two of Hooker's brigadiers, George Meade and John Gibbon, arrived from different directions. Gibbon's brigade was fighting west of the Hagerstown Pike.

---

and within the East Woods. But the small 10th Maine and Robbins's detachment were the only units firing across the East Woods. DeRosset wrote that the Federals on his flank opened fire before he checked with Doles and started changing front, and Thruston noted that his advance after changing front was on these very troops. These details suggest that the 128th Pennsylvania was both the unit on his flank and the one that attacked his regiment, diverging from Carman's conclusion. The large 128th had been in column while still in the northwest corner of the East Woods before its botched deployment.

44 OR 19, pt. 1, 487, 493; Carman, *Maryland Campaign: Antietam*, 120, 123; Allardice, *Confederate Colonels*, 372; Thruston to DeRosset, July 28, 1886, APD; Thruston to Carman, September 3, 1898, NA-AS; Thruston to DeRosset, May 11, 1891, and Brown to Carman, August 27, 1897, APD; *Reading Daily Times*, September 27, 1862.

The last regiments of Meade's division of Pennsylvania reserves were withdrawing from the Cornfield. Both sought help to protect threatened batteries. Gordon's brigade was deploying toward the Cornfield, relieving Meade's regiments. Williams told Hooker he would detach Greene's last brigade, under Col. William Goodrich, to support Gibbon west of the pike.[45]

Crawford's deployment had not gone as intended. Most of the brigade had shot its bolt, and a yawning gap existed in the center of his assigned line. One positive outcome was that Crawford's men had sustained the Pennsylvania reserves' left flank. However, that flank was not seriously threatened by Robbins, whose intention was merely to defend his position in the East Woods. It was not until multiple brigades from D. H. Hill's division arrived over the next hour that a Confederate advance through the East Woods was contemplated. By then, Crawford's brigade was finished on that part of the field. All of the events, from the initial deployment at about 7:20 a.m. until Gordon's regiments went into line, transpired in 30 to 40 minutes.

Williams left to coordinate the corps's remaining deployments. He first rode to George Greene, whose division approached from behind Gordon's brigade. Greene immediately dispatched William Goodrich's brigade to the right with orders to report to any general officer he found west of the pike. Per Williams's directions, Greene proceeded with his two remaining brigades farther east to cover the space between the J. Poffenberger Lane and the burning Mumma house. In other words, Greene would be in position to assault the full breadth of the East Woods from the northeast. After meeting with Greene, Williams sought Colonel Knipe to tell him that, with Crawford elevated to division command, he was now in charge of Crawford's brigade. Knipe was in the woods, unraveled and in tears over the casualties in his regiment, which had recently suffered severe losses at Cedar Mountain. The death that morning of Capt. George A. Brooks, who fell with a Confederate ball through his head, particularly affected Knipe. Sensing that action was the best cure for the moment, Williams told Knipe to find Crawford's new Pennsylvania regiments and get the brigade "in order." Williams wrote that the mission gave Knipe "new life and he dashed off full of zeal." Knipe left the woods

45 Williams to Carman, May 16, 1877, NYPL; Quaife, *From the Cannon's Mouth*, 126. There was some disagreement between Williams's letter to his daughter days after the battle and one he sent to Carman in 1877. In the 1862 letter he indicated that he had initially met with Hooker before learning of Mansfield's death and that Meade arrived during that meeting. It also indicated that he deployed the 124th Pennsylvania after learning of Mansfield's wound. The version of events in the 1877 letter, used here, appears more likely and is in line with other sources.

and found the 128th Pennsylvanians; he called out to them, "Will you follow me boys?"[46]

Williams sent his aide, Colonel Pittman, to ascertain the situation near the pike. He sent orders to the 124th Pennsylvania to advance south and attempt to take and hold the West Woods "as long as practicable." This was a tall task for a single green regiment. In fact, this whole day was full of untried XII Corps regiments being assigned overwhelming tasks while isolated from leadership and other units. Given the circumstances, these regiments stood up creditably. As the 124th tossed blankets and knapsacks behind the gully in which it crouched at the northwest corner of the Cornfield, preparing to advance, Gordon's brigade deployed on the high ground behind and to the left of it. The Pennsylvanians tore down the fence at the north edge of the Cornfield to be ready for a charge. Ransom's battery and Gordon's veterans, meanwhile, unleashed a torrent of fire into the Cornfield.[47]

Gordon's brigade was originally intended as a reserve for Crawford's new Pennsylvania regiments. Prior to being hit, Mansfield rode as far to the rear as the head of the 107th New York's line, asking after Gordon. Lieutenant Colonel Alexander S. Diven was at the head of the 107th and told Mansfield that the brigade commander had just ridden toward the rear of the column. Mansfield told Diven to find him and tell him, "hurry up." Holding the 107th New York in reserve, Gordon sent his aide, Capt. Charles Wheaton, to retrieve the 13th New Jersey, which had not yet returned after Mansfield diverted it to cover the column's flank on the march. Gordon then led his three veteran regiments at the double-quick up the hill toward the eastern edge of the North Woods. En route, one of Hooker's aides rode up and urged them to make haste. After knocking over the post and rail fences on either side of Poffenberger's Lane, the regiments paused briefly in the eastern fringe of the North Woods to toss off their knapsacks. The 27th Indiana deposited its belongings near a large gum tree. As Ripley's brigade filled the air with exultant shouts, Gordon's veterans deployed on the plowed field as coolly as if on the parade field at Little Washington. A panoramic view opened before the veterans' eyes as they continued south into Miller's meadow.[48]

46 OR 19, pt. 1, 475; Williams to Carman, May 16, 1877, NYPL; Gould to Carman, January 7, 1898, APD.

47 OR 19, pt. 1, 475, 488; Williams to Carman, May 16, 1877, NYPL; Green, One Hundred and Twenty-fourth Pennsylvania, 30.

48 OR 19, pt. 1, 494-495; Alexander Diven to John Gould, January 7, 1891, APD; Bryant, Third Wisconsin, 126; Brown, Twenty-Seventh Indiana, 242; W. F. Goodhue, "Memoranda Concerning 3rd Wisconsin Infantry Movement on the Field at Antietam," January 12, 1895, NYPL.

"The battle of Sharpsburg from the extreme right," Alfred Waud. The 3rd Wisconsin's position is depicted in the center. *Library of Congress*

The Federals advanced through Captain Ransom's battery of four 12-pounder Napoleons. These smoothbores were ideal for fighting infantry at close range. The 2nd Massachusetts formed between the battery and the Hagerstown Pike. General Hooker rode up to Colonel Andrews and told him they had the Confederates where they wanted them and that all they needed to do was press their attack. Andrews pushed the 2nd Massachusetts 75 yards beyond Ransom's battery and the other regiments, deploying in perpendicular lines along the south and east faces of Miller's orchard. This deployment facilitated an enfilading fire down the line of Confederate units attacking the brigade's other two regiments farther east. It proved highly effective. Fifty yards in front of the 2nd Massachusetts's right, the 124th Pennsylvania was on the lower ground at the Cornfield's edge. The 3rd Wisconsin stood in the center Gordon's line, at the fullest height of the ridge overlooking the Cornfield. The sky backlit its silhouette, making the soldiers clearly visible to the Rebels below. With Colonel Colgrove riding ahead of the regiment, the 27th Indiana deployed east of the Badger Staters. As it advanced, one Hoosier was killed and several were wounded. The 27th Indiana's right was on ground sloping upward to the 3rd Wisconsin. Lacking a major, Colonel Colgrove posted Lt. Col. Abisha Morrison on the left, which terminated near a stone chimney or lime kiln on lower ground near the East Woods. For the time being, the Hoosiers' left was in the air. A gap of about 350 yards of the eastern cornfield and the East Woods stood between the 27th Indiana and the 10th Maine. The 3rd and 27th both deployed in line with Ransom's Battery. Captain John Reynolds's Battery L, 1st New York Light Artillery, and Matthews's Battery, 10 three-inch rifles, unlimbered behind the 27th Indiana.[49]

---

49 OR 19, pt. 1, 500; Bryant, *Third Wisconsin*, 127-128; Rupert Sadler to sister, September 24, 1862, Dwight Family Papers, MHS; Green, *One Hundred and Twenty-fourth Pennsylvania*, 30-31;

Below Gordon's brigade, the Cornfield had been trampled or shot down in places, though the corn still stood thickly in much of the field. Over those sections, regimental flags betrayed movements within the field. With Thruston's 3rd North Carolina on its heels, the 128th Pennsylvania fell back, filing past the left of the 27th Indiana and offering the relieving brigade cheers and hat tosses. The Indiana veterans were in no humor for time-wasting niceties. They had to stand and take fire from Ripley's brigade for two to three minutes until the field was clear to fire. The 27th Indiana's regimental history described the moments after the 128th Pennsylvania cleared its front:

> [T]he voice of the Colonel rings out like a clarion: "Battalion, make ready!" Instantly a hush falls upon the line. From one end of it to the other can be heard the click of the locks, as the hammers are pulled back. Before giving the rest of the command, the Colonel says: "Now, aim good and low boys!" "Aim low, boys, aim low!" is repeated by the line officers. Then the Colonel: "Take aim, fire!"[50]

The resulting volley was so effective that Ripley's advance stalled almost immediately. The 3rd North Carolina was the only unit to actually enter the Cornfield, so much of the fire passed over the Cornfield into the open field beyond. When the 3rd North Carolina recoiled to the south side of the Cornfield, it and some of the 1st North Carolina rallied with their right at a large brushy outcropping that contained a boulder, eight feet tall and up to four feet in diameter, surrounded by a heap of piled fieldstones. This position was 150 yards from the southwest corner of the East Woods. Meanwhile, Col. Alfred H. Colquitt's brigade marched in front and requested that the North Carolinians cover his left. After rallying, the remnants of the 1st and 3rd North Carolina near the rock pile marched left until uncovering past Colquitt's left. These troops then joined one final Confederate assault through the Cornfield.[51]

Brown, *Twenty-Seventh Indiana*, 243; John Bresnahan, "Battle of Antietam," *National Tribune*, February 21, 1889; Bresnahan to Gould, January 9, 1893, APD; Carman, *Maryland Campaign: Antietam*, 125, 130-131; Johnson and Anderson, *Artillery Hell*, 69-71. According to Bryant, Ruger suggested to Andrews that he advance the 2nd Massachusetts and enfilade the Confederates. During a portion of this engagement, Gordon was away positioning the 107th New York (Gordon to Gould, January 19, 1871, APD). Ruger would have commanded the brigade in his absence.

50 OR 19, pt. 1, 498; Hinkley, *Third Wisconsin*, 55; Position Report Summary, 3d Wisconsin, undated, NYPL; Carman, *Maryland Campaign: Antietam*, 126; Brown, *Twenty-Seventh Indiana*, 247.

51 Thruston to Carman, September 3, 1898, NA-AS; Brown to Carman, August 27, 1897, APD; Thruston to Gould, May 11, 1891, NA-AS.

*   *   *

Alfred Holt Colquitt had a varied and successful career before the war. After graduating from Princeton, he had served as a staff officer in the Mexican War. He then practiced law until 1852, when he was elected to Congress. He voted to leave the Union during Georgia's secession convention. Shortly afterward, he was named colonel of the 6th Georgia, and served on the Peninsula. Like the rest of D. H. Hill's division, Colquitt's brigade missed Second Manassas. It completed the last-minute forced march from Richmond's defenses to join the invasion of Maryland and fought at Turner's Gap on South Mountain.[52]

On the evening of September 16, Colquitt's men burnt fence rails and roasted corn near the Sunken Road. They were occasionally told to extinguish the fires, but Colquitt allowed his men to relight them. His aide-de-camp, Capt. George G. Grattan, watched the evening's skirmishing from nearby high ground. Members of the 27th Georgia raided cider from a farmhouse cellar and become quite drunk. At about 7:00 the next morning, Colquitt's brigade, less its skirmish battalion, started from its bivouac and followed Ripley's brigade. It took heavy artillery fire from guns across the Antietam while passing the Mumma house. It then skirted the edge of the East Woods by the left flank. Colquitt's regiments, from front to back, were the 13th Alabama and the 23rd, 28th, 27th, and 6th Georgia. D. H. Hill met the brigade at the Smoketown Road and personally directed its movement. Captain Nehemiah Garrison, then commanding the 28th Georgia, was wounded while on the road and fell out. With the 13th Alabama leading, Colquitt's brigade moved northwest then west by the left flank, in front of the 3rd North Carolina's rock pile, until the whole brigade was south of the Cornfield. It then faced right and engaged Gordon's brigade. Initially, the 6th Georgia and the 27th's right were within the East Woods. These units took fire from the Mainers on the far side of the forest. As the brigade advanced, Stephen D. Lee sent two guns under Capt. George Moody behind Colquitt's left.[53]

52 Warner, *Generals in Gray*, 58.

53 OR 19, pt. 1, 845; Carman, *Maryland Campaign: Antietam*, 126, 128, 130; Ben Milikin to John Gould, March 14, 1895, Grattan to Gould, December 9, 1890, George Cain to Gould, July 13, 1895, Cobb to Gould, February 23, 1892, Ben Witcher to Gould, May 25, 1891, and June 25, 1891, and Jeremiah Stallings to Gould June 18, 1892, APD. While participants concurred as to the locations of the 6th Georgia and 13th Alabama, they disagreed regarding the middle three regiments. No evidence sufficiently undermines Carman's description, which is what this narrative uses.

Col. Alfred Holt Colquitt, CSA.
Library of Congress

After firing for several minutes from rock ledges below the Cornfield's southern edge, Colquitt's brigade advanced. Captain Grattan rode to each regiment to pass along the order. As he reached the 13th Alabama, a ball hit Col. Birkett D. Fry. Grattan then sought out Lt. Col. William Betts. As Colquitt's line advanced through the Cornfield, smoke from the burning Mumma house rolled over it. Eventually, enough space opened for the 6th and 27th Georgia to oblique out of the woods. Lieutenant Hinkley admired the "steady courage" of the "gallant fellows" in Colquitt's brigade. The canister from Ransom's Napoleons tore holes in its line, and Gordon's destructive fire stalled Colquitt's advance. A veteran of the 28th Georgia wrote after the war that whomever the regiment faced "knew how to handle rifles very well." Colquitt's right continued to push forward until the 6th Georgia, firing on the move, reached the fence at the northeast corner of the Cornfield with its right 50 to 75 yards from the woods. Before reaching the fence, Maj. Philemon Tracy fell at the feet of Lt. Thomas J. Marshall of Company E. Tracy had been wounded in the face and upper leg at Seven Pines on June 1. He cut his convalescence short and reached the regiment on the morning of September 17. He told Marshall that the artery in his thigh was severed. Marshall bandaged Tracy's leg and started helping him to a safer spot when he, too, was shot. Helped by a comrade, Marshall eventually made it to the rear. Tracy died in the Cornfield.[54]

54 Witcher to Carman, September 8, 1897, NA-AS; Cain to Gould, March 4, 1893 and July 13, 1895, George Gratton to Gould, July 20, 1895, W. H. H. Simmons to Gould, August 8, 1895, Witcher to Gould, May 25, 1891, and June 25, 1891, J. A. Hunt to Gould, July 18, 1892, and Thomas Marshall to Gould, February 23, 1892, APD; Carman, *Maryland Campaign: Antietam*, 130-131, 615; Hinkley, *Third Wisconsin*, 56; Bryant, *Third Wisconsin*, 127; Robert Rodgers Statement, October 2, 1899, and unidentified newspaper transcript entitled "The Daring Southern Hero Sleeps in Northern Clime—Interesting Story of Philemon Tracy, Killed in Battle at Sharpsburg, and Who Was Buried in Batavia, New York," NYPL.

The two western regiments and Colquitt's brigade exacted a fearful toll on each other. From their advanced position at the fence, the Georgians delivered such a pernicious fire that, to Colonel Colgrove, "It seemed that our little force would be entirely annihilated." The Hoosiers suffered 209 casualties out of 443 men it took into battle. Colgrove's claim would have been even more aptly applied to the 3rd Wisconsin, which presented an inviting target on the high ground. The 3rd bore the highest casualty rate of any XII Corps regiment at Antietam. Of 340 men engaged, it suffered 59 percent casualties, including 27 killed and 173 wounded. All but four of Ruger's 12 officers were killed or wounded with most being seriously injured. One Wisconsin soldier recollected that men "fell like grass before the scythe." This was reflected in the 3rd's color guard, where a sergeant was hit and turned to pass the colors to a corporal. There was none; three of them were dead and the rest had been wounded. A private stepped forward and caught the flag before it fell to the ground. In the 27th Indiana, men exchanged their muskets for those that had been dropped by dead or wounded comrades. Some of their own barrels were too fouled to drive the balls down, while others had become too hot to hold. Officers gathered rounds from the dead and wounded for those on the firing line. The 3rd Wisconsin's rapid firing resulted in a solid line of discarded cartridge papers that remained weeks after the battle as a testament to its tenacity.[55]

Though the western regiments' losses were severe, their veterans fought with stubborn determination. The 27th Indiana's history described a soldier, "tall, gaunt, and slow-spoken, but every inch a hero." Badly wounded, he placed his weapon on the ground and walked behind the line. After coolly looking himself over, he said, "Wall, I guess I'm hurt about as bad as I can be. I believe I'll go back and give 'em some more." The man slowly walked back and took his place in the firing line. In his official report, Colonel Andrews graciously commented on the, "Gallant manner in which the Third Wisconsin, under Colonel Ruger, sustained and replied to a destructive fire." Andrews's comment was quite magnanimous, since the 2nd Massachusetts's well-chosen position allowed it to deliver the brigade's most effective punishment against the Rebels. Despite a head wound, Ruger remained

55 OR 19, pt. 1, 499, 504; Carman, *Maryland Campaign: Antietam*, 130-131; Hinkley, *Third Wisconsin*, 56; Brown, *Twenty-Seventh Indiana*, 247, 249; *Janesville Daily Gazette*, September 26, 1862, Quiner Scrapbook, 3:62; Bryant, *Third Wisconsin*, 127.

on the field. As Gordon's and Colquitt's brigades struggled, another Confederate brigade had an opportunity to clear the East Woods and turn Gordon's left.[56]

* * *

In the East Woods, Captain Robbins's mixed command continued to hold off the 10th Maine. Robbins went to the right of his line at about 8:00 a.m. and found the 5th Texas there. He was unaware that the Texans had formed on the right of Captain Marcus R. Ballenger's mostly Georgian detachment. In any event, unit cohesion had eroded, as soldiers from the three commands were considerably intermingled. Despite the welcome news of these unplanned reinforcements, Robbins's situation worsened. Ammunition ran low. Soldiers searched the dead and wounded for cartridges. By this time Robbins had requested reinforcements from Colonel Law, who told him to hold on. Reinforcements did arrive, but not from Hood's division. Colonel Duncan McRae's brigade of D. H. Hill's division trailed Colquitt by about 15 minutes. En route, Hill cautioned McRae not to fire into Colquitt's men, who could be in his front. The brigade halted in line facing the East Woods from the south.[57]

Across the woods from McRae and Robbins, the 10th Maine held fast despite dwindling numbers and a worsening leadership vacuum. Parties of two to four began joining wounded men who were headed to the rear, and they did not return. The regiment steadily evaporated. Its acting commander inspired no confidence. With a dearth of higher leadership, each captain was left to his own devices. First Lieutenant Edwin W. Fowler of Company A notified Capt. George Nye in neighboring Company K of orders to leave. Nye had just a few men with him, and the only officer present besides Nye and Fowler was 2nd Lt. Albert E. Kingsley of Nye's company. They all fell back. When Nye found Maj. Charles Walker and suggested that they find more ammunition and prepare to go back into the fight, Walker objected. He told Nye that he was wounded and should not return to the battle. Walker, however, was not listed among the wounded officers in the regimental history. Captain Charles S. Emerson then took command of the regiment and returned to the woods to look for anyone left there. He only found

56 OR 19, pt. 1, 500; Brown, *Twenty-Seventh Indiana*, 249; *Janesville Daily Gazette*, September 26, 1862.

57 OR 19, pt. 1, 936; Robbins to Gould, March 25, 1891, and Smither to Gould, March 24, 1891, APD; Duncan McRae to Gould, December 27, 1870, NA-AS.

Capt. George H. Nye, 10th Maine.
Nicholas Picerno Collection

Private Martin. The 10th Maine suffered 71 casualties during this action, including three officers killed and four wounded out of 277 engaged.[58]

Minutes before Captain Nye headed rearward, Sgt. Henry F. Smith decided he had better leave his advanced position in the woods to avoid capture. He turned and found few bluecoats around him, and those he did see were moving quickly to the rear. After exiting the woods and moving halfway up the hill to the northeast, toward Samuel Poffenberger's house, he heard someone call for help. He discovered Sgt. Henry M. Smith of Company C with a gruesome knee wound. Smith and Charles Milikin carried the wounded sergeant behind the hill. There, Smith found Major Walker commanding the regiment while "lying down as close to the ground as the grass would allow." Smith later recalled, "When I saw one of our officers high in command as this one and the Regiment disorganized and flying. I exclaimed, for God sake is there no one to command us today?" At that moment, Smith spotted General Greene deploying his column behind the 10th's former position. Smith and others from the 10th Maine fell in with the 28th Pennsylvania. Orders went out to anyone still in the woods to get out of the way.[59]

58 Gould, *10th Maine*, 243, 258, 261; George Nye to John Gould, March 15, 1891, and January 25, 1870; Turner to Gould, April 8, 1891, APD.

59 Smith to Gould, March 24, 1870, and Milikin to Gould, December 20, 1897, APD. Charles Milikin's cousin, Ben Milikin of the 27th Georgia, had been fighting about 200 yards away at the southwestern edge of the East Woods, taking fire from the 10th Maine.

Chapter 9

"I found it a wonderfull busy day."[1]

— Milton Wing, 3rd Maryland

Greene's Division Breaks the Stalemate

8:30 to 9:20 a.m., September 17, 1862

Facing the fence at the northeast corner of the Cornfield, the 6th Georgia stood ahead of the rest of Colquitt's brigade, clearly exposed to the 27th Indiana's fire in front and the 2nd Massachusetts's enfilading fire on its left. Lieutenant Colonel James Mitchell Newton stalked along the 6th Georgia's line. Tall and well built, Newton was liked by his men and by Colonel Colquitt, who had led the 6th before assuming brigade command. Colquitt thought Newton, "A gentleman of the purest character . . . [and] a brave and gallant officer." With his hat raised in his left hand and a sword in his right, Newton's thunderous voice rose above the maelstrom whirling about the 6th Georgia. Gordon's men on the high ground saw a steady stream of Confederate wounded walking and crawling away. Their fire was taking its toll. After the Georgians exchanged several rounds with the Hoosiers in their front, Capt. John Hanna, commanding the 6th's rightmost company, approached Newton, who stood behind Company I. Just as Hanna announced that the regiment was being flanked, a volley from the trees to its right front tore through the line, killing both men. Captain William Plane and a man from Plane's Company H, both of whom stood

1 Milton Wing to John Gould, June 9, 1892, APD.

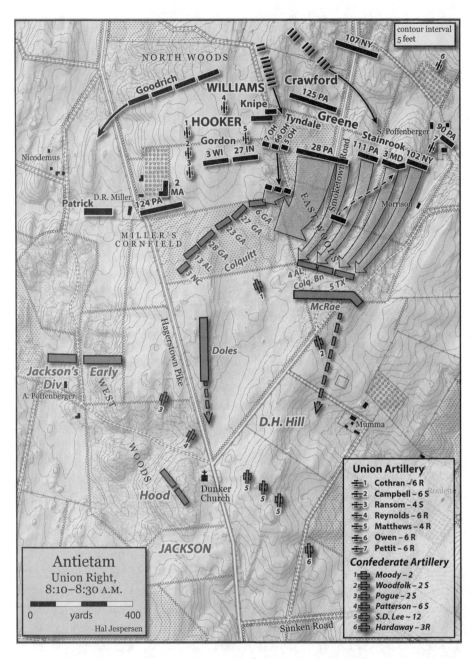

nearby, caught Newton and started rearward with him. Balls quickly felled both men. Minutes before this volley hit Newton in the arm, leg, and bowels, two brigades of Greene's division, numbering 1,727 officers and men, had begun deploying north and east of the East Woods.[2]

* * *

Greene's division had deployed at about the time that Col. Duncan K. McRae's brigade of North Carolinians arrived behind Robbins's mixed command. A flank attack at South Mountain three days earlier had badly abused McRae's men, who were still rattled. At that battle, they also lost their commanding officer, and McRae took charge of the brigade. Once it crossed the southern East Woods fence, the brigade's discipline quickly deteriorated. Men in the ranks began repeating orders and the officers did not put an end to it. As a result, no one really knew whether an order was legitimate, and the brigade lurched with tottering movements.[3]

The men took cover behind a rock ledge. While the captain commanding McRae's rightmost regiment, the 5th North Carolina, deployed flankers to guard against the kind of horrifying flank attack it had experienced at South Mountain, Greene's men appeared on the other side of the woods, in the direction of the brigade's right. Another captain in the 5th shouted to the commanding officer, "They are flanking us! See, yonder is a whole brigade." The man was told to keep silent and return to his post, but the damage was done. Terror surged through the brigade. McRae's men were already apprehensive about firing over fellow Confederates in their front. The thought of volleys again raking their open flank sent the brigade running after firing a single volley. McRae called it a "most unutterable stampede." He and a handful of officers were left standing in the woods, watching them go. More importantly, the brigade's retreat left the Alabamians, Georgians, and Texans to maintain a line they had precariously held for over an hour. Bewildered and understandably frustrated, Captain Turner ordered his Texans to fire into the fleeing North Carolinians. He soon canceled the order but angrily confronted one of the regimental commanders and demanded to know which unit was his. The man responded, "I'll be damned if I tell you!" and followed his regiment rearward. The situation for the mixed detachment degenerated rapidly.[4]

Tyndale's brigade approached the eastern cornfield from the north, still closed in column with a company front. As it approached the northern face of the East Woods, Maj. Ario Pardee's 28th Pennsylvania encountered the retiring Mainers. Under heavy fire from Robbins's men, the 28th deployed column left on the first

3 OR 19, pt. 1, 1,026, 1,044; Carman, *Maryland Campaign: Antietam*, 132-133.

4 OR 19, pt. 1, 1,023, 1,044; McRae to Gould, December 27, 1870, NA-AS; Smither to Gould, March 24, 1891, APD.

company when within 60 paces of the woods and became the left of the brigade. The first Confederate volley brought down two men in Sgt. William H. H. Fithian's Company M. As each company deployed, it halted, and officers ordered, "charge bayonets."[5]

To the Pennsylvanians' right, the Ohio regiments fanned out promptly after taking fire from the Rebels in the woods. The three regiments got into line quicker than the Pennsylvanians due to their small size. Powell moved the 66th Ohio right to avoid a length of high fences bordering J. Poffenberger Lane. The 66th formed on the left of the 7th Ohio. Both regiments advanced through the northwest corner of the woods, with the 5th Ohio on their left. The Ohioans climbed a slight elevation while, below them, the battle between Gordon and Colquitt raged. The 7th Ohio's Pvt. Joseph Clark found a Confederate sitting at the foot of a tree in the East Woods with part of his head shot away. The man was still alive, and Clark gave him water before pressing on.[6]

Lieutenant Colonel Eugene Powell and Maj. Orrin Crane, commanding the 66th and 7th Ohio regiments, respectively, rode together through the woods

---

5 Carman, *Maryland Campaign: Antietam*, 135-136, 140; John Foering to John Gould, June 22, 1891, William Armor to Gould, May 6, 1891, Harrison Lowman to Gould, January 20, 1892, Luke Behe to Gould, April 11, 1892, and Carman to Gould, January 19, 1899, APD; William H. H. Fithian, Diary (typescript), September 17, 1862, AMP; Foering Diary, September 17, 1862, HSP. Carman's narrative places the 28th Pennsylvania entirely west of the Smoketown Road. Armor put its position in the same field as the 10th Maine, east of the Smoketown Road. Foering's two accounts, used here, agree with Carman, but describe the leftmost companies as crossing the road and its snake rail fence to deploy. Foering's diary is particularly clear on this: "We formed at the edge of the woods, in doing which, the left companies lost severely in crossing the Sharpsburg Road." He was mistaken about the name of the road but corrected himself in the 1891 letter: "before all of the companies of our regiment could cross the worm fence on the Smoketown Road." The fence along Poffenberger's Lane, on the west side of the field, was a post-and-rail fence. Foering's account reconciles Armor's perspective, since Armor belonged to Company B on the left flank. Gould, quoted by Behe in a response letter, asserted, "There is no doubt at all that the 28th came in behind our [the 10th Maine's] extreme right man." Regarding the brigade's disposition, Foering and Tyndale put the 28th Pennsylvania on the right instead of the left; Armor placed at least the 5th Ohio on the 28th's left as well. The correct interpretation is uncertain, but the order listed by Carman seems most convincing, given the flank fire received by the 28th, where Armor exited the woods, and the relative position of the Ohio regiments and the 6th Georgia: the 28th Pennsylvania and the 5th, 66th, and 7th Ohio, from left to right.

6 OR 19, pt. 1, 509; Eugene Powell to John Gould, November 18, 1893, and Joseph Clark to Gould, March 18, 1892, APD; Powell, Memoir, chap. 6, OHC; Carman, *Maryland Campaign: Antietam*, 136. The whole brigade had to cross the Poffenberger Lane, and its two fences, to deploy. Crawford's regiments must have already taken one section down.

Maj. Orrin Crane, 7th Ohio
Library of Congress

between their two regiments. They soon reached the crest of the hill, still among the trees. Through the smoke of the two firing lines, Powell saw the 6th Georgia about 30 yards ahead along the Cornfield fence. Though the Ohioans were largely in front of the Georgians, the Southerners' attention was fixed toward the 27th Indiana and the 3rd Wisconsin. Powell immediately ordered the regiment to fire. Crane shouted that the men were Northerners. Sure of what he saw, Powell nosed his horse forward into the ranks and repeated the command. A volley from the 66th tore through the unsuspecting Georgians, killing their commanding officer. Disabused of his error, Crane ordered the 7th to join the firing line.[7]

When the 28th Pennsylvania's 15th company uncovered near the Smoketown Road, it loosed a massive volley, its first in a major battle. With bayonets fixed, the Pennsylvanians double-quicked into the woods. The 28th's right moved swiftly through the woods and bore down on Colquitt's unsuspecting right and rear. Meanwhile, Robbins created havoc in the 28th's left. Stainrook's brigade had not yet come up on its left. Exposed for a time to Robbins's fire, the companies on that side of the 28th Pennsylvania's line stalled and lost heavily. A 5th Texan observed, "There was some low ground about the center of the timber. This large Regt ceased to advance when they reached the low land and took to the trees & rocks." A volley then swept the woods beyond the 28th's left. The 111th Pennsylvania's woodsmen arrived behind the 28th's open flank in support. The two regiments would spend

7 Wood, *Seventh Regiment*, 138; Powell, Memoir, chap. 6, OHC; Carman, *Maryland Campaign: Antietam*, 136. Powell's account suggested that a misty fog had not yet burned off and that he had to peer through the haze to see the Confederate line. While fog may have remained, it likely did not impede vision, since the 10th Maine had seen D. H. Hill's brigades beyond the woods, and McRae's men watched Greene deploying. It seems Powell embellished the story a bit, though the substantive parts of his account accord with others' recollections. In any event, there was likely a great deal of smoke.

Maj. Thomas M. Walker,
111th Pennsylvania
University of Kentucky

the rest of the battle together, more closely associated with each other than either was with its own brigade. Sustained by the 111th's fire, the 28th's left sprang forward at the Alabamians.[8]

Henry Stainrook's deployment, in the field east of the Smoketown Road, was muddled. Directly in front of, and closer to the 5th Texas, his brigade took position under a more severe fire than had met Tyndale's brigade. The 111th Pennsylvania deployed first, nearest to the Smoketown Road, and was most successful; its soldiers entered the battle sanguine. The men thought well of Maj. Thomas Walker. One of them recalled that despite the hardships of the previous campaign, "We were in good cheer, and the confidence that existed between 'our brave little Major' [and] his officers and men, gave us all a feeling of strength and significance, even in the vast multitude that we were about to engage." They deployed under fire, behind the 10th Maine's former position, with each company opening fire as it uncovered. As Capt. Arthur Corrigan of Company B faced front, preparing to move around the left of his unit for the advance, a Confederate ball crashed into the center of his forehead. When the last company uncovered, Walker ordered a charge, and the regiment hustled to connect with the 28th Pennsylvania's left. Walker's horse could not cross the high rail fence at the edge of the woods so he continued on foot.

8 Armor to Gould, May 6, 1891, Foering to Gould, June 22, 1891, and W. T. Hill to Gould, July 21, 1891, APD; Carman, *Maryland Campaign: Antietam*, 137. A comparison of letters by those on the left flank (William Jordon to Gould, April 28, 1892, APD, and Armor's letter) with those at the center (Joseph Addison Moore, "A Rough Sketch of the War," 6, FNMP, and Fithian Diary, September 17, 1862, AMP) shows that a few companies on the 28th Pennsylvania's left broke away from the regiment to engage Robbins and continued with the 111th Pennsylvania, with both exiting the woods into open fields toward the Mumma house. The balance of the 28th continued to the west, exited into the Cornfield, and engaged Colquitt's men before eventually moving left and reuniting the regiment south of the Smoketown Road.

Beyond the fence, the Pennsylvanians' cheers resounded in the forest. The men hurried through the timbered ravine and up its south face toward the 4th Alabama. Before driving the Alabamians out of the woods, they nabbed prisoners from both the 4th Alabama and 5th Texas and, reportedly, a portion of the 4th's battle flag. Colonel Stainrook initially advanced with the 111th Pennsylvania.[9]

To the Pennsylvanians' left, the Marylanders and New Yorkers initially benefitted from taking position in the swale that stretched northeast from the 10th Maine's former line. The swale shielded their initial advance from Captain Turner's Texans. With ammunition almost gone, the Texans' situation was critical. Fortunately for Turner, Stainrook's left stalled. When the 3rd Maryland deployed, the Texans' and Georgians' fire caused its left to swing backward. A north-south fence bisected the open field. Once the Marylanders' left reached the woods, the men had to tear down the intersecting fences before entering. The 3rd's deployment jumbled the 102nd New York, which formed on its left.[10]

Unlike the 111th Pennsylvania, the 102nd New York did not enter the battle with the same confidence in its commander. Some of the men referred to Lt. Col. James Lane as "Black Jack" and, sarcastically, "the Fighting Major." Captain Lewis R. Stegman called Lane an "incubus" and complained that he never gave commands. A faction of the 102nd, however, supported Lane. Private Lyman B. Welton called it a, "Brigade of coffee cooling sneaking hospital bummers, both officers and privates." Fortunately, the regiment had a collection of able and respected company commanders. Captains Daniel M. Elmore, Walter R. Hewlett, Lewis Stegman, and M. Eugene Cornell were remembered for their animated leadership at Antietam. Stegman, who absconded from the hospital with a head injury suffered at Cedar Mountain to rejoin the regiment before the battle, later prepared formal charges against Lane for cowardice at Sharpsburg. General Geary

9 OR 19, pt. 1, 512; *Erie* [PA] *Weekly Gazette*, October 9, 1862; Thomas Walker to John Gould, April 18, 1891, and Howard to Gould, February 4, 1892, APD; Boyle, *Soldiers True*, 61. The fate of the Alabamians' flag created a heated disagreement between Walker and Robbins after the war. Robbins maintained that the 4th Alabama left the field with the flag intact and shredded it at Appomattox. The Pennsylvanians initially claimed that they took the whole flag, but later moderated their claim to only a piece of the flag that someone tore from its staff. Robbins still did not agree with this (Stocker, 70). Walker told Gould that he personally brought three-quarters of the flag off the field.

10 OR 19, pt. 1, 511, 936; Wing to Gould, June 9, 1892, APD.

convinced him to withdraw the charges. Private Charles P. Smith wrote of Captain Cornell that "a braver man never carried a sword."[11]

The 102nd took fire within 100 yards of the woods and went into line. While deploying, the men were ordered to fix bayonets, then move at the double-quick. Casualties mounted while the companies ran into line. When the 3rd Maryland's left swung back, it muddled the 102nd New York's right. Captain Cornell complained loudly about the Marylanders crowding his men. The New Yorkers wavered for a moment after coming fully into line, their left swinging back just as the Marylanders' left had. Captain Elmore and the acting adjutant, 1st Lt. Aaron Bates, moved ahead of the regiment. Other company officers followed Elmore's example and rushed for the woods, cheering their men. The regiment followed. As it reached the northern edge of the wood line, Captain Cornell rallied the men behind him. He turned forward to climb the high rail fence, and a Confederate sharpshooter put a ball through his head. Several others fell around him. Lieutenant Colonel Lane was to the rear, as Private Welton described, "laying with his nose in a cornhill." He later rejoined the regiment at the Dunker Church plateau.[12]

Robbins termed the 28th Pennsylvania's initial contact "overwhelming." After Stainrook hit the woods, Robbins felt he was being attacked from all directions at once and ordered his regiment to withdraw after his left and right were beginning to be turned. Robbins feared being wounded in the back. He and his soldiers fired while walking backwards, with men dropping all around them. They continued doing so until they got over the fence on the south end of the woods. The fighting came to close quarters in some places, however. Turning from the fence, the

11 Stegman to Gould, March 25, 1892, and April 4, 1892, Bates to Gould, March 18, 1892, Smith to Gould, undated, and Welton to Stegman, undated, APD.

12 Smith to Gould, undated, Stegman to Gould, April 4, 1892, Van Steenbergh to Gould, March 27, 1892, Welton to Stegman, undated, Bates to Gould, March 18, 1892, and Albert Baur to Gould, March 4, 1892, APD. Welton accused the 3rd Maryland of firing into them while flustered. Walter Hewlett (Stegman to Gould April 1, 1892) noted that the 3rd "busted us." This could mean firing on or crowding the 102nd. If the Marylanders did fire on the New Yorkers, the 3rd would have had to stall sufficiently for the New Yorkers to advance past them. Several members of the 102nd New York asserted that the Texans had sharpshooters in the trees. J. D. Roberdeau of the 5th Texas told Gould (April 22, 1891, APD) that "there was no time for anything but cold blooded, hard fighting. On our part—Therefore leave all such theories as . . . tree climbing out of your catalogue." Several stories from the 10th Maine, however, recounted earlier, substantiate the New Yorkers' claims.

Alabamians moved quickly down the Smoketown Road to the Dunker Church, firing irregularly.[13]

Captain Turner had sent to Hood four times for support. His acting adjutant, Sgt. J. A. Murray, delivered the last message, which stated that Turner's men were out of ammunition, that the Federals were turning their left, that their right was in the air, and that they would need to withdraw. Hood responded, "Go back and tell Captain Turner he must hold his position!" Nevertheless, with little ammunition, with no relief in sight, and with Stainrook's left bearing down on his right, Turner found it "prudent" to fall back.[14]

After crossing the East Woods, Colonel Stainrook's brigade halted briefly to reform. Major Walker stopped the 111th Pennsylvania for several minutes at the south edge of the woods to realign. Just a few Rebels were ahead of the 111th Pennsylvania when it emerged from the woods, and those departed quickly. Sharpshooters behind a fence to the southeast delivered scattered fire at the Pennsylvanians, and a reformed Confederate line in Mumma's field made a brief stand before retiring. To the right, 1st Sgt. Gideon Woodring witnessed "a grand sight" as Tyndale's brigade drove Colquitt's men toward the Smoketown Road and the West Woods. Many in the 111th moved into the field and opened a crossfire on the retreating Southerners. While beneficial to their neighbors on the right, this activity slowed Walker's realignment. Once reformed, the 111th exited the woods south of the Smoketown Road, advanced to the Mumma haystacks, wheeled right, and crossed the ravine west of the Mumma house to the low plateau across the Hagerstown Pike from the Dunker Church. Stainrook's other two regiments pursued elements of Robbins's detachment after leaving the woods, heading south or southeast. Lieutenant Colonel Joseph M. Sudsburg led the 3rd Maryland across the plowed field south of the woods, then halted near the Mumma house and reformed.[15]

Like the rest of Stainrook's brigade, the 102nd New York had moved southwesterly through the woods and exited into the plowed field north of the burning Mumma home. While still in the woods, 1st Lt. A. P. Bates found a 5th

13 Robbins to Gould, March 25, 1891, Bowles to Gould, February 25, 1891, and S. O. Hale to Gould, March 27, 1891, APD.

14 *OR* 19, pt. 1, 936; Smither to Gould, March 26, 1891, APD.

15 *OR*, 19, pt. 1, 511, 513; Walker to Gould, April 18, 1891, Howard to Gould, February 4, 1892, and Gideon Woodring to Gould, January 8, 1892, APD; *Erie Weekly Gazette*, October 9, 1862; Boyle, *Soldiers True*, 58.

Texas officer who had part of his head blown away. One of the New Yorkers near Bates shot a Confederate sharpshooter who lay prone, resting a telescopic rifle against a fence rail. On reaching the plowed field, the 102nd broke into squads and scattered across the fields to the south. The rightmost company right obliqued and drove away some Rebels that had rallied at the Mummas' fenced graveyard. It then obliqued back to the left, to the flaming house. The left of the regiment moved toward the Roulette house, where it engaged Confederates concealed along a fence line and among the outbuildings. By this time, General Greene rode across the field, redirecting scattered parties toward the Dunker Church plateau. He stopped one band of New Yorkers chasing a group of Rebels, calling, "Halt 102nd, you are bully, but don't go any farther. Halt where you are. I will have a battery here to help you." Near the haystacks west of the Mumma house, the New Yorkers started taking fire from Capt. George Patterson's Georgia battery on the high ground in the direction of the pike. Greene rode up and told them to "give it to" the Confederate gunners. The New Yorkers did as they were ordered, and drove them off. About this time, D. H. Hill ordered Stephen D. Lee to withdraw his batteries. The 102nd's disorganized drive to the south was not the only infantry threatening Lee's guns. Before Greene redirected the bands of New Yorkers, he was with Tyndale's brigade, which now converged on the Dunker Church plateau from the Cornfield.[16]

*　　*　　*

At the right of Greene's line on the edge of the Cornfield, Tyndale's and Gordon's combined fire had caused considerable trouble for Colquitt's troops, particularly the 6th Georgia. The Georgians, however, did not give way immediately. While attempting to maintain an active fire on both Federal brigades, the Georgians suffered terribly for their courage. Just after Lieutenant Colonel Newton fell, Lt. Thomas Dozier stooped over one of his fallen men in Company K. Private Stowers called to Dozier that the company was being flanked. When he

16 Bates to Gould, March 18, 1892, Baur to Gould, March 4, 1892, Stegman to Gould, April 4, 1892, Van Steenbergh to Gould, March 27, 1892, and Welton to Stegman, undated, APD; Carman, *Maryland Campaign: Antietam*, 147.

looked up, Dozier saw Federals and their colors behind the 6th Georgia's right and in the woods from which it had advanced. He was taken prisoner in short order.[17]

Ben Witcher of the 6th Georgia noticed a mounted Federal officer ride into view and then return behind his line. A fellow Georgian perceived that a charge was imminent and warned that he and Witcher should leave. Witcher gestured toward all the men lying along the fence and reassured his comrade, "We have a line, let them come." The other man disabused Witcher, pointing out that the prone men were all dead or wounded and jostled a few corpses to prove his point. Witcher then realized there were only three other men in the company. Another volley killed one and wounded two of them. Witcher helped one wounded man to the rear, reaching the Dunker Church as Stephen Lee's artillery withdrew from the nearby plateau.[18]

The Ohio regiments descended the wooded knoll and closed with the 6th Georgia at the fence. The 28th Pennsylvania enveloped Colquitt's right and rear. Private Tenney wrote that the Confederate line "began to waver." Tyndale shouted, "Charge Bayonets!" Tenney continued: "With a yell of triumph we started, with levelled bayonets; and, terror-stricken, the rebels fled." But Colquitt's withdrawal was not precipitous. The fighting degenerated into hand-to-hand combat. The 7th Ohio's commander, Maj. Orrin J. Crane, wrote that after exchanging a few shots with the Georgians, the fight "became general." Major John Collins, leading the 5th Ohio, saw some of his men "using clubbed guns," as they did not have bayonets. During this charge, the 7th Ohio's adjutant, Lt. Joseph Molyneaux, found his voice useless amidst the cacophony. He snatched a rifle and charged into the fray as an example to his men. Private Patrick McShay of Company A, 28th Pennsylvania, charged ahead intrepidly as well. He dashed 20 yards in front of the regiment and took a flag from a Georgia color bearer. For Lieutenant Colonel Powell, the effects of Tyndale's and Gordon's combined fire was immediately apparent after advancing. His 66th Ohio had toppled the Cornfield fence, but Powell's horse refused to trample the dead Georgians piled at the opening.[19]

17 John Gould, copy of extract from Thomas Dozier's letter to George Grattan, January 31, 1891, APD.

18 Witcher to Gould, June 25, 1891, APD.

19 *OR* 19, pt. 1, 506-507; Powell, Memoir, chap. 6, OHC; Wood, *Seventh Regiment*, 138; Tenney to "My Darling Addie," September 21, 1862, UVA; *Painesville* [OH] *Telegraph*, October 2, 1862; "28th Pennsylvania Volunteer Papers, 1861-1863"; Powell to Gould, November 18, 1893, APD.

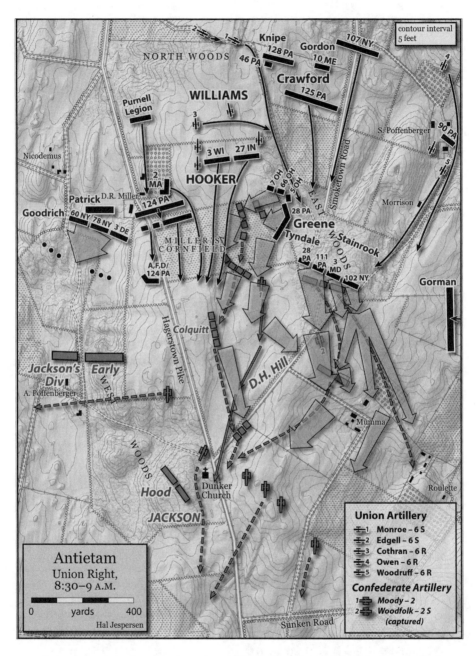

Colquitt's resistance within the Cornfield soon collapsed. As the Rebels' escape route grew tenuous, they obliqued southwest. From the ridge north of the Cornfield, Gordon's brigade saw Greene's division spill onto Colquitt's flank. The 27th Indiana's regimental history described Greene, "Leading them quite a distance . . . bareheaded, with drawn sword, and horse at a stiff trot, his was a figure to remember." Private Tenney wrote, "Like hounds after the frightened deer, we pursued them fully three-fourths of a mile, killing, wounding, and taking prisoners almost every rod." Though the Confederates' resistance during their retreat was more tenacious than Tenney suggested, Tyndale's brigade was flush with the spirit of success.[20]

Though his brigade's cohesion unraveled after the close combat and initial pursuit through the corn, Tyndale's men largely turned left oblique and chased the fugitive Confederates out of the Cornfield and into the hollow open field beyond. When Lieutenant Colonel Powell caught up with his troops after his delay at the Cornfield fence, he found them "madly rushing forward in a southerly direction." The 28th Pennsylvania's Sergeant Fithian described the pursuit: "They would load, then halt and give us a volley, then retreat, we pushing them as closely as possible." A 7th Ohioan recalled that the Confederates, "Rallied several times . . . but a few well-directed volleys and a charge would make them run, and then what a beautiful chance it gave us to shoot at them. I tell you we of the 7th took good aims with our Springfields." Private Clark, also of the 7th, remembered the fighting as, "Very fierce, and several times we were pushed back through the field and across the sunken road." The road Clark described was evidently the Smoketown Road, across which stood Stephen D. Lee's artillery.[21]

The 28th Pennsylvania temporarily halted due to Confederate artillery fire. Sergeant Fithian reported that the Rebel gunners, "Had complete range upon us, creating sad havoc among our brave fellows. They fell right and left; some with heads blown off others with legs, arms, and so on." Lieutenant Joseph Addison Moore, standing near the 28th's color guard, saw a shell strike one of the flag bearers under the arm; the man was cut in two. The next two soldiers to carry the flag were shot before the regiment made it across the open field. Federal artillery engaged in counterbattery fire and silenced the Confederates. Between the dueling guns, the Pennsylvanians took to the ground. The artillery most immediately in the 28th Pennsylvania's path was Captain Moody's two-gun section. From its advanced position behind Colquitt, Moody's gunners fell back stubbornly, repositioning two or three times and firing into their pursuers before finally

---

20 Witcher to Gould, May 25, 1891, APD; Brown, *Twenty-Seventh Indiana*, 250-251; Wood, *Seventh Regiment*, 138.

21 McLaughlin, *Memoirs of Hector Tyndale*, 55; Powell to Gould, November 18, 1893, and Clark to Gould, March 18, 1892, APD; Fithian Diary, September 17, 1862, AMP; *Jeffersonian Democrat* [Brookville, PA], October 3, 1862.

Lt. Col. Wilder Dwight, 2nd Massachusetts
Library of Congress

drawing off. After withdrawing, Stephen D. Lee's batteries fired briefly from west of the Hagerstown Pike and about 600 yards south of the Dunker Church. Tyndale's brigade then made a final push to clear the hollow field, driving the remaining Confederate infantry into the woods from their "strong position" at a rock ledge.[22]

Tyndale's ammunition began to dwindle. Major Crane reported that the 7th Ohio had to "slacken" its fire on the pursuit because of low ammunition, and the 5th Ohio completely ran out. That was not the only issue. Smaller and moving more quickly, the three Ohio regiments approached the high ground east of the Dunker Church ahead of the 28th Pennsylvania. The Ohioans were then so far beyond the earlier field of battle that they were unsure where to go. Their leader, Lieutenant Colonel Powell, described the confusion of their pursuit through the open valley; they were, "Moving upon the run . . . but where we were to go, and where we was to stop we did not know . . . passing on our route many wrecks of a previous struggle . . . broken caissons dead men and horses lay along our path." After reaching the crest of the plateau east of the Dunker Church, the Ohioans' decision was made for them. Stephen Lee's artillery, now south of the West Woods, drove the Buckeyes to ground behind the steep eastern face of the hill. The 28th Pennsylvania had shifted left after the assault on Colquitt, crossing the Smoketown Road north of the Mumma Lane and reuniting with its left, which rested near the burning Mumma house. Tyndale, accompanying the 28th Pennsylvania, soon led the regiment forward to join on the Ohioans' left. With its colors by a small walnut tree on top of the Dunker Church plateau, the brigade faced the West Woods. Stainrook's men deployed on the southern end of the ridge, which turned slightly to the southeast, in the same order as its initial deployment. With ammunition

---

22 OR 19, pt. 1, 845; Fithian Diary, September 17, 1862, AMP; Moore, "Rough Sketch of the War," 6; Carman, *Maryland Campaign: Antietam*, 139, 146; McLaughlin, *Memoir of Hector Tyndale*, 55, 102.

Maj. Gen. Joseph Hooker
Library of Congress

sparse and Lee's artillery rounds thick in the air, the men remained covered behind the plateau's eastern face.[23]

*   *   *

When Greene's division started across the Cornfield, Gordon's three veteran regiments ceased firing. They had done well, inhibiting the movements of nine Confederate regiments. To Capt. Robert Gould Shaw, recently returned from Gordon's staff to company command in the 2nd Massachusetts, their work above the Cornfield "was the prettiest thing we have ever done." Wanting to press that success, General Hooker arrived behind the 3rd Wisconsin and called for the brigade to fix bayonets and charge, which it did with loud hurrahs. Upon reaching the bottom of the slope to the Cornfield, the 27th Indiana passed the fence that was strewn with corpses and wounded from the 6th Georgia's stand. The men then marched forward between cornrows filled with blood. During the advance, Hinkley remembered that Hooker was, "leading like a Captain." The brigade wheeled right, stopping at that base of a ridge just east of the pike. Sergeant Henry Wheat in Company E of the 2nd Massachusetts found a wounded 11th Mississippi color-bearer in the Cornfield, left behind during Hood's retreat. The wounded man surrendered the colors, and Lieutenant Colonel Dwight rode up and down the 2nd's line to huzzahs and cap tossing. Captain Morse wrote that these cheers could be heard at Jamaica Plain in Boston.[24]

23 *OR* 19, pt. 1, 506-507; *National Tribune*, June 27, 1901; Powell, Memoir, chap. 6, OHC; Powell to Gould, November 18, 1893, and Foering to Gould, June 22, 1891, APD; Foering Diary, September 17, 1862, HSP; Carman, *Maryland Campaign: Antietam*, 139, 141.

24 *OR* 19, pt. 1, 498-499, 504; Carman, *Maryland Campaign: Antietam*, 142; Duncan, *Blue-Eyed Child of Fortune*, 240; Hinkley, *Third Wisconsin*, 57; Bryant, *Third Wisconsin*, 128; Brown, *Twenty-Seventh Indiana*, 250-251; Morse, *Letters*, 87; Comey, *A Legacy of Valor*, 77; John Fox to Gould, March 11, 1891, APD.

Gordon's men lay down to rest and tried to avoid flying shells. Captain Shaw described the scene in the hollow beyond the Cornfield, which was filled with dead and wounded: "[I]t was a terrible sight, and our men had to be very careful to avoid treading on them; many were mangled and torn to pieces by artillery fire. We halted right among them, and the men did everything they could for their comfort, giving them water from their canteens, and trying to place them in easy positions." Shortly after they halted, a staff officer arrived, telling them to clear out of the way. The brigade returned to its erstwhile position north of the Cornfield, from which Gordon's men would soon watch a fresh division march westward. They then moved to the East Woods, rejoining the green regiments. Gordon rode up to the 27th Indiana and announced, "Colonel Colgrove, I want to congratulate you and your men. You have covered yourselves all over with glory." Though much of the 27th Indiana would never have good feelings about Gordon, this compliment helped a bit and was reported widely. Sergeant Solomon S. Hamrick wrote that the men regarded Gordon's statement as, "Quite [a] compliment for our Gen is a Massachuts Yankey and has always acted toward us before as though he thought but little of us."[25]

*　　*　　*

About the time that Gordon's brigade advanced into the Cornfield, the 124th Pennsylvania moved forward, falteringly. After passing 20 to 50 yards into the corn, it halted. Here, at 8:45 a.m., a ball struck Colonel Hawley in the neck. The wound was not fatal, but his men had to carry him from the field. The regiment advanced 50 to 75 yards farther and halted again. Companies F and D then half-wheeled to the right, facing southwest, and crossed the pike to join Company A in a clover field near the Miller barn and haystacks. The 124th would stay cut in twain the rest of the day, with no coordination between the two parts. The seven companies on the left continued through the Cornfield in the wake of the 2nd Massachusetts and into the open field beyond. The Purnell Legion followed the Pennsylvanians. Someone was evidently displeased with the 124th's initial movements. As Goodrich's brigade moved west toward the pike, Maj. William Fulton was ordered to deploy the Legion behind the 124th Pennsylvania and drive

---

25 Brown, *Twenty-Seventh Indiana*, 254; Duncan, *Blue-Eyed Child of Fortune*, 240; Julian Hinkley to Ezra Carman, February 25, 1905, NYPL; Solomon S. Hamrick to father, September 26, 1862, F0085, and Josiah C. Williams to brother, September 18, 1862, IHS.

it forward. Nonplussed by the unusual order, Fulton simply maintained supporting distance behind the Pennsylvanians.[26]

West of the pike, Sgt. William Potts of Company F saw a "Colonel or General" ride to their line. The officer urged them to hurry because his men were being "cut to pieces." This did nothing for Potts's desire to pitch in, anxious at possibly meeting a similar fate. Nevertheless, Potts soon took de facto command of Company F. Captain Frank Crosby refused to advance, saying that it was too hot for him and that "he would be —— if he would" go in. As no one else took control of the company, Potts began directing its alignment until it moved forward.[27]

The three companies west of the pike—A, F, and D—pushed south about 150 yards through the clover field until fire from the West Woods stopped them. With their left on the road, 325 paces south of Miller's spring house, the company commanders ordered their men to lie down and return fire to their right oblique. The line curved back on the right in order to maintain a front against the Confederate line. Sergeant Potts and another man in Company F scouted the Rebel firing line. Potts found that they filled the "bushes along a ridge of rocks." His companion was hit; the shot buckled his Bowie knife, which saved him. A ball hit Potts in his instep, and he limped back to the company. The Pennsylvanians faced the same disadvantage as the 3rd Wisconsin. Their open field, higher than the Confederates' line, caused their silhouettes to stand out in sharp contrast, though they were allowed to fight prone. The Rebels benefitted from their smoke-filled

26 Green, *One Hundred and Twenty-fourth Pennsylvania*, 31, 196; C. D. M. Broomhall to John Gould, July 13, 1891, and Broomhall to Joseph Hawley, March 19, 1891, APD; Broomhall to Carman, March 1, 1899, and William T. Fulton to Carman, December 21, 1899, NYPL. The relative timing of the 124th Pennsylvania's advance and that of the 2nd Massachusetts is not firmly established. Carman wrote that the Pennsylvanians followed Gordon's brigade into the Cornfield (2:157). The Pennsylvanians, however, were already ahead and to the right of the 2nd. Given the size of the new regiment, it would have covered part of the 2nd Massachusetts's line at the Miller orchard, creating an obstacle to its advance. This would not have seriously interfered with the fire from the 2nd, because of its elevated position and the fact that its fire was principally left oblique. It seems most likely that the 124th Pennsylvania went forward either ahead of or coincident with the 2nd Massachusetts, but was passed when it halted. The timing of Colonel Hawley's wound after the brief advance, 8:45 a.m., is about when Gordon's brigade moved forward. Regardless of the timing, the 2nd would likely have had to move around or through the 124th's right. Carman also assigned the fire that hit Colonel Hawley to Jubal Early's men across the Hagerstown Pike in the West Woods. Broomhall stated that he could not see the left of the regiment when he crossed the pike, and Early's men would have had the same problem. While Early's Virginians may have fired on the 124th's left, it is likely that this volley came from the 3rd North Carolina or the 13th Alabama before those regiments retreated.

27 Green, *One Hundred and Twenty-fourth Pennsylvania*, 120-121.

position in the woods and inflicted a destructive fire on the Pennsylvanians. A bullet took off Cpl. David Wilkinson's cap and almost removed a finger, and another went through his coat sleeve. After he fired only three rounds, he was shot in the leg. The three companies held west of the pike until reinforcements from both armies arrived and created a maelstrom in the Pennsylvanians' midst.[28]

* * *

The carnage that occurred in the Cornfield during the XII Corps's engagement was horrific. An Ohioan wrote, "The sight at the fence, where the enemy was standing when we gave them our first fire was awful beyond description. Dead men were literally piled upon and across each other." Colquitt's brigade lost terribly, with 111 killed, 444 wounded, and 173 missing. Five of its nine field officers were wounded and three were dead. The 6th Georgia, trapped between Gordon and Tyndale, lost 81 killed and 115 wounded of 250 engaged. The 6th's 78 percent casualty rate was the second-highest at Antietam. In absolute numbers, its 81 killed was the most in any Confederate regiment. Lieutenant Colonel Powell paid the Georgians a genuine compliment in his memoir: "We had been enabled to pour a volley into an entire line, at a few rods distance, and striking them in flank at about the same time. No line of men in the world, of equal strength, could have done better than they tried to do." This respect went both ways. A prisoner asked a member of the 28th Pennsylvania what regiment of sharpshooters Colquitt's brigade had faced. In the same field, the 3rd North Carolina suffered the highest total casualties, 253, of any Southern regiment during its repulse of the 128th Pennsylvania and charge against Gordon's line. This heavy fighting ended the battle in the Cornfield.[29]

* * *

When Greene initially attacked into the East Woods, a Virginia battery under Capt. Pichegru Woolfolk moved forward from Lee's battalion at the Dunker Church plateau to a position near the southwest corner of the woods. As these guns

---

28 Green, *One Hundred and Twenty-fourth Pennsylvania*, 111, 121; Broomhall to Carman, March 1, 1899, NYPL.

29 Powell, Memoir, chap. 6, OHC; Carman, *Maryland Campaign: Antietam*, 608, 616, 618; Grattan to Gould, December 9, 1890, APD; Roberts to father, September 21, 1862, HSP.

deployed, Maj. Gen. D. H. Hill sat atop his horse in the Smoketown Road. Hill, an 1842 West Point graduate, was twice brevetted for gallantry in the Mexican War. He then taught mathematics at Washington College and Davidson College before superintending the North Carolina Military Institute for two years just prior to secession. He started the war as colonel of the 1st North Carolina, winning a small engagement at Big Bethel. He was quickly promoted to major general and fought on the Peninsula. Afterward, his division had remained to guard Richmond until Lee finessed it away from Jefferson Davis. Hill had a frightful day at Antietam, throughout which he coolly exposed himself to Federal fire. As a result, three horses were shot from under him, one of which lost its forelegs to solid shot from a Union battery. As he watched events unfold amid his three deployed brigades, the situation quickly deteriorated. He hurriedly ordered his troops to withdraw from the unfolding disaster, but was too late.[30]

Across the Cornfield from Hill's men, Joseph Hooker busily gathered forces for the pursuit. He later recalled the scene: "At that time my troops were in the finest spirits. . . . The troops almost rent the skies with their cheers; there was the greatest good feeling that I have ever witnessed on the field of battle." Besides pushing Gordon's infantry forward, Hooker advanced fresh batteries. He personally directed Capt. J. Albert Monroe and Lt. Frederick Edgell to take Battery D, 1st Rhode Island Light Artillery, and 1st Battery, New Hampshire Light Artillery, beyond the Cornfield and as near the West Woods as possible. He told Monroe that he would find infantry support there.[31]

Monroe's and Edgell's batteries headed south on the J. Poffenberger Lane into the East Woods. Turning west within the woods onto the Smoketown Road, they drove into the hollow field beyond the forest. After moving carefully through the field to avoid running over the dead and wounded, Monroe went into battery north of the road near the Mumma Lane, positioning his guns facing the West Woods. Lieutenant E. K. Parker, commanding the right section, told Monroe the position was not ideal. On the heels of this unsolicited advice, one of Hooker's staffers arrived and directed Monroe to the Dunker Church plateau. Monroe left his

---

30 Carman, *Maryland Campaign: Antietam*, 134, 274; Warner, *Generals in Gray*, 136-137; Henry E. Shepard, "D. H. Hill at Sharpsburg," *Confederate Veteran*, 26:72.

31 OR 19, pt. 1, 227; *Joint Committee on the Conduct of the War, 38th Congress*, 1:581; Carman, *Maryland Campaign: Antietam*, 160; J. Albert Monroe, "Battery D, 1st Rhode Island Light Artillery, at the Battle of Antietam, September 17, 1862," *Personal Narratives of Events in the War of the Rebellion, Being Papers Read Before the Rhode Island Soldiers and Sailors Historical Society* (Providence, 1886), 17; E. K. Parker to Gould, March 10, 1894, APD.

caissons behind and moved as ordered. Gaining the top of the ridge, he discovered Greene's men on their stomachs behind the plateau. He inquired whose brigade they belonged to, and soon saw Greene approaching him. Monroe asked for infantry support. In a hushed tone, Greene admitted that his men had no ammunition. Monroe wondered why they were so far ahead of the army if that were the case. Though justifiably anxious about going into battery in an advanced position without infantry support, he figured that if Greene's men stayed without ammunition, he could stay with fully provisioned limber chests.[32]

Monroe unlimbered with his rightmost guns down the slope toward the Dunker Church, within 70 yards of the Hagerstown Pike and the woods. Edgell went into battery to Monroe's left and rear. Both batteries, each with six 12-pounder Napoleons, were immediately employed. A Confederate battery west of the pike and south of the West Woods unlimbered ahead of Monroe. It opened fire on the Rhode Islanders, but its fire was, Lieutenant Parker wrote, "wild too high." Ignoring the ineffective enemy artillery at first, Monroe directed one section against Confederate infantry retreating about 125 yards from his left front. The remaining four guns fired canister and case shot against Brig. Gen. Jubal Early's infantry, which approached within the West Woods. Before long, all his sections fired at the latter target, which recoiled deeper into the open woodlot. Rebel sharpshooters emerged along a ridge diagonal to Monroe's front and began killing and wounding many of his horses and men. Two guns firing canister caused the sharpshooters to keep their heads down. Meanwhile, Edgell's and Monroe's remaining four guns engaged the battery south of the woods. Their fire blew up its caisson and soon drove the guns off. Out of ammunition and with caissons to the rear, Monroe ordered his battery to limber up and withdraw. At this point the Confederate sharpshooters returned and nearly prevented one of the guns from escaping. Horses fell faster than drivers could replace them. Greene's men were still without ammunition and could not help. The gun was eventually pulled off with a prolonge. Monroe returned to battery after collecting his caissons near the Mumma Lane. Four guns were near the southwest corner of the East Woods. The remaining section moved to the Cornfield. Greene's men were alone again, but another Rhode Island battery would soon arrive on the Dunker Church plateau.[33]

---

32 Monroe, "Battery D," 19-21; Parker to Gould, March 10, 1894, APD.

33 OR 19, pt. 1, 227-228; Carman, *Maryland Campaign: Antietam*, 160, 175, 189; Monroe, "Battery D," 24-25; Parker to Gould, March 10, 1894, APD; Jonathan Gibson to Carman, June 21, 1901, NA-AS; Johnson and Anderson, *Artillery Hell*, 107.

Col. William B. Goodrich,
60th New York

William Goodrich Collection, MSS no. 056,
Special Collections, St. Lawrence University Libraries,
Canton, NY

* * *

Over half a mile northwest, Col. William B. Goodrich's brigade crossed to the west of the pike. Alpheus Williams had detached it to the right to sustain the battery assigned to Gibbon's brigade. Goodrich was to report to any general officer that he found. When he arrived west of the pike, his brigade numbered only 572 men. The Purnell Legion had been detached to support the 124th Pennsylvania. Goodrich found neither Gibbon nor his battery. He did find Brig. Gen. Marsena Patrick, whose brigade had fought hard that morning in conjunction with Gibbon's brigade. Patrick's New Yorkers rested along an outcropping, facing south, and were awaiting ammunition and reinforcements. They made coffee under fire from Confederate horse artillery to the west. Their position, about 250 feet northeast of the West Woods, was also just across the road from the 124th Pennsylvania.[34]

Goodrich marched the 60th and 78th New York and 3rd Delaware in front of Patrick's brigade, which followed in support. Before advancing, Patrick debriefed Goodrich on the nature of the ground, including its copious rock ledges, and on Confederate positions. He suggested that Goodrich advance cautiously behind skirmishers. Meanwhile, Patrick would gather reinforcements to attack the corner of the woods ahead and to the left of Goodrich's attack. The trees hid a brigade under Jubal Early and another 200–300 men of Jackson's division. As Patrick unsuccessfully sought his division commander to request more men, Goodrich advanced, mounted at the head of his brigade. The 21st New York's Col. William Rogers hailed Goodrich. He asked Goodrich where he was going with such a small force and cautioned him not to go into the woods because they were full of

---

34 OR 19, pt. 1, 244; Sparks, *Inside Lincoln's Army*, 148-149; Carman, *Maryland Campaign: Antietam*, 158.

sharpshooters. Goodrich announced that he was ordered to go in but did not appear to have clear direction as to where to attack, Patrick's guidance notwithstanding. Rogers suggested that he dismount.[35]

Colonel Goodrich remained in the saddle and pressed forward. Resolute and self-possessed, he stimulated hearty exertions in his men. Bringing the brigade into line, skirmishers deployed to the left and right. Captain J. C. O. Reddington, commanding the 60th's Company C, covered the right, clearing sharpshooters from the tree line in his front. Major Arthur Maginnis's 3rd Delaware was on the left. Maginnis had divided the regiment into four 30-man companies, one of which skirmished ahead of the brigade's left. Three of Patrick's regiments—the 21st, 23rd, and 35th New York—followed in support. The right of the brigade entered the extreme northwest portion of the West Woods and soon came up behind Reddington's skirmishers.[36]

Goodrich rode 50 feet in the rear of the 60th New York atop his black horse, calling to the men, "Steady! Shoot low!" A Confederate ball struck the right of his chest, severing an artery close to his intestines and behind his stomach. Given the angle of impact, this shot likely was fired from a sharpshooter in a tree. Goodrich fell from his horse. Sergeant Major Lester S. Willson ran to Goodrich and raised him from the ground. Recovering from the shock of the wound, he called, "My God, I am hit!" before drifting in and out of consciousness. A few of his men carried him to a field hospital in a nearby barn. He came to, smiling as he recognized Willson. He occasionally spoke of family and entreated Willson to return his body to New York. At length, he asked about the brigade, anxious that the men do their duty. Before losing consciousness for the last time, Goodrich cried, "I have always tried to do my duty!"[37]

Returning to the field empty-handed, Marsena Patrick found Goodrich's brigade clinging to its position. The 78th New York's Lt. Col. Jonathan Austin had assumed command, and Patrick took charge of both brigades, which he ordered forward. They entered the forest, and skirmishers advanced to the fence along its western edge, bordering a cornfield. Its advance began to expose the brigade's left,

35 Sparks, *Inside Lincoln's Army*, 149; William Rogers, Statement, 4, NA-AS.

36 OR 19, pt. 1, 514-515; Eddy, *Sixtieth New York*, 180; Carman, *Maryland Campaign: Antietam*, 159; J. C. O. Reddington to Ezra Carman, January 4, 1900, NYPL. Carman wrote that the entire 3rd Delaware deployed as skirmishers; this narrative accepts the account in the *Official Records*.

37 Donald Brown, "Reminiscences of a Civil War Veteran," 60th New York Infantry, SLCHA; Eddy, *Sixtieth New York*, 181.

but this vulnerability was short-lived. A large body of Federal infantry soon appeared to the east, advancing directly toward Patrick's position and causing him to disengage and clear the way. Earlier, while Goodrich approached the north end of the West Woods, one of Crawford's regiments entered the southern end of the woods at the Dunker Church.[38]

*　*　*

After its aborted attempt at deploying, the 125th Pennsylvania stood fast north of the eastern cornfield. Shortly after Greene swept through the woods, Crawford ordered Colonel Higgins's 125th forward. It pushed through the woods and across the southeastern corner of the Cornfield, capturing a number of prisoners, some of whom were gathered at the outcropping that had sheltered Thruston's North Carolinians. Some had handkerchiefs tied around ramrods. As the Pennsylvanians neared the Smoketown Road, Higgins was ordered to support a battery that straddled the road. The 125th moved into line behind Monroe's battery, which had not yet advanced to the Dunker Church plateau and Higgins told his men to lie down. He and Lt. Col. Jacob Szink dismounted while there. Just after Szink alighted from his horse, a shell struck the saddle and disabled the animal. Another shell passed through the horse of one of Alpheus Williams's orderlies. The ball then vaulted over the 125th's line and lodged in the ground. Corporal William Homan of Company F saw a cannonball land about 100 yards in his rear, where it took "long jumps." Homan "felt somewhat bad" and got closer to the ground.[39]

Like Monroe's battery, the 125th Pennsylvania straddled the Smoketown Road. Company B was left of the road, and Company G was on either side. Two officers in Company G, Lt. Thomas McCamant and Capt. John McKeage, chatted with the battery commander. Stocky and wearing an India rubber coat, the artillerist leaned on his sword and complained that the former Army of Virginia, rather than the Army of the Potomac, was doing all the fighting. As they talked, a solid shot severed a gunner's leg below the knee. Soon, Monroe's and Edgell's batteries moved forward to join Greene, and portions of the two companies near

---

38 OR 19, pt. 1, 514; Sparks, *Inside Lincoln's Army*, 149.

39 OR 19, pt. 1, 492; Carman, *Maryland Campaign: Antietam*, 160-161; *One Hundred Twenty-Fifth Pennsylvania*, 68-69; Homan Diary, 10-11, USA.

Col. Jacob Higgins, 125th Pennsylvania
U.S. Army Heritage and Education Center

the road, B and G, tore down fences bordering it to allow the guns to advance toward the Dunker Church plateau.[40]

General Hooker approached Colonel Higgins, who was kneeling behind a fence corner. He asked Higgins which regiment this was and what infantry was in the woods in front. Higgins proclaimed that there was no infantry there but Confederates, and that his own regiment was the farthest in front. At that time, Higgins's claim was overstated. All of Greene's units had cleared the East Woods before the 125th entered, and some would have finished their fighting and moved on to the Dunker Church plateau, forward of Higgins's Mumma Lane position. As Higgins spoke to Hooker, a bullet struck Hooker's horse. Higgins brought this to Hooker's attention, but the untroubled general merely replied, "I see," and rode off. Lieutenant Witman of Crawford's staff rode up and told Higgins to move forward and occupy the West Woods.[41]

After crossing the Hagerstown Pike, the regiment halted to correct its alignment. Higgins ordered Captain McKeage's Company G forward as skirmishers. Seeing that he was alone and that Rebels were approaching his right and front, Higgins put his brother, 1st Lt. Joseph Higgins, on his horse and told him to find Crawford and procure reinforcements or they would have to fall back.

40 Thomas McCamant to Ezra Carman, October 26, 1899, and November 4, 1899, NYPL. A staff officer told McCamant that this was Lt. Edward Muhlenberg's Battery F, 4th U.S. Artillery, but the 8:30-8:40 a.m. and the 9:00-9:30 a.m. Carman-Cope Antietam Atlas maps place that battery about a mile and a half to the east of that point. It is more likely that this was Monroe's Battery D, 1st Rhode Island Light, in its first position, 160 yards from the East Woods. McCamant wrote that the artillery officer requested the 125th's support. The 125th's unit history identified it as Monroe's battery, which had been in the erstwhile III Corps, Army of Virginia.

41 OR 19, pt. 1, 492; *National Tribune*, June 3, 1886; Huyette, *Maryland Campaign*, 36-37; *One Hundred Twenty-Fifth Pennsylvania*, 71; Carman, *Maryland Campaign: Antietam*, 178.

He told Joseph that the last time he saw Crawford was when they passed through a cornfield. Higgins moved the regiment forward again to the northern face of the wooded hill west of the Dunker Church, facing west. His left was beyond the church and 20 yards north of it. The regiment extended to the north down the hillside, into a ravine, and up the other side. The regiment's skirmishers, who had come in and were sent back out, advanced nearly to the fence at the woods' western edge. They discovered a makeshift Confederate field hospital beyond the trees, in Alfred Poffenberger's fields. Higgins sent Capt. Ulysses Huyette with Company B back to the Dunker Church to watch the low ground south of the church on the regiment's left rear. Huyette positioned Company B about 20 yards north of the church, fronting south, with its left facing the building's northwest corner. The regiment had barely arrived before it began taking fire.[42]

* * *

Shortly after leaving the 125th Pennsylvania, a musket ball hit Hooker in the foot while he was scouting artillery positions. He remained mounted, encouraging soldiers and reportedly refusing surgical services. Hooker later claimed that he was unaware of the injury before he fainted from blood loss and fell from the saddle. He was removed from his horse and examined by surgeons before orderlies carried him to the Pry house, across the Antietam. Hooker's absence on the Union right transformed the simmering effects of leadership vacancies into an acute void that was never filled, though another veteran corps commander was en route.[43]

When Tyndale's and Stainrook's men took cover behind the Dunker Church plateau, they were isolated and without ammunition, and over a quarter mile ahead of most of the corps. The 125th Pennsylvania was in or approaching the southern portion of the West Woods. Goodrich's brigade and a portion of the 124th Pennsylvania approached the same woods from the north and northeast. These units were unaware of the others and did not operate in concert. At about that time, General Williams rode to the area southeast of the East Woods to watch a fresh column approach. Dissuaded by Confederate fire, he did not stay long to take in the

42 OR 19, pt. 1, 492; *National Tribune*, June 3, 1886; *One Hundred Twenty-Fifth Pennsylvania*, 71; Lylte to Gould, October 27, 1892, and Jacob Higgins, Map, February 1891, APD; McCamant to Carman, November 17, 1894, September 14, 1897, and October 26, 1899, NYPL; Carman, *Maryland Campaign: Antietam*, 179.

43 OR 19, pt. 1, 219; *Joint Committee on the Conduct of the War, 38th Congress*, 1:581; Matchett, *Maryland and the Glorious Old Third*, 22.

sights. It was about 9:00 a.m. when Williams spotted Maj. Gen. Edwin V. Sumner's II Corps, veterans of the Peninsula campaign. Sumner's was the first corps engaged at Antietam in which George McClellan had any real confidence.[44]

Sumner had already had a frustrating morning. Born in 1797, Sumner was the oldest corps commander in the Civil War. Despite his age, he suffered no lack of personal bravery. A dragoon and cavalry officer, he was brevetted twice during the Mexican War, where one of his dragoons was a young George Henry Gordon. Sumner still had the aggressive instincts of a cavalryman. As Francis Palfrey suggested, Sumner's cavalry background may have "done him positive harm" as an infantry commander. As will be seen, this comment applied to both his natural aggressiveness and to his cavalier's approach to infantry tactics. The night before the battle, Sumner put five of his batteries across the Antietam and into bivouac with the XII Corps. McClellan denied his request to advance II Corps infantry across the creek but told him to be ready to march an hour before daylight. The corps was ready when Sumner went to the Pry house just after 6:00 a.m. to get permission to move. The commanding general, however, was unavailable. With the sounds of battle growing west of the creek, Sumner paced outside the house as he awaited McClellan's orders. At 7:20 a.m., while Mansfield deployed Crawford's brigade, Sumner finally got orders to advance and immediately set Maj. Gen. John Sedgwick's division into motion. Sedgwick led his troops across Antietam Creek at the ford above the Pry residence.[45]

Sumner accompanied Sedgwick's division, pressing westward ahead of his other divisions under Brig. Gen. William French and Maj. Gen. Israel Richardson. Halting at the plowed field south of the East Woods, Sumner briefly surveyed the situation. He saw troops lying down to the left and discounted Tyndale's and Stainrook's brigades as cowed and helpless. One of his staff found Brig. Gen. James B. Ricketts, who erroneously indicated that only 300 men could be marshaled from the I Corps. Alpheus Williams sent a staff officer to inform Sumner of his corps's dispositions. Meanwhile, Sumner moved Sedgwick's men by the right flank into the East Woods, pushing portions of Crawford's brigade aside. The division faced to the west and dismantled the fence bordering the fields. Williams arrived and gave Sumner unsolicited and unwelcome guidance on the

44 *OR* 19, pt. 1, 476; Williams to Carman, May 16, 1877, NYPL.

45 *OR* 19, pt. 1, 217, 275; Warner, *Generals in Blue*, 489-490; Francis Palfrey, *The Antietam and Fredericksburg* (New York, 1996), 54; Carman, *Maryland Campaign: Antietam*, 43-44; 171-172.

position of his own corps and on how he might best advance. Carman wrote that these suggestions "were not well received."[46]

* * *

After pausing for a few minutes, Sumner pushed ahead at 9:10 a.m. Sedgwick's division advanced with a brigade front and with the three brigades deployed in line. In this formation, a change of front to the right or left would take time and space. That space did not exist, because the two rear brigades pressed closely on the heels of the brigade in their front. The corps's line of advance was due west, to the north of Greene's men and toward the middle section of the West Woods. Sumner's two remaining divisions would pass south of Greene. Sedgwick's division thus advanced along a different axis from the earlier Union attacks. Hooker had moved due south, and the XII Corps's axis of advance had been largely southwest.[47]

Sumner's assessment that the II Corps was on its own was understandable. His corps's advance, starting at a ford close to the Pry house instead of the Upper Bridge, oriented his advance westerly. Hooker's corps and elements of the XII Corps had recoiled to where they had started the battle, in and behind the woods on Sumner's right. Sumner's appropriate desire to engage the Confederates, however, kept him from understanding two important details. First, there were Federal units available for a coordinated attack. While Rickett's division was truly unable to be rallied, parts of Meade's and Doubleday's I Corps divisions may have been capable of further fighting. In the XII Corps, portions of Crawford's brigade were unlikely to continue, but it had two available and unused regiments. Gordon had the same, and Carman accurately wrote that Gordon's three previously engaged, veteran regiments were "not a bit wanting in aggression." Finally, though Greene's division gave the impression of being beaten by lying down short of the Dunker Church, events would prove otherwise. The information that Sumner was able to gather and assess before advancing was insufficient for him to understand that his westerly movement was being made parallel to what had been the Confederate's front all morning.[48]

46 Carman, *Maryland Campaign: Antietam*, 172; *Joint Committee on the Conduct of the War, 38th Congress*, 1:368.

47 Carman, *Maryland Campaign: Antietam*, 189, 245; Palfrey, *The Antietam and Fredericksburg*, 83-84; Armstrong, *Unfurl Those Colors*, 178.

48 Carman, *Maryland Campaign: Antietam*, 165, 576.

The three veteran brigades hastened forward to the cheers of the men they relieved. The brigades, from front to rear, were commanded by Brig. Gens. Willis A. Gorman, Napoleon J. T. Dana, and Oliver O. Howard. General Patrick saw them pass "with rapid step under the belief that they were driving everything before them." As the division passed the three 124th Pennsylvania companies that were firing from behind a bank along the road, someone called on the Pennsylvanians to fall in. Sedgwick's men negotiated the fences on the Hagerstown Pike and traversed the open ground west of the road and into the West Woods' middle section while under fire from Jeb Stuart's horse artillery. The open forest grove permitted a quick advance. Without room for the second and third brigades to maneuver, the head of the column emerged from the western edge of the woods. Sumner rode directly behind the lead brigade as its right emerged from the tree line into a western cornfield. The 13th Virginia, which Early had detailed to guard some of Stuart's artillery, opened fire in front of Gorman's right. The left of the brigade exited the woods into the open field south of the western cornfield. Suddenly, volleys savaged its ranks.[49]

---

49 OR 19, pt. 1, 476; Francis A. Walker, *History of the Second Army Corps in the Army of the Potomac* (New York, 1887, reprint, Gaithersburg, MD, 1985), 101, 104-106; Sparks, *Inside Lincoln's Army*, 149; Broomhall to Gould, July 13, 1891, APD; Carman, *Maryland Campaign: Antietam*, 193-194.

Chapter 10

"What the Ohio and Pennsylvania boys can't do, nobody can!"

— Hector Tyndale

McLaws's Counterattack from the West Woods

9:00 to 10:00 a.m., September 17, 1862

. . . [W]e had won a great battle. I did not suppose [upon being carried from the field] that anything could happen by which any drawn battle could be made out of it. . . . I supposed that we had everything in our own hands.[1]

— Joseph Hooker

Before occupying the Dunker Church plateau, part of the 28th Pennsylvania's left wing halted south of the Smoketown Road. From behind the fence borering the East Woods, the men shot at fleeing Confederates. They soon discovered an abandoned section of Southern artillery 30 to 40 paces away. The 12- and six-pounder pieces were iron smoothbores from Woolfolk's Virginia battery of Stephen D. Lee's battalion. The Pennsylvanians swiftly seized the obsolete Model 1841 guns, whose cannoneers had had the misfortune of deploying just as Greene's assault began. After nabbing the guns, this left portion of the 28th Pennsylvania executed a left oblique and headed for haystacks west of the Mumma house, a few hundred yards east of the high ground across the Hagerstown Pike from the Dunker Church, where it would soon take position. It paused there and found several wounded Confederates. Among the

---

1 *Joint Committee on the Conduct of the War, 38th Congress*, 1:582.

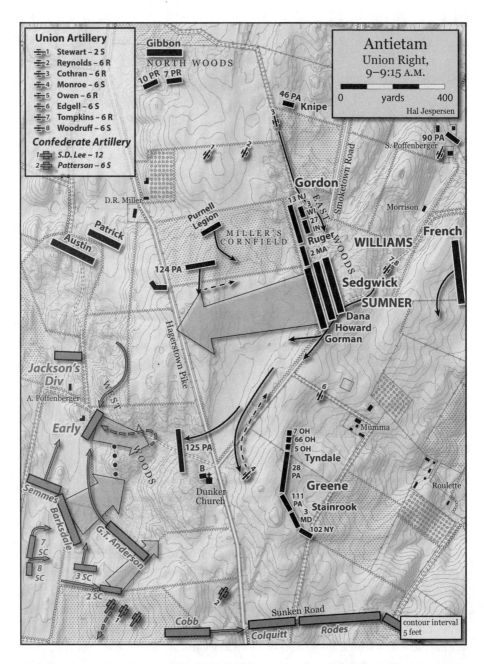

Federals was Sgt. Henry Smith of the 10th Maine, who had joined the Pennsylvanians as his regiment withdrew. He spoke with a loquacious Southerner who fabricated various details, either to deceive or have a laugh at his captors. He boasted that Stonewall Jackson had captured Harpers Ferry and that they were expecting him any time. When Jackson arrived, "You d——d Yanks will have to get out of this." Using the Federals' bugbear was nothing new and might have been effective, but it was by no means accurate on September 17, 1862. Jackson was not en route from Harpers Ferry. He was less than half a mile away in the West Woods, facing potential catastrophe. All but three of his brigades on the field, plus one relief division, were already spent from the morning's fighting and had become largely disorganized. Two of those available brigades, from D. H. Hill's division, guarded Robert E. Lee's fragile center alone. Three other brigades from the same division—Ripley's, Colquitt's, and McRae's—had already shifted left to shore up Jackson's front. The only fresh brigade in close proximity to Jackson belonged to Brig. Gen. Jubal Early.[2]

Just after dawn, Jackson had detached Early's brigade to support artillery and cavalry under Jeb Stuart on the army's extreme left flank. After heavy casualties among the commanders in Ewell's division, and as the Confederate left was about to collapse, Jackson ordered Early to return. Early left the 13th Virginia behind and marched his brigade to the West Woods, where he found Colonels Grigsby and Stafford organizing about 200–300 men of Jackson's division. Grigsby then drove Yankee skirmishers under Brig. Gen. Marsena Patrick from the northern reaches of the West Woods.[3]

A description of the West Woods is necessary at this point. The main body of this open woodlot measured approximately 450 yards from east to west and 550 yards from north to south. This section of the woods was immediately west of the Dunker Church. The meetinghouse sat on the eastern side of a large knoll, along the west and north sides of which ran two ravines. One ravine started in the low southwest corner of the woods and ran northeast for about 250 yards, where it converged with another ravine coursing eastward from near Alfred Poffenberger's house. These ravines bordered the northern edge of the Dunker Church knoll and connected with the swale in the open field between the Smoketown Road and the Cornfield. South from the church, the southern wood line angled away from the Hagerstown Pike slightly before turning west. A path ran through the woods from just north of the Dunker Church to the northwest corner of this section of woods. The southern and western borders of the woods were fenced. To the south, open

2 Armor to Gould, May 6, 1891, Foering to Gould, June 22, 1891, and Smith to Gould, March 24, 1870, APD; Carman, *Maryland Campaign: Antietam*, 134, 139; Johnson and Anderson, *Artillery Hell*, 22, 107.

3 Early, *Autobiographical Sketch*, 141-142.

ground stretched for 200 yards, beyond which stood corn that will be referred to here as the "southern cornfield." North of the ravine, the ground rose to another rail fence at the edge of the woods. North of the fence, an area 400 yards north to south and east to west bordered the pike. A north-south fence bisected it, with woods west of the fence. This rectangular wooded area is the middle section of the West Woods. The woods continued to the northwest of this lot for another 400 yards. Between the middle section of trees and the pike was a gently undulating meadow that was a little higher than the woods to the west and south. Rock ledges dotted both woods and field, creating excellent cover.[4]

Early's brigade deployed halfway up the middle section of the woods, facing north. Early saw Goodrich's brigade advancing toward his left front and directed the remnants of Jackson's division to form there in defense. He then rode east of the pike, seeking the rest of Ewell's division. Failing to find any of his new command and only discovering D. H. Hill's men falling back, Early sent an aide to the rear to locate the division. Realizing that his brigade of scarcely 1,100 men, plus fewer than 300 troops under Grigsby, were all that was left to defend the Confederate left, Early rode to find Jackson, who was on the hill west of the church. He told Early to resist any advance until reinforcements arrived.[5]

The Federals soon threatened Early and Grigsby from opposite directions. Goodrich and Patrick advanced toward Early's left front. The three westernmost companies of the 124th Pennsylvania were along the pike on Early's right front, while the balance of the regiment moved further toward his flank, east of the road. A battery opened fire from his right rear. Early supposed it was friendly, but soon learned that it was shooting into the West Woods behind him. This was Monroe's battery. He then discovered Greene's two brigades near it. Goodrich's men entered the northwest portion of the West Woods at his left front. Almost immediately after this, a more critical threat emerged. Early rode south to investigate and promptly returned, quite animated. With the large 125th Pennsylvania's move behind him into the woods near the church, Early could no longer remain concealed among the trees.[6]

Leaving Grigsby's men to face Goodrich's and Patrick's brigades and the 124th Pennsylvania, Early started to counter the threat to his rear. Using woods

---

4 Carman-Cope, *Antietam Atlas*, LC.

5 Early, *Autobiographical Sketch*, 142-144; Carman, *Maryland Campaign: Antietam*, 157.

6 Carman, *Maryland Campaign: Antietam*, 179; Early, *Autobiographical Sketch*, 145-146; Jonathan Gibson to Carman, September 6, 1899, NA-AS.

and outcroppings for concealment, he moved his brigade by the right flank. Paralleling the 125th Pennsylvania's path, Early's men descended into low ground east of the A. Poffenberger farm and continued south to the western side of a rock ledge just inside of the wood's western boundary. When the 49th Virginia, leading the column, cleared the ledge, Early ordered it to engage the Pennsylvanians' right skirmishers. As the remaining regiments came up, Early ordered them to face left and open fire. After two volleys, Early's men started after the Pennsylvanians, but their pursuit was disjointed. On his right, Early led the 49th Virginia uphill through the woods but was stopped by the 125th's main line. He directed the 49th up and down the hill two more times. Lieutenant Colonel Jonathan Gibson of the 49th questioned Early about these eccentric movements. Early claimed that he was trying to throw off the range of Monroe's guns. The irregular movements of his right disarranged the entire brigade. In his official report, however, Early suggested that his brigade had caught the scent of its prey and could not be stopped. Whatever the cause, he soon recalled the brigade to near the western edge of the woods and allowed inbound reinforcements to have their turn. As Early waited, he turned his leftmost regiment, the 31st Virginia, to the north to guard his flank against Sedgwick's approaching division, a burgeoning threat of greater moment than the Pennsylvanians. Those reinforcements to which Early deferred, from James Longstreet's Corps, deployed south and west of Early's troops.[7]

*   *   *

After experiencing heavier fighting than any other unit during the reduction of Harpers Ferry, Maj. Gen. Lafayette McLaws's division deployed across Pleasant Valley, facing north. After Franklin's corps captured Crampton's Gap and descended into Pleasant Valley, it isolated McLaws from Lee's main army. At 2:00 a.m. on September 16, McLaws withdrew from the southern end of the valley and crossed the Potomac into Harpers Ferry. At this point, his men had been without food for three days. He made an unsuccessful effort to secure rations before pushing upriver to Shepherdstown, under orders to reach Sharpsburg as quickly as possible. The clutch of Federal prisoners that A. P. Hill's division had to process in Harpers Ferry delayed McLaws's passage, and his troops reached the outskirts of

7 OR 19, pt. 1, 971; Early, *Autobiographical Sketch*, 146-147; Gibson to Carman, September 6, 1899, and June 21, 1901, NA-AS.

Shepherdstown after dark. After briefly bivouacking two miles short of the town, it recrossed the Potomac at Boteler's Ford by torchlight.[8]

When McLaws's rundown division arrived in the vicinity of Sharpsburg before sunrise, Lee took personal control of it, telling McLaws that he would be subject only to Lee's direct orders. The entire Confederate line, having already shifted forces from the center and right to stanch scattered waves of Federals toward the left, was now vulnerable. McLaws would be available to respond to any threatened point. The few men with food cooked and ate it, and McLaws slept in a patch of tall grass.[9]

Just before 9:00 a.m., a member of Lee's staff rousted McLaws from his slumber. The division had moved without him. He mounted and hurried forward, finding his troops halted a few hundred yards southwest of the West Woods, in the field west of the southern cornfield. Brigadier General George "Tige" Anderson's brigade had arrived shortly before McLaws's division and was in line along the southwest edge of the woods. Earlier that morning, Anderson's Georgians were positioned behind the Washington Artillery, east of Sharpsburg. When called to the left wing, Anderson had no guide and found his own way, homing toward the sounds of battle. He eventually found Hood, who sent him forward to the woods. When within 200 yards of the tree line, his men took fire from the 125th Pennsylvania, which had just moved up. Anderson ordered sharpshooters forward, and the brigade advanced to the edge of the woods. The Georgians dismantled the fence and stacked its rails into a makeshift breastwork. These were the first reinforcements that Early saw. Anderson's men remained there, lying behind rails, exchanging fire with unseen Pennsylvanians up the wooded ridge.[10]

McLaws's division deployed with the brigades of Cobb, Kershaw, Barksdale, and Semmes arranged from right to left. McLaws, seeing the Pennsylvanians in the woods and wanting to prevent their further advance, ordered Brig. Gen. Joseph B. Kershaw to cover the division's deployment. Kershaw called on his former regiment, the 2nd South Carolina, to provide the necessary cover and enter the southern portion of the woods. The 2nd's commander, Col. John Kennedy, double-quicked his men toward the pike, by the flank. Fences crossed Kennedy's

8 *Lafayette McLaws, "The Capture of Harpers Ferry," Philadelphia Weekly Press*, September 12 and 19, 1888, handwritten copy in NA.

9 *Philadelphia Weekly Press*, September 19, 1888.

10 OR 19, pt. 1, 909; W. H. Andrews, "Tige Anderson's Brigade at Sharpsburg," *Confederate Veteran*, 16:578-579.

path at unfortunate angles, and the 2nd became entangled southwest of its assigned entry point. Just then, shots from the Pennsylvanians hit the regiment. Kennedy faced the 2nd South Carolina front into line and headed for the 125th Pennsylvania's left front. The 2nd's left passed through Tige Anderson's brigade. To its left rear, Kershaw's other three regiments got into position.[11]

The rest of the division deployed with varying success. Lieutenant Colonel Christopher Sanders, commanding Brig. Gen. Howell Cobb's brigade, was to move to Kershaw's right and face north to enter the woods. The lead regiment's commander did not hear the command to face left and pressed on across the pike and past the front of Stainrook's brigade until joining the left of what remained of D. H. Hill's division in the soon-to-be-infamous Sunken Road. Brigadier General Paul Semmes moved his brigade north along a high ridge several hundred yards west of the West Woods on the Hauser farm, where Confederate artillery was going into battery. From this position, he was south of the cornfield that Sedgwick's lead brigade, under Brig. Gen. Willis A. Gorman, had entered. Northwest of Semmes, the 13th Virginia and one of Stuart's batteries on the western side of this cornfield kept Gorman's line busy in front.[12]

The four Mississippi regiments of Brig. Gen. William Barksdale's brigade, positioned between Kershaw and Semmes, advanced to the left of Tige Anderson's line. His rightmost regiments, the 17th and 21st Mississippi, moved along the ravine, which coursed northeasterly through the woods and temporarily concealed their movement from the Pennsylvanians. The Rebels would use the ravine regularly over the next three hours. Other units trailed in Barksdale's wake. The 3rd South Carolina, the only regiment in Kershaw's brigade to move left, or north, of Anderson's brigade, followed one of Barksdale's regiments through the trees. After Barksdale and the 3rd South Carolina passed, Tige Anderson moved his Georgians double-quick by the left flank, along the fence at the edge of the woods, for about 200 yards. Anderson's brigade then faced front, leapt the fence, and followed roughly behind Barksdale and the 3rd South Carolina.[13]

---

11 OR 19, pt. 1, 865.

12 OR 19, pt. 1, 859, 871; Carman, *Maryland Campaign: Antietam*, 199.

13 OR 19, pt. 1, 868, 883, 909; Carman, *Maryland Campaign: Antietam*, 200; Andrews, "Tige Anderson's Brigade at Sharpsburg," 579; Marion V. Armstrong, *Opposing the Second Corps at Antietam: The Fight for the Confederate Left & Center on America's Bloodiest Day* (Tuscaloosa, AL, 2016), 36.

* * *

After Early's first volley, Colonel Higgins's skirmishers returned to the regiment, firing as they retreated. Higgins saw Confederate brigades stacking up beyond the open woodlot. Sumner rode up and asked Higgins what command his was, then returned to Sedgwick's division. Soon, General Gorman arrived from Sedgwick's lead brigade. He told Higgins that his brigade was on the march and was just a few minutes away. Captain Huyette arrived with Company B and informed Colonel Higgins that two regiments were moving toward their left from the low ground south of the Dunker Church. The 2nd South Carolina approached from that direction. The 34th New York from Gorman's brigade then marched up. It had gone astray, continuing straight when the rest of its brigade right-obliqued. The New Yorkers arrived at the double-quick behind the 125th and moved by the left flank, deploying on the Pennsylvanians' left. But it uncovered only two of its companies. The rest of the regiment was unable to assist initially. These two companies were south of the Dunker Church and refused the regiment's flank, facing southwest. The 7th Michigan, from the left of Brig. Gen. Napoleon J. T. Dana's brigade, then took a position near the Pennsylvanians' right. Almost immediately after the regiment halted, the 17th and 21st Mississippi were seen moving up the ravine toward it. The Michiganders had been cautioned against shooting into their own men and held their fire as the Mississippians approached.[14]

Higgins ordered a retreat, but the green troops would not budge. Company officers were occupied firing rifles alongside the men, and most of them did not hear the order. Their rootedness added to the mounting peril. Higgins's major was absent, his lieutenant colonel had been wounded before entering the woods, and his brother, functioning as a makeshift aide, was fetching reinforcements. Only his adjutant, Robert M. Johnston, remained. After a few attempts at yelling to his men to fall back, Higgins sent Johnston down the line to pass the word to move out. Before moving far, Johnston fell, mortally wounded. Higgins likened the several advancing columns to an "avalanche that threatened to sweep all before it." Eventually, the Mississippians fired into both Higgins's right and the 7th Michigan's left. This volley quickly convinced the 125th's right to break rearward. After Barksdale's men attacked, the 2nd South Carolina neared the 125th's left

---

14 Thomas McCamant to Ezra Carman, September 14, 1897, NYPL; J. Fletcher Conrad to John Gould, February 20, 1897, APD; *One Hundred Twenty-Fifth Pennsylvania*, 72; Carman, *Maryland Campaign: Antietam*, 191, 197-198; *National Tribune*, June 3, 1886, and July 1, 1886; Huyette, *Maryland Campaign*, 39.

flank. With both flanks overlapped and Rebels sweeping to its rear, the whole 125th ran, soon followed by its supports. Though the Pennsylvanian's flight was precipitous, 2nd South Carolina Pvt. Creswell A. C. Waller later wrote solicitously that the 125th had not been driven so easily. He explained that the 2nd South Carolina's two right companies were "crack rifle companies . . . composed of good shots." Two more, from Charleston, were on the left. The 2nd next pitched into the 34th New York.[15]

Robert W. Shand of the 2nd South Carolina left a vivid description of this phase of the fighting in the West Woods:

> Men were falling all around me, and I could see numbers of the enemy falling in my front. There would be volleys and more scattering firing. Cannons were belching forth on our side and on their side. Officers were yelling to men, and men shouting. Orders were heard but unheeded; some leaped forward; others drew back. . . . Lieut. Lovick jumped to the front, called to his men to follow, moved his sword, and fell badly wounded in the face, disfigured for life. Lieut. Goodwyn fell mortally wounded. I thought I would make sure that I had killed a man; so I aimed at the one who stood third from the color bearer in my front and pulled trigger. He threw up his arms and fell to the ground.[16]

After the 17th and 21st Mississippi drove the Pennsylvanians, they turned north toward the 7th Michigan, and were followed by the 3rd South Carolina. Tige Anderson's brigade continued east out of the Mississippians' wake and attacked the right of the 34th New York. The 2nd South Carolina continued to the northeast and attacked that regiment's left. The New Yorkers put a volley into the South Carolinians that briefly halted their advance. Two to three volleys from the Georgians and South Carolinians in turn drove off the New Yorkers and the 72nd Pennsylvania, which had approached the rear of the 125th Pennsylvania and 34th New York.[17]

The 125th Pennsylvania's retreat was precarious. Some of it took place amid groups of Confederates in the smoke. Leaving the woods, five color guard members were shot down. Color Sergeant George A. Simpson was killed instantly. Private Eugene Boblitz of Company H snatched the flag and he was badly

---

15 OR 19, pt. 1, 492; *National Tribune*, June 3, 1886; Carman, *Maryland Campaign: Antietam*, 200-201; McCamant to Carman, November 4, 1899, NYPL; *One Hundred Twenty-Fifth Pennsylvania*, 72; C. A. C. Waller to Carman, June 13, 1901, NA-AS.

16 Robert Shand, Memoir, 37, SCL-USC.

17 Carman, *Maryland Campaign: Antietam*, 201-202.

wounded after moving a short distance. Sergeant Walter W. Greenland of Company C saw the colors on the ground, tossed his rifle aside, and ran for the flag. The Southerners were then within 50 yards, but he left the woods with only a shot through his ear, which "stung considerable." Greenland passed the colors to Capt. William W. Wallace behind Monroe's guns, which had returned to its caissons north of the Smoketown Road. Wallace waved the flag furiously and called on the men to rally. A Confederate officer recalled that Wallace "must have led a charmed life, as one hundred rifles were aimed at him without effect." As the Pennsylvanians approached, Monroe motioned with sword in hand to lie down or break to the sides. Most obliqued out of the way. Once clear, Monroe's gunners discharged double canister into the gray ranks. The battery then withdrew to just in front of the southwest corner of the East Woods, north of the Smoketown Road. Higgins's men joined the two sections that remained there, supporting batteries into the afternoon.[18]

James Randolph Simpson, whose brother George died carrying the 125th's colors, narrowly escaped. The regiment had fought in open order, taking cover behind trees. He told the men behind him to be careful not to shoot him. Before long, firing faded around him. Simpson looked around, saw that he was nearly alone, and hurried to the rear. Crossing the dismantled fence on the pike, he saw Confederates in the road on either flank shooting into the retreating regiment. He considered lying on the rails and pretending to be a casualty until the Confederates moved on, but preferring to risk being shot over going to a Southern prison camp, he continued across the open field. After about 50 feet, he stopped and joined another Pennsylvanian shooting from behind a tree. Hundreds of Rebels now lined the road, firing on his withdrawing regiment. As Simpson placed a percussion cap, his rifle dropped from his hand. He looked down and found blood spurting from his chest. Simpson hurried rearward. After 300 feet, a comrade helped him go another 50 feet before he collapsed and was carried away in a blanket.[19]

*   *   *

18 *National Tribune*, June 3, 1886; *One Hundred Twenty-Fifth Pennsylvania*, 74; Huyette, *Maryland Campaign*, 40; Parker to Gould, March 10, 1894, APD; Walter Greenland to "Dear Bro," September 18, 1862, 125th Pennsylvania Infantry Enlisted Man's Letters, USA.

19 "Recollections of J. R. Simpson Relating to His Participation in the Battle of Antietam on the Seventeenth Day of September, 1862," USA.

With the 125th Pennsylvania out of the woods, much of the weight of McLaws's assault fell on Sedgwick. After Barksdale, Anderson, and the 3rd South Carolina passed, Early turned his reformed brigade and headed north to the west of Barksdale and the 3rd, toward Gorman's and Dana's left. Gorman was already fully occupied with the 13th Virginia and Stuart's horse artillery in his front. Then, Semmes's brigade and the line of Rebel batteries on Hauser's Ridge fired into Gorman's brigade. Gorman soon noticed Confederates descending on the division's flank and notified Sumner, who exclaimed, "My God, we must get out of this!" Gorman's brigade managed to maintain a stiff resistance before wavering and withdrawing to the north.[20]

Meanwhile, Barksdale's brigade, with the 3rd South Carolina on its right, pitched into Dana's and Howard's vulnerable flanks, sweeping toward their rear. Sumner rode rapidly down Howard's line, from left to right, shouting. Unable to make out what he was saying, the men thought he was urging a charge. They soon heard him, "Back boys, for God's sake move back; you are in a bad fix!" Volleys from the left soon disabused them of their initial impression. Stunned by the sudden fire, against which it was helpless, the left of each brigade disintegrated. Some units attempted to change front, but this was largely unviable. Badly mauled, the regiments fell away from the advancing Southerners in various states of order and disorder. Barksdale and the 3rd South Carolina advanced as far as the open field between the West Woods and the Hagerstown Pike. Early halted in the woods just to the west. Semmes's brigade pursued beyond the northern edge of the West Woods, and the artillery on Hauser's Ridge energetically repositioned to stay on the retreating Federals' flank. The retreating Yankees eventually halted near the North Woods, stanched by reformed I Corps units and fire from Federal batteries. Tige Anderson advanced eastward to the edge of the woods north of the church and halted. A mounted officer rode up and told Anderson that the Federals were threatening his right and directed him to withdraw.[21]

*   *   *

North of the 125th Pennsylvania's withdrawal, 1st Lt. George Woodruff's Battery I, 1st U.S. Artillery, had followed Sedgwick west and unlimbered south of

---

20 Early, *Autobiographical Sketch*, 147; Carman, *Maryland Campaign: Antietam*, 198-199, 207, 211-212.

21 Carman, *Maryland Campaign: Antietam*, 204-209, 215-221.

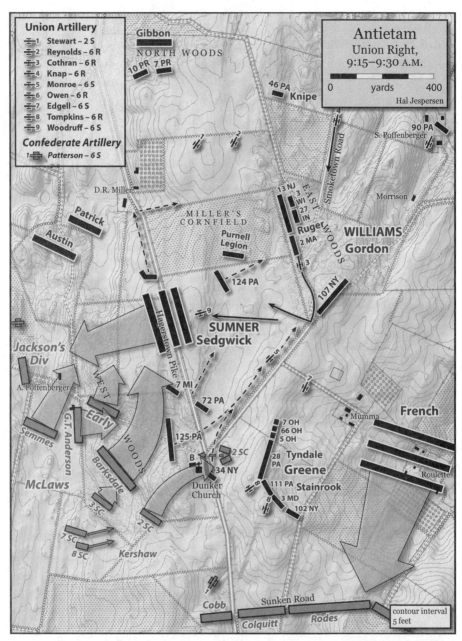

the Cornfield and east of the pike. Going into battery about 300 yards from the West Woods on high ground northwest of the swale, Woodruff enfiladed Barksdale and the 3rd South Carolina. XII Corps artillery soon joined Woodruff.[22]

22 *OR* 19, pt. 1, 309, 869; Carman, *Maryland Campaign: Antietam*, 214.

Captain George Cothran had ridden with Alpheus Williams south through Miller's Cornfield after Greene's attack. Williams sent Cothran back to his battery, which was south of the North Woods, and told him to be ready to move. No sooner had Cothran arrived than one of Williams's aides directed him through the East Woods via the Joseph Poffenberger Lane and the Smoketown Road. He was to meet another staffer there for orders. Cothran could not find a staffer, but saw Woodruff heavily engaged. Without waiting for orders, Cothran advanced his six Parrott guns to Woodruff's right and fired canister and spherical case at Confederates who were pursuing Federal fugitives between the Hagerstown Pike and the West Woods.[23]

Sedgwick's division, tumbling away from the West Woods, swept Goodrich's brigade with it. With the situation now "in the wildest disorder," Marsena Patrick ordered his men to return to the rock ledge parallel to the pike. They stayed there a short time, attempting to stem Sedgwick's rout, before marching north by the right flank. Captain Reddington kept control of his 60th New York skirmishers and formed a line behind which the regiment congealed.[24]

The three 124th Pennsylvania companies west of the pike also fell back. They paused at the Miller barn as a "hurricane of a cannonade" from their front and rear passed overhead. The Pennsylvanians eventually moved east along the fence at the north edge of the Cornfield. Halfway to the East Woods, Company D met a Confederate soldier asking for help to evacuate his wounded captain. Captain Norris L. Yarnall took Pvt. Jason Cheetham and entered the corn. They found the wounded captain and three more Rebels. Having been trapped in the Cornfield for some time, the fallen men were understandably anxious to reach safety. Yarnall withdrew to fashion a stretcher but soon learned of advancing Confederates. He recalled Cheetham, and continued to the East Woods, abandoning the Southerners in the corn. Company D then supported a battery west of the woods.[25]

After exiting the corn onto the ridge east of the Hagerstown Pike, the 124th Pennsylvania's other seven companies briefly returned fire across the road and fell back to the low ground east of the ridge, fronting nearly parallel with the pike. A

23 Carman, *Maryland Campaign: Antietam*, 214; George Cothran to Carman, March 24, 1898, and August 21, 1895, NYPL.

24 Carman, *Maryland Campaign: Antietam*, 216; Sparks, *Inside Lincoln's Army*, 150; Reddington to Carman, January 4, 1900, NYPL.

25 Broomhall to Gould, July 13, 1891, APD; Broomhall to Carman, March 1, 1899, and May 16, 1900, NYPL.

portion of Sedgwick's retreating division disordered these companies, which then returned to the East Woods. Companies H and I then went back to the Cornfield until late afternoon. Williams and Knipe gathered stragglers from the 124th and placed them under Captain Yarnall in the southern portion of the East Woods, from which they later deployed as battery support.[26]

When the eastern wing of the 124th Pennsylvania broke, the Purnell Legion, which had been prone in the Cornfield, rose and tried to keep the Pennsylvanians from withdrawing. They were unsuccessful, and took the 124th's place at the Cornfield's southern edge. The Marylanders maintained this position until late morning, when Major Fulton marched them to the East Woods for ammunition. A portion of the regiment had moved to the haystacks west of the pike and helped contain the surging Confederates at the rock ledges between the road and the West Woods.[27]

*   *   *

Aided by Federal command disorder, the immediate threat to the Confederate left had passed. Though Hooker's and Mansfield's replacements, Meade and Williams, were both capable officers, neither fought their corps that day with the same drive as their predecessors. Both were hobbled by the actions of underperforming subordinates. For instance, about the time that Gordon's brigade became engaged and Goodrich moved toward the right, Williams rode right to meet Brig. Gen. Abner Doubleday of Meade's corps. He reported finding Doubleday sheltered in a ravine, "Apparently in bland ignorance of what was doing on his front or what need he had of my troops, except to relieve his own." Williams faced a similar issue with Samuel Crawford, who took command of Williams's division. Crawford asserted in his official report that he rallied a portion of his command that fell back during Sedgwick's retreat, at which point a thigh wound took him out of the battle. Williams described the wound as "a minor puncture," though later complications may point to a bone injury. He added, "Not only did [Crawford] not form a line, but he did not give a command to either of the two Brigade commanders of the 1st Division during the day. I say this on their repeated

26 Carman, *Maryland Campaign: Antietam*, 157-158; Broomhall to Carman, March 1, 1899, NYPL; Broomhall to Hawley, March 19, 1891, and Broomhall to Gould, June 29, 1891, APD.

27 Fulton to Carman, December 21, 1899, David Herring to Carman, July 2, 1900, and Pennock Cole to Carman, October 13, 1900, NYPL.

assertions." Colonel Ezra Carman reported seeing Crawford once after the battle started. The general was "safely ensconced behind a ledge of rocks where nothing could touch him."[28]

Crawford cast shade on Gordon in his official report, writing that he took command of Williams's division and went forward to find Gordon's brigade as it advanced into the Cornfield. There he instructed Colonel Andrews "in the absence of the brigade commander." The 27th Indiana's history seconded Crawford's claim, alleging Gordon was absent during at least part of the fight above and the advance through the Cornfield. Hooker, however, had ordered Gordon to move the 107th New York to Samuel Poffenberger's woods, which it was to defend "at all hazards." It will be remembered that on that errand, Gordon was unable to send for a surgeon for Mansfield because he had no staff officers available. That point accounts for his guiding the regiment personally. Its commander, Col. Robert Bruce Van Valkenburgh, was ill. Though determined to take the field, he left maneuvering the regiment to Lieutenant Colonel Diven, who later admitted that he had no training and the regiment was new. Gordon oversaw its deployment into line and marched it by the left flank into the leading edge of the woods. Perceiving no Confederates ahead, Gordon rode briskly forward into the East Woods and along the Smoketown Road until he saw that the Cornfield had been cleared. This was an unusual reconnaissance duty for a brigadier.[29]

Throughout the XII Corps, critical staff shortages existed. Mansfield had a single staff officer, Capt. Clarence Dyer, and McClellan loaned him Capt. James Forsyth of his own staff. Mansfield kept them hurrying about during his short time in command. No one in the corps seemed to have any idea that Mansfield had a staff. Within the brigade staffs, many were killed or captured at Cedar Mountain. Some returned to their erstwhile regiments to fill gaps, and the hardships of the late August battles and marches debilitated others. This shortage certainly existed in Gordon's and Crawford's brigades. Tyndale had no regular staff at all, only using a few officers that he scraped together from his regiments. Geary's staff had left after his wounding, inhibiting effective coordination.[30]

---

28 Quaife, *From the Cannon's Mouth*, 128; Alpheus Williams to George B. McClellan, April 18, 1863, NA-AS; Welsh, *Medical Histories*, 81. McClellan's official report was markedly Crawford-centric; Williams believed that Crawford sent a self-serving account directly to McClellan.

29 OR 19, pt. 1, 477, 485, 494; Brown, *Twenty-Seventh Indiana*, 254; Diven to Gould, January 7, 1891, and George Gordon to Gould, January 19, 1871, APD.

30 Gould, *Mortal Wounding*, 27; McLaughlin, *Memoir of Hector Tyndale*, 58.

Edwin Sumner might well have been expected to bring the same energy that propelled Hooker throughout the morning and to wrest coordinated effort from the far-flung units, but Sedgwick's precipitous collapse shattered Sumner's confidence. In his history of the II Corps, Francis Walker explained that the intrepid Sumner had lost moral courage after Sedgwick's repulse. Walker wrote that while Sumner would still have been ready to face personal danger, he lost, "The courage which, in the crash and clamor of action, amid disaster and repulse, enables the commander coolly to calculate the chances of success or failure. He was heartbroken at the terrible fate of the splendid division on which he had so much relied, which he had deemed invincible, and his proximity to the disaster had been so close as to convey a shock from which he had not recovered." Simply put, Sumner was no longer capable of making hard decisions, and in a few hours would enable McClellan's proclivity for caution. In any event, if anyone expected Sumner to effectively command the Army of the Potomac's right wing, such hopes were dashed when he retrenched into sorting out his own corps's problems. With no one on the right capable of tending to matters beyond their own immediate concerns, an isolated Federal salient under George Greene stood exposed and unsupported well beyond the main Federal line.[31]

* * *

At the Dunker Church plateau, Greene's men were tired from the morning's fighting. They had driven Colquitt and Robbins from the Cornfield and East Woods and had fought a running battle for nearly half a mile. Private Joseph Clark of the 7th Ohio recalled their condition as they waited behind the ridge. Their throats "were parched from the heat of the weather, the continuous and exhausting effects of the battle, and the awful thirst produced by the powder in biting off cartridges." Clark's company was particularly affected. Early that morning at their bivouac on the Hoffman farm, two men were given the company's canteens to fill. They never returned. Clark, who was afraid to relinquish his canteen, was the only man in the company with water during the battle. To make matters worse, almost everyone in the two brigades was without ammunition. The possibility of defending with bayonets must have been on the men's minds. Yet they remained, sheltering from Confederate artillery. Shortly after reaching the plateau, a shell landed amid the 5th Ohio's color guard. According to Powell, "all at that point

31 Walker, *History of the Second Army Corps*, 117.

seemed swept out of existence." Other Ohioans raised the colors immediately. Officers ordered the men to lie behind the ridge, which protected them from direct hits. Still, shells burst overhead, throwing shrapnel amongst them without causing harm.[32]

Despite thirst, hunger, fatigue, and empty cartridge boxes, the men exulted. They knew they had fought well. After the taste of so much defeat, largely handed to them by their own leaders, they had driven the Confederates back, clearing the Cornfield for good and occupying the ground that had held Southern artillery since dawn. After one of their charges, a man in Company M shouted, "I'd rather be a member of the 28th than king of the whole world." Sheltered behind the ridge, they recounted the prisoners, colors, and artillery they had captured. Hector Tyndale rode by and called to them, "Boys don't, yourselves, boast of what you have done, let others speak of it; it is ill manners to talk of it yourselves." Someone called for three cheers for their lieutenant colonel, which roared from the ranks. In doing so, the men flung aside the ill feelings that they had for their despised commander after a few hours of hard and successful fighting. A member of the 28th pondered after the war, "Who would have believed a month before that the 28th would ever cheer that officer? He, the over-strict, yet kind hearted, but misunderstood Tyndale. No officer ever received a greater compliment from his men than did Tyndale on that day. And I desire to say, that in all twenty-four battles and nineteen skirmishes in which the regiment and brigade participated in during the War of the Rebellion, in none was it so well handled as at the battle of Antietam by Lieut.-Colonel Tyndale." Another 28th Pennsylvanian wrote soon after the battle, "Col. Tyndale is as brave as steel. All his faults are forgotten. He is brave."[33]

The 28th Pennsylvania was not alone in its improved opinion of Tyndale. A soldier in the 7th Ohio remembered that, during an early lull in the fighting, Tyndale rode up to the regiment and called, "Boys, you have fought nobly; and by the Great God who looks down upon us, you shall have your reward! What the Ohio and Pennsylvania boys can't do, nobody can!" Another 7th Ohioan remembered, simply, that Tyndale "did bully."[34]

---

32 Clark to Gould, March 18, 1892, APD; Powell Memoir, chap. 6, OHC; Powell to Gould, November 18, 1893, APD; Wood, *Seventh Regiment*, 139.

33 McLaughlin, *Memoir of Hector Tyndale*, 102; *Grand Army Scout and Soldiers Mail*, September 22, 1883; *National Tribune*, June 27, 1901; William Roberts, Jr., to father, September 21, 1862, HSP.

34 *Painesville Telegraph*, October 2, 1862; *Cleveland Morning Leader*, October 2, 1862.

Tyndale behaved conspicuously despite being physically hindered. He suffered from fever and diarrhea acquired on Pope's retreat. During the latter part of the battle, a glancing shot hit his hip, which became quite sore. This wound was exacerbated by being on foot after having three horses shot from under him. In the 28th Pennsylvania, Major Pardee's horse was shot. As Sedgwick's men rushed for the rear, Tyndale ordered the brigade's only remaining mounted officer, Lt. Col. Eugene Powell, to ride to them and have them reform on the right. This action yielded few recruits.[35]

Tyndale was not the only officer to earn respect at Antietam. General Greene behaved vigorously for a man his age. The sixty-one-year-old led the advance through the Cornfield before energetically gathering the command together at the Dunker Church plateau. As it assaulted the Cornfield, Greene sent his son, Charles Greene, to procure ammunition. Young Charles returned to the rear of the plateau with much-needed ammunition wagons. At about 9:00 a.m., a battery arrived. Battery A of the First Rhode Island Artillery, rifled Parrotts under Capt. John Tompkins, was one of the II Corps batteries that crossed the Antietam with the XII Corps late on September 16. It parked overnight on the Hoffman farm near Greene's division. On the day of the battle, Tompkins advanced past the Mumma farm. Passing Monroe's withdrawing battery near the Smoketown Road, Tompkins hurried his men onto the plateau, guided by General Greene. Tompkins's posted his rightmost gun where Monroe's left gun had been.[36]

Greene buoyed his men by bringing up Tompkins's guns and by his comportment. Lieutenant Colonel Powell wrote, "Gen. Greene's bearing was so heroic and knightly and his exposure so signal and conspicuous that the men of Tyndale's brigade turned towards him and gave him a cheer amidst the heavy fire, which he politely recognized by standing in his stirrups and taking off his cap. As there was not the best of personal relations then between Gen. Greene and these men, that cheer was won by his exhibition of heroism and not by any personal

---

35 McLaughlin, *Memoir of Hector Tyndale*, 68; Foering Diary, September 17, 1862, HSP; Powell Memoir, chap. 6, OHC.

36 *OR* 19, pt. 1, 308; Carman, *Maryland Campaign: Antietam*, 177; Charles T. Greene to sister, September 19, 1862 (transcript), CWD Collection, USA; Powell to Gould, November 23, 1893, APD. Tyndale wrote (McLaughlin, 56) that a battery first went into position on his right and swept the woods at his request before repositioning more to the left. He identified it as Lt. Evan Thomas's Battery A, 4th U.S. Artillery. It is most likely that Tyndale meant Woodruff's battery in its original, advanced position across the pike from the middle section of the West Woods. Woodruff reported (*OR* 19, pt. 1, 310) using solid shot on the Confederates at the Dunker Church. In line with Tyndale's description, Woodruff would soon reposition to the left, just not to Tyndale's left.

favoritism of the men for him." Powell, who thought Greene commanded the corps that day, wrote that he heard nothing but praise for Greene after Antietam. A 10th Mainer who fought for a time with the 28th Pennsylvania wrote that he "was one of the bravest of men." An Ohioan wrote that Greene, "Whom we all hissed and hooted whenever he passed, acted so bravely that when we halted and sent back for ammunition, we really got up three cheers for him." Private Tenney wrote that Greene "was very cool and collected on the field," and added that the boys in the 7th were no longer "so fierce for 'hitting him with a brick.'"[37]

Arriving at a run, someone in Tompkins's battery shouted to the infantry, which had been without artillery support or ammunition for a short time, "Hold to your place, there, boys, and we will stand by you while there is a shot in the locker." Greene's men found this most encouraging. They were more materially encouraged when Tompkins engaged a Confederate battery to the south of the West Woods and infantry in the Sunken Road to the southeast. When ammunition arrived, a detail from the 102nd New York moved it from the wagons. After being resupplied, some in the 28th used the downtime to take shots at Rebels moving through a cornfield between the Piper farmhouse to the Sunken Road. This long-range fire was to the left rear, assisting Sumner's remaining two divisions to the southeast.[38]

General French arrived at the East Woods about 9:15 a.m., with only Greene's men and Tompkins's battery visible. The gunners were plugging away at Confederates in the Sunken Road. French turned to assault left of Greene. Israel Richardson joined on French's left. Between 9:30 a.m. and 1:30 p.m., these divisions attacked and eventually shattered D. H. Hill's two remaining brigades under Brig. Gens. Robert Rhodes and George B. Anderson and Maj. Gen. R. H. Anderson's division. Though these attacks left the Confederate center virtually defenseless, Richardson was mortally wounded, and the Federals spent themselves in the effort. No further advance occurred.[39]

The Dunker Church plateau offered a fine view of the burgeoning attack against the Sunken Road. Lieutenant Colonel Powell had just returned from

37 Carman, *Maryland Campaign: Antietam*, 177; *National Tribune*, June 27, 1901; Powell Memoir, chap. 6, OHC; Smith to Gould, March 24, 1870, APD; *Cleveland Morning Leader*, October 2, 1862; Tenney to "My Darling Addie," September 30, 1862, UVA.

38 *National Tribune*, June 27, 1901; Van Steenbergh to Gould, March 27, 1892, and Armor to Gould, May 6, 1891, APD.

39 Carman, *Maryland Campaign: Antietam*, 245-246, 263-294.

attempting to corral Sedgwick's fugitives. From his position behind the 66th Ohio's line, he looked southeast. Past the smoldering Mumma house and along the Sunken Road, Powell could see, "The several lines of opposing troops with banners flying, arms and field pieces glistening in the sun as they moved, come closer and closer together." More pressing events ended this diversion. In the 28th Pennsylvania, Major Pardee had ordered Capt. James Fitzpatrick to move his Company A forward as skirmishers to clear Confederate sharpshooters from their front. The skirmishers hardly left the lines when they discovered a body of Southern infantry approaching.[40]

The 2nd South Carolina was leading this advance. Federal fugitives soon streamed rearward past Tyndale's right, north of the Smoketown Road. The 2nd South Carolina's Colonel Kennedy fell early, hit in the foot at the fence south of the West Woods, and Maj. Franklin Gaillard assumed command of the regiment. Captain William Wallace acted as major on the left and Capt. George B. Cuthbert oversaw the right. After driving off the Federals in the West Woods, Gaillard and Wallace disagreed about how the regiment should pass the Dunker Church. It ultimately split, maneuvering around both sides of the church and crossing the fences bordering the pike. The South Carolinians halted at a rock ledge just south of the Smoketown Road, from which they fired on retreating Yankees north of the road. Few targets appeared to the south. Indeed, it seemed a gap existed in the Federal line on the high ground to the east and southeast. While Gaillard took a handful of men to another bench-like rock to fire on Monroe's battery at its transient position near the Mumma Lane, Captain Cuthbert determined to exploit the opening and formed the right into line, oriented nearly east-west. Wallace's men faced a line at an angle with Cuthbert. With Gaillard's small detachment, the regiment resembled a "broken V." Cuthbert attempted to advance up the slope to the right.[41]

At this point, the Ohioans at the top of the slope, nearest Wallace, executed a ruse on the South Carolinians. The 7th Ohio threw forward the colors and the front rank of Company H, which began firing on the Rebels below, presenting an

---

40 *National Tribune*, June 27, 1901; *Grand Army Scout and Soldiers Mail*, September 22, 1883. The Dunker Church plateau was such a fine vantage point that the National Park Service chose the spot for its visitor center.

41 C. A. C. Waller to Ezra Carman, December 14, 1899, NA-AS; Carman, *Maryland Campaign: Antietam*, 234. The rock ledge is next to the Maryland Monument. The battery that received Gaillard's attention was either Monroe's, in its temporary position near the Mumma Lane, or Woodruff's.

apparently weak front that might be easily driven. When the Confederates advanced against it, the rest of the regiment joined the line and pushed Wallace back.[42]

Meanwhile, the Pennsylvanians to the Ohioans' left initially hesitated. Some of the Confederates in their front reportedly wore dark uniforms. At length, Sgt. James F. Knight of Company F called out, "Why, they're all greybacks." Someone shouted, "Give 'em hell." Major Pardee's men poured a destructive volley into the South Carolinians from the high ground, and Tompkins's right section soon joined in. Tompkins had been firing southward and was unaware of Kershaw's approach until about 50 South Carolinians diverted toward his rightmost gun and fired into the battery. Caught unawares, Tompkins's men turned the guns and fired double canister right oblique into the attacking infantry, causing it to recoil.[43]

A South Carolinian remembered it was "very hot" for those farthest east. Each man began to shift to the west of the man on his left to get away from the cannon fire. The Southerners soon recrossed the road and reformed in the woods south of the church. There they saw the 7th and 8th South Carolina approaching, still in column in order to keep a narrow front as long as possible. The 7th moved east along the southern edge of the West Woods with the 8th on its right, and the 2nd unfurled and waved its colors. The three regiments, recognizing one another, shouted wildly and headed toward the pike.[44]

The 7th and 8th South Carolina marched directly toward Greene's front. Colonel Wyatt Aiken of the 7th fell wounded at the eastern edge of the woods. Major William Capers White then vaulted to the head of the regiment and led the men forward. An overhead spherical case explosion had already thrown White to the ground, leaving his face covered with blood and dust. White's men advanced straight up the hill toward Tompkins's guns, believing that the Federals were in headlong retreat.[45]

42 Wood, *Seventh Regiment*, 140; *Jeffersonian Democrat*, September 18, 1862.

43 OR 19, pt. 1, 308; McLaughlin, *Memoir of Hector Tyndale*, 102-103; *Grand Army Scout and Soldiers Mail*, September 22, 1883; Henry C. Burn to father, September 18, 1862, Burn Family Papers, 1740-1974, SCL-USC, copy at AMP. Tompkins's report suggested that the battery was caught off guard during a subsequent attack by the 7th South Carolina that nearly overwhelmed the battery and its infantry support. The 2nd South Carolina's Henry Burn, however, clearly recollected firing on the battery at close range during this initial assault.

44 Waller to Carman, December 14, 1899, NA-AS; Carman, *Maryland Campaign: Antietam*, 234.

45 Waller to Carman, June 7, 1901, and H. W. Addison to Carman, November 3, 1898, NA-AS; Obituary of William Capers White, *Charleston Mercury*, December 3, 1862.

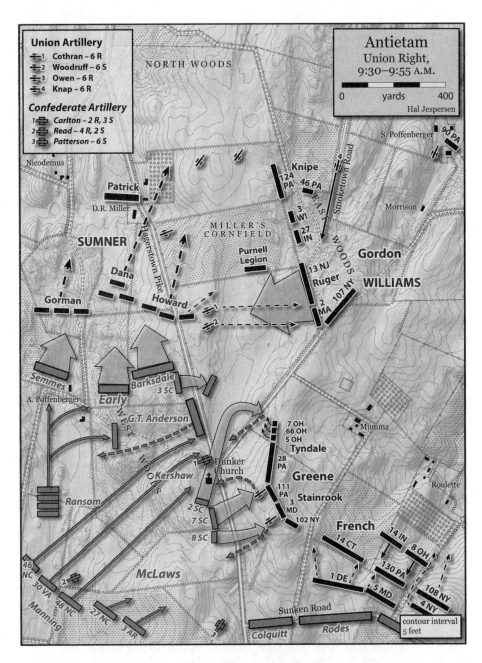

The greatest threat to Greene's line was in the center, at the obtuse-angle intersection of the 28th and 111th Pennsylvania behind Tompkins's rightmost section. Tompkins's cannoneers, aware of the South Carolinians' advance this time, gave Major White's men their full attention. A member of the 111th

Pennsylvania remembered hearing the battery commander calling for shorter fuses, set at three and then two seconds, before switching to canister. Some of Lane's New Yorkers carried ordnance to Tompkins's guns. As Kershaw's men charged the battery, these New Yorkers were told to bring canister, which James Wheeler remembered doing in a "lively" fashion. Meanwhile, the 111th Pennsylvania lay on the ground awaiting Major Walker's command. When the South Carolinians came within 60 yards of the guns, Walker called, "Now boys, up and forward. Do your duty." The Pennsylvanians rose and ran to the gun axles. Before the infantry advanced, Tompkins's situation became critical, and he ordered the battery to limber to the rear. But his command went unheard. The two regiments of Pennsylvanians slowed the Confederates and gave the gun crews time to reload, which they did faster than they could have withdrawn the guns. This difficulty in hearing the order possibly saved the guns.[46]

The 7th South Carolina's right slowed under the 111th's and Tompkins's fire. Major White led the left forward, calling on his men to take the guns in their front. A Pennsylvanian shot him in the cheek, but he pressed on to within 20 yards of the nearest gun. A blast of canister from it killed the major and several others near him. As a result of White's surge, the action on the 28th Pennsylvania's left briefly degenerated into a hand-to-hand fight. Corporal Jacob George Orth of Company D captured the 7th South Carolina's battle flag, an act that earned him the Medal of Honor.[47]

It looked like a hand-to-hand fight would take place on the 111th Pennsylvanian's line as well. The South Carolinians got to within 10 feet of the battery. First Sergeant Gideon Woodring thought the Confederates would "run over us." But "the charging line lacked weight" and evaporated under the Federal fire. Farther left, the 3rd Maryland and part of the 102nd New York, covering Tompkins's left sections, temporarily recoiled. One Southern officer reached a gun near the 102nd. He placed a hand on the tube and demanded its surrender, but the

46 OR 19, pt. 1, 513; Boyle, *Soldiers True*, 59; Wheeler to Gould, January 22, 1892, APD; Theodore Reichardt, *Diary of Battery A First Rhode Island Light Artillery* (Providence, RI, 1865), 65.

47 *Charleston Mercury*, December 3, 1862; McLaughlin, *Memoir of Hector Tyndale*, 104; *The Medal of Honor of the United States Army* (Washington, 1948), 117. Members of the 28th captured seven Rebel flags at Antietam, and the brigade as a whole took nine. Other men noted for capturing Confederate colors were Pvt. Patrick McShay of Company A and 1st Lt. Charles W. Borbridge of Company I, both of the 28th, and Pvt. John P. Murphy of the 5th Ohio. Murphy captured the 13th Alabama's flag during the fighting in the Cornfield. OR 19, pt. 1, 507; Foering Diary, September 17, 1862, APD; Cornet, "28th Pennsylvania."

gunner fired canister into him. Some of the crews left their pieces but soon returned. Shortly after the 7th South Carolina began backing away slowly, the smaller 8th South Carolina also withdrew. The 3rd Maryland's Lt. Col. Joseph Sudsburg led his men back to the line and regained the gun positions.[48]

The Federal fire was devastating. Private Charles Smith of the 102nd New York said he, "Never saw such slaughter for the rest of the war. It seemed whole companys were whipped out of existence." Henry W. Addison of the 7th South Carolina remembered, "We were confronted with Artillery and any numbers of lines of Infantry that belched forth such destruction as I had never seen before." He recalled the Federal fire being very rapid and thought that it killed or wounded three-quarters of the regiment in 15 minutes. In reality, the 7th suffered just over 50 percent casualties.[49]

As the 7th and 8th South Carolina receded, Tompkins's gunners engaged two new targets. A three-gun Georgia battery commanded by Capt. Henry Carlton arrived in the woods north of the Dunker Church after the 2nd South Carolina withdrew from its first engagement. Jeb Stuart ordered Carlton to hold the line alone until Kershaw's brigade passed through the woods, even if all his men were killed or his guns destroyed. Lafayette McLaws, to whose division Carlton was assigned, objected but was overruled by Jackson. Farther south, Capt. John Read's battery followed the 8th South Carolina and went into position south of the West Woods. Tompkins directed his four guns on the left against Read and his remaining two guns against Carlton, who also took fire from several batteries ranged in front of the East Woods. Both lost severely. Tompkins silenced Read's battery within 20 minutes after exploding one of Read's caissons and killing or wounding 14 officers and men and 16 horses. Kershaw recalled this battery. Carlton had lost 18 horses

---

48 OR 19, pt. 1, 865; Woodring to Gould, January 8, 1892, John Powers to Gould, March 23, 1892, John Keigan to Gould, January 22, 1892, and Joseph Carter to Gould, April 5, 1892, APD; Boyle, *Soldiers True*, 59; Reichardt, *Diary of Battery A*, 65; Duncan McIntyre to Carman, February 19, 1895, NA-AS. McIntyre wrote that he was not sure how far the 8th advanced, but that it got as far as a stand of apple trees, which does not appear in the Antietam atlas. Carman wrote (*Maryland Campaign: Antietam*, 247) that the 8th continued to the right and opened fire on the right flank of a regiment in French's division during the latter's attack against the Sunken Road. Such a movement would have exposed the 8th's left flank to four of Tompkins's guns at short range. This is unlikely. Lieutenant Colonel Sudsburg was armed with a homespun Bowie knife he had taken from a member of the 5th Texas in the East Woods. Joseph Sudsburg to Gould, July 4, 1891, APD. Charles Smith to John Gould, undated, APD; Waller to Carman, June 7, 1901, and Addison to Carman, July 4 and November 3, 1898, NA-AS; Carman, *Maryland Campaign: Antietam*, 616.

49 Charles Smith to John Gould, undated, APD; Waller to Carman, June 7, 1901, and Addison to Carman, July 4 and November 3, 1898, NA-AS; McLaughlin, *Hector Tyndale*, 616.

while traveling through the woods en route to his position, so his men lugged the pieces in by hand. The three batteries facing Carlton soon disabled all his guns.[50]

The 2nd South Carolina had left its brief reunion with the 7th and 8th South Carolina in the southeast corner of the woods and moved north. Its leftmost companies passed on either side of the church before the regiment crossed the Hagerstown Pike to the north side of the Smoketown Road. Avoiding a second frontal assault on the plateau, the 2nd moved northeast, within the swale in the hollow field and then up a knoll to the fence bordering the Smoketown Road.[51]

Meanwhile, the 3rd South Carolina had spilled into the open field east of the West Woods' middle section alongside Barksdale's Mississippians. Enfiladed by Woodruff's and Cothran's Federal batteries on his right, Colonel Nance changed front to the east and directed his men to lie in a shallow depression that shielded them from the batteries. Nance waited, watching for a Federal movement to counter. After seeing the 7th and 8th advancing "most beautifully through the woods up the open slope beyond," Nance led the 3rd from its covered position and "up the hill across a small road, climbed a fence, and passed to the summit of a hill in a freshly plowed field." The 3rd South Carolina advanced after the 2nd South

---

50 OR 19, pt. 1, 308, 858, 865; Carman, *Maryland Campaign: Antietam*, 235; Henry Carlton to Henry Heth, May 26, 1893, and Carlton to Carman, December 2, 1899, NA-AS.

51 Waller to Carman, December 14, 1899, and June 7, 1901, NA-AS. Tyndale described a massed assault on his right; the 3rd South Carolina, however, may not have approached as near as the 2nd. Waller's June 7 letter placed the 3rd farther left, "pretty much out of sight of the enemy . . . and not fully satisfactory to the members of the brigade." As to the position and direction of the 2nd South Carolina's attack, every other history of the battle has placed the 2nd's second assault south of the Smoketown Road. Carman's manuscript contains a gap from the end of the 2nd's initial movement until after Greene's men advanced again, but his atlas reflects this interpretation. This appears to be based on Waller's June 7 letter, which reads, "the 3 regiments 2nd, 7th, and 8th made a magnificent charge. The left of the 2nd touched + enveloped the church." This can be plausibly interpreted as the three regiments in a continuous line, and in fact may have been the case. Neither that letter nor any other primary source, however, places the 2nd South Carolina south of the Smoketown Road. Moreover, that interpretation contradicts Waller's December 14, 1899, letter, which explicitly described an advance that "went by church over Pike across or to north or northwest of the road forking with the Pike + up another swale hollow or depression over clover field to + up to a fenced thrown or knocked." This is further supported by the initial direction of the 2nd's second advance. If the 2nd left the other two regiments in the southeast corner of the woods, it would have had to go north to envelop the church. Passing the building to its left, heading mostly north, would have taken it north of the Smoketown Road and into the swale as noted in the December 14 letter. Additionally, Waller's description of hurtling fence rails fits along the Smoketown Road but not in the field next to the 7th South Carolina.

"View Where Sumner Charged," Alexander Gardner. *Library of Congress*

Carolina, approaching but ultimately stopping short of the 2nd's path toward Tyndale's right flank.[52]

Woodruff's battery fired solid shot at the 2nd South Carolina as it exited the West Woods. As the regiment advanced into the swale, it was protected from Woodruff's fire and was able to get on his left flank. Unable to change front without exposing his right flank to the western side of the Hagerstown Pike, Woodruff limbered up and withdrew to the front of the East Woods, north of the Smoketown Road. This cleared the 3rd South Carolina's path. Cothran remained forward briefly, repelling infantry across the pike before also withdrawing toward the East Woods. Cothran's battery discharged about 20 canister rounds per gun and suppressed another infantry assault later in the day, which accounted for some of this antipersonnel fire.[53]

52 OR 19, pt. 1, 310, 869; D. Augustus Dickert, *History of Kershaw's Brigade, with Complete Roll of Companies, Biographical Sketches, Incidents, Anecdotes, etc.* (Dayton, OH, 1976), 156; Carman, *Maryland Campaign: Antietam*, 214.

53 OR 19, pt. 1, 310, 869; Cothran to Carman, March 24, 1898, NA-AS; Leander E. Davis to Wife, October 2, 1862, Leander Davis Letters, USA, copy at AMP. Woodruff reported he had no "supports," which made the position untenable with his flank threatened. Cothran's letter suggested that after Woodruff retired, he was left without infantry support.

Soon after the 7th and 8th South Carolina recoiled from the Federal line, the 2nd marched up and ascended the knoll across the Smoketown Road from Tyndale's right flank. A few trees grew near the Hagerstown Pike–Smoketown Road intersection that concealed the 2nd's initial movement north of the Smoketown Road from the Ohioans. Private Clark of the 7th Ohio recorded that the Rebels advanced, "Across the field directly in our front, passing obliquely to a point where they were sheltered by the woods, and for a time hidden entirely from our view." The arriving Palmetto infantry "completely surrounded" the Buckeyes on the right, but the Ohioans quickly changed front and repelled the assault. The 3rd South Carolina fired on Tyndale's brigade from its hill near the turnpike. Its adjutant remembered seeing a Union officer with the colors five paces or more in front of his line, encouraging his men. Lieutenant Henry Brinkman, commanding the 5th Ohio's Company B, grabbed the national colors after two color-bearers fell at once. He wrote that he led the regiment in countercharging two Confederate regiments that attacked it. A 7th Ohioan wrote that the right of the brigade did most of the fighting while at the Dunker Church.[54]

As the Ohioans changed front, the regiments to their left filed right to close the line. After repulsing the 7th South Carolina's assault on the guns, Major Walker marched the 111th Pennsylvania by the right flank to counter a threat to the north. He reported that his troops suppressed it only after "some very heavy fighting." Walker behaved with conspicuous bravery at Antietam. A few weeks after the battle, an Erie newspaper account ended with a high plaudit for the 111th's major: "We ask for no *braver* man to lead us anywhere."[55]

54 OR 19, pt. 1, 513; Y. J. Pope to Ezra Carman, March 20, 1895, NA-AS; Henry Brinkman to John Brinkman, September 24, 1862, Henry C. Brinkman Papers (Mss 1075), CHA; Clark to Gould, March 18, 1892, and Charles Bentley, January 31, 1892, APD; Alexander Gardner, Antietam, Maryland, *View where Sumner's Corps Charged*, Sept. 1862, Photograph, https://www.loc.gov/item/2018671467/. The trees concealing the 2nd's advance through the swale can be seen in a picture taken a few days after the battle. It is unclear whether they are north or south of the Smoketown Road, but they are near where the trees around the Maryland Monument exist today. Standing at the Ohioan's position, it is clear how they could have lost track of the 2nd South Carolina's movement north of the Smoketown Road. Tyndale described this assault as coming "en masse down a hill and through a cornfield." The high knoll across the Smoketown Road from the Ohioans' flank appears to be the hill up which the South Carolinians advanced and down which they attacked. Tyndale also may have meant the high ground north of the swale from which the 3rd South Carolina fired on his brigade. The cornfield is a mystery. Accounts mention several unsubstantiated cornfields being located in this area.

55 Walker to Gould, April 18, 1891, APD; *Erie Weekly Gazette*, October 9, 1862. Walker's description of the 111th's move north to support the right flank could be interpreted as a

Tyndale wrote that the flank attack, "Was met by a terrific oblique fire, which melted down their ranks like wax." Woodruff's and Cothran's batteries, now repositioned near the East Woods and on the Rebels' left flank, proved more pernicious than Tyndale's fire. A 2nd South Carolinian remembered that the Federal artillery, "Began furiously to burst forth hurtling rails, dust and shells and we began to fall back sullenly at first then rapidly until we reached the church." Tyndale described, "The terror and agony of the men in the front and centre of [the Confederates'] lines, who endeavored to push their way from this dreadful fire, back through their own advancing columns, is most memorable." The 3rd South Carolina, also under artillery fire, returned to the pike and then to the woods. As Kershaw's brigade backed away, Greene's men saw a fresh line of gray-clad infantry emerging from the woods.[56]

movement behind Tyndale's brigade onto the Ohioans' right flank. Another member of the 111th wrote that the regiment went to support the right of the line after repulsing the attack on the guns, and "joined in their line." (Howard to Gould, February 4, 1892, APD) This is possible, but unlikely. It would have created an imprudent gap in the line. Both Walker and Howard described the ensuing advance past the Dunker Church as occurring immediately after this move to the right. The 111th made that advance on the 28th Pennsylvania's left, meaning it would have needed to march back to the left before advancing. It is more likely that both the 28th and 111th Pennsylvania merely closed ranks to the right, along the ridge, to support the Ohioans when the 2nd South Carolina, and later Manning's brigade, attacked the right. Another interpretation of the 111th's movement right is in Armstrong, *Opposing the Second Corps at Antietam*. Maps on pages 57 and 60 of that work depict the 111th fronting south at first, then moving right to counter the 7th South Carolina. Walker recollected moving to the top of the ridge overlooking the pike; but he also described moving north after defending Tompkins's guns from the 7th, which means the regiment was already fronting southwest to support the guns.

56 OR 19, pt. 1, 310; Waller to Carman, December 14, 1899, NA-AS; McLaughlin, *Memoir of Hector Tyndale*, 55-56. According to Tyndale, this was the third assault on his line. The first was the isolated attack by the right of the 2nd South Carolina, and the second was by the 7th and 8th. According to Tyndale, the third attack was on his flank and immediately preceded his advance. It included the movement by the 2nd and 3rd South Carolina, followed closely by the assault of Manning's brigade against Tyndale's right front, as we shall soon see.

Chapter 11

"An Ominous and Suggestive Pause"

— Alpheus Williams

To the Dunker Church

9:50 a.m. to Midnight, September 17, 1862

The new line approaching Greene's men, through the West Woods behind Kershaw, was part of Brig. Gen. John Walker's two-brigade division. On the night of September 16, Walker's men bivouacked on Lee's extreme right, overlooking Snavely's Ford. About 9:00 a.m. on the day of the battle, Col. A. L. Long of Lee's staff arrived and told Walker to move quickly to the extreme left, two and a half miles as the crow flies. Walker's division covered that distance in no more than an hour. Private Isaac Hirsh of the 30th Virginia remembered moving at a double-quick for about three miles, arriving at the fields near the West Woods where Lafayette McLaws's division had deployed. Walker left two of Col. Van Manning's regiments, the 27th North Carolina and 3rd Arkansas, at the northern edge of the southern cornfield to cover the gap between his division and D. H. Hill's left in the Sunken Road. Colonel John R. Cooke of the 27th commanded the detachment. The 3rd Arkansas was on the right. The rest of Manning's brigade moved into the West Woods.[1]

---

1 *OR*, 19, pt. 1, 914-915; J. A. Graham to Ezra Carman, December 16, 1899, NA-AS; Isaac Hirsh, Diary, September 17, 1862, LV.

Walker's other brigade, North Carolinians under Brig. Gen. Robert Ransom, deployed to Manning's left. Marching north to the west of the West Woods in column of regiments, each regiment executed a right wheel after it passed the one ahead of it. This put three regiments facing east along the fence on the western edge of the woods, centered on the A. Poffenberger farm. Ransom's fourth regiment, the 24th North Carolina, did not turn but continued north and became ensnared in the pursuit of Sedgwick's division. The 25th, 35th, and 49th North Carolina, in line from north to south, advanced through the woods until they reached the eastern edge, where they halted. Ahead, two Federal regiments, one small and one large, approached from the east.[2]

After allowing the II Corps to pass, Gordon's veteran regiments withdrew to the East Woods. The 13th New Jersey, which Gordon had ordered forward when Colquitt's troops broke, soon joined the brigade. After Sedgwick's repulse from the West Woods, Williams passed a request for reinforcements from Sumner to Gordon. The 2nd Massachusetts and 13th New Jersey were nearby and in much better condition than either of Gordon's western regiments, so Gordon started them toward the West Woods. As Gordon understood the situation, Sedgwick's division was holding on there. Colonel Ezra Carman's orders were to move into the West Woods, report to the first general officer that he found, and avoid firing on Federals in front. After passing this admonition to company commanders, Carman ordered his regiment to load its weapons for the first time.[3]

The two regiments advanced in line. The 13th New Jersey arrived at the high post-and-rail fence along the Hagerstown Pike just south of the Cornfield on the ridge where Woodruff's and Cothran's batteries had stood. The 13th's alignment was muddled, and Carman planned to reform it between the fences bordering the pike. Seeing no Confederates in front, the regiment climbed the first fence and entered the road. A few eager men, including Capt. Hugh C. Irish, scaled the second fence. Irish had apprenticed with The Guardian newspaper in Paterson, New Jersey, and established that town's first successful daily paper. The move across the fences immediately drew fire from the Rebels that had driven Sedgwick, who were lying behind substantial outcroppings parallel to the pike, about 150

---

2 OR 19, pt. 1, 915; Carman, *Maryland Campaign: Antietam*, 228-229.

3 OR 19, pt. 1, 495; Carman, *Maryland Campaign: Antietam*, 230-231.

Capt. Hugh C. Irish, 13th New Jersey
Courtesy of The Passaic County Historical Society,
Patterson, NJ

yards distant. While scattered puffs of smoke issued from the rocks, a portion of the Southern line rose and volleyed, flustering the untried Yankees.[4]

Adding to its angst, part of the command became convinced the Confederates in front were friendly, and officers passed conflicting orders. Eventually, Capt. John H. Arey of Company G stood on the fence rails to look down on the men in their front. Positively identifying the Southerners, Arey shouted to his company, "They are Rebs, boys! Give them hell!" The men returned fire, but it was largely ineffective. The Confederates went back to the cover of the rock ledges to reload. Besides difficulties finding targets, many Garden Staters were still unsure how to load their weapons. Carman's casualties mounted. Captain Irish was killed while directing his company's fire beyond the second fence. After a color bearer was hit, a private in Irish's company, James Kilroy, took the flag. Colonel Carman observed Kilroy "always pressing forward" through the day until he was severely wounded. Carman ordered the regiment to the rear shortly after it arrived.[5]

4 Carman, *Maryland Campaign: Antietam*, 231; Smith, "My First Campaign," 284; *Historical Sketch of CO "D," 13th Regiment*, 15; Susan Irish Loewen, "The Captain and Mrs. Irish," *The Castle Genie: Newsletter of the Passaic County, New Jersey Historical Society and Genealogy Club*, vol. 10, no. 1, Fall 1999. Smith wrote that a mounted Confederate officer approached the line and announced the men were firing into friendly units. This part of the account is unsubstantiated, though confusion regarding who was in front appears in other sources.

5 OR 19, pt. 1, 502; Carman, *Maryland Campaign: Antietam*, 231; Smith, "My First Campaign," 284.

Officers frantically tried to maintain order on the retreat. Private James Smith thought his comrades in the 13th New Jersey distinguished themselves as "sprinters rather than fighters." Smith's dash through the Cornfield to the East Woods stalled temporarily when he tripped over a cornstalk and face-planted into what he thought was a Confederate corpse's stomach. As he looked up, the man's eyes opened. With renewed urgency, Smith hastened rearward. Not long after the 13th gathered in the East Woods, Gordon galloped up to it. Seeing their dejected faces, he urged Lt. Col. Robert Swords to tell the men that "the enemy were licked" and to give three cheers. Swords waved his hat in the air as he executed Gordon's suggestion. The men bellowed. One remembered their renewed spirit "ran like an electric spark through the whole command." They would soon need this sanguine temperament.[6]

The 2nd Massachusetts had arrived at the turnpike fence before the 13th New Jersey. The two regiments never connected but were near each other. The 2nd was closer than the New Jerseyans to Ransom's brigade, which had halted at the edge of the middle section of the West Woods, roughly in line with the rock ledges to the north. The Bay Staters crossed the first fence, and Sergeant Comey's Company B went over the second fence. Colonel Andrews spotted men that he could not identify in the trees ahead. He ordered Francis Lundy, a color sergeant, to wave his flag. The Confederates in the woods replied with a hail of musketry.[7]

This brief clash quickly added to the 2nd Massachusetts's relatively low casualties from its earlier engagement. Several recently arrived replacement officers were hit. A ball passed through both of Lt. Charles Mills's thighs, and Capt. James Francis lost two fingers from a shot through his hand. Spent Confederate balls caused two minor injuries that were not registered in the returns. One hit Capt. Robert Gould Shaw in the neck. Another struck Captain Morse in the temple, laying him flat on his back and producing an angry bruise. With understandable concern, Morse wrote, "I thought at first it was all up for me."[8]

The loss of one officer provoked widespread grief in the regiment. Colonel Andrews was in his place near the center of the regiment when Lieutenant Colonel Dwight arrived from the left. Just then, Dwight's horse was hit. He dismounted and attempted to calm the animal, holding it by its head, but it struggled too

6 Smith, "My First Campaign," 284; *Historical Sketch of CO "D," 13th Regiment*, 16-17.

7 *OR* 19, pt. 1, 500, 920; Comey, *A Legacy of Valor*, 77.

8 *OR* 19, pt. 1, 500-501; Morse, *Letters*, 88; Coco, "Through Blood and Fire," 39-40, USA; Andrews to Wife, September 23, 1862, USA.

forcefully and broke away. Moments later, Dwight was standing about six feet from Colonel Andrews and was about to shout something to him when a ball shattered his left hip. He collapsed to the ground, uttering, "That's done for me." Andrews soon decided it would be "a useless sacrifice of life to keep my position" and ordered a withdrawal. Dwight was in intense pain and would not allow the men to carry him from the field. The 2nd Massachusetts's stand cost it 12 killed and 51 wounded. This was slight compared to the 27th Indiana's 209 total casualties or the 3rd Wisconsin's 200 losses. Heading for the East Woods, the 13th New Jersey and 2nd Massachusetts crossed paths with the two Midwestern regiments, heading for the pike to support them. Learning of the situation there, these regiments also returned to the East Woods.[9]

*　　*　　*

Gordon's brigade still contained one regiment that had not yet seen action. After Gordon positioned the green 107th New York at the southern end of the Samuel Poffenberger Woods, its left extended down the slope toward Poffenberger's limestone house. Men in the right companies, on higher ground, gazed intently toward the fighting still raging in the Cornfield. An occasional artillery shell or sharpshooter's bullet passed through the treetops. In the plowed field ahead, wounded men littered the ground, slowly moving rearward. A handsome, riderless bay horse galloped across the field. Soon one of Crawford's small regiments left the East Woods and passed to the rear.[10]

Gordon soon returned from his solitary reconnaissance in the East Woods. As he approached the 107th, the brigadier waved his cap and bellowed that they were driving the Confederates, eliciting thunderous cheers from the men. One of the officers later reported that Gordon's manner at that moment inspired the troops. This was after Greene's division drove Colquitt and Robbins from the East Woods, and after the 125th Pennsylvania followed Greene from the south edge of the plowed field in front of the 107th. Gordon ordered the New Yorkers toward the East Woods at the double-quick. The 13th New Jersey had just arrived, and

9 OR 19, pt. 1, 499, 501, 504; Chaplain Quint's account of Wilder Dwight's death, undated, Dwight Family Papers, MHS; Carman, *Maryland Campaign: Antietam*, 233; John Rankin to John Gould, March 19, 1892, APD.

10 William F. Fox to Carman, February 9, 1899, NYPL; Fox to Gould, December 31, 1890, APD.

Gordon sent it in the same direction before returning to the veteran regiments, which were crossing the Cornfield. The 107th incurred its first casualties while crossing the plowed field. A Confederate shell exploded within Company G, at the left center of the regiment, killing or wounding an officer and 13 men. A shell fragment hit Cpl. Asa Brownell's rifle, tearing off a finger as it knocked the rifle to the ground. The right advanced through the eastern cornfield, which was covered with dead, and entered the woods, still cheering and enthusiastic. After a left half wheel, its three right companies were in the Smoketown Road. The left of the regiment extended to the east beyond the point where the road turned north. It remained there for an hour, viewing the fields to the south between the smoldering Mumma house and the Hagerstown Pike. Sedgwick's division passed to the west while it waited. During this time in the woods, a Confederate shell struck near the colors, tearing the flags.[11]

After Sedgwick's repulse, Gordon ordered the 107th to recover to the brigade, which was gathering at the north end of the East Woods. It faced right and moved through the trees by fours along the J. Poffenberger Lane. A general arrived and redirected the regiment to support Cothran's battery, which had just repositioned to the front of the East Woods facing west. Knap's Battery soon arrived and unlimbered northeast of Cothran. The 107th deployed about 50 yards from the East Woods and north of the Smoketown Road. Its left wing was behind Cothran's Battery, while its right was in front of Knap's guns. On higher ground, the men on the right could see the Dunker Church, but kept to their stomachs to avoid Knap's fire. The left wing was also behind the large, brush-covered outcropping that previously sheltered Thruston's North Carolinians. The 107th remained there several hours. Its proximity to two Federal batteries made the regiment a target for Confederate artillery fire. Captain William Fox, commanding the color company at the center of the regiment, had a close call. A Confederate shell struck a caisson horse that threatened to fall on him. Rebel artillery was not the only cause for anxiety. Fox could feel the concussion of one of Knap's guns on his face "like the flapping of a handkerchief" as it fired over him. Two companies to Fox's right, Pvt. Patrick Callaghan was hit by a gun discharging behind him. In Company F, one to the right of Callaghan, Sgt. John D. Hill described the experience of lying in front of the Federal battery: "We laid down flat on the ground, and they fired over us

11 Fox to Carman, February 9, 1899, and A. S. Fitch to Carman, February 5, 1895, NYPL; George Henry Gordon to Gould, January 19, 1871, Hull Fanton to Gould, May 9, 1870, and Fox to Gould, December 31, 1890, APD; John D. Hill to "Dear Friends at Home," September 18, 1862 (transcript), CWDoc Collection, USA.

about two hours which was anything but pleasant. The rebels, of course, replied briskly, and such a whizzing and buzzing I never heard before." Hill wrote that a Confederate artillery round hit the foot of a man in his company, "mangling it horribly."[12]

* * *

The 46th North Carolina was the first of Col. Van Manning's three regiments that followed Kershaw into the West Woods. It fulfilled an early request for support from Colonel Nance of the 3rd South Carolina. When the 3rd had emerged from the West Woods and lay down under Woodruff's fire, watching for an opportunity to advance, the gap between it and the 2nd South Carolina was significant, and Nance sent his adjutant, Y. J. Pope, to Kershaw for a regiment to fill it. Pope subsequently guided the 46th North Carolina to the eastern edge of the West Woods, north of the Hagerstown Pike–Smoketown Road intersection and south of the 3rd South Carolina's earlier position. Colonel Edward D. Hall of the 46th observed Greene's men "in heavy force on an elevation" about 200 yards away. He also saw the fences bordering the Smoketown Road that ran diagonally between his men and the Federal infantry and artillery and thought it "inexpedient" to advance farther. He ordered his troops to take cover behind a breastwork of fence rails and open fire from the edge of the pike.[13]

The 30th Virginia deployed to the right of Hall's North Carolinians. As the Virginians emerged from the West Woods at the intersection, Manning, "Came tearing up on horseback and waving his sword around his head and clearing the fence at a bound called to us to follow him. . . . [W]e charged over the fence and across the field with a yell fixing bayonets at a full run," remembered one member of the 30th. The regiment's right quickly crossed the Smoketown Road fence by file and pressed on to within 40 to 50 yards of Tyndale's line. According to the same Virginian's account, Tyndale's men wavered but recovered and "poured a perfect hail of bullets into us." Isaac Hirsh recalled that the men in his company fell "thick and thin" to his right and left. It had not taken long for the 30th's Lt. Col. Robert S. Chew to order a retreat. Hirsh had only fired two rounds when his weapon fouled. As he worked to extract the ball, a spent shot hit his heel and knocked him senseless

12 Carman, *Maryland Campaign: Antietam*, 303; Fitch to Carman, February 5, 1895, and Fox to Carman, December 31, 1890, and March 17, 1898, NYPL; John D. Hill, Letter, September 18, 1862, USA.

13 *OR* 19, pt. 1, 918; Pope to Carman, March 20, 1895, NA-AS.

with shock for a few minutes. He soon recovered and saw the regiment falling back with Tyndale's men "firing volley after volley after us." Hirsh was amazed that anyone escaped. A part of the regiment lingered behind the cover of the large rock ledge around which the 2nd South Carolina had huddled during its first advance, but the Virginians soon fell back to the church. While the 30th had advanced over the fences boldly, the 48th North Carolina's initial movement on the Virginians' right was less intrepid.[14]

The 48th lost several men while advancing through the West Woods, and canister from Tompkins's battery began pouring into it. Much of the regiment hesitated at the fence and sheltered behind trees. At first, it could not be coaxed beyond the fence. Lieutenant Colonel Samuel Walkup scolded and threatened to shoot the men, to little avail. He eventually mounted the fence and pushed on toward the slope, leading at least a portion of the regiment approximately 75 yards beyond the fence. By then the 30th Virginia had fallen back, leaving the 48th North Carolina isolated in Greene's front. Alone in the open field below two Federal brigades, it soon began to waver.[15]

At 10:30 a.m., with the North Carolinians in front of the Dunker Church showing signs of impending collapse, both of Greene's brigades advanced. The 28th Pennsylvania held briefly while the Ohioans approached the 48th North Carolina's flank. As Tyndale snatched the 28th's colors, the Pennsylvanians delivered a volley. Then, "A momentary pause and our whole brigade belched forth a concentric and simultaneous fire, which in the twinkling of an eye swept that devoted regiment from the earth. The enemy lay in long, straight lines—the heads of the front in the laps of the rear rank," recalled Tyndale. In Stainrook's brigade, Sgt. Isaac Van Steenbergh of the 102nd New York wrote, "If you ever saw a flock of sheep who had just been frightened by some unknown enemy, you can conceive the appearance of these Rebels as the Battery poured double charges of canister in their ranks and our division rising up poured a volley in their flank at short range.

14 Robert Knox to Ezra Carman, undated, and November 10, 1897, NA-AS; Hirsh Diary, September 17, 1862, LV.

15 Samuel Walkup, Diary, September 17, 1862, SHC; William F. Beasley, "The Forty-Eighth N. C. Troops at Sharpsburg," *Our Living and Our Dead*, vol. 1 (1874-75), 330; Walter Clark, *Histories of the Several Regiments and Battalions from North Carolina in the Great War, 1861-1865*, 5 vols. (Raleigh, 1901, reprint, Wendell, NC, 1982), 3:116; Wood, *Seventh Regiment*, 140.

As they ran back toward the woods we started in pursuit." The 3rd Maryland, on the left of the advance, right-obliqued toward the church.[16]

By the time the 48th reentered the woods, it had seen enough. Lieutenant Colonel Walkup frankly recounted that the 48th broke and "the whole gave way in confusion & retreat in disorder." He tried to rally the regiment behind the crest of the wooded hill. Neither Walkup's commands nor imploring calls from members of the 2nd South Carolina, which still retained some organization in the woods, could deter the North Carolinians. Despite its faltering start and precipitous flight, the 48th North Carolina cannot be charged with shirking at Antietam. It suffered the third-highest Confederate loss, with 31 killed and 186 wounded. Though sustaining fewer total casualties, the 30th Virginia, on the 48th's left, had 39 killed and a total loss of 68 percent of those engaged. All nine of the 30th's color-bearers were killed or wounded. In the earlier assault on the Dunker Church plateau, the 7th South Carolina suffered 140 casualties, or 52 percent of those engaged.[17]

Greene's men swept down the slope after the remnants of Manning's and Kershaw's brigades. Pockets of these Confederates continued firing from behind piled fence rails along the road. Others attempted to reform along rock ledges on the western slope of the hill on which the church stood. Both the 28th and the 111th Pennsylvania split in two, with part of each regiment going on either side of the Dunker Church. Once the 28th Pennsylvania passed the building, Tyndale directed the regiment to right-oblique, bringing it back to the right of the 111th Pennsylvania. Two companies of the 111th moved to the right of the church, while the rest passed to the south. A member of the 111th remembered its entry into the West Woods, "Where we had some fun gobbling up prisoners. Every man was for himself and everyone wanted to be ahead. I suppose we captured at least 3 to every man." The Federals disarmed prisoners and sent them to the rear without guards. Passing south of the church, Major Walker found dead and wounded Confederate officers covering the ground.[18]

Cutting through pockets of resistance, Greene's men advanced to the west side of the woods before halting. Quickly recalled, all of his units then deployed on the

16 OR 19, pt. 1, 505, 513; McLaughlin, *Memoir of Hector Tyndale*, 103; Wing to Gould, June 9, 1892, and Van Steenbergh to Gould, March 27, 1892, APD.

17 Walkup Diary, September 17, 1862, SHC; Carman, *Maryland Campaign: Antietam*, 616-618; Knox to Carman, December 10, 1899, NA-AS.

18 Woodring to Gould, January 8, 1892, and Walker to Gould, April 18, 1891, APD; McLaughlin, *Memoir of Hector Tyndale*, 57.

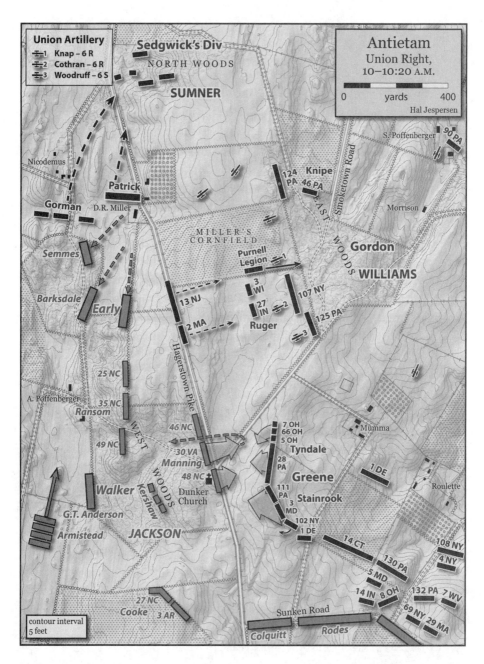

wooded western slope of the Dunker Church hill. On Greene's right, the 28th Pennsylvania, with the Ohio regiments to its right, faced west by southwest. These regiments were nearly 200 yards west of the church, and about 100 yards beyond the 125th Pennsylvania's erstwhile position. The ravine was north of, and perpendicular to, Tyndale's line. To the 28th Pennsylvania's left, the 111th Pennsylvania and 3rd Maryland faced south. Major Walker's 111th was within the tree line along the fence at the southern edge of the West Woods. The 3rd Maryland and a portion of the 102nd New York were behind the same fence as the Pennsylvanians but positioned in the open ground south of the church. When the advance from the Dunker Church plateau began, Captain Tompkins rode to Greene and asked whether he intended to leave his battery unattended. All but a few companies from the right of the 102nd New York remained with the guns, as did the 66th Ohio.[19]

With Greene's men in the woods, Tompkins shifted his attention to other targets. Before his guns expended their ammunition, they materially affected the fighting on the II Corps's front to the southeast with fire directed against Maj. Gen. R. H. Anderson's division, Brigadier General Rodes's brigade of D. H. Hill's division, and several Confederate batteries. This was in addition to the central role the battery played in repelling Kershaw's and Manning's attacks. In all, Thompson's guns fired 1,032 rounds. 83 rounds of which were canister shot during the close-in fighting against Kershaw and Manning.[20]

Colonel Manning had been wounded early in the advance and told Colonel Hall to command the brigade. Hall remained with the 46th North Carolina and could only see the 30th Virginia. As the 48th North Carolina and 30th Virginia fell back, he observed Greene's men flooding through the chasm that opened on his right. Though the 46th North Carolina briefly maintained what its commander called "a galling fire on their advancing line," he soon decided it was best to fall back as his right flank and rear had become exposed. Hall withdrew the 46th beyond the western boundary of the woods and reported to Stonewall Jackson, who told him to report to McLaws, who in turn ordered Hall to hold the woods "at all hazards." But the forest was thick with Federal infantry. Hall deployed the regiment along the western edge of the woods, joined by Company F of the 30th Virginia and a company from the 3rd Arkansas, both of which had just arrived from picket duty on the extreme right overlooking Antietam Creek. Ransom's 25th, 35th, and 49th North Carolina were still along a rock ledge in the middle section of the West Woods. The 27th North Carolina and 3rd Arkansas

---

19 OR 19, pt. 1, 505-507; McLaughlin, *Memoir of Hector Tyndale*, 57; Van Steenbergh to Gould, March 27, 1892, and Wing to Gould, June 9, 1892, APD; Stegman to Carman, January 10, 1905, NYPL; Carman, *Maryland Campaign: Antietam*, 303, 308.

20 Carman, *Maryland Campaign: Antietam*, 303.

detachment, commanded by Colonel Cooke, continued to defend the southern cornfield. Finally, the remnants of the 48th North Carolina and 30th Virginia; Barksdale's, Kershaw's, Semmes's, and Early's brigades; and a fresh brigade under Brig. Gen. Lewis Armistead, were all in the vicinity of the field west of the woods. Of all these units, which were in various states of readiness after fighting Sedgwick and Greene, only Ransom's brigade, Cooke's two-regiment command, and the two recently arrived companies under Colonel Hall contributed further to the action covered in this narrative. All presented a looming threat largely beyond Greene's gaze.[21]

After Tyndale's and Stainrook's brigades drove the Confederates from the woods, Hector Tyndale, flush with enthusiasm, told one of his regimental commanders, "If they'll give me ten thousand men, I'll win this battle in an hour." This was not quite idle boasting, given the widespread ignorance within the Confederate army regarding Greene's presence in the woods. Neither official reports and accounts from brigade and division commanders nor Jackson himself mention Greene's foothold in the West Woods. A few were aware. Colonel Hall, who cited Greene's advance as his cause for withdrawing, knew of Greene's presence. Likewise, Colonel Cooke saw the Federals across from his position. Otherwise, Confederate commanders busily addressed immediate problems of reforming and rearming their gravely worn brigades and apparently were unaware that Yankees were in the woods. Indeed, Confederate regiments soon were a stone's throw from Greene's right, with neither side aware of the other's presence.[22]

Though Greene's outpost posed little threat to the Confederate right in and of itself, it presented a Federal opportunity that, if pursued, might have facilitated the victory that Hooker envisioned before he was carried from the field. Greene possessed the objective of Hooker's assault but could do nothing further on his own. With respect to the threat from Goodrich and the 125th Pennsylvania earlier in the morning, Jubal Early wrote:

> The situation was most critical and the necessity most pressing, as it was apparent that if the enemy got possession of this woods, possession of the hills in their rear would immediately follow, and then, across to our rear on the road leading back to the Potomac,

21 OR 19, pt. 1, 918; Carman, *Maryland Campaign: Antietam*, 312; J. M. Hudgin to Carman, undated, NA-AS.

22 OR 19, pt. 1, 918, 865, 956; McLaughlin, *Memoir of Hector Tyndale*, 70.

would have been easy. In fact, possession of these hills would have enabled him to take our whole line in reverse, and a disastrous defeat must have followed.

After retrenching to the western slope of the hill, Greene's men were only 700 yards away from the high ground on Hauser's Ridge and 400 yards from a high spot in the southern cornfield that commanded the flank of Lee's center along the Sunken Road. Taking either of these points would open the Confederate rear and precipitate a headlong flight for the Potomac. Lee had deftly forestalled such a crisis all morning through the timely use of interior lines to shuffle his limited manpower. Despite his outstanding position, Greene could do little. Not unlike Crawford's isolated assault at Cedar Mountain, Greene's men retained their eagerness to fight, but had lost striking power. Even after the addition of the large 13th New Jersey and about 200 men from the Purnell Legion, Greene's force was down to approximately 1,350 men.[23]

In addition to Greene's inability to press this opportunity on his own, his little command was in a woefully precarious situation that threatened to engulf it at any moment. Worse still, Greene did not at first realize the extent of his exposure. He had seen Sedgwick's attack, but not its collapse. Much of the division had fled north, though a few regiments retreated toward the East Woods. Greene did not see this, and no one to the rear bothered to tell him. As a result, he thought Sedgwick's men occupied the woods somewhere to his right. As such, the gathering threat about both of his flanks drew his gaze only to the left. Alpheus Williams was not overly dramatic when he wrote that at this time, "an ominous and suggestive pause" settled over the battlefield, broken only by artillery fire.[24]

While Greene was out of the minds of his superiors, he was also beyond their sight. His two brigades were 100 yards down the western slope of the Dunker Church hill in the West Woods, out of visual contact with Williams, Sumner, and Maj. Gen. William Franklin, whose VI Corps began arriving at the East Woods about 11:30 a.m. Franklin's arrival created a throng of available troops behind Greene that ultimately stretched from the East Woods to the North Woods. Sumner sought immediate assistance from Franklin for a threatened battery near the northwest corner of the East Woods. Reinforcements continued to divert in this manner, covering points well out of the way of immediate threat. Meanwhile,

23 Early, *Autobiographical Sketch*, 146; Carman, *Maryland Campaign: Antietam*, 308.

24 Carman, *Maryland Campaign: Antietam*, 308; Alpheus Williams, *U. S. Army Generals' Reports of Civil War Service, 1864-1887*, Record Group 94, 476, NA.

Greene's detachment, disconnected on both flanks from Federal forces and half a mile in front of the nearest units with ammunition, carried on out of Sumner's view. Tyndale urgently requested reinforcements several times, "Stating mine and the enemy's positions. . . . [T]he ground was held, which was of vital importance, and yet no officer of commanding power came near us to see what had been done, or to learn the results of our fighting, although it could not have been wholly unobserved." The juxtaposition between Hooker's intrepid behavior in the morning with the anemic activity by his successors was striking.[25]

Greene also appealed to Alpheus Williams for reinforcements. Williams attempted to gather what Greene needed, sending an aide to Sumner, who could not be found. Williams was never able to get II Corps support. But Sumner did provide reinforcements to cover the flank of a relieving VI Corps brigade. Greene then sent his son, Lt. Charles Greene, scrounging for extra men. The younger Greene found Gordon and relayed his father's request. Gordon turned the 13th New Jersey over to him, and Lieutenant Greene led the regiment through a gap in the fences across the Hagerstown Pike, to the right of the Dunker Church, and into the woods. The 13th deployed north of the 28th Pennsylvania, relieving the 5th and 7th Ohio, both of which were out of ammunition. The 5th and 7th rejoined the 66th Ohio and the 102nd New York on the Dunker Church plateau. Ammunition once again ran low throughout Greene's detachment, which had used much of its resupply defending the plateau and attacking the West Woods.[26]

The last of Greene's reinforcements soon arrived. Williams unsuccessfully attempted to recall Goodrich's brigade, whose 200-man Purnell Legion had already been detached. Before noon, it moved to the edge of the East Woods for ammunition and was soon ordered to join Greene by one of his aides, who directed the Legion past the right of the Dunker Church. It deployed in echelon north of and about 80 yards behind the 13th New Jersey. Tyndale directed these Marylanders and the 13th New Jersey to front west-northwest, facing the ravine

25 OR 19, pt. 1, 67; Carman, *Maryland Campaign: Antietam*, 304-306; McLaughlin, *Memoir of Hector Tyndale*, 71. As Sumner reported (OR 19, pt. 1, 276), "the circumstances of the battle prevented me from witnessing the conduct of Banks's corps."

26 OR 19, pt. 1, 505; Moore, "Rough Sketch," 7; Charles Greene to sister, September 19, 1862, USA; Williams, *Generals' Reports*, 476; Smith, "My First Campaign," 285; Carman, *Maryland Campaign: Antietam*, 302, 306, 308; *Historical Sketch Company D*, 17. Charles Greene wrote that he initially returned with the 27th Indiana, that it left after firing its 40 rounds, and that he then returned with the 13th New Jersey.

Col. John R. Cooke, 27th North Carolina
U.S. Army Heritage and Education Center

and effectively refusing his overall line on the right. The Legion faced Alfred Poffenberger's house. Its left never connected to the 13th New Jersey's right.[27]

A second 40-round ammunition resupply was brought up, and the detachment settled into skirmishing. This began almost immediately on the left against Colonel Cooke's two-regiment command. As Stainrook's men reached the southern edge of the woods, they found the 27th North Carolina and 3rd Arkansas in the open field between the West Woods and the southern cornfield and opened fire. Stainrook's men benefited from the cover of the trees, and Cooke withdrew his command into the southern cornfield. The Southerners maintained a lively skirmish with Stainrook's brigade from behind the fence at the edge of that field. The three leftmost companies of the 27th North Carolina briskly engaged the Yankees in the woods.[28]

The center of the Federal line fired on Cooke's men in the southern cornfield to the left and at skirmishers in the woods ahead and to the right. As soon as the 13th New Jersey reached the scene, it fired to the west toward unseen Confederates. A New Jersey private remembered the "gentle purr of the swift moving minié balls" that soon confirmed the Southerners' presence. "The air became thick with smoke and the roar of musketry continual and deafening." The new recruits, their attention fixed ahead of them, continued shooting until between 11:30 and 11:45 a.m. The fire on Greene's left then slackened and Colonel Cooke

27 Cole to Carman, October 13, 1900, Herring to Carman, July 2, 1900, and William T. Fulton to Carman, December 21, 1899, NYPL; McLaughlin, *Memoir of Hector Tyndale*, 57.

28 *OR* 19, pt. 1, 915; Clark, *Histories of the Several Regiments and Battalions*, 2:434.

withdrew his men about 20 paces into the corn, where he told them to lie down. Cooke kept vigil by a small hickory tree at the edge of the corn rows.[29]

After scattering gun crews from a battery on the far side of the field beyond the woods, Tyndale determined to attack a rock ledge in that field that sheltered firing Confederates. He called the 28th Pennsylvania's third battalion from the left and sent it forward through the ravine. The ledge was roughly parallel with the western wood line and ran at an angle to the ravine. Before the Pennsylvanians reached their destination, Southern infantry rose from another rock ledge at the edge of the woods and unleashed a volley that returned the Federals to their lines.[30]

These Confederates were the 46th North Carolina. After Lafayette McLaws ordered Hall to "hold the woods at all hazards," Hall moved the 46th forward to a rock ledge at the western edge of the West Woods. Soon, presumably after repelling the Pennsylvanians' advance, Hall sent one company each from the 46th North Carolina and 30th Virginia forward, up the ravine. He told them to fall back on the balance of the regiment if they met a strong line, which they did. After suffering several killed and wounded against the 28th Pennsylvania and 13th New Jersey, the skirmishers retreated to the rock ledge. Regular firing then ceased. By that time, Private Smith of the 13th was down to his last round, which he had to drive down his fouled barrel by pushing the ramrod against a tree.[31]

At the center of Greene's line, dwindling ammunition and overused rifles became a problem for the 28th Pennsylvania as well. After starting the day with 60 rounds and being resupplied twice with 40 rounds, most men's guns were too fouled to load. They used stones and tree trunks to drive their ramrods home. For some, this no longer worked, so they exchanged these useless muskets for ones on the ground. Still, ammunition was short for the filched rifles, and the men scavenged from the cartridge boxes of the dead and wounded. Lieutenant Moore asked Tyndale about getting more ammunition, but none could be had. Asked what

29 Carman, *Maryland Campaign: Antietam*, 306; Smith, "My First Campaign," 285; Clark, *Histories of the Several Regiments and Battalions*, 2:434.

30 McLaughlin, *Memoir of Hector Tyndale*, 57; Armor to Gould, May 6, 1891, and Smith to Gould, March 24, 1870, APD. Armor noted that volunteers were called to bring two guns to the same spot that Tyndale described. It appears that the rock ledge from which Confederate infantry repulsed the Pennsylvanians was either across the field near the artillery or at the western boundary of the West Woods, where Hall's North Carolinians took position. The latter is more likely. Tyndale's statement of service suggested that a Rebel probe occurred before his skirmishers were able to go forward, but the accounts listed here suggest that they did advance.

31 OR 19, pt. 1, 918-919; Carman, *Maryland Campaign: Antietam*, 310; Hudgin to Carman, undated, NA-AS; McLaughlin, *Memoir of Hector Tyndale*, 70; Smith, "My First Campaign," 287.

they were supposed to do, Tyndale told Moore they would have to use their bayonets.[32]

While the 28th Pennsylvania and 13th New Jersey drove off Hall's skirmishers, the new regiments on the right of the line began to realize the seriousness of Greene's situation. Colonel Ezra Carman needed little convincing. Hours earlier, while at their earlier position across the pike, his New Jerseyans had taken fire from the woods to the north. Carman was well aware that no Federal forces occupied those woods and sent word to Greene that his flank was in the air. Greene did not suppose that any Federals were tied into his right, but he still labored under the impression that friendly forces were somewhere out there, creating both a modicum of security and a need to avoid friendly fire. Greene responded to Carman's courier, "Tell your Colonel not to be uneasy about his flank, the whole of Sedgwick's division is in the woods on his right."[33]

While Carman communicated with Greene, Maj. William Fulton, commanding the Purnell Legion in Carman's right rear, sent a half dozen skirmishers to the right to discover what was on his open flank. Private Pennock J. Cole was in front. Before moving far, they passed a cordwood pile. Beyond the ravine, Cole's party stumbled upon the 49th North Carolina lying in the woods. Fortunately, the North Carolinians were as oblivious to Cole's presence as the Northerners were to the North Carolinians roughly 100 yards away. Private Cole used hand motions to tell the scouting party to back away. The Marylanders quietly returned to Major Fulton, who informed Greene and sent Cole to locate the Confederate position ahead of the Legion's left.[34]

Soldiers in the 13th New Jersey now saw men moving in the woods on the right. They were certain these were Confederates. Edward Warren, a sergeant in Company B, had moved to a position ahead and to the right of the regiment, where he took cover and sniped at any injudiciously concealed Rebels. When the regiment's adjutant, Charles A. Hopkins, approached the rear of Company B, Warren called him over and pointed out glistening gun barrels that were intermittently visible through the trees in the dappled sunlight beyond the

32 McLaughlin, *Memoir of Hector Tyndale*, 56; Moore, "Rough Sketch," 7.

33 Carman, *Maryland Campaign: Antietam*, 308.

34 Pennock Cole to Ezra Carman, October 13, 1900, NYPL; Carman, *Maryland Campaign: Antietam,* 310. Cole's letter to Carman suggested that the group ended up between two Confederate regiments spaced 25 yards apart. The second was lying down. This narrative sticks with Carman's description of a single regiment. If Cole's accounting is correct, the 35th North Carolina would have been the second Rebel regiment.

Col. Ezra Ayers Carman, 13th New Jersey
U.S. Army Heritage and Education Center

regiment's right. Hopkins relayed this information to Carman, who sent Hopkins to inform Greene again. Greene decided to have a look for himself and spurred his horse downhill beyond the 13th New Jersey's right. He soon returned and told Hopkins, "Adjutant, do not let your men fire to the right under any circumstances as [Sedgwick's division] is in there and it is impossible to flank you." He made the same assertion to Colonel Carman and instructed him to maintain an oblique fire to the left. Greene then rode back to the left to attend to that threat. Hopkins carried out Greene's order and cautioned the men. However, he took little comfort in Greene's assertion and posted himself by the right flank so as to keep "a sharp lookout."[35]

When Greene went back to his left, a staff officer from corps headquarters approached him. In apparent exasperation, Greene informed the staffer that some of his officers on the right were "laboring under the delusion" that Sedgwick had been repulsed and was not in the woods. The surprised staff officer fired back, "Why, yes, General, didn't you know it?" Astonished and suddenly aware of the peril his troops could be facing, Greene ejaculated a "picturesquely sulfurous" response at the officer, according to Carman.[36]

Even before the disturbing revelation about Sedgwick, Greene was dissatisfied with the reinforcements he had received. About the time that the reconnaissance efforts occurred (not long after 11:30 a.m.), Lieutenant Greene rode to Captain

35 Charles A. Hopkins to Ezra Carman, January 15, 1900, NA-AS; Carman, *Maryland Campaign: Antietam,* 309. Hopkins's letter read "Smith's brigade"; Carman penciled through it with the correction "Sedgwick's division."

36 Carman, *Maryland Campaign: Antietam,* 310. This officer was likely one of Williams's division staff members. Carman did not use quotation marks around the first quote, indicating that they may not have been Greene's exact words, but the manuscript reads like that is what Greene said.

Knap, whose battery had redeployed south, to the right of Lt. Evan Thomas's Batteries A and C, 4th U.S. Artillery and to the left of Cothran's Battery. Greene ordered Knap to move two guns toward the church.[37]

Knap advanced his right section, commanded by Lt. James D. McGill, south of the Smoketown Road and to the top of the Dunker Church plateau. Hector Tyndale rode up and ordered McGill into the woods west of the church to address the threat from Cooke in the cornfield. David Nichol, who was with that section, thought it "no place for artillery." McGill tried to push back on this order, explaining that the guns would be at high risk in the woods, which would hinder their maneuverability. If infantry killed his horses, the guns would be lost. Prickly as ever, Tyndale was not dissuaded. McGill thus moved his pieces into the Smoketown Road and then into the Hagerstown Pike about 100 yards south of the intersection. He positioned one Parrott in the woods and kept the other in the pike. As the gun crew entered the trees, its erstwhile mates in the 28th Pennsylvania gave three cheers. McGill met with Tyndale for guidance on enemy positions. As branches crashed to the ground from Confederate artillery fire, Tyndale pointed out a group of mounted Southerners on high ground to the southwest, offering, "Just take my glass lieutenant and you can see them." McGill then moved his gun to elevated ground amid the trees.[38]

After learning the truth about his right, Greene rode to the rear to solicit help from Alpheus Williams. Further reinforcements were refused. Williams suggested that Greene go to Brig. Gen. Winfield Scott Hancock, who was commanding a nearby VI Corps brigade. Before returning to his men, Greene directed Colonel Van Valkenburgh to send two companies of the large and unused 107th New York into the woods. Companies I and E started forward but came back quickly when they discovered the woods and open ground near the Smoketown Road full of Confederates. Greene had been away only a few minutes when someone directed his attention to his troops, which were streaming toward the Mumma house.[39]

*   *   *

---

37 Carman, *Maryland Campaign: Antietam*, 306, 310.

38 Carman, *Maryland Campaign: Antietam*, 310-311; David Nichol to "Father and Home," September 21, 1862, USA; McGill, Statement to P. B. Shriver, November 4, 1897, NYPL.

39 George Sears Greene, "Battle of Antietam," Greene Papers, MSS 460, RIHS.

The deluge burst swiftly but without coordination upon both flanks of Greene's detachment. Colonel Matthew Ransom, commanding the 35th North Carolina to Greene's right, temporarily led the brigade while his brother, Brig. Gen. Robert Ransom, went to retrieve the wayward 24th North Carolina. Colonel Ransom saw McGill's section enter the woods and acted reflexively to capture the guns. He ordered the 49th North Carolina to descend the hillside to the ravine by file and charge toward the Dunker Church. The 25th and 35th North Carolina were to trail and keep pace with the 49th. When the decision to advance was made, neither Ransom nor anyone in the 49th had the slightest intimation that Federal infantry was in the trees. Greene's and Ransom's men were both on high ground. Though the woods were open, the foliage of the trees in the low ground between the combatants obscured each side's line of sight. As they advanced into the ravine, the North Carolinians saw troops ahead, but were not yet sure to which side this infantry belonged.[40]

On the 13th New Jersey's right, adjutant Hopkins kept seeing light reflecting off muskets through the forest on the high ground beyond the ravine to the right. He again reported to Colonel Carman, who directed him to refuse the right flank by drawing back the three rightmost companies. With Greene's last command in mind, Hopkins thought it best to be sure whose infantry he saw before firing. He bounded down the hillside. Looking downhill through the tree branches, he could not confirm his suspicions until the North Carolinians neared the bottom of the ravine. Hopkins dashed back up the hill, yelling, "They are Rebs, let them have it!" He had not yet reached his line when both sides fired simultaneously. He took to the ground, trapped between the firing lines. Private Cole of the Purnell Legion had gone forward as well, in front of the left of his regiment. After passing 50 yards to the front, he saw the North Carolinians advancing. Cole was also trapped between the lines.[41]

A parallel effort occurred on the Confederate side. Surprised to find infantry ahead, the 49th North Carolina's colonel sent Capt. Cicero Dunham up the hill to determine whether it was friend or foe. He stumbled into the Federal line, and the Northerners ordered him to surrender. Dunham wheeled his horse and beat a hasty retreat to his regiment. These investigations by both sides concluded at the same

---

40 Carman, *Maryland Campaign: Antietam*, 315-316. Carman listed two undiscovered letters from members of the 49th North Carolina as a note. In his publication of the Carman manuscript, Dr. Thomas Clemens included these passages in footnotes.

41 Hopkins to Carman, January 15, 1900, and Cole to Carman, October 13, 1900, NYPL; Carman, *Maryland Campaign: Antietam*, 315.

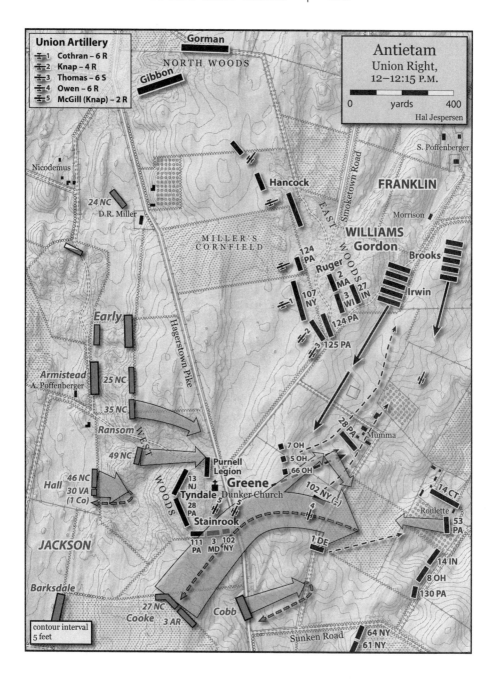

Antietam
Union Right,
12–12:15 P.M.

Union Artillery
1 Cothran – 6 R
2 Knap – 4 R
3 Thomas – 6 S
4 Owen – 6 R
5 McGill (Knap) – 2 R

Antietam
Union Right,
12–12:15 P.M.

0   yards   400

Hal Jespersen

Gorman

NORTH WOODS

Gibbon

Nicodemus

24 NC
D.R. Miller

Hancock

S. Poffenberger

FRANKLIN

Morrison

Smoketown Road

MILLER'S
CORNFIELD

WILLIAMS
Gordon

EAST WOODS

124
PA

Ruger

2
MA

27
IN

3
WI

Brooks

Irwin

107
NY

124 PA

1

2

3 125 PA

Early

25 NC

Armistead
A. Poffenberger

35 NC

Ransom

WEST WOODS

49 NC

Hagerstown Pike

28 PA

Mumma

7 OH

5 OH

66 OH

Purnell
Legion

Greene

102 NY

14 CT

Hall

46 NC
30 VA
(1 Co)

13
NJ

Tyndale

Dunker Church

4

Roulette

53
PA

28
PA

Stainrook

JACKSON

111
PA

3
MD

102
NY

1 DE

14 IN

8 OH

130 PA

Barksdale

27 NC

Cooke   3 AR

Cobb

contour interval
5 feet

Sunken Road

64 NY

61 NY

moment, and simultaneous volleys erupted at close range through the open forest.[42]

The 49th North Carolina continued toward the Purnell Legion's right flank. Seeing this, Major Fulton ordered three volleys, then turned the Legion by the right flank and filed it right. Cole eventually withdrew to the Mumma house. With the Legion gone, the 49th North Carolina's right contacted the 13th New Jersey's right. Threatened with envelopment, the New Jerseyans also headed east of the pike after firing two or three volleys. Its rearward movement precipitated cheers from the 49th North Carolina. Adjutant Hopkins watched the Southerners advance. Looking up the hill, he saw his own regiment withdrawing and decided it was time to take his chances and head for the rear. He was the last Union soldier to leave the woods on the right.[43]

The 28th Pennsylvania was next in line. The sound of Confederate cheers moved behind its right. The crisis was obvious and unavoidable. Meanwhile, fire from Rebels in front continued. Lieutenant Joseph C. Markle, who was in front of his Company B observing Confederates positioned behind the limestone ledge, was struck in the forehead by a ball. Members of his company carried his body to the rear. William Raphael, who commanded the 28th after Ario Pardee was wounded, ordered the Pennsylvanians to fall back. Ransom's regiments halted at a fence-rail breastwork at the edge of the woods about 130 yards north of the church, like the 46th North Carolina had done earlier.[44]

*   *   *

While Ransom's three regiments descended on Greene's right, Colonel Cooke's two regiments burst from the corn as McGill concluded his conference with Tyndale and unlimbered his first gun. As with Ransom, Greene's infantry was not Cooke's intended target. Israel Richardson's II Corps division had stalled in a cornfield south of the Sunken Road. Nevertheless, Maj. Gen. James Longstreet took this perceived threat to his center seriously. Though he had little material with

42 Carman, *Maryland Campaign: Antietam*, 316.

43 OR 19, pt. 1, 916; Cole to Carman, October 13, 1900, and William Fulton to Carman, December 21, 1899, NYPL; Carman, *Maryland Campaign: Antietam*, 316-317; Hopkins to Carman, January 15, 1900, NYPL.

44 OR 19, pt. 1, 509; Carman, *Maryland Campaign: Antietam*, 317; William Roberts, Jr., to father, September 21, 1862, HSP; McLaughlin, *Memoir of Hector Tyndale*, 70; Fithian Diary, September 17, 1862, AMP.

which to craft a counterstroke, he directed Cooke's command, totaling 675 men, to advance through the gap on Greene's left and attack the II Corps's flank. Cobb's brigade, which by then had just 250 men, would join on Cooke's right.[45]

After Cooke pulled his line back into the corn, firing on the southern front abated. Sharpshooters on the left of the 27th North Carolina exchanged a few shots with Greene's men. This fixed Greene's attention to the south. The 3rd Arkansas's right fired on Tompkins's battery and received unwelcome canister in return. This situation persisted for about 30 minutes when Cooke spied McGill's guns going into position about 400 yards away in the trees across the open field that separated the two lines. He quietly ordered his four leftmost companies forward to the fence. At that moment, Ransom's men began engaging the right of Greene's line. With orders to direct fire at the two artillery pieces, especially their horses, Cooke's men sprung from the cornfield. Their first volley dropped some of McGill's men, and killed one horse and wounded another. A shot also badly mangled the pintle hook, preventing McGill from quickly unlimbering the gun and bringing it into action, despite a handful of Stainrook's infantrymen trying to help. The Marylanders and New Yorkers in Cooke's front began to waver. At that moment, Longstreet ordered Cobb's brigade and Cooke to advance. McGill decided that he had to leave in order to save the other gun and the two caissons. The one in the pike fired without unlimbering, slowing Cooke's infantry before making its way to the rear, followed by the two caissons. Ransom's North Carolinians along the pike north of the church fired on the fleeing gunners, drawing the attention of the Union batteries near the East Woods. Ten guns from Knap's and Cothran's batteries opened a torrent of fire, causing heavy casualties among the North Carolinians, who recoiled into the woods. McGill suffered one man killed and four wounded in this action.[46]

*   *   *

Alpheus Williams saw Greene's two brigades burst from the woods, "scampering to the rear in great confusion." Illustrating Williams's description, Private Smith of the 13th New Jersey raced for the pike fence. He faced a dilemma. He needed to change course and head for a gap in the fence, which he might reach

45 OR 19, pt. 1, 915; Carman, *Maryland Campaign: Antietam*, 263-291, 320, 342, 616-617.

46 McGill, Statement to Shriver, November 4, 1897, NYPL; Carman, *Maryland Campaign: Antietam*, 317-318.

Cpl. Ambrose Henry Hayward,
28th Pennsylvania
U.S. Army Heritage and Education Center

after Ransom's North Carolinians, who coursed behind him and to the north, or he had to make an inviting target by climbing over the fence nearest him. He chose to scale the fence, tossing his musket over while he ran. As he went over, his knapsack got ensnared on a splintered fence rail. He slipped his head from the bag and raced east.[47]

Moments before Greene's men fell back, Battery G of the 1st Rhode Island Light Artillery, commanded by Capt. Charles Owen, relieved Tompkins's battery. Owen's attention was fixed to the south, beyond the Sunken Road. Suddenly, Owen heard a clamor from his right. Looking west, he saw Greene's infantry 150 yards away, streaming toward him, with Cooke's troops close behind. Owen's men limbered their guns and withdrew at a trot. Reaching the Dunker Church plateau, Greene's officers attempted to rally their regiments on the favorable ground that they had used so effectively hours before. The men brushed off these efforts. The flight continued to the Mumma house. A member of the 27th North Carolina remembered that Cooke's detachment broke six Federal regiments and that only one of those came off the field in any semblance of order.[48]

Though slowly giving ground, the 28th Pennsylvania continued to fight beyond the Dunker Church plateau. Some men gathered ammunition from the nearby dead. The regiment stopped to make a stand at the haystacks west of the Mumma house. The 13th New Jersey's Private Smith, recovered from his fence-rail confinement, made his way to the Mumma property. There, in the low valley, he

47 Quaife, *From the Cannon's Mouth*, 129; Smith, "My First Campaign," 287.

48 Carman, *Maryland Campaign: Antietam*, 318; Clark, *Histories of the Several Regiments and Battalions*, 2:435.

saw part of Greene's detachment rallying. Lieutenant Colonel Tyndale was reforming part of his line west of the haystacks when a Confederate ball crashed through the back of his head and lodged in his neck between his right jaw and sternum. He dropped unconscious. The Rebels were within 100 yards when Cpl. Ambrose Henry Hayward, who had been on the reconnaissance mission behind enemy lines earlier in the month, and 1st Lt. Charles W. Borbridge, who had earlier captured a Confederate flag, raced to Tyndale. Both men were long familiar with Tyndale and his odious demeanor. Nevertheless, they risked their lives to recover the body of a brigade commander whose passing would have been little mourned by anyone in the brigade until that morning. Borbridge and Hayward dragged Tyndale, who they thought was dead, 50 yards under fire to the haystacks. Lieutenant Colonel Powell had been shot in the neck and cheek during Manning's attack against the Dunker Church plateau and, with Tyndale's fall, brigade command shifted to the 7th Ohio's Major Crane. In Stainrook's brigade, the 111th Pennsylvania lost eight men during its retreat, which continued until it, and most of Greene's men, reached the East Woods.[49]

Cooke's men advanced swiftly and determinedly behind a pair of eager color-bearers. Firing on the run and only stopping to bag prisoners, the two regiments passed to the right of McGill's abandoned gun. Reaching the top of the Dunker Church plateau, they saw Greene's men beginning to reform in the low ground to the east. Their objective, however, was farther to their right. The fire of several Federal batteries, including Thomas's and Cothran's and likely Knap's two remaining sections, also helped steer Cooke to the right. These guns savagely raked Cooke's left flank. To Private Smith, "The sight was almost sickening, with even the very prevalent thought that they were the enemy." He also used the oft-written simile "like grain before the reaper" to describe the carnage. After Cothran's first discharges of grapeshot into Cooke's men, a clowning member of the 107th New York, supporting Cothran's guns, reportedly jumped atop an outcropping, waved his cap, and called out, "Bully, ten strike, set 'em up on t'other alley!" The two Confederate regiments wheeled right and advanced into the cover of the cornfield to the south of the Mumma farmhouse. Before reaching the corn, the 27th North Carolina's two leftmost companies spotted a handful of Greene's command still

49 Foering Diary, September 17, 1862, HSP; Fithian Diary, September 17, 1862, AMP; *Grand Army Scout and Soldiers Mail*, September 22, 1883; Smith, "My First Campaign," 287; Welsh, *Medical Histories*, 346; Ambrose Henry Hayward to brother, September 21, 1862, Hayward Papers, GC; McLaughlin, *Memoir of Hector Tyndale*, 58; Powell Memoir, chap. 6, OHC; Boyle, *Soldiers True*, 62.

behind the haystacks near the house. The North Carolinians moved there at the double-quick, sent those Federals to the rear, and double-quicked back to the regiment within the cornfield, where Cooke's men briefly faced portions of French's and Smith's divisions from the II and VI Corps. His men were hurled back to the West Woods under a severe fire. A fresh VI Corps brigade under Col. William Irwin followed close behind Cooke. As the Confederates retraced their steps to the West Woods, Irwin's men followed as far as the Dunker Church plateau. After attempting to move beyond the plateau and into the woods, reformed Confederates stifled Irwin's brigade.[50]

* * *

With Cooke's assault broken, the XII Corps's active involvement in the battle of Antietam ended. Cothran's and Knap's guns, still supported by the 107th New York and the 125th Pennsylvania, remained on the line until early afternoon, firing into the West Woods. The 107th was the only XII Corps unit to pass the day without firing a shot, though it once fixed bayonets and rose to face a portion of McLaws's advance that appeared to threaten Cothran's guns. It also had withstood the stress of lying in the open field, shackled to a target for counter-battery fire. Knap's business was not yet complete. He was down one rifled gun. To make his battery whole, he appropriated the iron 12-pounder howitzer and caisson the 28th Pennsylvania had captured from Woolfolk's battery. The obsolete Model 1841 piece was a poor replacement for his lost Parrott, but was still a fortuitous find, given the circumstances. At least one other member of Knap's Battery left the field with a trophy: James Stewart cut a star from Lieutenant Colonel Newton's coat.[51]

Colonel Knipe also reached the area near Cothran's guns at about the time McLaws attacked. Knipe, then in command of Crawford's brigade, brought along the 46th Pennsylvania's color guard and a handful of additional troops, ostensibly from the 46th. Likely full of sincere fervor following his pep talk with Williams,

50 OR, 19, pt. 1, 477; Carman, Maryland Campaign: Antietam, 319-320, 322-324; Smith, "My First Campaign," 288. Thomas's battery is the only one specifically named by Carman as suppressing this charge. Carman's official report (OR 19, pt. 1, 502) referenced Cothran's involvement. Smith's account did so indirectly with the account from Cothran's infantry support. With Knap located between Cothran and Thomas, it is likely that his guns fired on Cooke as well. Clermont Best's report, however, mentioned neither Cothran nor Knap firing during this assault. Cothran's report (OR 19, pt. 1, 483) described repulsing two charges in his front.

51 OR 19, pt. 1, 482, 503; Fox to Gould, December 31, 1890, APD; James Stewart to "Dear Mother," September 21, 1862 (typescript), USA.

Knipe endeavored to form a second line on the 46th Pennsylvania's colors. Captain William Fox of the 107th New York watched this take place behind where he lay with his regiment, among Cothran's caisson horses. Knipe's diminutive force departed shortly after it arrived. As fresh VI Corps units appeared on the field, Knipe received orders to withdraw. He then officially executed what had for some hours been a de facto withdrawal of the brigade. His small force returned to its bivouac on the Line farm, where it found the 28th New York, the 10th Maine, and the 128th Pennsylvania. There the men occupied themselves with ambulance duty and with raiding gardens as far away as Antietam Creek. Knipe told them to stay put and went looking for the 124th and 125th Pennsylvania, which he found supporting Franklin's line. They remained and bivouacked near the East Woods.[52]

The rest of the corps sprawled between the East Woods and Samuel Poffenberger's house. Greene's division had moved from the Mumma farm to behind the East Woods, where it regrouped for two hours before continuing north about a half mile. The men received rations and refreshed themselves with the frigid spring water rising from beneath the Poffenberger house. They cleaned their rifles in case they were needed again.[53]

As it happened, they were *not* needed. Shortly after Irwin's movement toward the West Woods, Franklin intended to assault that area with his next division to arrive. Sumner rode up to Franklin shortly thereafter. Franklin described Sumner's demeanor during the afternoon as "much depressed." He directed Franklin to call off his attack. One of McClellan's aides was also there, and Franklin told him what was happening. The commanding general soon arrived and followed Sumner's lead, deeming it imprudent to make another assault on the right. Fighting in the center also ended. Richardson's division had captured the Sunken Road, but no further assault was made there. As McClellan declined to press hard-earned opportunities on the right and center, Maj. Gen. Ambrose Burnside's IX Corps finally gained the Antietam's right bank at about 1:00 p.m.[54]

---

52 OR 19, pt. 1, 488; Fox to Gould, December 31, 1890, APD; Williams to Carman, May 16, 1877, NYPL; Gould, *10th Maine*, 243. In his official report, Knipe claimed that he rallied the 107th New York to his colors, but Fox insisted that a mounted general officer directed the 107th to Cothran's guns. Knipe also said he did not learn of his move to brigade command until late in the afternoon. Williams's letter to Carman appears to suggest, however, that he told Knipe just after Gordon's brigade began to advance into the Cornfield.

53 OR 19, pt. 1, 505, 512.

54 William Franklin, "Notes on Crampton's Gap and Antietam," *Battles and Leaders*, 2:597.

At 9:10 a.m., McClellan had ordered Burnside to assault the lower bridge, which would bear Burnside's name after the fighting there. Burnside made sluggish progress in establishing a foothold on the Confederate side of the creek, allowing Lee to draw resources such as Walker's division from his right to deal with the chain of emergencies erupting near the Dunker Church. After crossing the creek early in the afternoon, Burnside began to move toward town only to meet the same fate, on a much larger scale, that Crawford's brigade had incurred at Cedar Mountain. Late that afternoon, Maj. Gen. A. P. Hill's division arrived from paroling the Harpers Ferry garrison just in time to accost Burnside's flank. The IX Corps fell back to the Antietam.[55]

As the impact of Hill's counterstroke became apparent, orders came from McClellan for the XII Corps to form and take position behind Franklin. Greene's division and Gordon's brigade, then commanded by Colonel Colgrove, returned to the East Woods, where they rested on their arms for the night. The day had been eventful. Many of Greene's men had fired 140 shots and run out of ammunition three times. Second Lieutenant Hinkley of the 3rd Wisconsin remembered, "I know that I, for one, was completely exhausted. The sun had scarcely set before I had wrapped myself in my overcoat, and with my haversack for a pillow, was sound asleep, quite oblivious of the fact that the field of the dead was only a few steps away." The bloodiest day in American history had ended.[56]

---

55 Carman, *Maryland Campaign: Antietam*, 416-487.

56 OR 19, pt. 1, 499, 505; *Pottsville Miners' Journal*, October 4, 1862; Hinkley, *Third Wisconsin*, 62. From Colgrove's report, it appears that he was only in command of the brigade for a short period that evening and possibly night. This may have been the result of Colonel Ruger going to the rear to have his head wound examined.

Beyond the Antietam

September 18 to 30, 1862

After such service as they had rendered and the broken condition in which their gallant and heroic fighting [at Cedar Mountain] had left them they should for a time have been withdrawn from the presence of the enemy until they could be rested and their officers replaced. I should have done so at once, but that it was impossible at that time[1]

— Maj. Gen. John Pope

[R]egiment, brigade and division faded away under a terrible fire, leaving long lines of dead to mark where stood the living. Fields of corn were trampled into shreds, forests were battered and scathed, huge limbs sent crashing to the earth, rent by shell or round shot. Grape and canister mingled their hissing scream in this hellish carnival, yet within all this and through it all the patriots of the North wrestled with hearts strong and nerve unshaken. . . . We slept upon the bloody field of our victory.[2]

— Brig. Gen. George H. Gordon

If there is one thing more painful than many others to a commander in action, it is to lose the lives of men over whom he exercises almost unlimited power, and to whom he owes more than life itself to lose them uselessly in a barren or resultless, even though glorious battle. If war consists merely in killing men (which I do not believe), then, my regrets are unfounded; but unless that killing, leads to a higher end for humanity, all wars are merely damnable, and without justification of God or man. But Antietam is not alone among fields, fertilized with blood, which yielded little or no harvest of visible results. [3]

— Lt. Col. Hector Tyndale

1   OR 12, pt. 3, 827.

2   OR 19, pt. 1, 497.

3   Hector Tyndale to Ezra Carman, April 7, 1877, AMP.

Not long after returning from its futile struggle along the Hagerstown Pike, the 2nd Massachusetts grew anxious for its lieutenant colonel. Soon, Pvt. Rupert Sandler went looking for him. Nearing the road with a full canteen, Sadler began crawling. He saw what he thought was Wilder Dwight's horse and headed for it. After he examined the animal for a few moments, Confederate fire sent him ducking to the ground until the Southerners lost interest. He moved on and found Dwight lying with his head on a fence rail. Sadler gave him water and asked about his wounds. He soon discovered two more men approaching and called them over. They drew more Confederate fire, and Dwight said they should leave. But, persisting, his men carried him to the Cornfield, and one of them sought out their surgeon, Lincoln Stone. Captain Shaw wrote that Stone and a few others "pluckily" went to get Dwight. While Dwight lay on the field between the lines, he took out the note that he had started to his mother on the way to the front. To the bloodstained page, he added:

> DEAREST MOTHER,—I am wounded so as to be helpless, Good bye, if so it must be; I think I die in victory. God defend our country. I trust in God, and love you all, to the last. Dearest love to father and all my dear brothers. Our troops have left the part of the field where I lie.
> Mother, yours,
> Wilder[4]

As the Bay Staters carried Dwight into the East Woods, George Gordon rode up to him. Dwight saluted his friend. He had been the third volunteer to join Gordon in forming the 2nd Massachusetts and had thrown himself into the effort with exceptional energy. Gordon alighted from his horse and knelt by Dwight's side, holding his hand. He said, "My dear fellow I am very sorry for this." When asked if he thought the bone broken, Dwight replied, "I don't know—I fear it is—I fear it is—I've tried to . . . " Minié balls flew through the canopy, interrupting Dwight. Gordon said he would need to get his friend out of the woods. Dwight replied, "Never mind me—only whip them." Gordon assured him they would, and in fact were already doing so.[5]

---

4 Rupert Sadler to sister, September 24, 1862, Dwight Family Papers, MHS; Duncan, *Blue-Eyed Child of Fortune*, 241; Dwight to mother, September 17, 1862, MHS; *Harvard Biographies*, 1:288.

5 Extract from George H. Gordon letter, undated copy that appears to be by Dwight's mother, Dwight Family Papers, MHS; Gordon, *Brook Farm*, 4, 6-8.

Soldiers removed Dwight to a field hospital, and officers called for volunteers to move him to a house in Boonsboro. Private Richard Henry Lee Jewett, one of several new recruits who had arrived before the battle and were not permitted to fight, was among them. The 12 volunteers found Dwight in a farmhouse yard that night. They put him in an ambulance and drew the curtains until morning rather than move him in the dark. Setting off at dawn with a stretcher, they got to Boonsboro at 2:00 p.m. Dwight asked that a hot meal be cooked for the men, who greatly appreciated it. Early on September 19, Colonel Andrews learned that Dwight was failing and requested permission to go to him. Though marching orders had been issued, Gordon allowed the visit. Andrews reached the house a half hour after Dwight had quietly passed. Dwight had said his only regret was that he could no longer serve the cause of his country, and he requested a soldier's burial. Years later, Andrews reflected that, "The only effect of the order [to advance to Sumner's support] was to send the regiment into a hornets' nest to no good purpose."[6]

With respect to medical care, most of the wounded were not treated so considerately. Soldiers from two of the new regiments found themselves at field hospitals on September 17 and described the horrific conditions they encountered there. A member of the 125th Pennsylvania remembered, "My visit to the barn hospital when darkness set in left some unfading memories. The amputated limbs strewn around outside made a ghastly sight under the glare of the torchlights, and the audible sufferings of the maimed and wounded comrades and the comatose condition of others would have made the vocation of a soldier for empty honor or fame utterly abhorrent to me." Private Smith of the 13th New Jersey wrote, "I stood and watched the surgeon's knife as it cut its relentless way down to the bone; saw the 'flap' turned back, baring the bone for the merciless little ribbon; saw that twined around and into it until the poor, bleeding, shattered remnant of a once good leg or arm dropped to the floor, leaving a clean-cut stump, over which I saw, with a sort of horrid fascination, the flap once more turned, the arteries having been carefully picked up, and a 'neat job' accomplished."[7]

* * *

6 Richard Jewett to wife, September 21, 1862, Richard Jewett Letters, BA; *Harvard Biographies*, 1:291; Andrews to wife, September 23, 1862, and Andrews to Gould, March 5, 1891, APD.

7 *One Hundred Twenty-Fifth Pennsylvania*, 175; Smith, "My First Campaign," 288.

The next morning, Lt. Julian Hinkley committed to his diary, "We are all wondering why the battle is not resumed today. Our force is much weakened but the rebels must be more so." Putting the downtime to good use, many members of Hinkley's 3rd Wisconsin discarded antiquated muskets and collected new Springfield rifles from the dead. McClellan called off a planned assault by Franklin against the West Woods, and burials commenced. As the soldiers went over the field, they found thronging macabre sights. Lieutenant Colonel David Strother described the scene near the East Woods:

> In every direction around men were digging graves and burying the dead. Ten or twelve bodies lay at the different pits and had already become offensive. In front of this wood was the bloody cornfield where lay two or three hundred festering bodies, nearly all Rebels, the most hideous exhibition I had yet seen. Many were black as Negroes, heads and faces hideously swelled, covered with dust until they looked like clods. Killed during the charge and flight, their attitudes were wild and frightful. One hung upon a fence killed as he was climbing it. One lay with hands wildly clasped as if in prayer. From among these loathsome earth-soiled vestiges of humanity, the soldiers were still picking out some that had life left and carrying them in on stretchers to our surgeons. All the time some picket firing was going on from the wood on the Hagerstown turnpike near the white church. . . . In the midst of all this carrion our troops sat cooking, eating, jabbering, and smoking; sleeping among the corpses so that but for the color of the skin it was difficult to distinguish the living from the dead.[8]

On September 19, Gould noted a "death-like stillness" that covered the field. Lee's army had withdrawn across the Potomac overnight. Gould reported that the 10th Maine was being marched and countermarched, much to the men's frustration. The regiment finally halted and waited in a "blazing sun" for three hours, "Near the dead and putrefying horses of Hooker's batteries. There were also dead cattle and sheep, swollen and boiling, making a fine nosegay." Private James Guinn of the 7th Ohio had an opportunity to walk the field:

> Gods what horrible sights. The dead rebels were not burried yet. They were swelled up as big as three men and as black as the ace of spades. Some . . . are not burried yet nor never will be. It looks horrible to see a man eaten up by buzzards and maggots but such sights were common enough on that battlefield.

---

8 Hinkley, Diary, September 18, 1862, WHS; Hinkley, *Third Wisconsin*, 62; Bryant, *Third Wisconsin*, 135; Franklin, *Battles and Leaders*, 2:597; Eby, *Virginia Yankee*, 112-113.

At length the 10th Maine formed a burial detail. Soon after starting its work, however, the regiment received marching orders. After noon, Williams's division passed through Sharpsburg and moved east across the lower bridge, which Burnside's corps had captured. Greene's division followed, clearing Sharpsburg at 9:00 p.m. On September 20, the XII Corps climbed Elk Ridge along a path. Many unburied dead from McLaws's fighting the previous week still littered its slopes. The corps then moved south along its crest to Maryland Heights. From there, the men saw the tents of Lee's army. Williams's division, under Gordon, established a fortified camp on Maryland Heights. Colonels Knipe and Ruger now commanded the brigades. On September 21, Greene's division waded the Potomac and occupied the heights on the Virginia side. Six days later, Brig. Gen. John Geary, his arm in a sling from his Cedar Mountain wound, visited the division at Loudon Heights and was greeted with much enthusiasm. The soldiers rushed him and flooded the air with hurrahs, and the general delivered a speech. Corporal Ambrose Hayward wrote that, "Such a crazy set of boys could not be found in the Union army."[9]

A series of leadership changes followed the battle of Antietam. Geary assumed 2nd Division command on October 1, returning Greene to his brigade. Hector Tyndale survived his wound, which included a compound skull fracture. After regaining consciousness but thinking himself mortally wounded, Tyndale sent a message to his soldiers: "Thank the officers and men for their great courage and endurance this day; and tell them that, though I have always been very strict with them, it was for their own good, and I love and respect them." Tyndale was removed to a hospital in Hagerstown and then by freight car to Philadelphia; he returned to service in 1863, but transferred from the corps, leaving command of his brigade to the 66th Ohio's Col. Charles Candy. Before the next battle, Brig. Gen. Thomas Kane, who had energetically resisted Stuart's raid at Catlett's Station, took over Stainrook's brigade. Alpheus Williams returned to the 1st Division. George Gordon was transferred and led a division during the Confederate siege of Suffolk and the Union siege of Charleston. He subsequently served in Florida, Arkansas, and the Eastern District of the Department of Virginia. He mounted an earnest and nearly successful effort to return to the XII Corps with his new division in July

---

9 Gould, *10th Maine*, 262-264; Bryant, *Third Wisconsin*, 135-136; James Guinn to Brother, October 1, 1862, James Miller Guinn Papers, HL; Foering, Diary, September 19, 1862, HSP; Fithian, Diary, September 19, 1862, ANB; Tenney to "My Darling Addie," September 25, 1862, UVA; Hayward to Brother, September 28, 1862, GC; Powell, Memoir, ch. 6, OHC.

1863. Colonel Thomas H. Ruger replaced Gordon and remained with the corps until the fall of 1864. Samuel Crawford never returned after Antietam, but soon commanded the Pennsylvania Reserve division that Meade had led there. Colonel Joseph Knipe assumed command of Crawford's brigade.[10]

From their aeries around Harpers Ferry, the men of the XII Corps enjoyed magnificent views into Virginia. Up to then, most of them had entered the Old Dominion twice, only to be chased from the state on each occasion. The latter defeat, Cedar Mountain, was followed six weeks later by a triumphant effort within a wider Union victory north of the Potomac. While not lethal to Lee's army, the limited success at Antietam sustained Northern fortunes. Gould recorded that his enthusiasm over the victory at Antietam was minimal; too great an opportunity had been lost. It portended another venture into the "deserts of Virginia."[11]

Before returning to Virginia to begin the next stage of its history, the XII Corps garrisoned Harpers Ferry and missed the next big battle along the Rappahannock in December. Then, in April 1863, events unfolded that paralleled its experience of the summer of 1862. A hard-fought effort by this corps nevertheless resulted in defeat at Chancellorsville. Nine weeks later, it turned in another signal performance in Union territory that contributed to the Northern triumph at Gettysburg.

---

10 OR, 27, Pt. 3, 778-779; Warner, *Generals in Blue*, 178, 257, 416, 517; Welsh, *Medical Histories*, 346; McLaughlin, *Memoir of Hector Tyndale*, 13-14; Williams, *Generals' Reports*, 478.

11 Gould, *10th Maine*, 264.

Appendix A

Orders of Battle[1]

Skirmish at Orange Court House, August 2, 1862

Confederate

Col. William E. Jones
6th Virginia Cavalry
7th Virginia Cavalry—Col. William E. Jones
17th Virginia Cavalry Battalion, Company F—Capt. Foxhall Daingerfield

Union

Brig. Gen. Samuel Wylie Crawford
5th New York Cavalry
1st Vermont Cavalry

Battle of Cedar Mountain, August 9, 1862

Confederate

Jackson's Corps—Maj. Gen. Thomas J. Jackson

Ewell's division—Maj. Gen. Richard S. Ewell

Early's brigade—Brig. Gen. Jubal A. Early
12th Georgia—Capt. William F. Brown
13th Virginia—Col. James A. Walker
25th Virginia—Maj. John C. Higginbotham
31st Virginia—Lt. Col. Alfred H. Jackson (w)
52nd Virginia, 58th Virginia

---

1 Regimental commanders are provided for units within the II Corps, Army of Virginia, for batteries supporting the corps's infantry and, where known, for Confederate units that engaged the corps. Sources for this appendix include the *Official Records*; Krick's *Stonewall Jackson at Cedar Mountain*; Carman's *The Maryland Campaign: Antietam*; and the National Park Service's online *Soldiers and Sailors Database*.

Forno's brigade—Col. Henry Forno
5th Louisiana, 6th Louisiana
7th Louisiana, 8th Louisiana
14th Louisiana

Trimble's brigade—Brig. Gen. Isaac R. Trimble
15th Alabama—Maj. Alexander A. Lowther
21st Georgia, 21st North Carolina

Division Artillery—Maj. Alfred R. Courtney
Brown's (Maryland) Battery (Chesapeake Artillery)— Capt. William D. Brown
D'Aquin's (Louisiana) Battery—Capt. Louis E. D'Aquin
Dement's (Maryland) Battery—Capt. William F. Dement
Latimer's (Virginia) Battery—Capt. Joseph W. Latimer
Terry's (Virginia) Battery (Bedford Artillery)—Lt. Nathaniel Terry

Hill's division—Maj. Gen. Ambrose Powell Hill

Archer's brigade—Brig. Gen. James J. Archer
5th Alabama Battalion, 19th Georgia
1st Tennessee—Col. Peter Turney
7th Tennessee, 14th Tennessee

Branch's brigade—Brig. Gen. Lawrence O'Bryan Branch
7th North Carolina—Col. Edward G. Haywood
18th North Carolina, 28th North Carolina
33rd North Carolina, 37th North Carolina

Field's brigade—Brig. Gen. Charles W. Field
40th Virginia
47th Virginia
55th Virginia
22nd Virginia Battalion

Pender's brigade—Brig. Gen. William D. Pender
16th North Carolina, 22nd North Carolina
34th North Carolina, 38th North Carolina

Starke's brigade—Col. Leroy A. Stafford
1st Louisiana, 2nd Louisiana
9th Louisiana—Col. Leroy A. Stafford
10th Louisiana, 15th Louisiana

Thomas's brigade—Brig. Gen. Edward L. Thomas
14th Georgia—Col. Felix L. Price (w), Lt. Col. Robert W. Folsom
35th Georgia, 45th Georgia
49th Georgia

Division Artillery—Lt. Col. Rueben L. Walker
Braxton's (Virginia) Battery (Fredericksburg Artillery)
Davidson's (Virginia) Battery (Letcher Artillery)
Fleet's (Virginia) Battery (Middlesex Artillery)
Latham's (North Carolina) Battery
Pegram's (Virginia) Battery (Purcell Artillery)—Capt. William J. Pegram

Jackson's division—Brig. Gen. Charles S. Winder (k), Brig. Gen. William B. Taliaferro

Stonewall Brigade—Col. Charles A. Ronald
2nd Virginia—Lt. Col. Lawson Botts
4th Virginia—Lt. Col. R. D. Gardner
5th Virginia—Maj. Hazael J. Williams
27th Virginia—Capt. Charles L. Haynes
33rd Virginia—Lt. Col. Edwin G. Lee

Garnett's brigade—Col. Thomas S. Garnett
21st Virginia—Lt. Col. Richard H. Cunningham (k), Capt. William H. Witcher
42nd Virginia—Maj. Henry Lane (mw), Capt. Abner Dobyns
48th Virginia—Capt. Y. C. Hannum (k), Capt. James H. Horton
1st Virginia Battalion—Maj. John Seddon

Taliaferro's brigade—Brig. Gen. William B. Taliaferro, Col. Alexander G. Taliaferro
47th Alabama—Lt. Col. James W. Jackson
48th Alabama—Col. James L. Sheffield (w)
10th Virginia—Maj. Joshua Stover
23rd Virginia—Col. Alexander G. Taliaferro, Lt. Col. George W. Curtis (mw),
Maj. Simeon T. Walton
37th Virginia—Col. Titus V. Williams (w), Maj. Henry C. Wood

Division Artillery—Maj. Richard Snowden Andrews
Poague's (Virginia) Battery (Rockbridge Artillery)—Capt. William T. Poague
Carpenter's (Virginia) Battery (Alleghany Artillery)—Lt. Joseph Carpenter
Caskie's (Virginia) Battery (Hampden Artillery)—Capt. William H. Caskie

Corps cavalry—Brig. Gen. Beverly H. Robertson
6th Virginia
7th Virginia—Col. William E. Jones
12th Virginia, 17th Virginia
2nd Virginia (detachment)
4th Virginia (detachment)
Chew's (Virginia) Battery

Union

Army of Virginia—Maj. Gen. John Pope

II Corps—Maj. Gen. Nathaniel Prentiss Banks

1st Division—Brig. Gen. Alpheus S. Williams

1st Brigade—Brig. Gen. Samuel Wylie Crawford
5th Connecticut—Col. George Chapman (w/c)
10th Maine—Col. George L. Beal
28th New York—Col. Dudley Donnelly (mw), Lt. Col. Edwin F. Brown (w)
46th Pennsylvania—Col. Joseph F. Knipe (w)
3rd Brigade—Brig. Gen. George Henry Gordon
27th Indiana—Col. Silas Colgrove
2nd Massachusetts—Col. George L. Andrews
3rd Wisconsin—Col. Thomas H. Ruger
Zouaves d'Afrique Company (Attached to 2nd Massachusetts)

2nd Division—Brig. Gen. Christopher C. Augur, Brig. Gen. Henry Prince,
Brig. Gen. George Sears Greene

1st Brigade—Brig. Gen. John W. Geary (w), Col. Charles Candy
5th Ohio—Col. John H. Patrick
7th Ohio—Col. William E. Creighton (w)
29th Ohio—Capt. Wilbur F. Stevens
66th Ohio—Col. Charles Candy, Lt. Col. Eugene Powell

2nd Brigade—Brig. Gen. Henry Prince (c)
3rd Maryland—Col. David P. DeWitt
102nd New York—Lt. Col. James C. Lane
109th Pennsylvania—Col. Henry J. Stainrook (w)
111th Pennsylvania—Maj. Thomas M. Walker
8th and 12th U.S. Infantry Battalion—Capt. Thomas Pitcher (w)

3rd Brigade—Brig. Gen. George Sears Greene
1st District of Columbia—Lt. Col. Lemuel Towers
78th New York—Lt. Col. Jonathan Austin

Corps Artillery—Capt. Clermont L. Best
4th Battery, Maine Light Artillery—Capt. O'Neil W. Robinson
6th Battery, Maine Light Artillery—Capt. Freeman McGilvery
Battery M, 1st New York Light Artillery—Capt. George Cothran
Battery L, 2nd New York Light Artillery—Capt. Jacob Roemer
Battery E, Pennsylvania Light Artillery—Capt. Joseph M. Knap
Battery F, 4th U.S. Artillery—Lt. Edward Muhlenberg

III Corps—Maj. Gen. Irvin McDowell

2nd Division—Brig. Gen. James B. Ricketts

1st Brigade—Brig. Gen. Abram Duryée
97th New York, 104th New York
105th New York, 107th Pennsylvania

2nd Brigade—Brig. Gen. Zealous B. Tower
26th New York, 94th New York
88th Pennsylvania, 90th Pennsylvania

3rd Brigade—Brig. Gen. George L. Hartsuff (w)
12th Massachusetts, 13th Massachusetts
83rd New York, 11th Pennsylvania

4th Brigade—Col. Samuel S. Carroll
7th Indiana, 84th Pennsylvania
110th Pennsylvania, 1st West Virginia

Division Artillery
2nd Battery, Maine Light Artillery—Capt. James A. Hall
5th Battery, Maine Light Artillery—Capt. George F. Leppien
Battery C, 1st Pennsylvania Light Artillery—Capt. James Thompson
Battery F, 1st Pennsylvania Light Artillery—Capt. Ezra W. Matthews

Action at Beverly Ford, August 21, 1862

Confederate

5th Virginia Cavalry—Col. Thomas L. Rosser
Robertson's brigade—Brig. Gen. Beverly Robertson (crossed at Freeman Ford)
2nd Virginia Cavalry, 6th Virginia Cavalry
7th Virginia Cavalry, 12th Virginia Cavalry
17th Virginia Cavalry Battalion
Brockenbrough's (Maryland) Battery—Capt. John Bower Brockenbrough
Carpenter's (Virginia) Battery (Allegheny Artillery)—Capt. Joseph Carpenter
Poague's (Virginia) Battery (Rockbridge Artillery)—Capt. William T. Poague
Wooding's (Virginia) Battery (Danville Artillery)—Capt. George Wooding

Union

Initial force (dispersed)
II Corps, 2nd Division, 2nd Brigade, 3rd Maryland—Col. David P. DeWitt
2nd Battery, Maine Light Artillery—Capt. James A. Hall

Reinforcements

I Corps

Independent Brigade—Brig. Gen. Robert H. Milroy
82nd Ohio, 2nd West Virginia
3rd West Virginia, 5th West Virginia
12th Battery Ohio Light Artillery

III Corps, 1st Division

3rd Brigade—Brig. Gen. Marsena Patrick
21st New York, 23rd New York
35th New York, 80th New York

4th Brigade—Brig. Gen. John Gibbon
19th Indiana, 2nd Wisconsin
6th Wisconsin, 7th Wisconsin

Catlett's Station Raid, August 22, 1862

Confederate

Maj. Gen. James Ewell Brown Stuart, commanding

Robertson's brigade
Brig. Gen. Beverly H. Robertson
2nd Virginia Cavalry, 6th Virginia Cavalry
12th Virginia Cavalry, 17th Virginia Cavalry Battalion

Lee's brigade—Brig. Gen. Fitzhugh Lee
1st Virginia Cavalry, 4th Virginia Cavalry
5th Virginia Cavalry, 9th Virginia Cavalry

Union

13th Pennsylvania Reserve Battalion—Lt. Col. Thomas Leiper Kane
Purnell Legion (Maryland) Infantry (five companies)—Col. William J. Leonard (c),
Lt. Col. Benjamin L. Simpson

Action at Beverly Ford, August 23, 1862

Confederate

Longstreet's Corps, Jones's division—Brig. Gen. David R. Jones

Drayton's brigade—Brig. Gen. Thomas F. Drayton (artillery support)
50th Georgia, 51st Georgia
15th South Carolina, Phillips Legion
3rd Company, Washington (Louisiana) Artillery—Capt. Merritt B. Miller
Loudon (Virginia) Artillery—Capt. A. L. Rogers
Thomas (Virginia) Artillery—Capt. Anderson

Union

II Corps, 1st Division—Brig. Gen. Alpheus Williams

3rd Brigade—Brig. Gen. George H. Gordon (artillery support)
27th Indiana—Col. Silas Colgrove
2nd Massachusetts—Col. George L. Andrews
3rd Wisconsin—Col. Thomas H. Ruger
Zouaves d'Afrique Company (Attached to 2nd Massachusetts)
Battery M, 1st New York Light Artillery—Capt. George Cothran

III Corps Artillery
16th Battery, Indiana Light Artillery—Captain Naylor
2nd Battery, Maine Light Artillery—Capt. James A. Hall
Battery L, 1st New York Light Artillery—Capt. John A. Reynolds

Battle of Antietam, September 17[2]

Confederate

Army of Northern Virginia—Gen. Robert E. Lee

Longstreet's Corps—Maj. Gen. James Longstreet

---

[2] Includes only the Union corps and Confederate divisions involved in this narrative. Confederate commanders, where known, are listed only for regiments and batteries that engaged the XII Corps. Commanders are also shown for Union regiments and batteries outside the XII Corps that are important to this narrative.

McLaws' division—Maj. Gen. Lafayette McLaws

Kershaw's brigade—Brig. Gen. Joseph B. Kershaw
2nd South Carolina—Col. John D. Kennedy (w), Maj. Franklin Gaillard
3rd South Carolina—Col. James D. Nance
7th South Carolina—Col. D. W. Aiken (w), Maj. William C. White (k), Capt. John S. Hard
8th South Carolina—Lt. Col. Axalia J. Hoole

Cobb's brigade—Lt. Col. Christopher C. Sanders, Lt. Col. William MacRae
16th Georgia, 24th Georgia
Cobb's (Georgia) Legion, 15th North Carolina

Semmes's brigade—Brig. Gen. Paul J. Semmes
10th Georgia, 53rd Georgia
15th Virginia, 32nd Virginia
Barksdale's brigade—Brig. Gen. William Barksdale
13th Mississippi
17th Mississippi—Lt. Col. John C. Fiser
18th Mississippi
21st Mississippi—Capt. John Sims, Col. Benjamin G. Humphreys

Division Artillery—Col. Henry C. Cabell
Manly's (North Carolina) Battery
Pulaski (Georgia) Artillery—Capt. John P. N. Read
Richmond (Fayette) Artillery
Richmond Howitzers (1st Company)
Troup (Georgia) Artillery—Capt. Henry H. Carlton

Jones's division—Brig. Gen. David R. Jones
Toombs's brigade
Drayton's brigade
Garnett's brigade
Kemper's brigade
Jenkins's brigade

Anderson's brigade—Col. George T. "Tige" Anderson
1st Georgia (Regulars)—Col. W. J. Magill (w), Capt. R. A. Wayne
7th Georgia—Col. G. H. Carmichael
8th Georgia—Col. John F. Towers
9th Georgia—Lt. Col. John C. F. Mounger
11th Georgia—Maj. F. H. Little

Division Artillery—Wise (Virginia) Artillery

Walker's division—Brig. Gen. John G. Walker

Walker's brigade—Col. Van H. Manning (w), Col. Edward D. Hall
3rd Arkansas—Capt. John W. Reedy
27th North Carolina—Col. John R. Cooke
46th North Carolina—Col. Edward D. Hall, Lt. Col. William A. Jackson
48th North Carolina—Col. Robert C. Hill, Lt. Col. Samuel H. Walkup
30th Virginia—Col. Robert S. Chew (w)

Ransom's brigade—Brig. Gen. Robert Ransom, Jr.
24th North Carolina
25th North Carolina—Col. Henry M. Rutledge
35th North Carolina—Col. Matt W. Ransom
49th North Carolina—Lt. Col. Lee M. McAfee

Division Artillery
French's (Virginia) Battery
Branch's (Virginia) Artillery

Hood's division—Brig. Gen. John Bell Hood

Hood's brigade—Col. William T. Wofford
18th Georgia
Hampton's (South Carolina) Legion
1st Texas, 4th Texas
5th Texas—Capt. Ike N. M. Turner

Law's brigade—Col. Evander M. Law
4th Alabama—Lt. Col. O. K. McLemore (mw), Capt. Lawrence H. Scruggs (w),
Capt. William M. Robbins
2nd Mississippi, 11th Mississippi
6th North Carolina

Division Artillery—Maj. B. W. Frobel
German (South Carolina) Artillery
Palmetto (South Carolina) Artillery
Rowan (North Carolina) Artillery

Lee's Artillery Battalion—Col. Stephen D. Lee
Ashland (Virginia) Artillery—Capt. Pichegru Woolfolk, Jr.
Bedford (Virginia) Artillery—Capt. T. C. Jordan
Brooks (South Carolina) Artillery—Lt. William Elliot
Eubank's (Virginia) Battery—Capt. J. L. Eubank
Madison (Louisiana) Artillery—Capt. G. V. Moody
Parker's (Virginia) Battery—Capt. W. W. Parker

Jackson's Corps—Maj. Gen. Thomas J. Jackson

Ewell's division—Brig. Gen. Alexander R. Lawton (w), Brig. Gen. Jubal A. Early

Lawton's brigade—Col. Marcellus Douglass (k), Maj. John H. Lowe
13th Georgia, 26th Georgia
31st Georgia, 38th Georgia
60th Georgia, 61st Georgia

Early's brigade—Brig. Gen. Jubal Early, Col. William Smith (w)
13th Virginia—Capt. Frank V. Winston
25th Virginia—Capt. Robert D. Lilley
31st Virginia
44th Virginia—Capt. David W. Anderson (w)
49th Virginia—Col. William Smith (w)
52nd Virginia—Col. Michael G. Harman
58th Virginia

Trimble's brigade—Col. James A. Walker
15th Alabama, 12th Georgia
21st Georgia—Maj. Thomas C. Glover (w), Capt. James C. Nisbet[3]
1st North Carolina Battalion Sharpshooters

Hays's brigade—Brig. Gen. Harry T. Hays
5th Louisiana, 6th Louisiana
7th Louisiana, 8th Louisiana
14th Louisiana

Division Artillery—Maj. A. R. Courtney
D'Aquin's (Louisiana) Battery, Dement's (Maryland) Battery
Johnson's (Virginia) Battery, Staunton (Virginia) Artillery

Jackson's division—Brig. Gen. John R. Jones (w), Brig. Gen. William E. Starke (k),
Col. Andrew J. Grigsby

Stonewall Brigade—Col. Andrew J. Grigsby, Lt. Col. Robert D. Gardner (w),
Maj. Hazael J. Williams
4th Virginia, 5th Virginia
27th Virginia, 33rd Virginia

Jones's brigade—Capt. John E. Penn (w), Capt. Archer C. Page (w),
Capt. Robert W. Withers

3 See Chapter 8 for a discussion as to whether the 21st Georgia or Colquitt's skirmish battalion fought Crawford's brigade.

21st Virginia, 42nd Virginia
48th Virginia, 1st Virginia Battalion

Taliaferro's brigade—Col. Edward T. H. Warren, Col. James W. Jackson (w),
Col. James L. Sheffield
47th Alabama, 48th Alabama
23rd Virginia, 37th Virginia

Starke's brigade—Brig. Gen. William E. Starke (k), Col. Jesse M. Williams (w),
Col. Leroy A. Stafford (w), Col. Edmund Pendleton
1st Louisiana, 2nd Louisiana
9th Louisiana, 10th Louisiana
15th Louisiana

Division Artillery—Maj. Lindsay M. Shumaker
Brockenbrough's (Maryland) Battery
Carpenter's (Virginia) Battery (Alleghany Artillery)
Danville (Virginia) Artillery
Lee (Virginia) Battery
Poague's (Virginia) Battery (Rockbridge Artillery)

D. H. Hill's division—Maj. Gen. Daniel Harvey Hill

Ripley's brigade—Brig. Gen. Roswell S. Ripley (w), Col. George P. Doles
4th Georgia—Col. George P. Doles, Maj. Robert Smith (k), Capt. William H. Willis
44th Georgia—Capt. John C. Key
1st North Carolina—Lt. Col. Hamilton A. Brown
3rd North Carolina—Col. William L. De Rosset (w), Maj. Stephen D. Thruston (w)

Rodes's brigade—Brig. Gen. Robert E. Rodes (w)
3rd Alabama, 5th Alabama
6th Alabama, 12th Alabama
26th Alabama

Garland's brigade—Col. Duncan K. McRae (w)
5th North Carolina—Capt. Thomas M. Garrett
12th North Carolina—Capt. Shugan Snow
13th North Carolina—Lt. Col. Thomas Ruffin, Jr. (w), Capt. Joseph H. Hyman
20th North Carolina—Col. Alfred Iverson
23rd North Carolina—Col. Daniel H. Christie

Anderson's brigade—Brig. Gen. George B. Anderson (mw), Col. Charles C. Tew (k),
Col. Risden T. Bennett (w)
2nd North Carolina, 4th North Carolina
14th North Carolina, 30th North Carolina

Colquitt's brigade—Col. Alfred Holt Colquitt
13th Alabama—Col. Birkitt D. Fry (w), Maj. Algernon S. Reaves (w)
6th Georgia—Lt. Col. James M. Newton (k), Maj. Philemon Tracy (mw), Lt. Eugene P. Burnett
23rd Georgia—Col. William P. Barclay (k), Lt. Col. Emory F. Best (w), Maj. James H. Huggins (w)
27th Georgia—Col. Levi B. Smith (k), Lt. Col. Charles T. Zachary (w), Capt. William H. Rentfro
28th Georgia—Capt. Nehemiah J. Garrison (w), Lt. James E. Banning

Division Artillery—Major S. F. Pierson
Hardaway's (Alabama) Battery
Jeff Davis (Alabama) Artillery
Jones' (Virginia) Battery
King William (Virginia) Artillery

Union

Army of the Potomac—Maj. Gen. George Brinton McClellan

I Corps—Maj. Gen. Joseph Hooker (w), Brig. Gen. George Gordon Meade

1st Division—Brig. Gen. Abner Doubleday

1st Brigade—Col. Walter Phelps, Jr.
22nd New York, 24th New York
30th New York, 2nd U.S. Sharpshooters

2nd Brigade—Lt. Col. J. William Hofmann
7th Indiana, 76th New York
95th New York, 56th Pennsylvania

3rd Brigade—Brig. Gen. Marsena Patrick
21st New York—Col. William F. Rogers
23rd New York—Col. Henry C. Hoffman
35th New York—Col. Newton B. Lord
80th New York—Lt. Col. Theodore B. Gates

4th Brigade—Brig. Gen. John Gibbon
19th Indiana, 2nd Wisconsin
6th Wisconsin, 7th Wisconsin

Division Artillery—Capt. J. Albert Monroe
1st Battery, New Hampshire Light Artillery—Lt. Frederick M. Edgell
Battery L, 1st New York Light, Artillery—Capt. John A. Reynolds
Battery D, 1st Rhode Island Light Artillery—Capt. J. Albert Monroe
Battery B, 4th US Artillery—Capt. Joseph B. Campbell (w), Lt. James Stewart

2nd Division—Brig. Gen. James B. Ricketts

1st Brigade—Brig. Gen. Abram Duryée
97th New York, 104th New York
105th New York, 107th Pennsylvania
2nd Brigade—Col. William A. Christian, Col. Peter Lyle
26th New York, 94th New York
88th Pennsylvania, 90th Pennsylvania

3rd Brigade—Brig. Gen. George L. Hartsuff (w), Col. Richard Coulter
12th Massachusetts, 13th Massachusetts
83rd New York, 11th Pennsylvania

Division Artillery
Battery C, Pennsylvania Light Artillery—Capt. James Thompson
Battery F, 1st Pennsylvania Light Artillery—Capt. Ezra W. Matthews

3rd Division—Brig. Gen. George Gordon Meade, Brig. Gen. Truman Seymour

1st Brigade—Brig. Gen. Truman Seymour, Col. R. Biddle Roberts
1st Pennsylvania Reserve, 2nd Pennsylvania Reserve
5th Pennsylvania Reserve, 6th Pennsylvania Reserve
13th Pennsylvania Reserve
2nd Brigade—Col. Albert L. Magilton
3rd Pennsylvania Reserve, 4th Pennsylvania Reserve
7th Pennsylvania Reserve, 8th Pennsylvania Reserve

3rd Brigade—Lt. Col. Robert Anderson
9th Pennsylvania Reserve, 10th Pennsylvania Reserve
11th Pennsylvania Reserve, 12th Pennsylvania Reserve

Division Artillery
Battery A, 1st Pennsylvania Light Artillery
Battery B, 1st Pennsylvania Light Artillery—Capt. James H. Cooper
Battery C, 5th U.S. Artillery—Capt. Dunbar R. Ransom

II Corps—Maj. Gen. Edwin V. Sumner

1st Division—Maj. Gen. Israel B. Richardson (mw), Brig. Gen. John C. Caldwell,
Brig. Gen. Winfield Scott Hancock

1st Brigade—Brig. Gen. John C. Caldwell
5th New Hampshire, 7th New York
61st New York, 64th New York
81st Pennsylvania

2nd Brigade—Brig. Gen. Thomas F. Meagher (w), Col. John Burke
63rd New York, 69th New York
88th New York, 29th Massachusetts

3rd Brigade—Col. John Brooke
2nd Delaware, 52nd New York
57th New York, 66th New York
53rd Pennsylvania

Division Artillery
Battery B, 1st New York Light Artillery
Batteries A and C, 4th U.S. Artillery—Lt. Evan Thomas

2nd Division—Maj. Gen. John Sedgwick (w), Brig. Gen. Oliver Otis Howard

Brig. Gen. Willis A. Gorman
15th Massachusetts, 1st Minnesota
34th New York, 82nd New York
Massachusetts Sharpshooters
Minnesota Sharpshooters

2nd Brigade—Brig. Gen. Oliver Otis Howard, Col. Joshua T. Owen,
Col. De Witt C. Baxter
69th Pennsylvania, 71st Pennsylvania
72nd Pennsylvania, 106th Pennsylvania
3rd Brigade—Brig. Gen. Napoleon J. T. Dana (w), Col. Norman J. Hall
19th Massachusetts, 20th Massachusetts
7th Michigan, 42nd New York
59th New York

Division Artillery
Battery A, 1st Rhode Island Light Artillery—Capt. John A. Tompkins
Battery I, 1st U.S. Artillery—Lt. George A. Woodruff

3rd Division—Brig. Gen. William B. French

1st Brigade—Brig. Gen. Nathan Kimball
14th Indiana, 8th Ohio
132nd Pennsylvania, 7th West Virginia

2nd Brigade—Col. Dwight Morris
14th Connecticut, 108th New York
130th Pennsylvania

3rd Brigade—Brig. Gen. Max Weber (w), Col. John M. Andrews
1st Delaware 5th Maryland
4th New York

Division Artillery
Battery C, 1st New York Light Artillery

Battery B, 1st Rhode Island Light Artillery
Battery G, 1st Rhode Island Light Artillery

XII Corps—Brig. Gen. Joseph King Fenno Mansfield (mw),
Brig. Gen. Alpheus S. Williams

1st Division—Brig. Gen. Alpheus S. Williams, Brig. Gen. Samuel Wylie Crawford (w),
Brig. Gen. George Henry Gordon

1st Brigade—Brig. Gen. Samuel Wylie Crawford (w), Col. Joseph F. Knipe
10th Maine—Col. George L. Beal (w), Lt. Col. James S. Fillebrown (w),
Maj. Charles Walker, Capt. Charles S. Emerson
28th New York—Capt. William H. H. Mapes
46th Pennsylvania—Col. Joseph W. Knipe, Lt. Col. James L. Selfridge
124th Pennsylvania—Col. Joseph W. Hawley (w), Maj. Isaac L. Haldeman
125th Pennsylvania—Col. Jacob Higgins
128th Pennsylvania—Col. Samuel Croasdale (k), Lt. Col. William W. Hammersly (w),
Maj. Joel B. Wanner

3rd Brigade—Brig. Gen. George Henry Gordon, Col. Thomas H. Ruger (w)
27th Indiana—Col. Silas Colgrove
2nd Massachusetts—Col. George L. Andrews
13th New Jersey—Col. Ezra Ayers Carman
107th New York—Col. Robert Van Valkenburg
3rd Wisconsin—Col. Thomas Ruger (w)
Zouaves d'Afrique Company (attached to 2nd Massachusetts)

2nd Division—Brig. Gen. George Sears Greene
1st Brigade—Lt. Col. Hector Tyndale (w), Maj. Orrin J. Crane
28th Pennsylvania—Maj. Ario Pardee, Jr. (w), Maj. William Raphael
5th Ohio—Maj. John Collins
7th Ohio—Maj. Orrin J. Crane, Capt. Frederick A. Seymour
66th Ohio—Lt. Col. Eugene Powell (w)

2nd Brigade—Col. Henry J. Stainrook
3rd Maryland—Lt. Col. Joseph M. Sudsburg
102nd New York—Lt. Col. James C. Lane
111th Pennsylvania—Maj. Thomas M. Walker (w)

3rd Brigade—Col. William B. Goodrich (mw), Lt. Col. Jonathan Austin
3rd Delaware—Maj. Arthur Maginnis (w), Capt. William J. McKaig
Purnell Legion (Maryland) Infantry—Lt. Col. Benjamin L. Simpson
60th New York—Lt. Col. Charles R. Brundage
78th New York—Lt. Col. Jonathan Austin

Corps Artillery—Capt. Clermont L. Best
4th Battery, Maine Light Artillery—Capt. O'Neil W. Robinson

6th Battery, Maine Light Artillery—Capt. Freeman McGilvery
Battery M, 1st New York Light Artillery—Capt. George Cothran
10th Battery, New York Light Artillery—Capt. John T. Bruen
Battery E, Pennsylvania Light Artillery—Capt. Joseph M. Knap
Battery F, Pennsylvania Light Artillery—Capt. Robert B. Hampton
Battery F, 4th U.S. Artillery—Lt. Edward Muhlenberg

Appendix B
Casualties, Cedar Mountain and Antietam

II Corps, Army of Virginia, Casualties: Cedar Mountain						
	Killed		Wounded		Captured/Missing	Aggre.
II Corps, 1st Division	Officers	Enlisted	Officers	Enlisted	Officers	Enlisted	
1st Brigade							
5th Connecticut	3	18	8	63	2	143	237
10th Maine	2	22	5	140	1	8	178
28th New York	1	20	6	73	10	103	213
46th Pennsylvania	2	28	8	94	8	104	244
1st Brig. Total	**8**	**88**	**27**	**370**	**21**	**358**	**872**
3rd Brigade							
27th Indiana	1	14	1	28	1	5	50
2nd Massachusetts	5	35	6	87	3	37	173
Zouaves d'Afrique		2		3	1	7	13
3rd Wisconsin ·	1	26	4	65	1	24	121
3rd Brigade Total	**7**	**77**	**11**	**183**	**6**	**73**	**357**
1st Division Total	**15**	**165**	**38**	**553**	**27**	**431**	**1229**
II Corps, 2nd Division							
2nd Division Staff			1		2		3
1st Brigade							
1st Brig. Staff			1				1
5th Ohio		14	11	93		4	122
7th Ohio	3	28	7	142		2	182
29th Ohio		6	6	44		10	66
66th Ohio		10	4	77	1	2	94
28th Pennsylvania							
1st Brigade Total	**3**	**58**	**29**	**356**	**1**	**18**	**465**

II Corps, Army of Virginia, Casualties: Cedar Mountain, continued							
	Killed		Wounded		Captured/Missing		Aggre.
II Corps, 1st Division	Officers	Enlisted	Officers	Enlisted	Officers	Enlisted	
2nd Brigade							
2nd Brig. Staff	2		1				3
3rd Maryland	1	11	3	39	1	15	70
102nd New York	1	14	8	77	1	14	115
109th Pennsylvania		14	3	69	2	26	114
111th Pennsylvania		7		74	1	8	90
8th and 12th Batt U.S. Regulars		8	6	31	1	14	60
2nd Brigade Total	4	54	21	290	6	77	452
3rd Brigade							
3rd Brig. Staff							
1st District of Columbia			1	2		1	4
78th New York					1	21	22
3rd Brigade Total			1	2	1	22	26
2nd Division Total	7	112	52	648	10	117	946
4th Battery Maine Light		1		6		1	8
6th Battery Maine Light		4		9		5	18
Battery M, 1st New York Light							
Battery L, 2nd New York Light			1				1
Battery E, Pennsylvania Light		1	1	6			8
Battery F, 4th U.S.		1		4			5
Artillery Total	0	7	2	25	0	6	40
II Corps Total	22	284	92	1226	37	554	2215

XII Corps, Army of the Potomac, Casualties: Antietam							
	Killed		Wounded		Captured/Missing		Aggre.
XII Corps, 1st Division	Officers	Enlisted	Officers	Enlisted	Officers	Enlisted	
1st Brigade							
10th Maine	2	19	4	46		1	72
28th New York		2	1	8		1	12
46th Pennsylvania	1	5		13			19
124th Pennsylvania		5	2	40		17	64
125th Pennsylvania	1	27	7	108		2	145
128th Pennsylvania	2	24	1	85		6	118
1st Brigade Total	**6**	**82**	**15**	**300**		**27**	**430**
27th Indiana	1	17	5	186			209
2nd Massachusetts		12	4	52		2	70
13th New Jersey	1	6	3	72		19	101
107th New York		7	2	49		5	63
Zouaves d'Afrique				2		1	3
3rd Wisconsin	1	26	7	166			200
3rd Brigade Total	**3**	**68**	**21**	**527**		**27**	**646**
1st Division Total	**9**	**150**	**37**	**827**		**54**	**1077**
XII Corps, 2nd Division							
1st Brigade							
5th Ohio		11	2	33		2	48
7th Ohio		5	1	32			38
66th Ohio		1	1	22			24
28th Pennsylvania	2	42	9	208		5	266
1st Brigade Total	**2**	**59**	**13**	**295**		**7**	**376**

XII Corps, Army of the Potomac, Casualties: Antietam, continued						
	Killed		Wounded		Captured/Missing	Aggre.
XII Corps, 1st Division	Officers	Enlisted	Officers	Enlisted	Officers	Enlisted	
2nd Brigade							
3rd Maryland		1	2	23		3	29
102nd New York	1	4		27		5	37
111th Pennsylvania	1	25	5	71		8	110
2nd Brigade Total	2	30	7	121		16	176
3rd Brigade							
3rd Delaware	1	5	2	9			17
Purnell Legion (MD) Infantry		3	3	20			26
60th New York	1	3		18			22
78th New York	1	7	1	18		7	34
3rd Brigade Total	3	18	6	65		7	99
2nd Division Total	7	107	26	481		30	651
Battery M, 1st New York Light				6			6
10th New York Battery							
Battery E, Pennsylvania Light		1		6		1	8
Battery F, Pennsylvania Light				3			3
Artillery Total		1		15		1	17
XII Corps Total	17	258	63	1323		85	1746

The casualties listed for Cedar Mountain are out of an estimated 6,946 infantry and artillery engaged. In the 1st Division, Crawford reported his strength at 1,767 officers and men (OR 12, pt. 2, 153). Gordon reported less than 1,500 infantry (Brook Farm to Cedar Mountain, 286). Both exclude cavalry and appear to exclude artillery. Williams wrote that his division sustained 1,222 casualties, which was "nearly one-third of the number engaged." Adding a nominal 100 officers and men per battery for Roemer's, Cothran's, and Muhlenberg's batteries puts the total for Williams's division at 3,567, excluding cavalry.

In the 2nd Division, Augur's report explicitly included the batteries attached to each brigade: Knap, Robinson, and McGilvery (OR 12, pt. 2, 157). Augur reported 1,121 enlisted men in Geary's brigade, 1,435 in Prince's, and 457 in Greene's. As for officers, each regiment would have had an estimated four field and staff officers, and each company, two. Half that total was used for the battalion of Regulars in Prince's brigade. Five officers were estimated for each battery. Adding those totals to the reports for enlisted men gives 3,292 officers and men to the 2nd Division, and 3,567 to the 1st—a total of 6,859 infantry and artillery for Banks's corps.

If the numbers in Greene's official report (Banks Papers, LC) were used instead of Augur's numbers, the total would perhaps be lower. Greene wrote that the 2nd Division took 169 officers and 2,685 enlisted men into action—2,854. It is unclear whether this number included the gun crews. If it did not, adding a nominal 100 officers and men per battery totals 3,154 for the 2nd Division and 6,721 for the II Corps. If Greene's number included the batteries, then he was claiming a considerably lower number present at the battle than the total calculated using Augur's numbers.

In sum, Banks's estimated strength in infantry and artillery was somewhere between 6,700 and 6,900 before accounting for straggling, which was excessive due to the heat.

The Cedar Mountain casualty figures are adjusted slightly from the *Official Records* returns. Gould's and Bryant's histories were used for Crawford's and Gordon's brigades, respectively.

For Antietam, the *Official Records* returns were used for the casualty figures. Dr. Thomas Clemens gives a sound synopsis of the XII Corps's strength (Carman, *Maryland Campaign: Antietam*, 538). Without recapitulating his entire summary, Clemens arrived at a total of 7,239 infantrymen and 392 artillerymen for the four batteries engaged. The infantry's numbers included 2,504 in Greene's division, 2,210 in Gordon's brigade, and 2,525 in Crawford's brigade.

Appendix C

Where the Advanced 3rd Wisconsin Battalion Fought at Cedar Mountain

In his 1913 book, *A Narrative of Service with the Third Wisconsin Infantry*, Julian Wisner Hinkley seemingly placed the 3rd Wisconsin's skirmish battalion in the Wheatfield. He described an "open field" as it emerged from the woods. Colonel Thomas Ruger's after-action report indicated that his companies were "placed on the right of [Crawford's] line." These references from Hinkley and Ruger, taken with accounts from the Stonewall Brigade about a right wheel by its three left regiments onto the edge of the Wheatfield, might suggest that the Virginians executed this right wheel and then enfiladed the 3rd Wisconsin. This is the generally accepted modern interpretation. Primary sources other than those mentioned above, however, suggest that this fighting likely occurred within the Scrub Field.[1]

Edwin Bryant's 1891 history of the 3rd Wisconsin placed it in the Scrub Field. Bryant's account matched every official report from the Stonewall Brigade. From these reports, it is clear that the 4th Virginia, in the woods to the north, was the only regiment without Yankees directly in its front. Reports from the 2nd and 5th Virginia described attacking the Federals straight ahead across the Scrub Field, and driving them back into the woods before wheeling right to engage Federals in the Wheatfield. The 27th and part of the 33rd were in the woods south of the Scrub Field and stopped when they reached the Wheatfield. Bryant echoed the Confederate reports, noting that the 2nd Virginia was directly ahead of the 3rd Wisconsin, and that the 4th and 5th fired on the right and left, respectively.[2]

---

1 Hinkley, *3rd Wisconsin*, 33-34; OR 51, pt. 1, 124, and 12, pt. 2, 193-198; Krick, *Stonewall Jackson at Cedar Mountain*, 164-167.

2 Bryant, *3rd Wisconsin*, 82-83; OR 12, pt. 2, 193-198.

In an 1895 *National Tribune* article, Hinkley stated that the action occurring within the "old bushy field." He likely referenced Bryant's history for this article. Hinkley's account of the relative positions of the Stonewall Brigade's regiments match Bryant's, going so far as to reference the 33rd and 27th Virginia engaging Crawford's brigade in the Wheatfield during the 3rd Wisconsin's fight with the 5th, 2nd, and 4th Virginia. It is initially unclear what changed Hinkley's mind between 1895 and his comparatively vague published account in 1912. The handwritten manuscript of the book in his personal papers, however, provides more detail. First, he described a "cleared field" rather than an "open field." This could mean the recently harvested Wheatfield, but additional details make clear that he meant the Scrub Field, a recently cleared woodlot. Hinkley's draft also mentioned the right company being "within a few yards of the bushes which skirted the field on the right" and receiving fire from these bushes. At first this suggests the Wheatfield as the position, with the Scrub Field to the right. But when describing the 4th Virginia, the *National Tribune* article put the regiment "close upon the right flank . . . but [they] were screened from us by the trees and bushes. . . . [T]hey fired from the woods, not 20 yards from the right." This virtually matches the language in Hinkley's manuscript, reconciling the two accounts and placing the regiment in the Scrub Field. Finally, the manuscript described the 3rd's temporary withdrawal "into the woods . . . following an old road and reformed . . . in rear of and about seventy five yards from the edge of the wheat field in which Crawford's brigade had been engaged." This makes a clear distinction between the two fields.[3]

Returning to Ruger's report, "the enemy's lines extended beyond the right of ours considerably, overlapping my regiment sufficiently to give by an oblique fire of that part of their line a most destructive cross fire on the right wing of my regt. The enemy also had a force on the right which opened a flank fire on the regt." This part of Ruger's report could support either interpretation with respect to location. But Hinkley's manuscript and his *National Tribune* article have clarified that description, reconciling it with the Scrub Field. A portion of Ruger's contemporaneous report further resolves this issue. Ruger included what he described as "a rough sketch of the relative position of the forces." That drawing was omitted from the published *Official Records*, but is included here. Like Bryant's history and Hinkley's *National Tribune* article, Ruger's drawing buttressed the Stonewall Brigade reports, though without the benefit of his having read them. The

---

3 *National Tribune*, February 28, 1895; Julian Wisner Hinkley, "Handwritten Essay on the Civil War," Julian Wisner Hinkley Papers, 20, WHS.

key aspect of the sketch is that it showed the 3rd Wisconsin north of the ridge that reportedly separated the Wheatfield and the Scrub Field. Moreover, it depicted the 46th Pennsylvania, which formed the right of Crawford's brigade, south of this ridge, over which Ruger could have seen on horseback. It also showed woods, rather than a field, on his right.[4]

4 Thomas Ruger, *Cedar Mountain Battle Report, August 13, 1862*, Union Battle Reports, 1861-1865 (Trifolded Segment) Unpublished, vols. 11-13 (Box 4), Record Group 94, NA.

Bibliography

NEWSPAPERS AND PERIODICALS

Charleston Mercury
      December 3, 1862
Cleveland Morning Leader
      August 18, 1862
      August 27, 1862
      October 2, 1862
Confederate Veteran
      Vol. 16: 1908
      Vol. 26: 1918
      Vol. 28: 1920
Danbury Times
      August 21, 1862
Erie Weekly Gazette
      October 9, 1862
Grand Army Scout and Soldiers Mail
      September 22, 1883
      September 4, 1886
Jeffersonian Democrat
      September 18, 1862
      October 3, 1862
Lewisburg Chronicle
      August 22, 1862
Macon Daily Telegraph
      December 19,1862
Montpelier Green Mountain Daily Freeman
      August 12, 1862
      August 13, 1862
National Tribune
      June 3, 1886
      July 1, 1886
      July 28, 1887
      October 11, 1888
      February 21, 1889
      June 27, 1901
      September 5, 1901
New Paltz Times
      September 10, 1862
Painesville Telegraph
      October 2, 1862
Philadelphia Weekly Press
      April 7, 1886

September 12 and 19, 1888
Pottsville Miners' Journal
October 4, 1862
Reading Daily Times
September 27, 1862
Richmond Daily Dispatch
August 13, 1862
August 14, 1862
Richmond Times Dispatch
October 19, 1902
November 8, 1903
July 17, 1904
Southern Historical Society Papers
Vol. 10, 1882
Vermont Watchman and State Journal
August 29, 1862
The Warren Ledger
August 13, 1862
August 27, 1862

MANUSCRIPT COLLECTIONS

The Confederate Memorial Literary Society Collection, under the management of the Virginia Historical Society, American Civil War Museum, Richmond, VA
R. T. Mockbee, "Historical Sketch of the 14th Tennessee Regiment"
Antietam National Battlefield Archives, Keedysville, MD
Regimental Unit Files
Frederic Crouse, "An Account of the Battle of Antietam," typescript
William H. H. Fithian Diary, typescript
Nicholas Pomeroy Memoir (original at Confederate Research Center)

Boston Athenaeum, Boston, MA
Richard Jewett Letters
Buffalo History Museum Library, Buffalo, NY
Sullivan McArthur Papers
Cincinnati History Library and Archives, Cincinnati Museum Center, Cincinnati, OH
Henry Brinkman Papers
Rauner Special Collections Library, Dartmouth College, Hanover, NH
Antietam Papers (Microfilm copy at the United States Naval Academy)
David M. Rubenstein Rare Book and Manuscript Library, Duke University, Durham, NC
John Mead Gould Papers
Lane Family Papers
M. J. Solomon Scrapbook
Erie County Historical Society, Erie, PA
C. H. Blanchard Memoir (copy at GNMP)
Fredericksburg and Spotsylvania National Military Park Archives, Fredericksburg, VA
Abbott Family Papers
John Blue Reminiscences (published in unidentified newspaper)
J. K. Boswell Unpublished Report (original at Library of Congress)

John Bresnahan—Sun (unknown city) Newspaper Account, August 26, 1902

Noah Collins Diary, typescript

George Hamman Diary, typescript

John W. F. Hatton Memoir (original at Library of Congress)

Jedediah Hotchkiss Letter to G. F. R. Henderson, July 30, 1896 (original at Library of Congress)

C. Lewis Letter to "Editors," August 18, 1862 (original at Yale University)

Abraham Marks Diary

Joseph Addison Moore, "Rough Sketch of the War"

Charles L. Pickard Letters (from various authors)

Michael Schuler Diary (original at Library of Congress)

Thompson A. Snyder Recollections

Georgia Archives, Morrow, GA

John Key Memoir, RG 57-1-2, 44th Infantry Unit File

Gettysburg College, Gettysburg, PA

Ambrose Henry Hayward Papers

Houghton Library, Harvard University, Cambridge, MA

Robert Gould Shaw Letters, MS Am 1910, Box 1 (26)

Historical Society of Pennsylvania, Philadelphia, PA

John O. Foering Papers

John White Geary Papers

John Gibbon Papers

George Gordon Meade Papers

Daniel D. Jones Papers

28th Pennsylvania Volunteers Papers, 1861-1863

William Roberts, Jr., Papers

The Huntington Library, San Marino, CA

James Miller Guinn Papers

John P. Nicholson, "Diary in the War"

Indiana Historical Society, Indianapolis, IN

Solomon S. Hamrick Letters

Josiah C. Williams Letters

Rare Books and Manuscripts Division, Indiana State Library, Indianapolis, IN

Lewis King Manuscript, typescript

Library of Congress, Washington, D.C.

Nathaniel Prentiss Banks Papers

Charles H. Boyce Papers

James Jenkins Gillette Papers

Chandler B. Gillam Papers

John Porter Hatch Papers

John Love Papers

Michael Shuler Diary

Lawrence Wilson Diary

Library of Virginia, Richmond, VA

Robert G. Davis Letters

Isaac Hirsh Diaries

Monocacy National Battlefield, Frederick, MD

John Bloss, Letter from Hospital Barn, typescript

Massachusetts Historical Society, Boston, MA

Richard Cary Letters

Goodwin Family Papers

Dwight Family Papers

George H. Gordon Papers

Newberry Library, Chicago, IL

C. C. Augur Papers

New York Public Library, Manuscripts and Archives Division, Astor, Lenox, and Tilden Foundations, New York, NY

Ezra Ayers Carman Papers

Ohio History Connection, Columbus, OH

Eugene Powell Manuscript, United States Army Ohio Infantry Regiment 66th
(1861–1865), 1862–1878, MSS 842

Thomas Church Haskell Smith Papers, MSS 158

Pennsylvania State Archives, Harrisburg, PA

Matthew Taylor Memoir

Rhode Island Historical Society, Providence, RI

George Sears Greene Papers

Special Collections and University Archives, Rutgers University, East Rutherford, NJ

Roebling Family Papers

St. Lawrence County Historical Association Archives, Canton, NY

Donald Brown "Reminiscences of a Civil War Veteran"

Tennessee State Library and Archives, Nashville, TN

"Military Reminiscences of Major G. Campbell Brown 1861–1863," Brown Ewell Papers

William L. Clements Library, University of Michigan, Ann Arbor, MI

James T. Miller Letters

William Ellis Jones Diary

Southern Historical Collection, the Louis Round Wilson Special Collections Library, University of North Carolina, Chapel Hill, NC

Samuel J. C. Moore Papers

Samuel Walkup Diary

South Caroliniana Library, University of South Carolina, Columbia, SC

Henry C. Burn Letters (copy at AMP)

Robert Shand Memoir

Albert and Shirley Small Special Collections Library, University of Virginia, Charlottesville, VA

Charles Tenney Letters

U.S. Army Heritage and Education Center, Carlisle, PA

"An Historic Flag," Clipping in James Garver Collection

George L. Andrews Letters

George E. Davis Memoir, typescript

Leander E. Davis Letters (copy at AMP)

John C. Ellis Letters

Charles Greene Letters

John D. Hill Letters

William Homan Diary, typescript

Charles J. Mills, "Through Blood and Fire: The Civil War Letters of Major
Charles J. Mills, 1862–1865," Gregory Coco, ed.

David Nichol Letters

Ariovistus Pardee, Jr., Letters

William Shimp Letters, CWDocColl

J. R. Simpson, "Recollections Relating to His Participation in the Battle of
Antietam"

James P. Stewart Letters

William H. H. Tallman Memoirs

Walter Greenland Letters

U.S. National Archives Records Administration, Washington, DC

Record Group 92:707—Antietam Studies
Record Group 94—U.S. Army Generals' Reports of Service, 1864–1887, M1098
    Samuel Wylie Crawford
    George Sears Greene
    Hector Tyndale
    Alpheus Williams
Record Group 94—Union Battle Reports, Unpublished
Record Group 153—John C. Walsh General Court-Martial Proceedings, October 9, 1862
Warren County Historical Society, Warren, PA
    George Cobham Letters (typescript), copy at GNMP, 111th Pennsylvania
Wisconsin Historical Society, Madison, WI
    Julian Wisner Hinkley Papers
    Quiner Scrapbook
    William Wallace Papers

MAPS AND PHOTOGRAPHS

Brown, S. Howell. *Map of Orange Court House*, U.S. Army Engineering Corps [1863]. Orange County Historical Society.

Dwight, C. S. Survey of Culpeper and a part of Madison counties, Virginia. 1863. Map. https://www.loc.gov/item/2002627432/.

Gardner, Alexander, photographer. *Antietam, Maryland. Captain J.M. Knap's Penn. Independent Battery "E" Light Artillery.* United States, 1862. Sept. 20. Photograph. Civil War Photographs, 1861–1865, Library of Congress, Prints and Photographs Division. https://www.loc.gov/item/2018671473/.

Gardner, Alexander, photographer. *Antietam, Maryland, View where Sumner's Corps charged.* United States, 1862. Sept. Photograph, Civil War Photographs, 1861–1865, Library of Congress, Prints and Photographs Division, https://www.loc.gov/item/2018671467/.

Hotchkiss, Jedidiah. *Map of Orange County, Va. [186-] Map.* Hotchkiss Map Collection, Library of Congress, https://www.loc.gov/item/2002627458/.

———. *Map of parts of Fauquier, Prince William, and Rappahannock counties, Va. [186-] Map.* Hotchkiss Map Collection, Library of Congress. https://www.loc.gov/item/2002627440/.

United States Army, Corps of Topographical Engineers and J Schedler. *Map of Culpeper County with parts of Madison, Rappahannock, and Fauquier counties, Virginia.* Washington, DC: U.S. Bureau of Topographical Engineers, 1863. Civil War Maps Collection, Library of Congress. https://www.loc.gov/item/99439135/.

United States War Department. *Atlas of the Battlefield of Antietam, Prepared under the Direction of the Antietam Battlefield Board, Lieut. Col. Geo. W. Davis, U.S.A., President, Gen. E. A. Carman, U.S.V., Gen. H. Heth, C.S.A. Surveyed by Lieut. Col. E. B. Cope, Engineer, and H. W. Mattern, Assistant Engineer, of the Gettysburg National Park. Drawn by Charles H. Ourand, 1899. Position of Troops by Gen. E. A. Carman. Published by authority of the SECRETARY OF WAR, under the direction of the CHIEF OF ENGINEERS, U.S. Army.* (Washington: Government Printing Office, 1904). Civil War Maps Collection, Library of Congress, https://www.loc.gov/item/map05000006/.

———. *Atlas to Accompany the Official Records of the Union and Confederate Armies.* Washington, DC: Government Printing Office, 2 vols., 1891, https://archive.org/details/atlastoaccompany00unit/page/n5.

PUBLISHED PRIMARY SOURCES

United States War Department. *Annual Report of the Adjutant-General of the State of New York For the Year 1899. Registers of the Twenty-Sixth, Twenty-Seventh, Twenty-Eighth, Twenty-Ninth, Thirtieth, Thirty-First, and Thirty-Second Regiments of Infantry.* Albany, NY: James B. Lyon, State Printer, 1900.

_____. *Annual Report of the Adjutant-General of the State of New York For the Year 1902. Registers of the One Hundredth, One Hundred and First, One Hundred and Second, One Hundred and Third, One Hundred and Fourth, One Hundred and Fifth, and One Hundred and Sixth Regiments of Infantry*. Albany, NY: The Argus Company Printers, 1903.

_____. *Annual Report of the Adjutant-General of the State of New York For the Year 1903. Registers of the One Hundred and Seventh, One Hundred and Eighth, One Hundred and Ninth, One Hundred and Tenth, One Hundred and Eleventh, One Hundred and Twelfth, and One Hundred and Thirteenth Regiments of Infantry*. Albany, NY: Oliver A. Quayle, 1904.

_____. *Harvard Memorial Biographies, Vols. I & II*. Cambridge, MA: Harvard University Press, 1866.

_____. *Historical Sketch of CO "D," 13th Regiment, N.J. Vols*. New York: D. H. Gildersleeve Printers, 1875.

_____. *History of the Fourth Maine Battery Light Artillery in the Civil War, 1861-1865*. Augusta, ME: Burleigh & Flynt, 1905.

_____. *John Hammond: In Memoriam*. Chicago: P. F. Pettibone, 1890.

_____. *Second Annual Report of the State Historian of the State of New York*. Albany, NY, 1897.

Allan, William. *The Army of Northern Virginia in 1862*. Dayton, OH: Press of Morningside Bookshop, 1984.

Anderson, T. M. "Civil War Recollections of the Twelfth Infantry," *Journal of the Military Service Institution of the United States*, Vol. XLI. Governor's Island, NY: Military Service Institution, 1907.

Andrews, George Leonard. "The Battle of Cedar Mountain, August 9, 1862," *Papers of the Military Historical Society of Massachusetts, Volume II*. Wilmington, NC: Broadfoot Publishing, 1989.

Bartlett, Napier. *A Soldier's Story of the War Including the Marches and Battles of the Washington Artillery and Other Louisiana Troops*. New Orleans, LA: Clark and Hofeline, 1874.

Bates, Samuel P. *History of the Pennsylvania Volunteers, 1861–1865*, 5 vols. Harrisburg, PA: B. Singerly, State Printer, 1869–71.

Beasley, William F. "The Forty-Eighth N.C. Troops at Sharpsburg," *Our Living and Our Dead*, vol. 1 (1874/1875).

Blackford, Charles. *Letters from Lee's Army*. New York: Charles Scribner's Sons, 1947.

Blackford, W. W. *War Years with Jeb Stuart*. New York: Charles Scribner's Sons, 1946.

Boudrye, Louis N. *Historic Records of the Fifth New York Cavalry*. Albany, NY: S. R. Gray, 1865.

Boyce, Charles. *A Brief History of the Twenty-Eighth Regiment New York State Volunteers*. Buffalo, NY: Matthews-Northrup Company, 1896.

Boyle, John Richards. *Soldiers True: The Story of the One Hundred and Eleventh Regiment Pennsylvania Veteran Volunteers, and of its Campaigns in the War for the Union, 1861–1865*. New York: Eaton & Mains; Cincinnati: Jennings & Pye, 1903.

Brown, Edmund R. *The Twenty-Seventh Indiana Volunteer Infantry in the War of the Rebellion, 1861–1865*. No publisher listed, 1899.

Bryant, Edwin E. *History of the Third Regiment of Wisconsin Volunteer Infantry, 1861–1865*. Madison: Veteran Association of the Regiment, 1891.

Buck, Samuel. *With the Old Confeds: Actual Experiences of a Captain in the Line*. Baltimore: H. E. Houck & Co., 1925. Reprint: Gaithersburg, MD: Butternut Press, 1983.

Carman, Ezra. *The Maryland Campaign of September 1862, Vol. I: South Mountain*, Thomas G. Clemens, ed. El Dorado Hills, CA: Savas Beatie, 2010.

_____. *The Maryland Campaign of September 1862, Vol. II: Antietam*, Thomas G. Clemens, ed. El Dorado Hills, CA: Savas Beatie, 2012.

Casler, John O. *Four Years in the Stonewall Brigade*. Dayton, OH: Morningside Bookshop Publishers, 1971.

Clark, Walter. *Histories of the Several Regiments and Battalions from North Carolina in the Great War, 1861–1865, vols. 1–5*. Raleigh: E. M. Uzzell, Printer and Binder, 1901. Reprint: Wendell, NC: Broadfoot's Bookmark, 1982.

Cockrell, Monroe F., ed. *Gunner with Stonewall: Reminiscences of William Thomas Poague*. Jackson, TN: McCowat-Mercer Press, 1957.

Comey, Richard Lyman, ed. *A Legacy of Valor: The Memoirs and Letters of Captain Henry Newton Comey, 2nd Massachusetts Infantry*. Knoxville: University of Tennessee Press, 2004.

Cullum, George W. *Biographical Register of the Officers and Graduates of the U. S. Military Academy at West Point, N.Y. from its Establishment, in 1802, to 1890 with the Early History of the United States Military Academy, Vol. II*. Cambridge, MA: Riverside Press, 1891.

Cunningham, D., and W. W. Miller. Report of the Ohio Antietam Battlefield Commission. Springfield, OH: Springfield Publishing Company, 1904.

Dabney, Robert L. Life and Campaigns of Lieutenant General Thomas J. Jackson. Richmond: Blelock & Co., 1866.

Davis, Nicholas A. Campaign from Texas to Maryland. Richmond: Office of the Presbyterian Committee of Publication of the Confederate States, 1863.

Dickert, D. Augustus. History of Kershaw's Brigade, with Complete Roll of Companies, Biographical Sketches, Incidents, Anecdotes, etc. Dayton, OH: Press of Morningside Bookshop, 1976.

Dickinson, Frank S. "Fifth New York Cavalry at Culpeper," The Maine Bugle Campaign 1, Call 3. Rockland, ME: The Maine Association, July 1894.

Dowdey, Clifford, and Louis H. Manarin, eds. The Wartime Papers of Robert E. Lee. Boston: Da Capo Press, 1961.

Duncan, Russell, ed. Blue-Eyed Child of Fortune: The Civil War Letters of Colonel Robert Gould Shaw. Athens, GA: University of Georgia Press, 1992.

Early, Jubal Anderson. Autobiographical Sketch and Narrative of the War Between the States. Philadelphia: J. B. Lippincott Company, 1912.

Eby, Jr., Cecil D., ed. A Virginia Yankee in the Civil War: The Diaries of David Hunter Strother. Chapel Hill: University of North Carolina Press, 1961.

Eddy, Richard. History of the Sixtieth Regiment New York State Volunteers, From the Commencement of its Organization in July, 1862, to its Public Reception at Ogdensburgh as a Veteran Command, January 7th, 1864. Philadelphia: published by the author, 1864.

"An English Combatant." Battlefields of the South, from Bull Run to Fredericksburg. New York: John Bradburn, 1864.

Folsom, James M. Heroes and Martyrs of Georgia: Georgia's Record in the Revolution of 1861. Macon, GA: Burke, Boykin & Company, 1864.

Gibbon, John. Personal Recollections of the Civil War. New York: G. P. Putnam's Sons, 1928.

Gordon, George H. A War Diary of Events in the War of the Great Rebellion: 1863–1865. Boston: James R. Osgood and Company, 1882.

_____. Brook Farm to Cedar Mountain: In the War of the Great Rebellion 1861–1862. Boston: James R. Osgood and Company, 1883.

_____. History of the Campaign of the Army of Virginia Under John Pope, Brigadier-General U. S. A; late Major-General U. S. Volunteers; from Cedar Mountain to Alexandria, 1862. Boston: Houghton, Osgood and Company, 1880.

Gould, John Mead. History of the 1st, 10th, and 29th Maine Regiment. Portland, ME: Stephen Berry, 1871.

_____. Joseph K. F. Mansfield, Brigadier General of the U. S. Army. A Narrative of Events Connected with His Mortal Wounding at Antietam, Sharpsburg, Maryland, September 17, 1862. Portland, ME: Stephen Berry, 1895.

Graham, C. R., ed. Under Both Flags. Richmond: B. F. Johnson, 1896.

Green, Robert M. History of the One Hundred and Twenty-fourth Regiment Pennsylvania Volunteers in the War of the Rebellion—1862–1863. Philadelphia: Ware Bros. Company Printers, 1907.

Hickerson, Thomas, ed. Echoes of Happy Valley. Letters and Diaries—Family Life in the South—Civil War History. Chapel Hill: Published by the author, 1962.

Hinkley, Julian Wisner. A Narrative of Service with the Third Wisconsin Infantry. Madison: Wisconsin History Commission, 1912.

Howard, McHenry. Recollections of a Maryland Confederate Soldier and Staff Officer Under Johnston, Jackson and Lee. Baltimore: Williams & Wilkins, 1914. Reprint: Dayton, OH: Press of Morningside Bookshop, 1975.

Humphreys, David. Heroes and Spies of the Civil War. New York: Neale Publishing, 1903.

Huyette, Miles Clayton. The Maryland Campaign and the Battle of Antietam. Buffalo, NY: 1915.

Johnson, Robert Underwood, and Clarence Clough Buel, eds. Battles and Leaders of the Civil War: Being for the Most Part Contributions by Union and Confederate Officers Based Upon "The Century War Series," Volume II. Secaucus, NJ: Castle Books, 1982.

Kelley, Tom, ed. The Personal Memoirs of Jonathan Thomas Scharf of the First Maryland Artillery. Baltimore: Butternut and Blue, 1992.

King, Horatio. Dedication of the monument to the 28th New York Volunteers, Culpeper, Va., Aug. 8, 1902.

Lindsley, John Berrien, ed. The Military Annals of Tennessee. Nashville: J. M. Lindsley, 1886.

Lloyd, William P. *History of the First Regiment Pennsylvania Reserve Cavalry*. Philadelphia: King and Baird Printers, 1864.

Longstreet, James. *From Manassas to Appomattox: Memoirs of the Civil War in America*. Philadelphia: J. B. Lippincott, 1896.

Marvin, Edwin E. *The Fifth Regiment Connecticut Volunteers: A History Compiled from Diaries and Official Reports*. Hartford, CT: Press of Wiley Waterman & Eaton, 1889.

Matchett, William B. *Maryland and the Glorious Old Third in the War for the Union: Reminiscences in the Life of her "Militant," Chaplain and Major Samuel Kramer*. Washington: T. J. Brashears, 1882.

McClellan, H. B. *I Rode with Jeb Stuart*. New York: Kraus Reprint Co., 1969.

McDonald, Archie., ed. *Make Me a Map of the Valley: The Civil War Journal of Stonewall Jackson's Topographer*. Dallas: Southern Methodist University Press, 1973.

McDonald, William N. *A History of the Laurel Brigade*. Baltimore: Mrs. Kate S. McDonald, 1907.

McLaughlin, John M. *A Memoir of Hector Tyndale, Brigadier-General and Brevet Major-General, U. S. Volunteers*. Philadelphia: Collins, Printer, 1882.

Middleton, Evan P. *History of Champaign County Ohio: Its People, Industries and Institutions, Volume I*. Indianapolis: B. F. Bowen, 1917.

Moore, Edward A. *The Story of a Cannoneer Under Stonewall Jackson*. New York: Neale, 1907. Reprint: Alexandria, VA: Time-Life Books, 1983.

Monroe, J. Albert. "Battery D, 1st Rhode Island Light Artillery, at the Battle of Antietam, September 17, 1862," *Personal Narratives of Events in the War of the Rebellion, Being Papers Read Before the Rhode Island Soldiers and Sailors Historical Society*. Providence, RI: published by the society, 1886.

Morse, Charles Fessenden. "From Second Bull Run to Antietam," *Sketches of War History. War Papers and Personal Reminiscences 1861–1865. Read before the Commandery of the State of Missouri, Military Order of the Loyal Legion of the United States, Volume 1*. St. Louis: Becktold, 1892.

_____. *Letters Written During the Civil War, 1861–1865*. Printed privately, 1898.

Nisbet, James Cooper. *Four Years on the Firing Line*, Bell Irvin Wiley, ed. Jackson, TN: McGowat-Mercer Press, 1963.

Owen, William Miller. *In Camp and Battle with the Washington Artillery of New Orleans: A Narrative of Events During the Late Civil War from Bull Run to Appomattox and Spanish Fort*. Boston: Ticknor, 1885.

Quaife, Milo, ed. *From the Cannon's Mouth: The Civil War Letters of General Alpheus S. Williams*. Detroit: Wayne State University Press, 1959.

Quint, Alonzo H. *The Potomac and the Rapidan: Army Notes from the Failure at Winchester to the Reenforcement of Rosecrans, 1861–1863*. Boston: Crosby and Nichols, 1864.

_____. *The Record of the Second Massachusetts Infantry, 1861–1865*. Boston: James P. Walker, 1867.

Palfrey, Francis. *The Antietam and Fredericksburg*. New York: Da Capo Press, 1996.

Paulus, Margaret, ed. *Papers of General Robert Huston Milroy*, 4 vols. Privately published, 1965.

Pyne, Henry R. *The History of the First New Jersey Cavalry*. Trenton, NJ: J. A. Beecher, 1871.

Regimental Committee. *History of the One Hundred and Twenty-fifth Regiment Pennsylvania Volunteers, 1862–1863*. Philadelphia: J. B. Lippincott, 1906.

Reichardt, Theodore. *Diary of Battery A First Rhode Island Light Artillery*. Providence: N. Bangs Williams, 1865.

Roemer, Jacob. *Reminiscences of the War of the Rebellion, 1861–1865*. Flushing, NY: The Estate of Jacob Roemer, 1897.

Schurz, Carl. *The Reminiscences of Carl Schurz, Vol. 2*. London: John Murray, 1909.

Se Cheverell, John Hampton. *Journal History of the Twenty-ninth Ohio Veteran Volunteers, 1861–1865*. Cleveland, 1883.

Smith, James O. "My First Campaign and Battles, A Jersey Boy at Antietam, Seventeen Days from Home," *Blue and Gray*, vol. 1, 1893.

Smith, Tunstall, ed. *Richard Snowden Andrews, Lieutenant Colonel Commanding the First Maryland Artillery Confederate States Army, A Memoir*. Press of the Sun Job Printing Office, 1910.

Sparks, David S., ed. *Inside Lincoln's Army: The Diary of Marsena Rudolph Patrick, Provost Marshal General, Army of the Potomac*. New York: Thomas Yoseloff, 1964.

Stocker, Jeffrey, ed. *From Huntsville to Appomattox: R. T. Cole's History of the 4th Regiment, Alabama Volunteer Infantry, C.S.A., Army of Northern Virginia.* Knoxville, TN: University of Tennessee Press, 1996.

Taylor, Jeremiah. *Memorial of Gen. J. K. F. Mansfield, United States Army, Who Fell in Battle at Sharpsburg, MD., Sept. 17, 1862.* Boston: T. R. Marvin & Son, 1862.

Thomas, Henry W. *History of the Doles-Cook Brigade, Army of Northern Virginia, C. S. A.* Atlanta, GA: Franklin, 1903.

Townsend, George Alfred. *Campaigns of a Non-Combatant and his Romaunt Abroad During the War.* New York: Blenlock, 1866. Reprint: Alexandria, VA: Time-Life Books, 1982.

Train, Arthur. *Puritan's Progress.* New York: Charles Scribner's Sons, 1931.

Turner, Charles W., ed. "Major Charles A. Davidson: Letters of a Virginia Soldier." *Civil War History* 22, no. 1 (1976): 16–40.

U. S. Congress. *Report of the Joint Committee on the Conduct of the War.* 3 vols. Washington, DC: Government Printing Office, 1863-66.

U. S. War Department. *The War of the Rebellion: A Compilation of the Official Records of the Union and Confederate Armies.* 128 vols. Washington, DC: Government Printing Office, 1880–1901.

Von Borcke, Heros. *Memoirs of the Confederate War for Independence.* Philadelphia: J. P. Lippincott, 1867.

Walker, Francis A. *History of the Second Army Corps in the Army of the Potomac.* New York: Charles Scribner's Sons, 1887. Reprint: Gaithersburg, MD: Butternut Press, 1985.

White, William S. *Sketches of the Life of Captain Hugh A. White, of the Stonewall Brigade.* Columbia: South Carolinian Steam Press, 1864.

Wilson, Lawrence. *Itinerary of the Seventh Ohio Volunteer Infantry, 1861–1864, with Roster, Portraits and Biographies.* New York: Neale, 1907.

Wood, George. *The Seventh Regiment: A Record.* New York: James Miller, 1865.

orsham, John H. One of Jackson's Foot Cavalry. New York: Neale, 1912. Reprint: Alexandria, VA: Time-Life Books, 1982.

Yeary, Mamie. Reminiscences of the Boys in Gray, 1861–1865. Dallas: Smith & Lamar, 1912.

SECONARY SOURCES

_____. *The Medal of Honor of the United States Army.* Washington DC: U. S. Government Printing Office, 1948

Allardice, Bruce S. *Confederate Colonels: A Biographical Register.* Columbia, MO: University of Missouri Press, 2008.

Armstrong, Marion V. *Opposing the Second Corps at Antietam: The Fight for the Confederate Left & Center on America's Bloodiest Day.* Tuscaloosa, AL: University of Alabama Press, 2016.

_____. *Unfurl Those Colors!: McClellan, Sumner, and the Second Army Corps in the Antietam Campaign.* Tuscaloosa: University of Alabama Press, 2008.

Datzman, Richard. "Who Found Lee's Lost Dispatch," 03 February 1973. Copy at Monocacy National Battlefield.

Eicher, John H., and David J. Eicher. *Civil War High Commands.* Stanford, CA: Stanford University Press, 2001.

Harsh, Joseph L. *Confederate Tide Rising: Robert E. Lee and the Making of Southern Strategy, 1861–1862.* Kent, OH; Kent State University Press, 1998.

_____. *Taken at the Flood: Robert E. Lee & Confederate Strategy in the Maryland Campaign of 1862.* Kent, OH: Kent State University Press, 1999.

Harrington, Fred Harvey. *Fighting Politician: Major General N. P. Banks.* Philadelphia: University of Pennsylvania Press, 1948.

Hartwig, D. Scott. *To Antietam Creek: The Maryland Campaign of September 1862.* Baltimore: Johns Hopkins University Press, 2012.

Hennessy, John J. *Return to Bull Run: The Campaign and Battle of Second Manassas.* New York: Simon & Schuster, 1993.

Hollandsworth, James G., Jr. *Pretense of Glory: The Life of General Nathaniel P. Banks.* Baton Rouge: Louisiana State University Press, 1998.

Hunt, Roger D. *Colonels in Blue: Michigan, Ohio, and West Virginia.* Jefferson, NC: McFarland, 2011.

380 | Cedar Mountain to Antietam: A History of the XII Corps

_____. *Colonels in Blue: Union Army Colonels of the Civil War.* New York. Atglen, PA: Schiffer Military History, 2003.

Hunt, Roger D., and Jack R. Brown. *Brevet Brigadier Generals in Blue.* Gaithersburg, MD: Olde Soldier Books, 2010.

Johnson, Curt, and Richard C. Anderson. *Artillery Hell: The Employment of Artillery at Antietam.* College Station, TX: Texas A&M University Press, 1995.

Krick, Robert. *Staff Officers in Gray: A Biographical Register of the Staff Officers in the Army of Northern Virginia.* Chapel Hill: University of North Carolina Press, 2003.

_____. *Stonewall Jackson at Cedar Mountain.* Chapel Hill: University of North Carolina Press, 1990.

Loewen, Susan Irish. "The Captain and Mrs. Irish," *The Castle Genie: Newsletter of the Passaic County [NJ] Historical Society and Geneology Club,* vol. 10, no. 1, Fall 1999.

Sears, Stephen W. *Landscape Turned Red: The Battle of Antietam.* Boston: Houghton Mifflin Company, 1983.

Schildt, John W. *Drums Along the Antietam.* Parsons, WV: McClain, 1982.

Warner, Ezra J. *Generals in Blue: Lives of the Union Commanders.* Baton Rouge: Louisiana State University Press, 1992.

_____. *Generals in Gray: Lives of the Confederate Commanders.* Baton Rouge: Louisiana State University Press, 2008.

Welsh, Jack D. *Medical Histories of Union Generals.* Kent, OH: Kent State University Press, 1996.

Index

Acknowledgments

I am full of gratitude to scores of folks who kindly helped in preparing this volume. Individuals at every one of the archives that I've used were very helpful, often going the extra mile to help this random researcher. I leaned quite heavily on the interlibrary loan system at my local library in southern Maryland and truly appreciate that service and everyone involved.

Many thanks to the historians who graciously shared or helped me track down sources. These include Stephanie Gray at Antietam National Battlefield, John Hennessy at Fredericksburg and Spotsylvania National Military Park, Dr. Thomas Clemens, and Eric Wittenberg. I very much appreciate the time that Michael Block generously spent with me at Cedar Mountain, sharing his knowledge of the ground and the feedback that Dr. Clemens and Scott Hartwig offered on the manuscript.

Diane Richard, Don Evans, and Jeanna Kinnebrew helped me collect sources and were indispensable.

Scott Hann and Nicholas Picerno made photos available from their personal collections for this book, helping to illustrate the story of the XII Corps.

Cartographer Hal Jespersen adroitly turned my research and crude scrawlings into a great set of maps. I very much appreciate his patience and skill.

I remain thrilled that Theodore P. Savas, managing director at Savas Beatie, saw something worthwhile in my manuscript, and I thank him for agreeing to publish it. Ted, Carl Zebrowski, and Joel Manuel offered incredible support and guidance throughout this process. Sarah Keeney, Sarah Closson, and Lee Merideth have been exceedingly helpful as well.

Most importantly, I am utterly grateful to my wife, Jen, and my kids, who allowed this book to develop over the past six years with patient support and encouragement. I discovered that my daughter Sophie has a sharp eye for deciphering 19th-century handwriting; she saved my bacon more than once.

Finally, I thank the subjects of this book for their underrepresented service and sacrifices. I am humbled to be able to share their story.

About the Author: M. Chris Bryan earned a Bachelor of Science in History from the United States Naval Academy; a Master of Arts in Liberal Arts from St. John's College, Annapolis; and a Master of Historic Preservation from the University of Maryland, College Park. A former naval aviator, Bryan works as a proj[ect] manager and lives in southern Maryland with his w[ife] and two children. *Cedar Mountain to Antietam* is his firs[t] book.